# Susan Sayers

## SPRINGBOARD TWO

# Susan Sayers
## SPRINGBOARD TWO

Ideas & Resources for All-Age Worship
A Weekly Companion to ASB

Kevin
Mayhew

First published in 1994 by
KEVIN MAYHEW LTD
Rattlesden
Bury St Edmunds
Suffolk IP30 0SZ

ISBN   0 86209 468 2
Catalogue No 1500011

Front cover: *Ancient Steps to High Priest's Palace.*
Reproduced by kind permission of the
Woodmansterne Picture Library.

Drawings by Arthur Baker
Cover design by Graham Johnstone
Typesetting and Page Creation by Anne Haskell
in Palatino (Linotype)
Printed in Hong Kong

# *Foreword*

Many churches now recognise the importance of providing for people of all ages and spiritual stages in Sunday worship. This book is a resource for such services, reflecting on a theme and readings and suggesting ideas for different parts of the worship, including an all stage talk. A separate, but thematically linked programme is also provided for the crèche, children and young people; all age worship does not necessarily mean everyone doing everything together all the time.

Increasingly there is at least one service in the month which draws those who are not yet baptised or confirmed Christians, and for whom eucharistic worship is not always appropriate. Also, many parishes are having to face the reality of some services being led by lay readers, rather than clergy. To help those in these situations, *Springboard Two* follows the Morning Prayer lectionary, and all the ideas in it are suitable for non eucharistic worship. Of course, the weekly themes are the same as for Communion, so the material can be used to supplement the resources of *Springboard to Worship*.

A thematic index is provided, so that the programmes can be used for planning informal, non liturgical and ecumenical services as well.

As with *Springboard to Worship*, the idea has been not to provide an exhaustive, detailed programme, but to start you off and help you plan. I have no doubt that having prayed for God's guidance, and read through a week's section, you will usually end up doing something different, and specifically suited to your congregation. And that is just as it should be.

May God bless you all, and all with whom you worship.

SUSAN SAYERS

# Contents

## HOLY WEEK

## EASTER

## PENTECOST

# How to use this book

## Planning

You can select from the week's material as much as you find useful for your particular needs on any one week, as all the ideas are independent of one another, although they are all linked to the weekly ASB theme.

All age worship is not about the entertainment business, nor is it child-centred worship, or 'watered-down' worship. Neither need it be noisy and extra hassle worship. There are usually many other age groups represented in our churches as well as children and our aim must be to provide for the middle aged and elderly as well as for the young, for the stranger as well as the regulars.

Since God is in a far better position to know the needs of your congregation than anyone, it is naturally essential to prepare for Sunday worship in prayer. I don't mean asking God to bless what we have already planned, but to spend time discerning the Father's priorities and listening as he tunes into the needs of those who will be there. Think about gathering a group of all ages to commit themselves to this each week, either together in church or separately at an agreed time. All the ideas in this book and other resource books are only secondary to this prayerful preparation.

Each week is set out as follows:

## Thought for the day

Use this on the weekly handout, or as a way of homing in on the theme when starting your planning.

## Reflection on the readings

There are ideas here for getting your mind going when sermon preparation jams. Or the reflections can be used for individual and group bible study.

## Discussion starters

These are provided for adult group work and could sometimes be used by adults in the sermon slot while toddlers, children and young people follow their own programme. Small group work within a service is rarely contemplated, but it can be a valuable way of involving everyone, avoiding the automatic pilot syndrome, and bringing the readings to life.

Some churches have parents present at the Sunday school; consider providing a parents' class within that programme for a short time as a way of reaching those who are wary of actually 'going to church'.

## All stage talk

In my experience the difference in faith stages is more important than the age differences, so these talks aim to present the teaching in ways that people of all ages and stages can relate to. There are so many ordinary experiences which are common to all of us and these can be used and enjoyed without anyone being excluded. Abstract thinking and reading skills are not necessarily common to all, but deep and abstract concepts can often be grasped if explained through concrete images, like three-dimensional parables.

In all these talks I want to encourage adaptation, so that the talks come across as fresh and owned by you rather than as another person's jacket, stiffly worn. Get the ideas, and then enjoy yourself!

## Intercessions

The main aim of those who lead the people's intercessions is to provide a climate for prayer, so that the congregation are not just listening passively, but are actively involved in the work of prayer. I have suggested times of silence, rather than pauses, so as to allow for this, and you could have music playing quietly during these times, open prayer or prayer clusters as well as individuals praying fervently together in the stillness of their Father's company.

During this time the young children can be praying through pictures, following a prayer trail, praying in pairs with an adult or singing some very quiet worship songs.

## Other ideas

I have suggested particular worship ideas for each week, but here are some more general guidelines to use to get your own ideas flowing.

*Dramatised readings:* Having read and prayed the readings, I find it helps to imagine myself sitting in the congregation, seeing and hearing the readings creatively expressed. If I imagine I am a child, a young adult, an elderly person and so on, I am more likely to pick up on what *won't* be helpful, and what *will* really make me think.

• Have a narrator to read, and simply mime what is read. Anyone not involved in the action at any one time freezes in his/her last position, like 'statues'.

• Give individuals their words to say. During the narration the characters act their parts and speak their own words.

• Have one or two instruments (guitar and flute, for instance, or organ) to play quietly as a background to the reading.

• Use a few materials as props and costumes. They need not be elaborate, just enough to aid imagination.

• Use live or taped music and depict not only the actions, but also the atmosphere, through mime or dance. Keep it natural, simple and controlled, and do make sure all types and ages are involved.

• Involve the whole congregation in the telling of a story, either by writing their words on the weekly sheet, or by displaying their words, noises and actions at appropriate places in the narration.

*Acts of worship:* Sometimes something very simple will speak deeply to people. As you prepare try to give the cerebral a break for a while, and listen to what the theme and readings make you feel. Then translate this into some music, communal action (or stillness), which will help people respond to God with their hearts as well as their minds.

*Church decoration:* The church building speaks. Our historical churches are visited and admired by many, and it is important that visitors see evidence of the living church of today as well as the beauty of the past. During services the mind and heart can be steered quietly towards the message of the day by means of a particular flower arrangement, exhibition of pictures, display or banner.

If those who arrange the flowers so faithfully, week by week, have access to the Thought for the day and the Reflection on the readings, they will be able to express these themes in an arrangement.

## In the crèche

This is often a rather neglected age group, so I have included suggestions for a programme which picks up on some of the important truths of the weekly themes which form a foundation to build on. This teaching can slot into a general play session, where the care, good humour and friendliness of those in charge of the children will continue to help them realise how much God loves them, and enable them to develop trust – the beginning of faith.

## Children

When planning for children's work it is advisable to read through the bible passages prayerfully. You are then in a better position to see how the programme relates to the theme, and also to enable you to supplement and vary the programme as a result of your own insights and the specific needs of your group.

A few general ideas about story telling:

• Tell the story from the viewpoint of a character in the situation. To create the time machine effect, avoid eye contact as you slowly put on the appropriate cloth or cloak, and then make eye contact as you greet the children in character.

• Have an object with you which leads into the story – a water jug, or lunch box, for instance.

• Walk the whole group through the story, so that they are physically moving from one place to another; and use all kinds of places, such as broom cupboards, under the stairs, outside under the trees and so on.

• Collect some carpet tiles – blue and green – so that at story time the children can sit round the edge of this and help you place on the cut outs for the story.

## Young people

Many churches are concerned about this age group feeling too old for children's ministry but not able to relate to what the adults are doing in church. We have a wonderful resource here which we tend to ignore; many young people are happy to be involved with a music or drama group, and are excellent at preparing role play material with a wit and challenge that is good for everyone.

As they move towards owned faith it is vital that the church provides plenty of opportunity for questions and discussion, in an atmosphere which is accepting and willing to listen. Although many will be very valuable on the children's ministry teams, I am convinced that they need feeding at their own level as well. Sometimes in their programme I have suggested that the young people put their ideas to the PCC. Do encourage the PCC to take such ideas seriously.

**BEFORE CHRISTMAS**

# 9th Sunday before Christmas

## YEAR 1

*Thought for the day:*
*This earth is God's earth.*

### Readings
Psalm 104
Proverbs 8:1, 22-31
Revelation 21:1-7, 22-end

### Reflection

In these readings we can watch the developing of a great spiritual truth. Growing directly out of the practical good sense of reverencing God in our lives, this passage from Proverbs actually personifies Wisdom.

It is almost as if we are reading about God himself as we reflect on the character of Wisdom. With the coming of Christ, such ideas grow to maturity, and with hindsight we can gaze back over the ages and see God's tender patience and amazing love as he breathes his precious creation into life, cares for it and saves it.

The passage from Revelation looks not at any one particular time, but at all time, rather as we will all be able to when we live entirely in eternity. From this standpoint it dawns on us that the Wisdom described in Proverbs is indeed the expression of God, shown to the world personally in Christ.

So there is no time, no thing and no place which is ever outside the sovereignty of our loving God, even for a moment. This earth is God's earth.

### Discussion starters

1  The Trinity is not mentioned by name in the Bible. Discover how it is described implicitly in these readings.

2  If we really believe that the earth belongs to our God so completely, why do we need to work at looking after it?

### All stage talk

*Theme:* Jesus makes sense of our lives.
Prepare beforehand seven pieces of paper or card, large enough to be seen by everyone. On one side of each write a coded word. Also prepare a codebreaker, either on an OHP or on a flip chart sheet. You can use any sort of code you like, but here is one suggestion if ideas are slow in coming today!

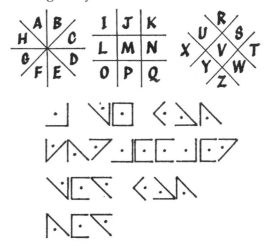

The words on the cards are: I AM THE BEGINNING AND THE END.
Give out the pieces of card to seven clusters of people, either mixed in age or not, but make certain people of all ages are included – it shouldn't be just the children involved.

While they are all working on the clues, draw everyone's attention to the way they are all working, though not on the same things. Also draw attention to the fact that some finish before others! As each group finishes, one group member brings up their card with their decoded message written clearly on the blank side of it.

Show how the message is not complete until everyone has finished, and some words were harder than others.

When the message is complete, everyone can proclaim it together, as it is a great truth about God. Often our life seems like a puzzle; we don't understand; we face terrible things like suffering and unfair things like not being as beautiful/clever/rich as someone else. We spend our lives cracking the code, and Jesus is the codebreaker – through constantly following him we begin to understand. And one day, which may be before or after we die, depending on what God has decided, everything will be complete and all will be made clear. Then we will know without any doubt at all that God is the beginning and the end, always loving and always there.

## Intercessions

Lord of the earth we stand on,
the air we breathe, the food we grow,
keep us in touch with this planet
we inhabit;
help us to tend it well and enjoy its beauty.
*Silence for prayer*

Lord of heaven and earth:
**let your kingdom come**

Lord of our past and our future,
Lord of our longings and disappointments,
teach us to recognise you in every moment
and know you are there through the good
and the bad times.
*Silence for prayer*

Lord of heaven and earth:
**let your kingdom come**

Lord of our fears and uncertainties,
our laughter and our foolishness,
fill us with thankfulness
and remind us of how great it is
to be alive.
*Silence for prayer*

Lord of heaven and earth:
**let your kingdom come**

Lord of our families and our friends,
of those we like and those we don't;
breathe into our loving the loving you
show to us.
*Silence for prayer*

Lord of heaven and earth:
**let your kingdom come**

## Other ideas

• Have a group of adults and children reading the Proverbs passage together chorally.

• Have instruments playing as a background to the reading from Revelation. If you try this, make sure the instrumentalists know the passage well and understand that they will be background, not enthusiastic foreground. Make sure the reader prepares the reading well and is sensitive to the music, so that s/he can alter the pace as appropriate.

• During the singing of a hymn, or while the collection is taken, have a willing flower arranger composing an arrangement. The finished arrangement can be placed near the altar, or near the door so that people will see it well on their way out. Have an inscription already written which can be placed beside it: ' "I am the beginning and the end" says the Lord'.

A short litany to link with this:

**Voice 1**  Father, did you know me when
I hadn't yet been born?

**All**  'I am the beginning and the end',
my child.

**Voice 2**  Father, are you with me at this
very moment, now?

**All**  'I am the beginning and the end',
my child.

**Voice 3**  Father, will you stay with me
until the day I die?

**All**  'I am the beginning and the end',
my child.
And I love you with a love that
lasts for ever!'

## In the crèche

*Aim:* To help children notice the variety of
God's creation.
Have a variety of things, both natural and
manufactured, to sort and enjoy; all the
*hard* things (like stones, wood, metal), all
the *red* things (such as leaves, rose-hips,
socks), all the *furry* things (which could
include some leaves and the cat as
well as teddies) and so on. Help them
pick out one or two things to thank
God for.

## Children

*Aim:* To help the children sense
something of God's creative power.
Play the 'Who made the ice-cream?'
game, so they can see that however man-
made something appears, if you trace it
back, it goes back to God. They like to
challenge this claim and can usually think
of some pretty unlikely starting points.
You can chart their ideas like this:

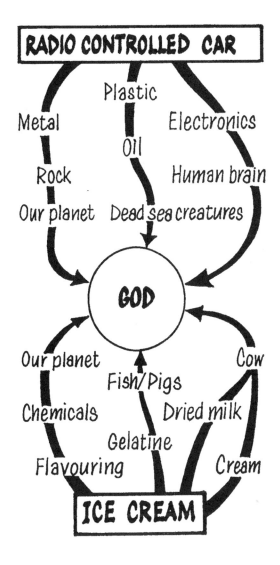

This leads on to the obvious question -
who made God? Such a deep question is
often asked by quite young children and
we can delight with them in the mind-
blowing answer: nobody made God! God
always was, always is and always will be.

Now spend some time examining with
magnifying glasses some of the clever
designs this amazing alive-for-ever God
thinks up. Have a selection of natural
objects and pass them round in small
groups getting everyone to notice
something different about each object.
This encourages the children to look

really carefully and become more sensitive to the details of design in such things as we often take for granted. Your selection of objects might include: a piece of evergreen, a stone, a twig of rose-hips, an apple, a cabbage leaf, their own hand. All the objects could be brought into church and displayed, with the title: Our God *is* wise and loving.

## Young people

*Aim:* To consider the vast and timeless nature of God.

Read both readings with the group, being sensitive to poor or embarrassed readers by having people read in twos or threes if necessary. After the Proverbs passage, guide them into seeing the link between Wisdom and the character of Jesus. Draw their attention to the words in Revelation: 'I am the beginning and the end'.

How can God not have a beginning? Surely everything starts somewhere? Allow doubts to surface and discuss them, respecting all opinions. In order to mature in faith it is essential that young people feel able to talk through their doubts without feeling criticised.

Have the word GOD written up on a large sheet of paper. Show how the very centre of God is like a circle - without beginning or end. After singing a quiet, worship chorus, sit together in complete stillness for a while to become aware of the present moment. Enjoy the peace of God which becomes noticeable in our stillness. While everyone is still relaxed and peaceful, tell them quietly how God living for ever doesn't mean that he's really old - it means that he always *is*, as we can feel him now. Whether we were living 500 years ago, or now, or in the next century, that wouldn't change. God loves us, and in every age, he *is*.

# YEAR 2

*Thought for the day:*
*This earth is God's earth.*

## Readings
Psalm 104
Job 38:1-21; 42:1-6
Acts 14:8-17

## Reflection

Job has been having a pretty rough time of it. Although a good and upright man before God, terrible disasters have all but broken him. This book in the bible tackles our bewilderment in the face of suffering. Several times Job has voiced his longing for a face to face meeting with God, a very human longing which was later provided in the person of Jesus. In the meantime, God speaks to Job in the mastery of his incredible creation, and as Job begins to grasp something of the infinite power and authority and tenderness of God, he is content to trust him, in both terrible and comfortable times.

Centuries later, Paul explains the healing of the lame man by directing the people's attention to that same mastery of creation. When we really understand that God actually brought all this into being and sustains it by loving it, then it becomes quite natural for such healing to take place. In both cases our hearts are led to worship God, whose creative power and creative loving are total.

## Discussion starters

1  Do you ever find God's power frightening? Should it ever be frightening?

2  Today's reading raises the question of God answering our prayers for healing. Sometimes he doesn't appear to. What factors may be involved here? Should we be going about things differently?

## All stage talk

*Theme:* Living in God's strength, not our own.

Have a very large, heavy suitcase or box, and make up a short, preferably funny, reason for it being there. Explain that it's extremely important to get this thing moved to the back of the church (or even up to the balcony, if you have one). Invite a small person to come out. Who thinks this person will be able to do it? Let them try, but intervene before any ruptures threaten! What we need is someone really strong. If there are any weightlifters among the uniformed organisations, now is the time for them to be put to the test.

Everyone watches as strength (or combined strength if necessary) achieves the desired effect.

In our lives we often find we have heavy weights to carry. Weights like being left out of the group at school; missing someone we love because they have moved away or died; weights like financial problems, illness or guilt about something we did years ago. (You could have heavy dustbin bags to represent all these.) We find them difficult because we try to lift them with our own strength and all we do is strain ourselves.

Our God is so powerful – he has all the strength needed to carry any weight, no matter how heavy. So the obvious, sensible thing is to let him. Stop saying to God, 'No thanks, I'm fine . . . I'll manage . . .' Stop saying to God, 'You lived ages ago, and I need help now!' Jesus *is* alive right now, full of power, full of good ideas, full of sympathy and understanding. He loves you, he knows your burden already, and he's happy to carry it so you can be free of it.

## Intercessions

We pray for everyone who has never yet heard of Jesus,
and all those who don't yet know
how much God loves them.
Enable us to use each opportunity
we are given
to show God's love in our behaviour.
*Silence for prayer*
With God:
**nothing is impossible!**

We pray for the Queen and those who govern our country;
we ask you to be among them as they make important decisions.
We bring to you the many problems
that are so difficult to solve lovingly.
*Silence for prayer*
With God:
**nothing is impossible!**

We pray for all who spend their lives feeling dissatisfied;
for those who are unhappy, lonely or overworked.
We ask you to lift their spirits and give them peace and joy.
*Silence for prayer*
With God:
**nothing is impossible!**

We pray for those in pain
and those whose peaceful lives
have suddenly been shattered.
Help them gather the fragments to start again; give courage and hope.
*Silence for prayer*
With God:
**nothing is impossible!**

*Continued overleaf*

Lord, we thank you that your grace is
sufficient for us,
no matter what happens to us.
In a time of silence
in God's company, let us thank him for
his many blessings.

*Silence for prayer*

With God:
**nothing is impossible!**

## *In the crèche*

*Aim:* To help the children understand that
when we're being loving we are passing
on God's love.

Play 'Pass the Hug' with several
cuddly toys going round the circle at
once, so no one has to wait too long for a
hug. As well as enjoying the cuddle
themselves they are learning to enjoy
sharing with the next person. Think about
what we can do to show people in our
family we love them.

## *Children*

*Aim:* To help the children realise that for
God nothing is impossible.

Show and talk about something you have
managed to make, but which you needed
a bit of help with. Let the children share
about something they have made and are
really proud of. Talk together about how
nice it is when you get to a really tricky
bit if someone is there to sort you out.

In the centre of the circle, have a few
children to help you tell the story by
acting it out. Now narrate today's Acts
reading, from the healing of the lame man
through to the people thinking Paul and
Barnabas had done the healing
themselves. Stop and ask the children
what they think – if it wasn't them, then
who had made the man better?

Can God really do something as
amazing as that?

Thank the volunteer actors and lay out
in the circle lots of pictures of our
beautiful creation – from stars and
planets to tiny insects. Put on some music
while you and the children wander round
very quietly, thanking God for each thing
he has made.

Now we can see that God is so great
that anything is possible for him, no
matter how difficult it may seem for us.

## *Young people*

*Aim:* To help them understand that God
can work through us with power.

Read the story in Acts together, with
people taking active parts if they enjoy
that sort of thing. Otherwise, have
different people reading, two at a time if
there are any with reading difficulties.
How could ordinary people like Paul and
Barnabas heal this lame man? Draw their
attention to the way the healing
happened, and the words that were said.
It was still Jesus doing the healing, just as
he had when he was there among people
in Galilee.

Now for a daft bit . . . have two model
cars – one a really smart, powerful car,
the other with a far less powerful engine.
Get everyone to make the right type of
engine noises for each one as you
push them along on the flat. The real
difference becomes apparent when you're
accelerating out of a roundabout up a hill.
Make a clipboard into the hill and try the
small car first. Now try with the powerful
model and see (and hear!) the difference.

To work powerfully for good in this
world we need the power of God right
inside our lives with God living in us we
shall all be 'powerful models'. The more
empowered Christians there are in this
area, the more powerful will be the effects
for good, and for healing.

# 8th Sunday before Christmas

## YEAR 1

*Thought for the day:*
*Sin destroys us; God can save us.*

### Readings
Psalm 25
Isaiah 44:6-22
1 Corinthians 10:1-13 (or 24)

### Reflection

We seem to have an inbuilt tendency to idolise. What we idolise depends on our age, taste and so on, but both individually and corporately we home in on some particular person or image judged by us to be 'the very best', for the moment at least. There are those who would rather die than be seen in a crimplene dress; there are others who grow weak with horror at the thought of nose studs or a different tune to the Lord's prayer.

People have been running after images for so long that we lose sight of the fact that this is really idolatry. Once we find time to stop and think about it, we discover that much of what we value so highly and spend such time cultivating is really very insignificant, and our obsessional delight in acquiring and preserving is somewhat pathetic. In contrast, the creative, living God is real; his accepting love and forgiveness break down our deep-seated anxieties at every stage of our journey through life, and his patience and mercy never run out.

So it is a better idea to fight against the temptations all around us to go image-hunting, and spend our lives instead in offering our instinctive worship in the right place – the vibrant centre of all that is loving, good and holy. God himself.

### Discussion starters

1 What is the difference between enjoyment and idolatry?
2 What practical steps can we take to deal with temptation?

### All stage talk

*Theme:* Recognising idolatry and allowing God to stamp it out.

Ask for four volunteers to carry four objects in procession from the back of the building, so that everyone can see them as they go past. There is a charm bracelet, or some other superstitious thing; a mirror; a clock; and a wallet. Have the objects displayed at the front.

Explain how God has warned us to be on our guard in case we are tempted to worship other things instead of the one true God. Sometimes we don't realise when we are going this, so today we are going to check our lives to make sure we really are worshipping God, and not some idol. We may not kneel down in front of trees or golden calves, but these objects give us a clue as to some other ways we may be just as full of idolatry.

Look at each object in turn. The charm bracelet: believing in luck ruling our lives, with the sense that there is no real order or point in it. God is there, but not actually able to do much.

The mirror: our image becomes extremely important to us. It is more vital to do/wear/have the same as everyone else than to be what God wants and plans us to be.

The clock: feeling that we are only valuable if our diary is full and we have to organise every second of our day. We have effectively blocked God from using our time, except for a little space which we control.

The wallet: we love our possessions and comforts, and forget that as Christians we are no longer owners of anything but stewards.

As the objects are slowly paraded again, ask people to think carefully as to whether any of them have become idols, and ask God to sort their lives out again.

## Intercessions

This can be sung as a round, to the tune of 'London's burning':

1   'You shall love the Lord your God with
2   all your heart and all your mind and
3   all your strength! All your strength!
4   And love your neighbour, love your neighbour.'

Children can do actions like this:

1   Hands on heart then pointing up to God.
2   Hands on heart; hands on brain.
3   Clenched fists, bulging muscles.
4   One arm out round neighbour, then other arm round other neighbour.

Father, we offer our selves
and our lives to you,
and long for those who do not yet know you
to receive your love with joy.
*Silence for prayer*

You are the one, true God:
**we trust you and adore you**

Father, release our grip
on all that prevents us
from living fully in your light;
alert our minds and hearts
to do your will.
*Silence for prayer*

You are the one, true God:
**we trust you and adore you**

Father, wherever there is pain or suffering
in our world, come and save us;
bring good out of every tragedy.
*Silence for prayer*

You are the one, true God:
**we trust you and adore you**

Father, we thank you for the refreshment
and encouragement you give us!
*Silence for prayer*

You are the one, true God:
**we trust you and adore you**

## In the crèche

*Aim:* To help children begin to recognise temptation, sin, repentance and forgiveness.

Have some soft toys and teddies, and help them act out various situations which involve:

1   being tempted and sometimes giving in to it.
2   saying sorry and putting things right.

The children can join in, saying 'Danger alert!', 'Whoops!' and 'I'm sorry' in the appropriate places.

## Children

*Aim:* To help them understand that in Christ they can fight against evil.

Give each child two matching sheets of paper. They create one picture gloomy and nasty, the other light and colourful, using paints, felts or collage. Draw lines the width of a ruler down one picture, place the other one behind it and cut both pictures into matching strips. On another sheet of paper or thin card, stick the strips alternately. Fold the completed sheet like a fan, keeping to the edges of the strips of pictures. When this is viewed from one side, you can only see the evil and darkness. But when you turn it a bit, you can see it change into brightness and joy.

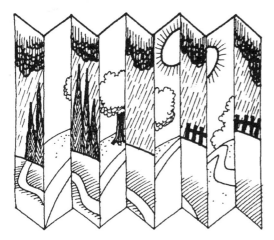

Explain that sometimes we can feel like the dark picture, with no power to avoid being unkind/jealous/angry etc. That's the time to remember to ask God to give us his power to put things right, and he will transform the way we are looking and help us sort things out.

## Young people

*Aim:* To remind them of their true birthright.

Prepare a short tape – audio or video – of a selection of adverts on television. Look at the ways they are persuading us to buy their product,

e.g. You will look beautiful if . . .
You will be successful if . . .
You will be acceptable if . . .

Talk together about some of the pressures they find themselves under to do what they know is wrong. Recognise the real difficulties here and offer sympathy, support and practical encouragement, not implied criticism or judgement.

Stress that God loves them and holds them very precious. That's why he has something far more lovely and fulfilling in store for them in their lives. Also, he completely understands all their temptations. If they stay close to God, he will protect them from being cheated out of the fulfilling life he has planned for them.

# YEAR 2

*Thought for the day:*
*Sin destroys us; God can save us.*

## Readings
Psalm 25
Jeremiah 17:5-14
Romans 5:12-end

## Reflection

Sin is distorted truth, rather like those fairground mirrors which reflect clearly, but grotesquely. It is only in comedy shows that the onlooker walking away actually resembles the elongated or squat reflection in the mirror.

These readings are looking at contrasts and, as we read them, we can see the startling comparison made between a life based on trust in humanity, and a life based on trust in God. In both there is trust; the distortion comes from trusting in things and people, both of which let us down and disappoint us because we are expecting them to act with the faithfulness of God, which of course they can't. Trust rightly placed, on the other hand, gives us access to the unlimited reserves of patience and forgiveness and mercy which God has in dealing with us. He is by nature totally faithful and so when we trust in him our lives will flourish and blossom. Shut God out of our human endeavours and our societies will collapse in destruction and death. Build our human endeavours on trust in the all powerful God, and life will burst out in glorious abundance.

## Discussion starters

1 Looking at our society/our world what would you think it was trusting in?
2 What would change in our society if people really trusted in God?

## All stage talk

*Theme:* The same, only different.
Bring in an ordinary mirror. Also make a distorting mirror using a sheet of the very shining wrapping paper. It can either be stuck on bent card or simply held by two volunteers. Invite a few people to see themselves in both mirrors, or walk the mirrors round the church reflecting people here and there. Which reflection looks most like them?

Sometimes we are like good mirrors, whenever we reflect God's loving, by being loving to others. Or we may reflect God's forgiving nature when we forgive someone who has been unkind to us. Or we may reflect God's faithfulness when we are trustworthy ourselves.

But sometimes we are like bad mirrors. We distort loving into possessiveness; we distort relaxing into laziness; we distort honesty into critical gossip; or pleasure into greed. Worst of all, we distort trust. We are designed to trust God, and when we trust in things and people instead of God, our lives get twisted and misshapen.

If we get our trust in the right place, everything else will start reflecting properly and our lives will be very beautiful and very fulfilling.

## Intercessions

We pray for all who are fearful
of being themselves;
for those whose lives seem pointless.

*Silence for prayer*

Lord, we trust in you:
**we trust you to respond in love**

We pray for those in ordained
and lay ministries;
for a deepening of our own commitment
to Christ.

*Silence for prayer*

Lord, we trust in you:
**we trust you to respond in love**

We pray for those who are going through difficult times at the moment;
those whose lives seem full
of pain and darkness.

*Silence for prayer*

Lord, we trust in you:
**we trust you to respond in love**

We thank you for all the special blessings
of our own lives;
for all your patience and gentleness
with us.

*Silence for prayer*

Lord, we trust in you:
**we trust you to respond in love**

## Dance of contrasts

This dance is a reflection on the way there is always hope in the middle of our sinfulness, and always a constant renewing of life in the middle of weakness.

While the chorus 'O Lord, your tenderness' is sung quietly and prayerfully by everyone, a group of about 6-8 people of all ages get completely tangled up together. Slowly they get untangled, raising their arms upwards in thanks and praise as they do so, and then helping to free those who are still 'knotted'. During the repeated 'O Lord, I receive your love', they slowly form first a circle facing inwards with their arms raised to God, and then a circle with their arms outstretched to one another and out to the congregation, so as to express the truth that when God fills us with his love it enables us to reach out in love to other people.

## In the crèche

*Aim:* To understand a little more what trust means.

Use two puppets, either bought or home grown from socks. You will also need a bowl of fruit. One puppet steals a banana from the other in full view of everyone. When the first puppet notices, he asks the thief if he has seen the banana and the thief says 'No!'.

Talk with the children at this point - do we trust him? No, we know he's seen it, so we can't trust him. Repeat the performance with other fruits. Then have the first puppet putting the fruit in a safe place and having a snooze. When he wakes up he has forgotten where he has put it and accuses the thief of taking it. The thief protests his innocence, but the first puppet says he has learnt not to trust him. If we want people to trust us we have to be trustworthy. God never ever lets us down, so we know for certain that we can trust him.

## Children

*Aim:* We can trust God to save us.
Play a trust game first. One idea is for the children to get into pairs, with one of the pair blindfolded. The blindfolded person is then led round an obstacle course.

Afterwards discuss with the children how they needed to trust their partner for the game, otherwise they would have been in danger of getting hurt. Talk about times they have felt let down by people, and recognise that because we are weak as humans, we can't expect humans never to let us down. But we can certainly trust God never to let us down, however, difficult or frightening life gets.

Show the children a length of cotton contrasted with a length of really strong rope. They can try pulling on each. God is like the strong rope, and whenever they feel frightened, or lonely, or tempted to do something cruel, they can hang on tight to the strong rope of God's love and it will never let them down.

## Young people

*Aim:* To understand the peace of mind which comes from trusting God.
Read Jeremiah together. Discuss what it means in practice to trust in man. Jot down all the ideas on a board or flip chart.

Now give the group some situations, such as:

- a school leaver can't get a job and likes dressing well.

- your best friend has moved away.

- Mum and Dad have split up and you don't get on with Dad's girlfriend.

Talk about each situation, seeing how it will look and how you might act if you are trusting in man/trusting in God. Make notes of people's ideas under the two headings.

# 7th Sunday before Christmas

## YEAR 1

*Thought for the day:*
*God chooses Abraham; Abraham*
*responds in faith.*

### Readings
Psalms 32, 36
Genesis 18:1-9
Romans 9:1-13

### Reflection

If you have ever braved a skating rink you will have noticed the tendency of nervous beginners to hug the surrounding bar. Those entrance and exit gaps become yawning wastes of fear to negotiate before the friendly bar returns. The other thing you notice is that no-one even starts to learn to skate until they learn to leave the friendly bar and venture out on to the middle of the ice.

I think faith is rather like this; we only start to discover the freedom and joy of God's loving mercy and faithfulness when we start trusting him.

That involves risk and the sense of travelling into the unknown. Most of the time we cling on so tightly to the bars we are familar with that we rarely feel the exhilaration of gliding round freely in God's Spirit.

Abraham's trust in God enabled him to live his life in God's freedom, fitting in with God's ideas and moving on to wherever God called him. That's the kind of faith we all need, and it's only as simple as stepping out and relying on God's hands and skills, rather than the cumbersome bars we try to erect for ourselves.

### Discussion starters

1   When we make ourselves available, God can use us – but on his terms. Do we believe in him enough to do this seriously, or do we really doubt that God can actually do things in our lives?

2   How honest are we with God about the things we feel he might be disappointed/hurt to discover?

### All stage talk

*Theme:* Being chosen and responding with faith.

Beforehand place a pair of scissors under one seat, a sheet of A4 paper under another, and a piece of paper with 'It's YOU!' stuck with blu-tak under a third seat. Make sure that these places are filled.

First choose someone, by telling everyone that the chosen person will find a message with 'It's YOU!' written on it stuck to the underneath of their chair. Now you know a little of how Abraham might have felt when he realised God had chosen him. When we find God choosing us, we tend to spend far too much time thinking 'Why me?' and 'I expect he really meant someone else!' Abraham was happy to let God do the choosing. He just got on with being chosen.

Now someone has been chosen, you have a task for them to do. The task is to make an A4 sheet of paper fit round four people. Can it be done? Collect people's suggestions as to what is certainly needed before it's even remotely possible. (Four people and a sheet of A4 paper.) Sometimes God's plans seem just as impossible at first, and we're tempted to give up. But if we trust him, possibilities gradually unfold . . .

Does anyone happen to have a sheet of A4 paper under their chair? What about four people – are there any willing to volunteer? Now we need some scissors – anyone able to help? Point out how an impossible task is gradually becoming possible. Last we need instructions. Hold out an envelope and point out that it has to be received and opened up before it's any use, which is like praying and listening to God. Now the instructions can be followed so that the sheet of paper actually does fit around four people. (And here are the instructions)

## Cut along the marked lines

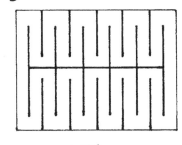

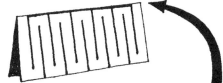

## It is easier to cut if you fold the paper like this

We may be asked to do what seems impossible. But if we trust God he will lead us to the time and conditions where the impossible can happen.

## Intercessions

Pray for all who have been chosen as spiritual leaders; pray for their encouragement and good health, pray that they stay attentive to God.
*Silence for prayer*
Teach us, Lord to trust you:
**let your will be done**

Pray for those setting out on new careers, or a new phase of life.
*Silence for prayer*
Teach us, Lord to trust you:
**let your will be done**

Pray for those whose bodies
don't work as well as they used to;
pray for people to befriend the lonely.
*Silence for prayer*
Teach us, Lord to trust you:
**let your will be done**

Pray for the people you would like
to spend more time with,
and those you would be relieved
to spend less time with;
remembering both are loved by God.
*Silence for prayer*
Teach us, Lord to trust you:
**let your will be done**

Think of your spiritual journey up to date, and thank God for the way he is teaching and guiding you.
*Silence for prayer*
Teach us, Lord to trust you:
**let your will be done**

## Other ideas

So as to affirm one another, have the two halves of the congregation facing one another, as each half says to the other:

'Do not be afraid, little flock. It is the Father's good pleasure to give you the kingdom.' (Luke 12:32)

and/or

'I will instruct you and teach you in the way you should go, says the Lord; I will counsel you and watch over you.'
(Psalm 32:8)

## In the crèche

*Aim:* To discover what it means to choose effectively.

Have available various toys which involve posting shapes through suitably shaped holes, and early learning jigsaws. Enjoy playing with these, bringing out in the conversation how we choose the right shapes. God chooses you – he has a special job for you to do in your life, and you are the only one who can do it.

## Children

*Aim:* To learn about choosing and responding.

Tell the children today's story about Abraham receiving his guests and being told that although he and his wife are old, they are going to have a son. Point out how God had chosen Abraham for something which must have seemed pretty impossible, but his trust in God made it possible. Then follow a recipe together so that by following the instructions you end up with something nice to eat.

## Young people

*Aim:* Choosing and responding.

Read the Abraham passage together, imagining how Abraham might have felt at the news. Think about how his reaction would depend on the relationship he already had with God and his experience of God so far in his life.

Now get everyone talking and chatting while one person has to try and tell them something. If the messenger can't make himself heard, he may try speaking louder. If that fails, he may go round getting each one's attention and even then they may not listen.

Notice how Abraham had already settled himself ready to listen to his guests, so he heard their message clearly. Unless we deliberately set out to listen to what God is saying, we may well miss what he is trying to tell us. When we are in tune with God speaking to us through the bible, through other people, through events in our lives and so on, we are still free to respond positively or negatively, as we wish. Pray together that you will all be able to recognise God's voice better, and be brave enough to go along with what he says.

# YEAR 2

*Thought for the day:*
*God chooses Abraham;*
*Abraham responds in faith.*

## Readings
Psalms 32, 36
Isaiah 55
Galatians 3:1-14

## Reflection

At all those times when we are made particularly aware of our sin, it can be tempting to give up, or to get thoroughly depressed trying to sort ourselves out and failing miserably. Then perhaps we start feeling guilty that we could have sorted ourselves out if only we'd tried a bit harder, done things differently or been more strict with ourselves. We end up rather like ingrowing toenails – causing ourselves great pain by growing in the wrong direction.

We are not able simply to complete a certain number of tasks to qualify for salvation. Salvation is not like collecting coupons for a hugh saving, nor like collecting modules towards a university degree. The marvellous thing about salvation is that God promises to give it to us as a free gift, and all we have to do is believe his promise enough to stretch out our hands to receive it. Can you imagine Woolworth's offering free videos (or even free inner soles) and no-one going in to take them up on their offer? Yet God offers us something we cannot manufacture and still in every generation people turn the offer down because they don't believe God is real enough to actually do such a thing. Our lack of faith prevents God from acting powerfully in our lives.

## Discussion starters

1 ✓ Earning seems better to us than freely receiving. How can we change this unhelpful attitude?
2  Why does Paul call the Galatians 'foolish'?

## All stage talk

*Theme:* Trying to earn salvation is a waste of time.
Beforehand, fix an apple or a bun on to a string.

Begin by setting an impossible task – who can eat the bun without using their hands while the string is being swung about? Several people can try, but make sure no-one succeeds!

Then have someone butting into the game and saying something like: 'You're never going to manage that, are you? That's impossible. I can give you a bun myself, if you really want one enough to make a fool of yourself in front of all this lot!'

If the person accepts the offer, they are given a bun from the intervener's pocket. If not, try with the next contender.

That is like we often are with God. We waste our time and energy trying to earn God's love and save ourselves, when actually it's an impossible task, and he's happy to give it to us free. All we have to do is *trust* God and *accept* his offer.

## Intercessions

Pray for all those whose faith
is worn or battered,
bringing to mind anyone known to you.
*Silence for prayer*
For with God:
**everything is possible**

Pray for a deepening of faith in all church-goers, particularly those in your own area.
*Silence for prayer*
For with God:
**everything is possible**

Pray for our society to be changed and renewed in God's way, bringing to mind the areas that particularly concern you.
*Silence for prayer*
For with God:
**everything is possible**

Pray for those who are in pain or anguish and those who are frightened.
*Silence for prayer*
For with God:
**everything is possible**

*Continued overleaf*

Thank God for what he is doing in your life, and for his living presence with us now and always.

*Silence for prayer*

For with God:
**everything is possible**

## Other ideas

Have people praying in clusters of three or four, either aloud or silently together. The leader of intercessions directs each prayer section as above.

## In the crèche

*Aim:* To plant in children the idea of seeking and searching for Jesus.

Play hide and seek, either in the normal way or like 'hunt the slipper /trainer'. Have a look at some pictures of Jesus healing, chatting, being born, at a party etc. When you've talked about them put them around the room. Then play another seeking game: 'go and seek Jesus when he's . . .' and the children go and find the right picture.

## Children

*Aim:* Helping children to understand that we don't earn God's love, as it's freely given.

Have a nice box of chocolates on display as a prize. For the group to win it everyone must answer one question right. With the atmosphere of a quiz show, give each person a question they can definitely answer until the last person. (Make sure this is someone fairly self confident to avoid anyone being upset.) Ask this person a question which is impossible to answer, rather than just hard. For instance: Who is driving past West Leigh school at the moment? Weather all the protests at the unfairness and impossibility of the question and savour the disappointment a little. Then explain that it's obvious they can't win the chocolates even though they all tried very hard, and that's the bad news. That's true with God's love as well – there's nothing we can do to earn it.

But there's good news too. Jesus told us that God loves us all the time already. He offers us his love for free. (As you say this, take the wrapping off the chocolates ready to hand them round.) What we have to do is choose whether to say 'Yes please' or 'No thank you'. Go round the group saying to each one, 'Will you enjoy one of my chocolates?' If they say 'Yes please' they can have one and you can all enjoy them together.

In a time of prayer, remind them that God offers each of us his love to make our lives full of love and peace and joy. All we have to do is to say to him 'Yes please'.

## Young people

*Aim:* To explore how God draws near to us and we to him.

Have ready some advertisements of expensive items from a mail order catalogue. Choose things your group would probably like to have but can't afford. Also have several calculators available.

In small groups ask them to work out how long it would take them to earn enough to buy a chosen item, by saving pocket money/paper money etc. For some things they'd probably be too old to enjoy them by the time they'd managed to earn enough.

Now read together the Galatians passage. We can sometimes get into the 'earning mode' with God. But Paul is saying it's more like some generous person offering to give us, as a free present, what we're struggling hard to earn.

Where does the 'faith' part come in?

When we're offered our present, we can choose whether or not to receive it. God offers us his love and forgiveness and constant 'presence' but it is only able to work in our lives if we receive it in faith, open it up, get to know it and use it daily.

# 6th Sunday before Christmas

## YEAR 1

*Thought for the day:*
*God is a rescuer and redeemer*
*of his people.*
### Readings
Psalm 66
Deut. 18:15-end
Acts 3

## Reflection

In the Deuteronomy reading our natural question is expressed: how can we ever know for certain that a prophet really is from God? Jesus warned us against false prophets, and on many occasions in the Old Testament false prophets would speak out what people wanted to hear rather than the truth. In our own society there is such an emphasis on self esteem and encouragement through praise, that we are sometimes in danger of assuming more truth in the affirming, comforting prophesies than in those which challenge and rebuke.

The answer given is that what the true prophet says is proved true by what happens. Or as Jesus said, a good tree can be known by its fruit. When Jesus came into the world he fulfilled in his life, death and resurrection what many esteemed prophets had foretold. He also took great national memories such as the freeing of God's people from slavery in Egypt, and filled them full of new meaning in the way he himself frees God's people from slavery of their sin.

When we allow God to work through us, as Peter and John were doing, he continues to be a rescuer and redeemer in all kinds of situations, setting people free from physical, mental, emotional and spiritual prisons so that they can live joyfully and lovingly.

## Discussion starters

1 People 'run to see' Jesus quite naturally when they notice dramatic changes in the lives of his followers. Should we be spending more time seeking God's total power in our lives and living out his love, and less on trying to get the crowds into our churches?

2 Does our church seriously seek God?

## All stage talk

*Theme:* Jesus fulfils what the prophets said. Prepare this crossword puzzle on the OHP or a large sheet of card.

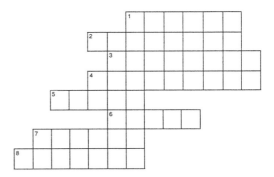

Give out each clue in turn; I have suggested who to allow to answer each one but do of course change this to suit the group. Make sure that everyone present has a chance to answer at least one clue.

Across:

1 (For uniformed people only)
  The plural of person.

2 (For those with long hair only)
  To say what will happen in the future.

3 (For those with short hair only)
  Truthfully.

4   (For those wearing green)
    Special and significant.
5   (For those with brown eyes)
    The real facts about something.
6   (For those without brown eyes)
    The name of Mary and Joseph's son.
7   (For those who like pizza)
    Christmas without the last three letters.
8   (For those who can/could skip)
    Fills with meaning; manages to
    accomplish something.

Down:

1   (Everybody)
    The hidden word in this puzzle.
    Solution to 1 down: PROPHETS

Now ask everyone to help you with your sermon notes by calling out the words as you point to them. Read the message so that everyone joins in at the right places, like this:

PROPHETS are PEOPLE. False PROPHETS FORETELL what PEOPLE are wanting to hear, but good PROPHETS FORETELL HONESTLY IMPORTANT TRUTH from God. To FORETELL doesn't just mean to FORETELL the future, it can also mean to speak out God's TRUTH even when PEOPLE don't want to hear it. JESUS CHRIST FULFILS the IMPORTANT TRUTH about God which the good PROPHETS were able to FORETELL HONESTLY. In everything JESUS does, both during his time on earth and ever since through PEOPLE who believe in him, JESUS shows the IMPORTANT TRUTH about God's love for PEOPLE. So who are PROPHETS? PROPHETS are PEOPLE who FORETELL HONESTLY IMPORTANT TRUTH from God, and JESUS CHRIST FULFILS it.

## Intercessions

Bring to God's love all who teach
the faith to others;
pray for their work
and their personal life.
*Silence for prayer*
Father:
**let your will be done**

Bring to God's affection all who feel
worthless or inadequate.
Pray for their lives to be freed
and transformed.
*Silence for prayer*
Father:
**let your will be done**

Bring to God's compassion the areas of
war and violence.
Pray for those caught up in the fighting
and for those trying to negotiate
a just settlement.
*Silence for prayer*
Father:
**let your will be done**

Bring to God's peace all the rush and
business of our world.
Pray for a right balance in our lives
between doing and being;
between speaking out and holding
our tongues.
*Silence for prayer*
Father:
**let your will be done**

Bring your thankfulness to God
for his constant love and faithfulness
*Silence for prayer*
Father:
**let your will be done**

## Other ideas

As part of the time of penitence, use these words with the actions which help the intentions to be thoroughly absorbed:

From now on,
let us speak only God's words
(touch mouth with both hands)
think only his thoughts
(hold head with both hands)
and express only his love
(place both hands on heart and then open
them out to those around).

## In the crèche

*Aim:* To help the children understand that God can use us as his messengers.

Use a Postman Pat toy van or something similar to drive around delivering letters to the children, or read with them one of the Jolly Postman books. Then let the children take turns in being a postman to take messages from one person to another.

Explain how God can use us as his messengers too. Perhaps your pet is frightened. You are being God's messenger when you cuddle it up and talk quietly to it. What about . . . when you've just been given a lovely tea? . . . when someone you love is feeling sad? . . . when your friend wants to play with one of your toys?

Finish with a time to draw a message and put it in an envelope to give to someone in the family.

## Children

*Aim:* To help the children see that Jesus fulfils the prophets.

Either begin with the crossword puzzle as explained in the All stage talk or, with younger children, have a game of messengers being sent from one person to another.

Then look at some of these things the prophets said (have them written out clearly on pieces of card) and see if the children can work out how the prophecies came true in Jesus. Have a selection of books and pictures for the children to search through and when the pictures have been matched up with the prophecies, display them all on the floor.

## Young people

*Aim:* To draw their attention to opportunities for spreading God's word.

Read together Acts 3, acting it out if the group enjoys this. If they are embarrassed by acting, try giving people different parts to read, with a clear reader as the narrator, or ask several people to read together at a time. Always have the 'double reader' way when there are poor readers or any with speech difficulties as it builds confidence. Talk about the episode together, pointing out that it was as unexpected then as it would be in the local High Street today. Notice how Peter and John used the opportunity to tell people about Jesus. Make a list together of occasions during our lives which might be opportunities we are given to tell people about Jesus. Look at them one by one to plan what would be appropriate and what might actually put people off. As you do this emphasise the importance of the undercurrent of listening prayer, so that we do God's will and aren't carried away by our own enthusiasm. Help them to see a balance between this danger and the danger of keeping quiet when we could help someone by speaking out.

# YEAR 2

*Thought for the day:*
*God is a rescuer and redeemer*
*of his people.*

## Readings

Psalm 66
Exodus 1:8-14, 22-2:10
Hebrews 3

## Reflection

We are reminded in today's psalm of how God is by nature a rescuer, and we can see this in practice in the story of baby Moses. One of the things I love about God's rescue plans is that they are always so economical – he never misses the chance to bless all kinds of people on the sidelines in the course of a rescue operation, somehow perfectly balancing the timing and placing with incredible delicacy. This story leads us to look beyond the events towards the nature of God.

Notice, too, how a baby floating secretly in a basket is a marvellous symbol of hope in the face of such appalling ethnic cleansing. No situation, however terrible, is out of God's sight or pain and, against ridiculous odds, he will mastermind rescue wherever our openness allows him access.

That baby hidden in the basket leads our eyes to look forward to another baby, born in a manger, who would be the greatest rescuer of all.

## Discussion starters

1  To what extent do we sometimes actively prevent God from rescuing or healing in some situations?
2  Bearing in mind the Moses story, sort out the difference/similarity between total trust in God and personal effort.

## All stage talk

*Theme:* Fixing our eyes on Jesus.

Rake out some nativity clothes so that you can dress a volunteer up as Moses. (Don't say yet that it's Moses) Now show a basket and remind everyone of the morning's story. Explain that this is what he looked like when he grew up. (At this point, give Moses a label to wear around his neck so everyone remembers who he is.) Ask Moses to stand with one arm pointing to a cross somewhere in the building.

Now show everyone a telescope (or long cardboard tube). Ask a volunteer to stand some distance from Moses and

focus on his face. Suggest that everyone else can make their hands into a telescope and do the same. Make some comment about what a nice face it is - so good and holy that we could look at it for ever.

Now ask everyone to look through their telescopes at Moses' hand. What is it doing? (If they can't see it pointing, they need to focus on the other hand!) If everyone carefully follows the direction of Moses' hand, they should find it leads them to focus on the cross. They have all just discovered a great truth - that Moses and all the prophets, and all the holy men and women ever since, may have beautiful lives themselves, but they always direct us on to see God more clearly.

## Intercessions

Let us pray together for the leaders
of the churches
and for the spiritual growth
of all Christians.

*Silence for prayer*

Father, in you we trust:
**work your will in our lives**

Let us pray for the areas of our world
where there is oppression and violence,
pleading for peace and justice.

*Silence for prayer*

Father, in you we trust:
**work your will in our lives**

Let us pray for our homelife,
for all the members of our families;
and for those who live
in our neighbourhood.

*Silence for prayer*

Father, in you we trust:
**work your will in our lives**

Let us pray for those who feel imprisoned by bad health or some kind of disability.

*Silence for prayer*

Father, in you we trust:
**work your will in our lives**

Let us remember those who have died –
those known personally to us
and those we have heard about –
and pray for all who are torn apart by grief.

*Silence for prayer*

Father, in you we trust:
**work your will in our lives**

Let us give thanks for all that is good
and honest, loving and refreshing.

*Silence for prayer*

Father, in you we trust:
**work your will in our lives**

## Other ideas

While a narrator reads the Exodus story of Moses, have a group of people to mime it. Perhaps there is even a real baby who could take part!

## In the crèche

*Aim:* To introduce the children to the baby Moses story.

There are some lovely versions of today's story available which you could look at, or tell the story simply with the aid of a baby's Moses basket and a doll. Go through the story several times with different children taking the parts.

## Children

*Aim:* To help the children see the difference between looking at God's creation and looking through it to God.

Have plenty of coloured cellophane toffee wrappers. (You may need to eat some toffees first). Ask everyone to look at their wrapper carefully and tell one another what they can see on it. There

may be the odd sticky patches, wrinkly bits, creases, slits or specks of dust.

Now try looking through the wrappers and notice how everything changes colour. If there is enough time, let them swap the wrappers around to see all the different colours.

Tell the story of Moses with the help of some visual aids and willing actors, drawing the story from the children if they are already familiar with it. Explain how we can look at Moses and learn a lot from him (just as we looked straight at our wrappers) but we can also find that, as Moses was God's friend, looking at his life helps us to see God in a new way (as we saw everything differently when we looked through our wrappers).

Make this model using a toffee wrapper and card.

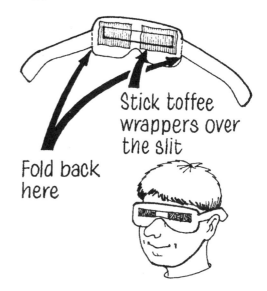

Fold back here

Stick toffee wrappers over the slit

## Young people

*Aim:* To familiarise them with the background to the Moses rescue.

Have a collection of library books providing information on the Israelites in Egypt and ask the group to find out what they can about:

1  how the Israelites came to be in Egypt;

2  how they were now being treated by the Egyptians and why.

They can do this in twos and threes.

Come together and discuss the findings, noting the main points on a flip chart. In the light of this discussion, read the Exodus passage together. Think together about:

1  why Moses' mother put her son in a basket;

2  why it would help for the Israelites' rescuer to have been familiar with the Egyptian way of life;

3  how God was responding to the Israelites' cries for help.

# 5th Sunday before Christmas

## YEAR 1

*Thought for the day:*
*God preserves a remnant,*
*whatever the surrounding evil.*

### Readings
Psalm 147
Genesis 18:20-end
Mark 13:14-end

### Reflection

Friendship with God is always a two-way process, which is something we need to bear in mind when we batter his ears with our prayers and don't let him get a word in edgeways. We can see a lovely example of his friendship in action with this conversation between God and Abraham.

God loves Abraham so much that he is prepared to waive his loathing of evil in order to answer Abraham's pleading. Even when the whole city is destroyed, Lot's family is saved for Abraham's sake. Whenever we pray in love it is actually the Spirit of God within us reaching out in communion with the Father; that's why prayer is so very powerful a source of transformation.

In God's purity and utter goodness, evil cannot survive, just as darkness cannot survive when we switch a light on. This truth brings us face to face with the unavoidable fact of evil in ourselves – however shall we survive in God's presence when we know we fall so far short of his purity and goodness?

The logical answer is that we can't hope to survive. God's answer is that if we will only allow ourselves to be rescued his mercy will manage to destroy the evil without destroying us. That's why Jesus was always concerned to get people trusting God; trust is the necessary climate for allowing oneself to be rescued. And without rescue there can be no survival.

### Discussion starters

1  Are we acquaintances, enemies or friends of God and are we sometimes unwilling to be rescued by him?

2  What evil in our lives, both individually and internationally, must God loathe and desire to destroy?

### All stage talk

*Theme:* God's purity and love cannot shine without destroying evil.

Have ready three dustbin bags labelled SODOM, YOUR TOWN and SAM. You will also need a grid of some kind, such as a cooling tray. Inside each dustbin bag have some cut up shapes of blue and orange card, making sure that the orange shapes will fall through the holes in the grid and the blue ones won't. Put many more orange shapes than blue in the Sodom bag, about equal in your town's bag and more blue in Sam's bag. Finally you need a clear blue sign with 'GOOD' written on it and an orange sign with 'EVIL' on it.

First of all introduce everyone to the three bags. They can imagine Sam to be either male or female. He or she is just a fairly ordinary Christian with 2.4 children. Introduce your town with any appropriate remarks and introduce Sodom as another city – the one we've just been hearing about, the one Abraham was pleading with God to save if a few good people could be found in it.

Can we see by looking at these bags how good or evil they are? No, we can't. But there's probably lots hidden from view which the light would show up to be good or evil. (Ask two volunteers to hold the good and evil signs so we know what we're looking for).

It's when God's bright love shines that we see clearly what is good and what isn't. When we do that . . . (tip the Sodom bag up over the grid) God filters out the evil so that only the good survives.

The volunteers can comment on how much of the city of Sodom survived. Allow God's light to shine on the contents of the other bags in the same way.

## Intercessions

Father, we pray through your Spirit
for those who do not know you;
for those who try to control you.

*Silence for prayer*

Great is our God:
**and great is his power**

Father, we pray through your Spirit
for a world which is bleeding and aching;
fighting and starving;
cruel and vulnerable.

*Silence for prayer*

Great is our God:
**and great is his power**

Father, we pray through your Spirit
for the hurting and hating;
for the damaged and the deluded;
for the ruthless and the wretched.

*Silence for prayer*

Great is our God:
**and great is his power**

Father, we pray through your Spirit
for those we love and cherish
and for those we work at loving.

*Silence for prayer*

Great is our God:
**and great is his power**

Father, through your Spirit
we thank you for the flow of your love
which fills our lives with colour and joy.

*Silence for prayer*

Great is our God:
**and great is his power**

## Other ideas

*A dance:* Give a group of six to eight people the challenge of preparing a mime to music to represent the few being led to safety through the surrounding evil. They can choose suitable taped music or have a go at creating their own sound effects. The dance would be particularly helpful if performed between the Exodus and Mark readings.

## In the crèche

*Aim:* Valuing the good.

Prepare a bowl of apples which includes some badly bruised ones, a box of pencils including quite a few blunt or broken ones, and a set of felt tip pens which includes several which have gone all feint and fluffy.

Work together sorting out the good apples from the bad ones, putting the good fruit in a nice bowl on a cloth. Sort out the sharp pencils from the blunt, putting the sharp ones in an attractive pencil holder on the cloth. Try out all the felt tip pens, putting all the workable ones in a box on the cloth.

What can we do with the bad apples? Cut out any good bits and put them in a dish, and throw the rest away. What about the broken pencils? Put the sharpenable ones in a bag to take home and sharpen, and throw the others away. What about the felt tip pens? We can't do anything with them so they get thrown away.

Now go over to the attractive good things and enjoy eating the apples, drawing and colouring. As you do so tell the children how God is always sorting through to find the good in people, and we can do the same.

## Children

*Aim:* Sorting out and rescuing the faithful. Bring along with you a pile of old greetings cards. Start by asking the children to sort these into ones which can be used for messages and those which can't be as they have writing on the back of the picture. Make a pile of the usable ones and put the others ready for recycling.

Tell the children the story from Exodus, bringing out the fact that although the city was so wicked, God still gathered Lot's family and saved them before the city was destroyed. He loves to rescue us from doing unkind, unloving things. When we turn a light on in a dark room the darkness can't survive. In the light of God's love evil can't survive.

Use the good cards to write this message: 'Jesus to the rescue!'.

## Young people

*Aim:* Falling away and being rescued. The three dustbin bags containing good and evil can be used first, before reading and/or dramatising the Exodus passage. Talk together about how evil takes root and grows in a person or a nation. Distribute the different lines of this rhyme and act it out as a discussion starter:

10 keen Christians trying to walk in line,

1 preferred to do as she liked and then there were 9.

9 keen Christians working late,

1 had no time left for God and then there were 8.

8 keen Christians seeking the kingdom of heaven,

1 couldn't be bothered and then there were 7.

7 keen Christians found their lives in a fix,

1 blamed it all on God and then there were 6.

6 keen Christians glad to be alive,

1 stopped praying and then there were 5.

5 keen Christians feeling pretty sore,

1 rejected the God of love and then there were 4.

4 keen Christians happy to be free,

1 lived to please himself and then there were 3.

3 keen Christians feeling frail and few,

1 gave up and then there were 2.

2 keen Christians enjoying all the fun,

living in the light of God which was made for everyone.

# YEAR 2

*Thought for the day:*
*God preserves a remnant, whatever the surrounding evil.*

## Readings
Psalm 147
Genesis 6:5-end
1 Peter 3:8-end

## Reflection

What a lovely world it would be if God could trust us to desire his will and keep his way just because it is good. As it is, law systems recognise that the good behaviour of many is mainly determined by the fear of consequences. But there is a limit to the effectiveness of externally imposed laws. At some point the whole system breaks down into anarchy unless there is some internal self control among most of the individuals in a society. Such times are noticeable throughout history by the widespread violence, the breakdown of family life, increasing mutual suspicion and lack of trust.

God is serious about sin and has designed us to live joyfully and freely with him, our Creator, at the centre of our lives, just as the tree of good and evil was planted in the centre of the garden.

If we keep abusing his leniency and placing ourselves at the centre of the universe, he will, for our own good, allow us to get hurt.

God grieves over the short-sightedness of our selfishness and pride, but out of love for us will always honour our free will. When we choose to live and work in harmony with him, joy and lightness of spirit can flood into our lives.

## Discussion starters

1 What do you think would happen if there were no laws or rules in society? What about in a Christian community?

2 What does this tell us about human nature?

## All stage talk

*Theme:* Rules.

Have a number of rules written out on large pieces of card. Choose rules appropriate to the experience of those present, such as:

Keep to the left in the corridors

No parking outside hospital entrance

Clear out pockets before dumping jeans for washing

Don't drink and drive

Hold up each in turn, asking people to work out what used to happen before the rule was made. Fill in the chart in each case, ticking as many columns as you like each time. Show how it is because we tend to be selfish/light-fingered/thoughtless that the rules need to be made. And in every case selfishness was to blame.

| People were being: | Rule 1 | Rule 2 | Rule 3 | Rule 4 | Rule 5 |
|---|---|---|---|---|---|
| SELFISH | | | | | |
| THOUGHTLESS | | | | | |
| LAZY | | | | | |
| LIGHT-FINGERED | | | | | |
| IRRESPONSIBLE | | | | | |
| FORGETFUL | | | | | |

It makes God very sad to see us behaving like this because he designed us, not with *self* at the centre, but *love* at the centre – love for God and love for one another. When we live like this, according to the maker's instructions, we feel free and happy, and the world is a better place to live.

## Intercessions

Father, we come to you
well aware of our habit of selfishness
which distorts your will
and wastes your opportunities;
and yet in trust we can lean on your love.

*Silence for prayer*

You are our God:
**the God who heals and restores us**

Father, we come to you
recognising the human weaknesses
of the church
and sorrowful at her divisions;
and yet in anticipation we can lean
on your love.

*Silence for prayer*

You are our God:
**the God who heals and restores us**

Father, we come to you
wearied and angered by the cruelty
and injustice
of a self-centred world;
and yet in hope we can lean on your love.

*Silence for prayer*

You are our God:
**the God who heals and restores us**

Father, we come to you
sharing the pain of all those who suffer,
sharing the grief of all those who mourn;
and yet in peace we can lean
on your love.

*Silence for prayer*

You are our God:
**the God who heals and restores us**

Father, we come to you
thrilled by your beauty and wisdom
and grace;
and filled with your joy we can lean
on your love.

*Silence for prayer*

You are our God:
**the God who heals and restores us**

## Other ideas

The Noah reading can be effectively dramatised, either by miming the actions while the passage is read, or by breaking the passage into parts which are read by different people.

In contrast to this very visual first lesson, try having quiet music playing as a background to the second reading.

## In the crèche

*Aim:* To make the children familiar with the story of Noah.

Use a toy Noah's ark or some cut out cardboard models to tell the story of Noah, bringing out the point that God wanted to keep Noah and the animals safe right through the flood.

The children can all act out being the animals coming into the ark and coming out on to dry land after the flood.

## Children

*Aim:* Sticking to what you know is right.

If you can bear the embarrassment, bring along a few things you have tried to make which have turned out badly, or something you loved which has got broken.

Begin by playing the 'sleeping lions' game, where everyone has to lie completely still, however much the others tempt them to move. Talk together about how difficult it is to keep lying still when you are being encouraged to move, and how difficult it is to keep on doing what you know is right when everyone around is persuading you not to bother. (e.g. not wanting to join in a 'be nasty to so-and-so' game; wanting to walk straight home from school when others want you to use a short-cut you've been told not to use.)

Now reveal to the children your disaster, to tell them about it. If any of them want to, they can share disasters they have had. Talk about how disappointed we feel when we try really hard to make something well and it turns out badly. Or how miserable it is when something we have made and are fond of gets broken.

That's how God felt and feels when he sees the people he has made so carefully all getting at one another and spoiling things. With the aid of pictures of models, get the children to help you tell the story of God rescuing Noah and the animals from the wicked world.

Help the children make this working model to remind them: DON'T GET SUCKED IN – STICK TO WHAT'S RIGHT.

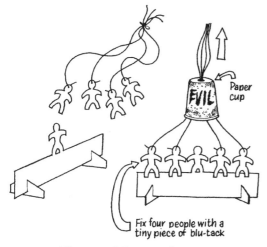

When you pull the strings, four people get tempted into evil, one stays where s/he is.

Read together the Genesis passage, then try a lucky-dip role play – put the following characters on folded slips of paper in a hat and each person takes one. They take up their positions and argue it out! The characters:

Noah (a friendly farmer who wants everyone to be happy)

Mrs. Noah (fed up with the hard work and missing her drowning friends)

Shem (rather bossy and wanting to get the animals organised)

Ham (happy to be on board so long as he doesn't have to do anything)

Esther (finding it hard to swim but refusing to be rescued)

a giraffe (who is frightened of going into the ark)

Rebecca (too engrossed with the way the water is affecting her hair style to hear an invitation to be rescued)

Jo and Ruth (still arguing over whose fault it was that their fire had gone out).

## Young people

*Aim:* To explore where rules work and fail and discover what rule we really need.

As in the All stage talk, have appropriate rules written out to start discussion on why rules are necessary. Look at the irritating truth that one person's selfishness can make life tedious for everyone else. Look at the way human nature tends towards self gratification unless love is involved.

# ADVENT

---

# *1st Sunday in Advent*

---

## YEAR 1

*Thought for the day:*
*Keep alert, because much is demanded*
*of those to whom much is entrusted.*

### Readings

Psalm 18:1-32
Isaiah 1:1-20
Luke 12:35-48

### Reflection

God's warnings are clear and unequivocal; lip-service gets us nowhere. It is the real, solid, practical loving and the tough, daily battling with evil that shows God our true feelings for him. One of the hardest and least fashionable things is perseverance – that willingness to carry on past the excitement stage, to keep reaching out when immediate rewards are negligible, to be as faithful completing a job as starting it.

Mind you, even here we need to be alert, in case what begins as perseverance isn't discreetly hardening into stubbornness. God is no brutal slave driver and if a task is turning impossible he may well offer an escape route. If we have been persevering in Christ's love we will be happy to carry on following in an escape plan; if our perseverance has hardened into self-directed stubbornness, we'll hang on for grim death and refuse to be rescued.

Whenever self muscles in on a gift of the Spirit such hardening happens – love hardens into possessiveness, joy into complacency and peace into self indulgence. This isn't a message of gloom, though. Recognising the danger is a considerable help in avoiding it, and our job is to co-operate willingly with the God of love. If we keep doing this daily, we won't be allowing the devil a foothold and then we will be ready when Jesus comes in glory.

### Discussion starters

1  Obedience is something most of us find very hard. How is it linked to selfishness and what factors make it easier/more difficult for us to do?

2  When is obedience a matter of life and death? How can we practise obedience in little ways so we're ready for the Big Event?

### All stage talk

*Theme*: Being watchful.
Beforehand make these two traffic signs from card, or draw them on acetates for an OHP.

First ask some volunteers to play a game. One stands at the front holding a stop sign and the others go to the back. They have to get up to the front without being noticed. If the person at the front sees them moving s/he shows the stop sign and they must go and sit down. While the game is being played, keep distracting the person at the front and see what happens! If someone thinks they can be even more vigilant, try the game once more, now that everyone realises you are deliberately trying to distract their attention to prevent them being watchful.

Make the point that sin creeps up on us like this, little by little. It's all the day-to-day acts of meanness, selfishness, unkindness, dishonesty and so on that gradually make us comfortable behaving with cruelty and lack of love, until we're completely bitter, cynical and destructive people. Jesus warns us to be watchful, so we can stop (show the stop sign) bad habits before they get very far.

The trouble is that Satan doesn't like us being watchful and will try to distract us, often in ways which seem very nice and reasonable (as you were doing). So don't be deceived by that. Make a point of learning what is right (show the other sign) by spending time with Jesus in prayer every day, and don't let yourself be distracted from being watchful.

## Intercessions

When the pressures of the day
fragment our peace,
keep us watchful and alert,
both for ourselves and for the world.
*Silence for prayer*
For who is God but the Lord:
**who is our rock but our God?**

When false values are paraded
among the true,
keep us watchful and alert,
both for ourselves
and for our young.
*Silence for prayer*
For who is God but the Lord:
**who is our rock but our God?**

When our tight schedules
leave no time for being merely available,
keep us watchful and alert,
both for ourselves and for those who
need a listener.
*Silence for prayer*
For who is God but the Lord:
**who is our rock but our God?**

When the injustice of the world laughs
at our insignificance,
keep us watchful and alert,
both for ourselves and for all who rely
on our solidarity with them.
*Silence for prayer*
For who is God but the Lord:
**who is our rock but our God?**

When we begin to take the wonder of
your creation for granted,
keep us watchful and alert,
both for ourselves and for every person
you cherish.
*Silence for prayer*
For who is God but the Lord:
**who is our rock but our God?**

## In the crèche

*Aim:* To explore the idea of keeping watchful.
Have some books to look at which involve searching for something (such as 'Where's Spot?') and play a game such as 'Peep-bo' for younger ones and 'What's the time, Mr. Wolf?' for older children.

We have to watch carefully so we don't fall over. (Some children may like to tell stories of when they fell over and hurt themselves because they weren't watching where they were going.) We need to watch carefully to stop ourselves being unkind, too.

Tape rolls together and tape string on to sides

## Children

*Aim:* To help the children recognise that sin creeps up on us if we aren't watchful. Give the children large labels to wear round their necks or headbands which have on them such things as: being greedy, being mean, being unkind, being thoughtless, being rude, being lazy etc.

Play the Mr. Wolf game with a difference, with all the evil creeping upon Mr. Wolf while he isn't looking. Mr. Wolf can only stop the evil getting at him by catching sight of someone moving. Point out that the more watchful he is, the less chance there is of them getting him. Now read the passage from Luke 12 to them, and help them make a pair of cardboard binoculars to remind themselves to keep watchful.

KEEP WATCHFUL

## Young people

*Aim:* To explore the practicalities for keeping alert for when Jesus comes. Read together the passage from Luke 12. Then give out copies of the following script to act out.

## What's in store

Characters: Manager, Assistant, Customer, Boss.

Provide a jacket and tie for the manager, various items of the store's produce and some authentic cardboard cartons. The manager and shop assistant are moving cartons from one place in the shop to another.

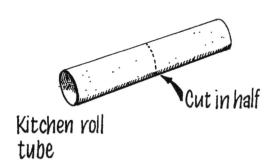

Kitchen roll tube

Cut in half

**Manager:** Easy does it, Fred.
**Assistant:** Yes, sir.
**Manager:** Always bend your knees, rather than your back.
**Assistant:** Yes, sir.
**Manager:** I take my responsibilities seriously, you know; and as shop assistant

your back is one of my heavy responsibilities.

**Assistant:** Yes, sir. These chocolate and nut cookies weigh a ton, don't they, sir?

**Manager:** Ah yes, more heavy responsibilities the boss left me with, eh . . . ha, ha!

**Customer:** Hallo, Harold! The boss gone away and left you in charge, has he? How about a packet of chocolate and nut cookies for friendship's sake? I'll buy you a pint this evening at the Crown.

**Manager:** You owe me a pint as it is, you old skinflint! And anyway, what do you think the boss would think if he came back and found me dishing out his stock. He's left me in charge because he reckons I'll look after things properly for him.

**Customer:** I don't think you'll see the boss in a hurry. He's languishing in the sun somewhere I expect. Anyway, I'll have some chewing gum.

*(He buys chewing gum, thanks the manager and leaves.)*

**Manager:** What's that grinding noise, Fred?

**Assistant:** That's my stomach, sir. It seems a long time since breakfast.

*(He strokes one of the packets of cookies.)*

**Manager:** Yes, I'm rather peckish, myself. Oh, come on, let's split a packet of these between us! Bill's probably right – the boss won't be back yet.

*(They do so and start eating.)*

**Boss:** *(Comes in and stares amazed at what is going on. Then he coughs to get their attention.)* So this is the man who was so sure I could trust him, is it?

**Manager:** *(Trying to hide biscuits)* Mr. Taylor! I . . . I wasn't expecting you!

**Boss:** Evidently. Mr. Woodman . . .

**Manager:** Yes, sir?

**Boss:** You're fired.

Discuss and list suggestions for practical ways to stay alert and avoid falling into temptation.

# YEAR 2

*Thought for the day:*
*Keep alert, because much is demanded of those to whom much is entrusted.*

## Readings
Psalm 18:1-32
Isaiah 2:10-end
Matthew 24:1-28

## Reflection

These passages make disturbing reading and force us to face ultimate issues which most of the time we prefer to ignore. But it is right that the church sets time aside in Advent to recognise the reality of an ultimate, cosmic event when God's purposes will be fully accomplished; a time when all evil must be finally obliterated as God's full glory is revealed. Knowing the power of evil, both outside us and within ourselves, we are bound to feel fearful at the inevitable violence of such a time.

We can't just hope we'll be dead by that time either, because it will involve everyone, both in time and in eternity. And our own disturbing times, with all the wars, famines and rising crime, make us aware of Jesus' words and remind us that we are already in the last age.

Yet in all three readings there is a great sense of hope welling out of the terror as the second coming approaches. In the psalm is the joyous experience of being rescued from annihilation; in Isaiah there is the excitement and anticipation of God's splendour, carrying with it the wise advice to put all our trust in this God of power and love instead of anything else; and in Matthew there is the tone of authority in Jesus which impressed many of his hearers, and which we can still sense centuries later. Jesus speaks with inside knowledge and experience of a God who is totally in control. The more we get to know him and trust in him now, the less fearful we need to be about the last days, however terrible they are.

## Discussion starters

1  Why are all 'end of the world' predictions futile?

2  How can we stop ourselves getting fed up with waiting?

## All stage talk

*Theme:* Being prepared and protected lessens our vulnerability.

Beforehand prepare a cardboard T.V. to frame a face. Have ready an umbrella, two rucksacks and several sets of waterproof clothing, and ask the organist or music group to prepare a short burst of 'cloudburst' sounds – violent and noisy. Or have percussion instruments given out and ask the whole gathering to practise being a huge cloudburst with instruments and clapping; they will be used later on.

First ask someone to switch on the telly and someone else to be giving the weather forecast: 'Some time today there will be very heavy rain.' Have two groups of people who are going out for the day. The first group decides that as it's such sunny weather they won't believe the forecast and set off as they are. (Set them off walking round and round the church). The other group takes waterproofs, just in case. (Set them off walking too. Everyone can wave to them.)

Tell them it's lunch time so they're going to sit down where they are and eat a picnic. Chat to each group about how they're getting on. But now there's - guess what – a cloudburst. (Everyone makes a very noisy violent cloudburst.) Shout over it that the first group are having to run for shelter back home, and the second group have put on their waterproofs and are really enjoying themselves. As the rain stops and the second group, wearing their waterproofs, come back up to the front, explain how Jesus has told us the second coming will involve some terrible things, but he offers us his complete protection so that when it all happens, whether before or after our death, we need not be afraid.

## Intercessions

Father, in love we stand alongside
all those who lead and minister
in your church.
We ask you to bless their lives
and their work.

*Silence for prayer*

God our Father:
**we want to walk with you**

Father, in love we stand alongside our
Queen and all the leaders of the nations.
We ask you to guide them in your ways.

*Silence for prayer*

God our Father:
**we want to walk with you**

Father, in love we stand alongside
all whose lives are bound up with ours.
Work with tenderness in the relationships
we bring before you now.

*Silence for prayer*

God our Father:
**we want to walk with you**

Father, in love we stand alongside
all whose bodies, minds or spirits
are hurting.
We ask you to minister to them now.

*Silence for prayer*

God our Father:
**we want to walk with you**

Father, in love we stand alongside
all who are close to death
and we pray now for your mercy,

*Silence for prayer*

God our Father:
**we want to walk with you**

Father, with love in our hearts
we want to thank you
for all you are and all you do in our lives.

*Silence for prayer*

God our Father:
**we want to walk with you**

## Other ideas

Have each side of the church praying silently in turn for the other, asking for God's blessing and protection in their lives.

## In the crèche

*Aim:* To explore the idea of being ready for something by getting ready.

If practical, give out instruments. After an initial clatter, get the children to put the instruments down on the floor in front of them. Then practise getting ready to play and then playing as an accompaniment to a song or two. Talk about and mime together how we get ready for other things – going to bed, cooking, going swimming etc. Then get ready to talk to Jesus by being still and quiet. Pray together.

## Children

*Aim:* To explore getting ready and being ready.

Have some different types of work clothing, such as a judo suit, Brownie gear, school uniform, football strip, overall etc. Also have a house plant and watering can and/or a small pet.

As you get different children to dress up, talk about how we have to get prepared to do things, and we enjoy it while we're feeling keen. Then we might start getting fed up with it. (Get them to undress back into ordinary clothes again.) Even if we're actually still going along, we're rather lazy about it now.

Talk about the importance in our Christian life not only of getting ready but of keeping ready. Show the children the house plant and/or small pet – the getting ready is exciting, but we also have to keep on with the feeding and watering and so on, or the plants and pets would die. If we want our faith to stay alive, we've got to look after that as well, feeding it with praying and reading the bible. This would be a good opportunity to have a few different bible reading schemes on show to look at, and on sale for parents afterwards.

## Young people

*Aim:* To think about what it means to be ready for Jesus.

Read the Isaiah and the Matthew passages, looking at how the present state of the world fits in, as have other times in history. Since Jesus, we are in the last age and at some point, either before or after we die, everything will be accomplished with evil inevitably being destroyed. When we see Jesus face to face, we will know all the ways we have hurt people but be unable to do anything about it. So how can we prepare ourselves to be ready?

Pray together for insight and guidance and then make a list of ideas; think about how your local church could help, and plan some constructive suggestions for developing and encouraging the faith in people of all ages.

# 2nd Sunday in Advent

## YEAR 1

*Thought for the day:*
*The Word of God has been gradually*
*unfolded all through the*
*Old Testament, throughout*
*the New Testament and ever since.*

### Readings
Psalm 119:137-152
1 Kings:22:1-28
Romans 10:5-17

### Reflection

I once attended a school service where the children were excellently disciplined, sitting quiet and good throughout. They were all obeying the rules, but that's all many of them were probably doing. Being in a right relationship with God does not just mean obeying the rules because we have been told to. When we live this way the imposed Law is right outside us, and the danger is that the letter of the Law will therefore become over-important, as it had done with some of the Pharisees. Ironically their misunderstanding had arisen because they were being ultra conscientious about internalising the Law; the sad truth was that internalising the rules this way could not nourish – any more than eating a piece of paper with 'spaghetti bolognese' on it would nourish our bodies.

So how can we properly write God's Law on our hearts, and sing its praises as if it is a living person? The answer is in the word 'Word'; the living Word of God is expressed in his Law and of course most profoundly in Jesus, the living Word. Having God's Law written on our hearts and minds is having the living Spirit of God active within us, so that we naturally come out with God's words and ideas and attitudes, as has happened ever since the prophets.

Life may not always be pleasant that way and there are bound to be conflicts, but it will be the way towards the world's healing, and that is the coming of the kingdom.

### Discussion starters

1  Who do we go to when we want to talk things over or get advice – people who know the Lord well, or people who are likely to agree with us? What are the advantages/disadvantages of both?

2  It's tempting to speak the truth only when it won't get us into difficult or embarrassing situations. But what does this suggest about who really is the Lord of our hearts and minds?

### All stage talk

*Theme:* Doing what comes naturally.
You will need to spend a little time making a cardboard 'machine'. Beg a washing machine/tumble drier carton and cut out a machine outline using a craft knife. It might look something like this:

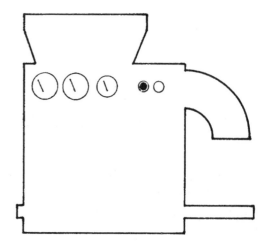

Set it up before the service, propped up against a table which has a washing up bowl on it. You will need bags of flour and sugar, a tin of chocolate powder and a packet of chocolate biscuits, a couple of large potatoes, a bottle of cooking oil and a packet of crisps. You will also need an old twisted piece of metal (a scrunched up metal clothes hanger will do fine) and a friendly, willing small accomplice to sit out of sight behind the machine.

Begin by explaining that you have brought along a machine which makes things. If you put in flour, sugar and chocolate powder (do so – just dumping the packets in, wrappers and all) the machine starts work with a low humming sound (which the children or everyone can do). And then the humming stops and out comes . . . (the child behind hands you a packet of chocolate biscuits) . . . these!

If you feed in potatoes and cooking oil, the machine starts humming and then produces . . . a packet of crisps. Explain that our lives are a bit like this machine; if we put into our lives lots of lies and arguments and thoughtless behaviour and gossip (drop in pieces of paper with these written on) then by the end of our lives we'll turn out like this . . . all hard and bitter and twisted (the scrunched up coat hanger).

But if we feed into our lives 'making an effort to be kind', 'forgiving people who hurt us', 'spending time with God' and 'reading the bible' we shall naturally turn out a happy, free, loving person . . . (at this point the small accomplice climbs out and runs to give his/her parent a big hug.) If we seek God and really believe that his love can make a difference to our lives, we're bound to become loving people quite naturally, and words and ideas will become increasingly in harmony with the God we worship.

## Intercessions

Father, we think of the difficulties facing the church;
and pray for all who minister your love.

*Silence for prayer*

We believe and proclaim:
**Jesus is Lord in every situation**

Father, we think of the way our world
is torn apart by war and lack of love

*Silence for prayer*

We believe and proclaim:
**Jesus is Lord in every situation**

Father, we think of those
whose lives are hard and twisted.

*Silence for prayer*

We believe and proclaim:
**Jesus is Lord in every situation**

Father, we think of the great pressures
on this generation to abandon your ways,
and of all those who feel lost
and without real value.

*Silence for prayer*

We believe and proclaim:
**Jesus is Lord in every situation**

Father, we think of those we find it hard
to relate to, and of those who sometimes
find us difficult to get on with.

*Silence for prayer*

We believe and proclaim:
**Jesus is Lord in every situation**

Father, we think of all
who fill our days with love and friendship.

*Silence for prayer*

We believe and proclaim:
**Jesus is Lord in every situation**

## In the crèche

*Aim:* To introduce the children to the bible.

Have one of the lovely children's bibles that are available now and show it to the children, browsing through the pictures to get an overall view of what it contains. Some pictures and stories they may recognise already. I think it is best if this is done in very small groups in a snuggly way. When they want to know about a particular story, tell them simply, or if it is one they have seen before, such as Noah or the birth of Jesus, tell it between you.

## Children

*Aim:* To explore the story in 1 Kings 22.

Tell the story with the children's help. They will be acting it out. Use dressing up clothes and appropriate props to make it realistic. Emphasise the importance of finding out God's will before we rush ahead and do things that we want to. Then make these badges to wear.

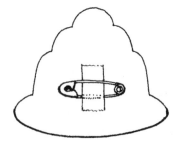

## Young people

*Aim:* To help them see the importance of having God's word in our hearts.

First read Romans 10:5-17 together. Talk about the difference between following rules and believing with your heart, and how these affect your actions in different ways. Give as examples such things as 'Don't smoke'; 'Don't drink alcohol in a pub unless you're 18'; 'keep your body for the person you marry'.

It may well be that one thing which crops up is that we often know what's right but still want to carry on our own way.

Now read 1 Kings 22:1-17, with different people taking speaking parts. Discuss this reading in the light of what was said earlier – look at the stages and consequences of Ahab's behaviour. Then pray together for God's word to take root in our hearts and change us from the inside.

# YEAR 2

*Thought for the day:*
*The Word of God has been gradually*
*unfolded all through the*
*Old Testament, throughout*
*the New Testament and ever since.*

## Readings

Psalm 119:137-152
Jeremiah 36:9-end (or 26)
Matthew 25:14-30

## Reflection

Today's readings are about the deliberate rejection of God's teaching through his word. It is there for our guidance and help, for our chastisement and our affirmation, but if we refuse to accept it, it will do us no good at all. What's more, it is a terrible waste, and so if we don't use what God gives us, or if we abuse it, he may well take it away from us.

The readings challenge us to check that we are actually listening attentively to the God we claim to worship. Listening is a skill we need to work at and master in ordinary life, and especially in our relationship with God. It involves being alert to seeing and hearing God's word in events and images he shows us – walking through each day expecting to have such communion with him. It also involves being willing to be taught even if we don't yet agree! It is accepting that God wants the best for us, so that we are content to follow his advice whether it comes to us through his word, his people or directly in our hearts.

## Discussion starters

1 Why did the king burn the scrolls? (List all reasons offered and explore each).

2 When do we as individuals/nations/ churches 'burn prophets' scrolls'?

## All stage talk

*Theme:* Receiving gracefully.

You will need:

A few books – a mixture of popular and little known

A bible

Walkman

First aid box containing some ointment labelled 'encouragement cream'

a bottle of 'refreshment'

a bandage labelled 'understanding'

an eye bath labelled 'grace to forgive'

a bible labelled 'handbook'.

The first aid box is wrapped like a present.

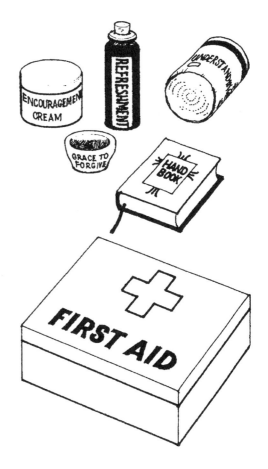

Begin by showing everyone some books. Involve their response – 'Do you like this one? . . . dislike that one?' When there is one they don't know whether they like or dislike, draw out that they can't tell you because they haven't read it. Show the bible – lots of people have one of these in their homes, but if we don't read it, it's as if we haven't got one.

Now ask for a willing helper and fit them up with the walkman, switching the tape on. Try to go on talking to them, but of course they won't be able to hear you. That's what happens to us – we don't hear God because we block out what he is trying to say to us and sometimes even accuse him of not speaking in our age. But if we really want to hear him, we've got to listen exclusively to him at least some time every day. (Turn off walkman and release volunteer).

And when we do read or hear God's word, what then? If we just put it away in a safe place and don't put it into practice, it will be just as if we haven't received anything. (Ask someone to offer you the present.) When they give it to you say 'thanks' but don't open it because it's too special. How does the giver feel when we do this? It hurts the giver and the present is no use to us, so he might as well give it to someone else. (Get him to do so.) Now this person opens it up and let's have a look at what's inside. (Go through the different items together, remarking how useful it would have been and how it's exactly what you needed.) so . . . make good use of what God offers – read his word, listen to him in prayer and put what you receive into action.

## Intercessions

Father, we pray for everyone
who reads the bible,
and those who could but don't.

*Silence for prayer*

Open our hearts:
**to recognise your will for us**

Father, we pray for your guidance
wherever decisions need to be made.

*Silence for prayer*

Open our hearts:
**to recognise your will for us**

Father, we pray for peace and
unselfishness
in every area of conflict.

*Silence for prayer*

Open our hearts:
**to recognise your will for us**

Father, we pray for greater love and
forgiveness
in all relationships.

*Silence for prayer*

Open our hearts:
**to recognise your will for us**

Father, we pray for your healing
and wholeness
in all those who suffer.

*Silence for prayer*

Open our hearts:
**to recognise your will for us**

Father, we lift our hearts in love
to praise you and give you thanks.

*Silence for prayer*

Open our hearts:
**to recognise your will for us**

## Other ideas

Have a small brazier burning during the first reading and through the time of intercessions.

## In the crèche

*Aim:* To explore the delight of giving and receiving.

As a preparation for Christmas, help the children wrap up gifts for a local centre for the homeless/battered wives and children etc. As you all work on this, chat about how lovely it is to give presents and how lovely it is when someone gives a present to you. Christmas cards could be made as well, possibly for the elderly and house bound.

## Children

*Aim:* Learning to listen.

First play this listening game. Tell the story from Jeremiah giving each person a part. Whenever they hear themselves mentioned, they stand up, turn around and sit down. At the mention of the fire, everyone moves. Afterwards point out how they had all needed to listen to do that so well. Who in the story didn't want to hear what God has to say? Did he succeed in destroying God's word when he burnt the scrolls? (For a little while, but not for long.) Who was good at listening to God?

Now try listening to hear a pin drop, first with your ears blocked and then normally. Try looking at something with your eyes closed and then with them open. Try feeling something with thick gloves on and then without. That's how we are, sometimes; God communicates with us in lots of ways, but if we want to notice, we'll have to listen carefully.

Check how the bible reading is going and help them make this pair of ears to remind themselves to listen to what God is saying.

## Young people

*Aim:* To explore the difficulties in listening to God.

Give out this dialogue for two people to read, which highlights our tendency to listen only when it's something we want to hear:

**Irene:** So I caught the 59 bus to the corner of the High Street and guess who I met? That Dora!

**Arthur:** Mmmm . . .

**Irene:** Her flu never got beyond her chest, you know?

**Arthur:** Really, dear . . .

**Irene:** She said she'd like us round to dinner next Monday.

**Arthur:** No, dear . . .

**Irene:** What do you mean, 'no, dear'? Arthur Harris, you haven't been listening to a thing I've been saying, have you?

**Arthur:** No, dear. Sorry, dear.

**Irene:** Her husband wondered if you could play bowls with him. Poor Dora's always stuck at home while her husband plays . . .

**Arthur:** Did you say bowls? Who wants to play bowls?

**Irene:** I told you . . . Dora with the chesty flu's husband.

**Arthur:** That's excellent – I could do with a game of bowls . . . I'll phone him straight away!

**Irene:** He caught it first, you see when he went out sailing in all that wind . . .

Now read the Jeremiah passage together and discuss why the king decided to burn the scrolls, how that made Jeremiah feel (remember the scrolls had been painstakingly written out by hand) and what God's reaction was.

Which parts of scripture do they sometimes wish they could ignore? Make a list of these and work out together why it is we would prefer to ignore them. Point out in the discussion that God always provides what we need, rather than what we want, and that we need to pray for our wills to be in harmony with his, so that eventually we shall want what God wants. Pray together about this and for strength in the times we're tempted to 'burn scrolls' rather than take them seriously.

# 3rd Sunday in Advent

## YEAR 1

*Thought for the day:*
*Through his messengers God prepares*
*the way for salvation.*

### Readings
Psalm 80
Amos 7
Luke 1:1-25

### Reflection

Since God works with full knowledge of everything in time and place, he is in a position to orchestrate events with perfect timing, even though the individuals involved may only see their own small part. Amos had been specially drawn from his farming in order to speak God's message to Israel, and he chose to go along with this calling, even though it made him extremely unpopular.

With hindsight we know that Elizabeth was to enable John the Baptist to come into the world, thereby providing the vital preparation of people's hearts for the arrival of the Messiah. Yet at the time, due to her husband's inability to communicate, Elizabeth must have seen her pregnancy in a less far-reaching way; for her, prayer had been answered and she was at last able to have the child she and her husband longed for.

So we, too, may be one small part of a great plan in God's heart at the moment; but unless we go along with him in our section, the plan will take far longer to be realised. We need to cultivate the art of saying 'Yes!' to God straight away, and

that ability is in direct proportion to the extent we trust him.

### Discussion starters

1   What are the similarities and the differences between the Jeremiah and the Luke readings?
2   Why was Zechariah so wary of believing Gabriel's good news?

### All stage talk

*Theme:* Preparing the ground is bound to cause disturbance.

Begin by explaining that to prepare for the talk today you will need everyone in each row to sit in reverse order from how they are sitting at the moment, so that those nearest the centre will end up nearest the sides. Give them a short time to organise that. (This should create mild chaos for a while which gradually settles into order again.) Thank everyone for their co-operation.

What they have just experienced is an important truth – when God prepares his people for his coming, that is bound to cause disturbance.

There they were sitting comfortably, and then they got messed about by you wanting them aligned differently; the people of Israel were living complacently until Amos came along and challenged the way their lives were aligned. John the Baptist's calling was to alert people to the way they were living and sort themselves out according to God's standards. When our own lives are challenged like this we have to set about checking the way we are living – are we in line with God's commandments and God's values? There may be drastic changes needed, (as there were for those sitting on the ends of the rows), or there may be minor changes (as there were for those few who have ended up sitting in the same place as before). But either way we need to get up, spiritually, and take a candid look at the way we speak and spend our time and money; we need to look at our relationships and attitudes, and at the extent to which we allow God to reign in us.

Now, as they realign themselves again in their rows, ask them to do so in silence, opening up their lives to be realigned in keeping with God's will.

## Intercessions

Father, into every situation of doubt and despondency,
among your followers,
breathe your faithfulness.

*Silence for prayer*

Prepare us, O Lord:
**to walk in your ways**

Father, into our strongholds of ambition and defensiveness
breathe your humility.

*Silence for prayer*

Prepare us, O Lord:
**to walk in your ways**

Father, into the prisons of guilt and revenge
breathe the grace of forgiveness.

*Silence for prayer*

Prepare us, O Lord:
**to walk in your ways**

Father, into the darkness of pain and fear
breathe your reassurance.

*Silence for prayer*

Prepare us, O Lord:
**to walk in your ways**

Father, into the flabbiness of complacency
breathe your zeal.

*Silence for prayer*

Prepare us, O Lord:
**to walk in your ways**

Father, into our homes and places of work
breathe your fellowship and love.

*Silence for prayer*

Prepare us, O Lord:
**to walk in your ways**

Father, into the whole of your creation
breathe your joy and peace.

*Silence for prayer*

Prepare us, O Lord:
**to walk in your ways**

## In the crèche

*Aim:* To help them sense the importance of preparing for Jesus.

Beforehand make the meeting area a tip, with everything in the wrong place, rubbish left around and so on. When you all arrive comment on what a mess it all is, and then work together making the place as beautiful as possible for Jesus. The children can help clear away and make an attractive area with candles, drawings, greenery and such like.

All enjoy how lovely it looks now and ask Jesus to make our lives beautiful and bright in the same way.

## Children

*Aim:* To introduce the children to John the Baptist.

Begin by enlisting everyone's help in getting the place ready for painting. When this is done, point out how we needed to change things in the room, putting them in new places, so that the room was ready. Today we are going to look at someone who helped people prepare their lives so they would be ready to meet Jesus.

Now tell the story of Zechariah and Elizabeth, adding that when the baby grew up he did just what the angel had said – he helped people get ready for Jesus. Ask them to think of one thing in their lives which they know is not right -

telling lies/not going to bed when they're told/being rude/not sharing/being a bad loser etc. and suggest they try and tackle that one thing through Advent.

Use the paints to make a large picture of John the Baptist baptising people in the Jordan. Call it: GETTING READY FOR JESUS.

## Young people

*Aim:* To help them look at the need to prepare themselves.

Begin by making several spirit levels and plumb lines. The spirit level is a square-sided squash bottle almost filled with water. The plumb line is a length of string with a heavy weight tied on to the bottom. In small groups everyone can try testing different surfaces and walls of the building to see if they are true or not. Gather again to share the findings.

Now read the plumb line section of the Amos passage together. We know what it means for building surfaces to be true – what does it mean for lives to be 'true'? Take note of the ideas raised, and in prayer, take time to measure your own lives up against God's spirit level and plumb line by looking at each idea in turn.

# YEAR 2

*Thought for the day:*
*Through his messengers God prepares*
*the way for salvation.*

## Readings
Psalm 80
1 Kings 18:17-39
Luke 3:1-20

## Reflection

This week we are given portraits of two extraordinary personalities – Elijah and John the Baptist. Both are fired with zeal to turn people's hearts back to God; both loathe the hypocrisy which worships God with the lips while the lives remain pagan. And both emerge from the austerity of the desert, visibly conscientious in self denial and self discipline.

It may help us to notice the two contrasting effects they have on people. Ahab's welcoming remarks speak for many in every age who have organised their lives comfortably and fitted religion into the convenient spaces left once the important things are catered for. To them (to us?) Elijah is a nuisance, because he churns up the well-padded conscience in us and threatens to disrupt our lifestyle, our working, reading and spending habits, our comforts and our rights. If, on the other hand, the words of Elijah or John the Baptist evoke a half-forgotten yearning in us for what is right and good, we will react like the hearers who said, 'What can we do about it?' To these people the words of the prophets are not bad but good news because they are like a glimmer of light in an existence of darkness – at last there is practical hope.

The changes needed in our lives may be just as disruptive, but we feel excited about putting them into practice because we can see they will do us good. In my experience, one of the marks of God working in people's lives is this excitement growing out of repentance; God reveals our sin to us in such a way that there is not only grief but a real itching to get things put right.

## Discussion starters

1  The people of Israel knew that Elijah would return to herald the coming of the Messiah. In what ways is John the Baptist similar to Elijah?
2  What makes us repentant? Why doesn't repentance lead to despair?

## All stage talk

*Theme:* Realigning ourselves to God frees us to live fully.

Beforehand you will need to collect six cartons of similar size and cover them back and front with plain paper. With the boxes arranged like this:

Draw a picture on one side of three people and write on the other: WE WORSHIP GOD. Write the same words on a long strip of paper which everyone will be able to see.

First of all remind everyone of how close Christmas is getting, and do a check on who has already made the pudding/got presents/wrapped them up/sent cards etc. So preparations are well under way. But the readings today are advising us to prepare our lives as well, and how is that going?

Arrange the boxes in the right shape but totally out of order and explain that it is a picture of the lives of Christians. Proudly drape a long strip of paper over the boxes and ask everyone if all is well as they look rather puzzled. When someone says the boxes are out of order, say something like, 'Well, these words say they worship God so they MUST be right, mustn't they?'

What both Elijah and John the Baptist were doing was challenging the people who said they worshipped God, but who lived as if they hardly gave him a thought. It happens today as well – we can get used to saying the words, but do our lives match up?

Ask a couple of volunteers to sort the words and pictures out so that they do match up with what they are saying. The whole thing can be viewed from both sides – when the words are really true, the people themselves are sorted out as well. And that's how it is with us – if we say we worship God, then we must sort our lives out so that they match up with what we are saying and, as we do so, we shall become more integrated, fulfilled people.

## Intercessions

Father, in all areas of weakness
and self-interest in your church,
both as individuals and collectively,

*Silence for prayer*

Lord, change us:
**from the inside out**

Father, in all areas of hardened resentment
and desire for revenge among the nations,

*Silence for prayer*

Lord, change us:
**from the inside out**

Father, in all areas of discord
and misunderstanding
in our relationships with one another,

*Silence for prayer*

Lord, change us:
**from the inside out**

Father, in all areas of guilt and regret
which haunt us from our past,

*Silence for prayer*

Lord, change us:
**from the inside out**

*Continued overleaf*

Father, in the time of our dying;
at the time of your coming in glory,

*Silence for prayer*

Lord, change us:
**from the inside out**

Father, enable us to praise you
not only with our lips
but in our lives,

*Silence for prayer*

Lord, change us:
**from the inside out**

## In the crèche

*Aim:* To continue preparing for Christmas. Talk together about getting ready for Christmas and all the things there are to do. Have a large green Christmas tree painted on paper or card and let everyone help decorate it with different stick-on shapes which are called love, happiness and peace.

## Children

*Aim:* To help them get their lives ready for Christmas.
You will need pieces of card, templates of crosses, coloured pens and scissors.

Tell them the story of John the Baptist helping everyone get ready for Jesus by making sure their lives were in line with the way God wanted them to live. How do they think God does want us to live? (Some of the answers may be very interesting!) Write up the main ideas inside the shape of a cross. We know God wants us to be like this because Jesus is like this, even though it brought him pain and suffering.

Show the children the height chart that we can check our height against. (Some children can demonstrate).

As Christians we have to check the way we are living against God's standard of LOVE. Help the children make these life-checkers:

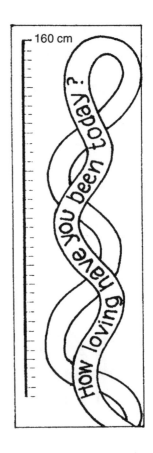

## Young people

*Aim:* To help them see the relevance of John the Baptist's teaching in their own lives.

Begin by asking them to line themselves up in order of height, then in order of shoe size, then by number of beans they can hold in one hand (dried, or baked if you are feeling adventurous or gross). They will find that the way they line up varies according to the standard or yardstick.

Now read the Luke passage together, asking them to look out for the standard John the Baptist wanted them to use in getting their lives lined up. Keep note of the suggestions made after the reading.

Have a look at yourselves and your church against this standard – God's standard of love and respect for one another.

# 4th Sunday in Advent

## YEAR 1

*Thought for the day:
After years of waiting, the Lord is
very near.*

### Readings
Psalm 40
1 Samuel 1:1-20
Luke 1:39-55

### Reflection

When things are done God's way so
many people are blessed in the process.
We need to remember that whenever we
long to crash in and force events to suit
our own short-sighted dreams. God does
things differently. He answers our prayer
at the time when various unrelated
circumstances can draw together to bring
widespread blessing and minimise hurt.

Hannah had many tears before she got
her son, but through the pain of her
waiting the love between her and
Elkanah was deepened, and Eli was made
more receptive so that he was better
prepared for dealing with Samuel's
calling. He was also given the grace to
pray for Hannah to have other children,
which she went on to do. And Samuel
was born at the right time to be able to
guide God's people and anoint the future
king David.

Typically for a God of order and care,
the birth of Samuel, who anointed King
David, is reflected by the birth of John the
Baptist, who one day baptised Jesus. As
Mary comes to visit her cousin, Elizabeth
is suddenly filled with the Spirit, the joy

of her unborn child radiating to her the
amazing truth that Mary's son is the
Messiah.

### Discussion starters

1  It was Hannah's deep pain which hurt
   her into praying so fervently. What
   does this suggest about the way we
   should pray, particularly in intercession?
2  Compare Mary's song of praise with
   Hannah's (in 1 Samuel 2).

### All stage talk

*Theme:* The perfect way God brings his
plans to fulfilment.

Beforehand either ask the music group
to prepare a short SATB hymn, chant
or anthem, or ask three of four
instrumentalists to prepare a short piece
of music.

First remind everyone that although
they are here partly because they chose to
come, they are also here because God
chose for them to be here, and people
praying for them opened the way for
God's will to be fufilled.

Ask everyone to sit back and enjoy the
prepared music. That is the composer's
original plan accomplished, but a lot of
people were involved in enabling the
composer's ideas to turn into the music
which helps us worship. There was the
composer, perhaps the composer's
teachers, the publisher and the editor, the
person at the warehouse who sent his score
to the shops, the sales person, and our
music director, even before we reach the
actual performers. (Have different people
to stand out as you mention each job.)

All this is like the way God prepared
the ground for the coming of Jesus, right
through from Abraham, and including
Samuel, who grew up to anoint David as
king.

But God also harmonises; he brings
things together in the best possible way

for everyone. We can get some idea of this if we hear just one strand of the music on its own (just the tenor part, for instance). It's interesting but not riveting! Try another part on its own. There may be times of silence in the separate parts when nothing seems to be happening, just as our prayers sometimes don't seem to be answered, but in fact if there weren't those silences, the whole piece of music wouldn't blend as well as it does.

Ask everyone to listen to the music again, noticing the harmony and remembering how we really can trust God to fulfill his plans in the best way for us.

## Intercessions

Father, we thank you for raising up leaders and ministers in your church, and we pray for them now.

*Silence for prayer*

In your way, Lord:
**let your will be done in us**

Father, we thank you for all that is good in our society and pray now for all in positions of authority.

*Silence for prayer*

In your way, Lord:
**let your will be done in us**

Father, we thank you for our homes and families, for our friends and neighbours.

*Silence for prayer*

In your way, Lord:
**let your will be done in us**

Father, we thank you for those who care for the sick, the distressed and the dying.

*Silence for prayer*

In your way, Lord:
**let your will be done in us**

Father, we thank you for all those who worked with you, in your plan of salvation for us. Work also in us for the good of your world.

*Silence for prayer*

In your way, Lord:
**let your will be done in us**

## In the crèche

*Aim:* To help the children prepare for Christmas.

Talk about Joseph and Mary starting their long journey with their donkey to Bethlehem where the baby Jesus would be born, and pack a bag with some of the things they would need – dried fruit and biscuits, water, baby clothes, a blanket etc. Help them make this crib for their homes:

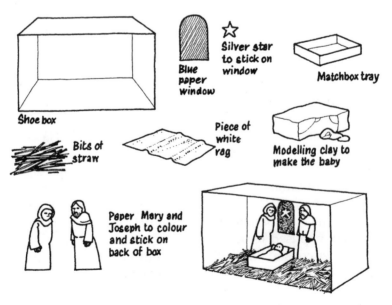

Shoe box

Blue paper window

Silver star to stick on window

Matchbox tray

Bits of straw

Piece of white rag

Modelling clay to make the baby

Paper Mary and Joseph to colour and stick on back of box

## Children

*Aim:* To meet some people who worked with God by trusting him.

Beforehand prepare card pictures of Zachariah, Elizabeth, Joseph and Mary; Elizabeth and Mary are both looking very happy. Also make a signpost which says 'To Nazareth', and Elizabeth's house. Put down the story mat, or green and blue sheets/carpet tiles.

Get the children to tell the story of Gabriel visiting Mary to tell her that she would have a son who would save his people. (This is something most will be familiar with already.) Point out how Mary said she was happy for it all to happen God's way, and how Joseph was prepared to marry her and help her look after the baby.

Now tell the children about Mary's cousin, Elizabeth; the way she had prayed for a child and was now six months pregnant with John, and how her husband had been told by an angel how his son would prepare the way for Jesus.

Using the story mat and figures, with the children adding trees and paths, tell how Mary went to visit her cousin, and what happened when they met. (Those with baby brothers and sisters may remember how babies move around in the womb.)

Help the children make these cards to remind them to say 'Yes' to God.

Front

 **Push in split pin to form a handle not at the front but at the BACK of the door.**

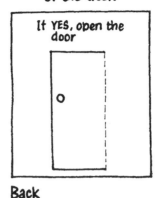

Back

## Young people

*Aim:* To think about doing things God's way.

First read the story of Hannah, with different people taking parts or acting it out. Look at why Hannah was so distressed and how that deep distress drove her to pray fervently. (Do we have to really care before we can really start praying?)

Now read the Luke passage, and how all these different life journeys (of Zachariah, Joseph, Mary and Elizabeth) had been brought together by God leading each of them so that his plan of saving the world could be carried out. Split the group into four to prepare a 'story of my life so far' of each person involved, trying to imagine the way each might express his/herself. Then have spokespeople reading each life story out in turn.

# YEAR 2

*Thought for the day:*
*After years of waiting, the Lord is*
*very near.*

## Readings
Psalm 40
Jeremiah 33:10-16
Revelation 22:6-end

## Reflection

Today we are hearing God's word in stereo, so to speak. In the Jeremiah reading we think of the promises fulfilled in the birth of Jesus at Bethlehem, and in Revelation of the promised second coming, when Jesus will come again in glory.

When you are looking forward to an arranged meeting with a loved relative or friend, the natural thing to do is to let your mind run over the happy times you had when you were last together – the words that were spoken and the way you passed your time. Although you know that this visit will be completely new, you will have some idea of what it will be like by looking back to the last visit as well as looking forward to this one.

Our way of looking back to the first Christians each year is a way of helping us prepare for the second coming of Jesus. We don't know when it will be, but we do know it will be the Jesus whose words of encouragement and challenge we cherish; whose delight in bringing people to wholeness fills us with hope; and whose dying proved an undying love for everyone.

We can learn, too, from the things which prevented people from accepting Jesus. We can work on holding our minds and hearts open to cope with God's surprises. And we can remember that it was those who knew the truth about themselves and their need of God who found in him such freedom and joy.

## Discussion starters

1   What do we know and what don't we know about the time when Jesus will come again?

2.  As you prepare to celebrate Christmas this and every year, what aspects of the Christmas story help you prepare for the second coming?

## All stage talk

*Theme:* Looking backwards and forwards at once.

Begin by explaining that we're going to conduct some scientific experiments, and ask everyone to cover one eye and look at you. They are to take note of exactly where you are in relation to the pillar/window behind you. Now they look again covering the other eye, and notice how you've changed postion. Our stereoscopic vision relies on us seeing a different picture with each eye, which the brain kindly fuses for us so we can judge distances better.

Now they can try closing their eyes and blocking one ear, and guessing where the shaking noise is coming from. If the experiment is repeated with eyes closed but both ears unblocked, it is likely that more people will be able to guess correctly. Hearing different sounds from each ear enables us to judge where things are around us.

What's all this to do with the second coming?

Jesus warned us that we will not know the exact time or conditions, but we need to be prepared because it will be a very nerve-wracking and confusing time, filled with terror for many as God bursts into everyday life and only what is of God will survive. But Jesus also says that those living in harmony with God and one another need not be afraid – to them it will be a time of great rejoicing.

Remembering how Jesus came last time can help us get ready for when he comes again. They are two different pictures, of course, but together help us see God more clearly.

## Intercessions

Father, we ask for your will to be accomplished in your church.

*Silence for prayer*

God in heaven:
**let your kingdom come**

Father, we plead for mercy on behalf of a petulant, self-seeking world.

*Silence for prayer*

God in heaven:
**let your kindom come**

Father, we ask your blessing on all who strive for peace and justice.

*Silence for prayer*

God in heaven:
**let your kingdom come**

Father, we welcome your presence in our families and friendships.

*Silence for prayer*

God in heaven:
**let your kingdom come**

Father we stand in your name against all that is evil.

*Silence for prayer*

God in heaven:
**let your kingdom come**

Father, we ask you to prepare us for the day when Jesus returns in your glory.

*Silence for prayer*

God in heaven:
**let your kingdom come**

## Other ideas

Have the crib prepared by the children while the music group are singing quietly, as a time of meditation for people to make their hearts ready to receive Jesus.

## In the crèche

*Aim:* to continue preparing for Christmas. Make a crib scene with the children talking together as you work about getting ourselves ready to welcome him, both at Christmas and when we meet him face to face.

## Children

*Aim:* To help children understand that we are both looking backwards and forwards at Christmas.

Talk about looking back to times we have enjoyed – you could show some holiday snaps to give them the idea. Ask them to think back to this year's summer holiday and then forward to the things they want to do again next year.

At Christmas we are looking back to the time when Jesus came to live among us as a human person. We're also looking forward to the time he has promised to come back again. (To many children this comes as a great surprise and they have lots of question about it. Answer them without surmising anything, recognising that even Jesus himself didn't know when it would be, but we do know it will happen, whether we are alive or dead at the time.)

Help them make this model (shown overleaf) to remember that we are preparing for both events.

**Colour and fold up**    **Colour, cut and fold up**    **Colour and fold up**

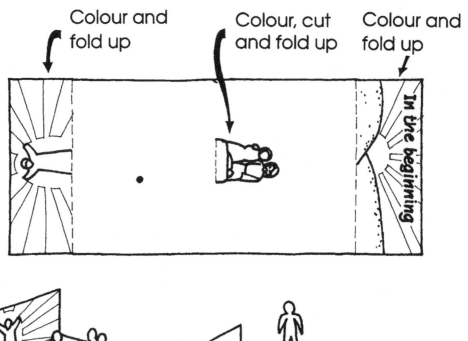

Move the person
to look back at the crib and
forward to the second coming

Colour yourself,
fold flap and fix
dot to dot with split pin

## Young People

*Aim:* To think about both the first and the second coming of Christ.

Try to get hold of one or two things which require two pieces before they make sense. I'm thinking of those 'I LOVE YOU' necklaces which don't make sense until you spin them round and round and both sides merge together; of messages which can only be read when you look through red cellophane (usually telling you how much you might have won); of combination cycle locks which only open when all the right numbers are lined up. If you haven't any of these, draw a bird on one side of the piece of card and a cage on another. Fix them on to a cocktail stick and roll the stick between your hands, so that people see a bird in a cage.

Talk together about these and then read the passage from Jeremiah. Who does this prophecy seem to refer to? Then read the passage from Revelation and have a time for discussion and questions about the second coming of Christ. Establish what we do know about it and what we don't; what we might look forward to about it and what might be frightening. Keep track of the conversation on two sheets labelled 'the first coming' and 'the second coming'. Work out from Jesus' life and teaching how best we can prepare for the time when Christ returns in glory.

# CHRISTMASTIDE

## *Christmas Day*

# *YEARS 1 AND 2*

*Thought for the day:*
*Jesus Christ is God's good news in*
*language humankind can understand.*

## *Readings*
Psalm 19
Isaiah 35
John 3:16-21

Christmas morning is very much a time for all God's children to worship together, so I have not included separate age-group programmes for today.

## *Reflection*

At the heart of all the festivities today is the marvellous truth of God's love for us, which spills out into our human need and weakness and at agonising cost is content to give up everything in order to set us free.

Every year we celebrate Christmas, we can learn something fresh about this amazing mystery of love; as our own life changes we shall find we are able to discern new insights, guided by the very Jesus whose birth we love to remember. Whatever our journey to the stable this year, we are welcomed by the beauty of its humility, the tenderness of its simplicity and the enormity of its glory. For God is here present among his people, and the world will never be the same again.

## *All stage talk*

*Theme:* The incarnation means that God is with us in person.

You will need some kind of transformer toy, a road map book of your country and a model car (preferably a sit-in one). Explain that you have brought along some Christmas presents to talk about.

First show the transformer and ask its owner to show how it changes from one thing into another. Perhaps some people expected the familiar 'Christmassy' readings of Mary and Joseph, the manger, and angels and the shepherds this morning. What we actually heard was the promise of impossible transformation taking place in our world due to God's complete love for us. Like this transformer, God coming in person into our lives means that he can change us from being selfish into being loving; he can change us from being trapped by guilt and fear into being free to live abundantly and enjoy life to the full.

Now show the road map. Anyone travelling over the Christmas holiday will really appreciate having one of these, because whenever you get to a confusing junction which suddenly stops sign posting the place you are trying to get to you can look here and see the whole picture, rather than just the muddy spray and tarmac around you. Now that God is with us in person our lives can be guided, and the best route taken.

As it's Christmas day we'll play a party game now. It's a sort of 'Give us a clue" and it will help us remember what Christmas really celebrates. One word, first syllable: IN (ask someone to climb into the pedal car). Second syllable: CAR (ask the person in the car to drive it around). Third and fourth syllable: NATION (get the road map book and point to the name of the country on the front, or show the complete map of the area in the front of the book). Whole word, which means the great news that God is with us in person: INCARNATION (In extrovert gatherings everyone can shout it. In more demure congregations, everyone can tell it to someone else).

## Intercessions

We pray for all the groups of Christians who are celebrating your birth today.

*Silence for prayer*

O God, we thank you:
**for loving us so much**

We pray for all babies,
that they may be given love and care.

*Silence for prayer*

O God, we thank you:
**for loving us so much**

We pray for all who are missing their loved ones,
and all who find Christmas difficult.

*Silence for prayer*

O God, we thank you:
**for loving us so much**

We pray for all those in pain
and those with debilitating illness.

*Silence for prayer*

O God, we thank you:
**for loving us so much**

We pray for those in prison
and for their families.

*Silence for prayer*

O God, we thank you:
**for loving us so much**

We pray for the homeless,
and all refugees.

*Silence for prayer*

O God, we thank you:
**for loving us so much**

We thank you for the joy of Christmas and welcome you in our homes.

*Silence for prayer*

O God, we thank you:
**for loving us so much**

## Other ideas

•  Have everyone joining hands during the Lord's prayer to emphasise God's real presence amongst us, his children.
•  Ask people to bring bells and ring them at the beginning of the Gloria.

# 1st Sunday after Christmas

## YEAR 1

*Thought for the day:*
*Laying his glory and majesty aside,*
*God is content to enter human life as*
*a vulnerable baby.*

### Readings
Psalm 132
Isaiah 40:18-end
Colossians 1: 1-20

### Reflection

So as to help us understand the incarnation better, this week's readings first take us on a guided tour of God's glory and majesty – the sheer size of the universe which he has created; his intimate knowledge of each fragile part of it; his delight and personal involvement; his controlled power and utter faithfulness. Then, as our imaginations are still reeling at the amazing reality of such a God, we are given an almost incredible truth – that Jesus, the baby just born in some very ordinary stable during a Roman census, is none other than the visible image of that unseen God.

As a loving parent crouches down to a toddler's eye level, so the God who has supreme command of the whole of life, crouches down to communicate with his created humanity by becoming human himself, putting himself at the mercy of their God-given ability to choose either good or evil. Immeasurably powerful must such love be.

## Discussion starters

1   What difference would it make to our world if more people realised the actual extent of God's power?
2   What does this way of saving people tell us about the character of God?

## All stage talk

*Theme:* Love that intervenes to rescue.
You will need a fairly large globe. You may choose to use a few slides of stars and planets (and a projector) as well.

Begin by talking about those times when you're watching a quiz programme or a football match and the people you are watching are making terrible mistakes. You may shout advice at them on the telly, but they don't seem to take any notice of you!

I suspect that might be a little like God feels, as he watches the people he has made messing up their own and other people's lives, and taking not a blind bit of notice of him, even though he could make their lives so much richer and more peaceful.

Now show some pictures of the extent of God's majesty and/or the globe, getting people's help with naming the other planets in our solar system, the name of our sun and our galaxy. Aim to get across the size, beauty and order of God's creation and therefore of the creator himself.

Use the globe to look at the littleness of our world and the separate countries. God has made us free to choose good and evil, and we were getting ourselves and each other into a mess we couldn't get out of. God was prepared to lay all that greatness and majesty aside so as to rescue us by being born, and walking around as a human, loving us back to freedom again.

## Intercessions

Father, breathe your life
into every worshipping community,
and heal all disunity in your church.
*Silence for prayer*
God of glory:
**we thank you for loving us**

Father, breathe your peace into our world
both in individuals and in nations.
*Silence for prayer*
God of glory:
**we thank you for loving us**

Father, breathe your joy into our homes
and places of work and leisure.
*Silence for prayer*
God of glory:
**we thank you for loving us**

Father, breathe your comfort into all
who suffer, whether mentally, physically,
emotionally or spiritually.
*Silence for prayer*
God of glory:
**we thank you for loving us**

Father, breathe your hope into those
who feel they have little to live for.
*Silence for prayer*
God of glory:
**we thank you for loving us**

*Continued overleaf*

Father, breathe your refreshment
and delight into our attitudes
until we live in thankfulness.

*Silence for prayer*

God of glory:
**we thank you for loving us**

## In the crèche

*Aim:* To enjoy the size and beauty of God's creation.

You will need picture books of all kinds of large animals, both living and extinct. Enjoy looking at them and measure up the length of the really big ones by pacing the length on the ground. Talk about some of the biggest things you have ever seen and draw pictures of these.

## Children

*Aim:* To help them appreciate the greatness and majesty of God. You will need a number of wildlife magazines, calendars and seed catalogues for cutting up, scissors, glue, pens and a large sheet of card. Also some reference books with good pictures of the universe and our planet viewed from space. A few percussion instruments may be used too.

First look at the reference books together, helping the children imagine the size and beauty of the universe God has made. Then make a working model of the solar system using one child to be the sun and nine others of varying size to be the planets. These children move slowly round the sun in their orbits while any remaining children play some quiet 'space music'. Or everyone can sing a worship song such as 'All that I am' (Spring Harvest – *Kid's Praise 1992*).

Then help the children to make a collage picture of the beauty of our created universe, including on it written truths about God, such as 'Our God loves what he has made'; 'Heaven and earth are full of his glory'.

## Young people

*Aim:* To help them appreciate the glory of God and his generous love.

Begin with a time of praise and worship, reading the Isaiah passage together with taped/live music playing quietly in the background. Then ask the group to plan some way of expressing the wonder of God which this passage describes. They can use art work, three dimensional structure, music, dance or mime, for instance, or a mixture of media. This can be incorporated into the worship either today or next week.

# YEAR 2

*Thought for the day:*
*Laying his glory and majesty aside,*
*God is content to enter human life as*
*a vulnerable baby.*

## Readings
Psalm 132
Haggai 2:1-9
1 Peter 2:1-10 or Luke 2:41-end

## Reflection

After their years in exile, the people of Israel are allowed to return home and, having established their own homes again, the time is right to start rebuilding the temple at Jerusalem. When we think back to the magnificence of the temple Solomon built we are able to feel with the older members of the community as they too remember, and look on what is now only a heap of rubble.

Perhaps you, too, have known that sense of desolation and hopelessness as you look on an area of your life which had once seemed so beautiful and permanent, and yet is now only rubble at your feet. Haggai was sent, both to them and to us as an encourager, to strengthen our hearts with hope. God does not look at anyone's pile of rubble and walk away; he does not look at our fallen nature and walk away. He is by nature a builder and rebuilder, and is able to make the rebuilt lives more beautiful than they were before.

The Incarnation is God's rebuilding programme, and this time the stones are alive with his Spirit. Through Jesus living in us, we can be restored to live freely in harmony with our creator in the way God originally intended.

## Discussion starters

1  Having read these two passages, what practical help can we find about the most effective restoration work whenever it is needed in our own lives, in our church community and in society?

2  In the light of the Haggai reading, what significance is there in the Luke story for this week?

## All stage talk

*Theme:* God's rebuilding programme.
You will need a lot of children's building bricks – separate and/or interlocking ones. Also make a stand-up notice in thin card which says on it: Our God rebuilds and restores us.

First tip all the bricks out on to the floor in front of everyone, and remind them of the rubble of stones which was all that was left of Solomon's glorious temple when the exiles returned to Jerusalem. Ask people to turn to someone near them and tell one another how they would feel in that situation. Now ask for

two or three very young people who enjoy building. Set them to work creating a magnificent building, arranging them to face the congregation so that everyone can watch the building progressing. Ask them to carry on building while you talk. Explain how God responded to his people's feelings of sadness/ depression/ despair/hopelessness etc. by speaking words of encouragement through his prophet, Haggai.

In a way the temple, so beautifully planned and made, and now in ruins, was rather like humanity – also beautifully planned and made, but also ruined through evil.

God decided on an extremely costly restoration plan: he sent his only Son into the world to put things right from the inside.  Through Jesus Christ living in us we are once again restored to the lovely relationship we were meant to have with God. Like living stones, we are all being built up into God's temple – and the temple is a place for God to live in. God is not far away somewhere, but right here in and amongst us now.

Thank the builders and place the notice beside their building.

## Intercessions

Father, we think of the variety of individuals who make up your church; make us quick to encourage one another and slow to criticise.

*Silence for prayer*

Thank you, Lord:
**for restoring us through love**

Father, we think of the responsibility we all have in looking after our world, and our desperate need for guidance.

*Silence for prayer*

Thank you, Lord:
**for restoring us through love**

*Continued overleaf*

Father, we think of the joys and sorrows among families and friends, and our need of the grace to forgive one another.

*Silence for prayer*

Thank you, Lord:
**for restoring us through love**

Father, we think of the pain
which so many suffer all over the world,
and of their thirst for comfort and
encouragement.

*Silence for prayer*

Thank you, Lord:
**for restoring us through love**

Father, we think of all those who dedicate
their lives to building with you,
and thank you for their faithfulness.

*Silence for prayer*

Thank you, Lord:
**for restoring us through love**

## Other ideas

During the second reading have a group of 8-10 people getting up from their seats and moving slowly and deliberately to form a human building. Spend a little time beforehand working out the structure (here is one idea from infinite possibilities!).

Then, since no one else knows what that finished shape is, the quiet and deliberate movements towards it are very effective, and bring out the meaning of Peter's word.

## In the crèche

*Aim:* To help them understand that when things fall down or go wrong we can build them up again, and help one another.

You will need lots of building bricks suitable for the children in your care. Play with the bricks, both building up and knocking down. With the older toddlers, try building a structure altogether, helping one another and learning co-operation.

## Children

*Aim:* To help them see that God works in us to put things right where they have gone wrong.

You will need a number of cartons and boxes and other interesting junk to build with, plenty of sticky tape and parcel tape, staples and pens.

First remind the children of how smart King Solomon's temple had been. Get them to make the temple with their bodies, bit by bit, like this:

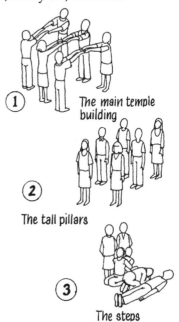

① The main temple building

② The tall pillars

③ The steps

Now explain how after many years of being unfaithful to God, the temple was attacked and reduced to rubble. (Everyone falls down.) Many people were taken off to Babylon.

Then, after 70 years, the people were allowed to return, and all they found was their beautiful temple in ruins. As the children lie there, read them Haggai's words, and then let them slowly rebuild themselves. Tell them how God can rebuild us whenever we fall down through doing or thinking or saying what is unloving or evil, and help them use some useless junk to build into a superb structure.

## Young people

*Aim:* To help them understand God's loving restoration programme.

You will need a selection of things which need restoring in some way, and the equipment for putting them right – e.g. tarnished silver, socks which need darning, guide/scout blackened pots and pans, and a badly wired plug.

First read the passage from Haggai and talk about the way God gets involved with people who are in ruins and lovingly restores them. It was for this reason that Jesus was born into our world.

Now set everyone restoring the things you have brought, and talk as you all work about the different ways that sin ruins people's lives and how there is always hope now that Jesus lives in and amongst us. When we offer to build with him we may be used in quite unexpected ways.

# 2nd Sunday after Christmas

## YEAR 1

*Thought for the day:*
*God's salvation is for all peoples and nations; everyone is eligible*

### Readings
Psalm 89:19-38
Isaiah 43:1-13
Matthew 2

## Reflection

It is always difficult to see any point in suffering when we are plunged in the middle of it, and the people of Israel were finding it very hard to see any presence of God in their state of exile in Babylon. Many felt their God had abandoned them and were changing their allegiance to the gods of the Babylonian people.

God speaks through his prophet a new concept of who he is – not merely Israel's national God, but the one and only God of all people, whatever their nationality. Within that overall picture, the people of Israel are chosen and cherished and they will be the means of bringing his light to the whole world. He will personally watch over them and protect them from annihilation, however unpromising things look to them at the moment.

In Matthew 2 we can see how God's plan is unfolding, as visitors from distant countries make their way with remarkable faith and persistence to find Jesus and honour him. Herod's jealousy is not allowed to block God's will due to the receptiveness and obedience both of Joseph and the wise men.

That is just as true now: evil in our time is powerful and threatening, but to the extent of our openness and obedience God can act to dodge it or turn it to blessing.

## Discussion starters

1  There are still so many who do not realise that God is their God and loves them. What are we/should we be doing about this?

2  Look up the Micah prophecy which the scribes at Herod's palace found. What prevented it from being good news for Herod? What kind of things can block our receptivity and obedience to God?

## All stage talk

*Theme:* God's promise to look after us and keep us safe.

You will need a couple of baby care items, designed for the child's protection (such as a playpen, stairgate, reins or baby alarm). You will also need large signs saying: EGYPT, BETHLEHEM and NAZARETH.

First show everyone the items you have brought, and ask some parents and babies to demonstrate how they are used, reminding people as they watch the two's and under that Jesus was about this age when Herod's soldiers came to kill him.

Parents spend a lot of effort making sure that their young are safe – as we get older we sometimes think they're fusspots, but their concern for our safety grows out of their love for us. It is because God, our parent, loves us so much that he promises to look after us for ever. Now ask for three volunteers to be Joseph, Mary and Jesus (young toddler) – preferably a family. Ask three other people to be road signs, standing in different parts of the building. (You could use a balcony for Egypt, if there is one.)

Ask the family to start at Bethlehem. King Herod felt threatened by this small boy, so God kept him safe by having him in a family and warning Joseph of the danger of staying in Bethlehem. Joseph listened and acted straight away, rushing his family off the Egypt. (They rush to Egypt.) While they were there Herod died, but his successor was just as cruel so they didn't go back to Bethlehem, they went to Nazareth, which is where they settled.

God may be trying to use us as part of someone's rescue plan. He won't be able to unless we listen to him and do what he wants, whether we understand the reasons or not.

## Intercessions

Father, into your care
we commit all Christians,
all in ministry and all church leaders.

*Silence for prayer*

O Lord, our God:
**it is good to be safe in your love**

Father, into your care we commit our world, with its needs and failures, hope and despair.

*Silence for prayer*

O Lord, our God:
**it is good to be safe in your love**

Father, into your care we commit those we love
and those we could love more.

*Silence for prayer*

O Lord, our God:
**it is good to be safe in your love**

Father, into your care we commit those of all ages who are in danger, and live in fear.

*Silence for prayer*

O Lord, our God:
**it is good to be safe in your love**

Father, into your care we commit those
who have recently died
and all who mourn for them.

*Silence for prayer*

O Lord, our God:
**it is good to be safe in your love**

Father, we rejoice in the way you look
after us, and thank you for providing for
all our needs.

*Silence for prayer*

O Lord, our God:
**it is good to be safe in your love**

## In the crèche

*Aim:* To think about what families are for.
You will need pictures/models/toys of
Mum, Dad and baby humans and animals.

Play with the toys/models/pictures,
sorting them into families and playing
out situations where Mum and Dad keep
the baby safe and look after it. Talk about
our own families – the people we live
with who look after us – bringing in the
wider family so they can see that they are
part of a group of people who look after
them and love them. If appropriate to the
age of those in your group, talk about us
all being in God's family, all looked after
and loved by him.

## Children

*Aim:* To teach them about the dangers of
Jesus' early life and God's protection
through his family.

You will need colouring pens, scissors,
staples and copies of the model pieces
shown opposite. Also slips of paper with
the names of different members of animal
families – enough to cover the number in
the group. First play the animal families
game. Each child is shown a slip of paper
which has on it the Daddy, Mummy or
baby form of an animal. When everyone
knows who they are they have to find the
other members of their family by making

the right noises. When they are a family,
Daddy stands behind a chair, Mummy
sits on the chair and baby sits on
Mummy's lap!

Now praise God and thank him for
our families, remembering each person
we live with. Tell the children the dangers
of Jesus' early life, and how he escaped
because of Joseph hearing God's warning
and rushing his family off – perhaps in
the middle of the night – as refugees.
(*Donkey's glory* by Nan Goodall includes a
classic retelling of this episode.) Help the
children to catch the very real danger and
fear there must have been, and the
support of the family in the time of
danger.

Help the children make this stand-up
model of the journey into Egypt.

## Young people

*Aim:* To reflect on the value of families,
and look at Jesus' family.

Read the Matthew passage together,
linking the events with the current
tragedy of refugees having to leave their
countries to avoid danger. Notice the
kind of character Joseph has, and talk
about why God had chosen him to bring
up his son.

Now show some pictures with different images of 'family' and talk about what they think of as an ideal family; which qualities they associate with a good father, or a good mother. In the discussion refer to the family God chose for Jesus, and don't let it degenerate into a moans session. Be open and sensitive to any real problems which are raised and bring these into a time of prayer for our own and all family life, which is so often difficult as well as beneficial. Remind everyone that we are also part of the wider family of God, who loves us like the very best parent, only more so.

# YEAR 2

*Thought for the day:*
*God's salvation is for all peoples and*
*nations; everyone is eligible.*

## Readings

Psalm 89:19-38
Isaiah 46:3-end
Romans 15:8-21

## Reflection

We are part of a natural system in which great things mature gradually from minute beginnings. We come across this model so often as we see trees and flowers develop from seed, one person's vision develop into a widespread ideology, mountain springs turn into majestic rivers and one tiny fertilised cell mature into a skilled, imaginative and intelligent human being.

All this reflects the nature of God , its creator, so it isn't surprising that the same pattern is there in God's calling and covenant with one man – Abraham – down through the growth of one small nomadic tribe, its development into a

nation and then, with the coming of Jesus, breaking out to flourish internationally until the whole world is brought in.

In this sense, we who are Gentiles are equally descendants of Abraham, and we share these marvellous promises of God to enfold us and take care of us right through our lives. God formed us and nurtured us not just in our individuality, but also as his chosen people; and now, in this last age, we are called to work very deliberately at spreading the good news of life in Christ. There are so many who do not yet know God's love and are still wasting their worship on idols. If our lives don't reflect God's light, then we are deliberately preventing them from knowing the joy of worshipping the one true God of love.

## Discussion starters

1  What kind of behaviour in Christians has helped you understand more about God?

2  What false impressions of God do Christian lives and church services sometime give to outsiders?

## All stage talk

*Theme:* Focusing on the real God who looks after us, rather than on idols.

You will need a loaded camera with a built-in light meter and flash. Begin by introducing everyone to your camera and taking two or three photos, focusing on different people and parts of the building each time. Explain that you don't need lots of complicated flash equipment with this camera because it has been designed with the light meter and flash facility built in. That means that whenever you go to take a picture, the camera automatically checks the light and provides extra light if necessary.

God has designed us with a built-in worship facility. Of course the idea is that we use this to worship our maker and, when we do that, the rest of our lives settles into a fully satisfying 'rightness' which is good and liberating. But the facility is still there, whether we use it like this or not and we all worship something because that is part of our design. The real question is 'what'?

Look again at the camera as it focuses on a particular person or thing to photograph. I may insist that I'm trying to get a picture of the organist, but if I'm actually focusing on Brown Owl, then that's the actual picture I'm taking and that's the picture I'll get. (Take the picture.) We may say we worship God, but if our hearts and minds are focused mostly on what we look like and wear, or on food, or the luxury bathroom we'd like, or our hobby, or our girl/boyfriends, or work, then the truth is that we are actually worshipping these things, and not God at all.

Today God is reminding us that all these other idols are very poor substitutes for the real thing; let's get our priorities right if the focus has slipped, and really enjoy using our worship facility in the way it was designed to be used – worshipping the God of enormous power who can work wonders in our characters; the God who has always loved us and cherished us right from our conception onwards; the God who loves and honours us even when our hair goes grey and we aren't as fit as we used to be. This God can provide everything we ever need; let's focus our worship on him alone.

## Intercessions

Father, work your love in the church, her ministers and all her members,
particularly where there is any hardness of heart, or misunderstanding of your will.
*Silence for prayer*
Lord, we know and believe:
**that you will keep us safe**

Father, work your love in our world,
guiding our leaders and redeeming good from all that is evil.
*Silence for prayer*
Lord, we know and believe:
**that you will keep us safe**

Father, work your love in our homes,
making them places of welcome,
understanding and forgiveness.
*Silence for prayer*
Lord, we know and believe:
**that you will keep us safe**

Father, work your love in all areas of pain and illness, anxiety and imprisonment.
*Silence for prayer*
Lord, we know and believe:
**that you will keep us safe**

Father, work your love in all areas of sadness and loneliness,
hopelessness and doubt.
*Silence for prayer*
Lord, we know and believe:
**that you will keep us safe**

Father, work your love in all that is beautiful, all that is growing
and all that touches our hearts with joy.
*Silence for prayer*
Lord, we know and believe:
**that you will keep us safe**

## In the crèche

*Aim:* To help them sense God's delight at gathering us up in his love.

You will need a large sheet of paper with a big heart drawn on it, and lots of cut-out people shapes in different colours. Beforehand, hide some of these around the area you are using. As you walk around showing the children these lovely cut-outs we are going to play with, accidentally on purpose keep letting them slip through your fingers, so they end up scattered all around and you end up holding only the last few. Then realise you have lost them and let the children enjoy finding them for you and gathering them up. Some you can drop several times. At last they are all safe. You count them up together and find there are still some missing. Now the children can go hunting for these and bring them to safe keeping as well.

That's how God keeps picking us up when we get things wrong, and looking for us when we feel lost or lonely. He looks after us because he loves us. They can draw themselves on the people and stick them inside God's love.

## Children

*Aim:* To help them realise that God looks after us all through our lives.
You will need some pictures of people of all ages, from birth to very old. Also include some pre-birth pictures and a pregnant woman.

Give the pictures out so that each child has one, and work together to stand with their pictures in order, starting with the youngest. (A fairly civilised way of doing this is to pick one person at a time, deciding where they should stand in relation to the others, gradually filling in the gaps. A less civilised way is to see if the children can work out the sequence for themselves.) In either case you should end up with a line of children holding pictures which show a growing and ageing person. The pictures are now stuck down in order on a long sheet of paper, labelled: ALL THE WAY THROUGH YOUR LIFE, GOD LOOKS AFTER YOU. Read the parts of the Isaiah passage which promise this and use the pictures to pray for all the different age groups.

## Young people

*Aim:* To check the focus of our lives and explore the nature of idol worship.
You will need a camera.

First read the Isaiah passage together, notice the amazing faithfulness, love and power of God and draw attention to the part about idols. We may feel that this sort of thing is irrelevant, as few of us would probably bow down before a home-made god. But there are many ways of worshipping idols, apart from bowing down in the dust before them.

Now, unless your camera has one of those clever automatic picture-taking facilities, ask one person to take a photo of all the rest of you. Then announce that you are going to take a picture of everyone as well, but in fact home in on a small item, such as the bin, or a pair of scissors or a tissue. Of course that's ridiculous – if we really want a particular picture, we'll have to focus on it. Talk together about some of the things we spend loads of time thinking about and make a note of these on a sheet of paper. It may well reveal to us how little time we focus on God and how much we are really worshipping these other things. As a group work out some strategies to help you all realign your worship.

# *Epiphany*

## YEARS 1 AND 2

*Thought for the day: In Jesus we see God's secret plan revealed.*

### Readings
Psalms 2,8
Isaiah 42:1-9
John 1:29-34

On this festival of Epiphany we take time to marvel at the majesty and wonder of a God who thought and loved our universe into being. So often we take for granted the magnificence and diversity of what we see, hear and touch each day. The sheer abundance of grass, foliage or insect life; the vastness of space, measured out by stars; the microscopic and the carefully ordered; the laws of physics and chemistry. As we pick up something of an artist's ideas when we look at an exhibition, so we can grasp something of God's nature when we bother to notice his creation.

In the Isaiah reading it is as if the almighty, all powerful God is reaching down to catch hold of us, to enable us to share in the celebration of generous life which streams from his nature. And with Jesus, this image becomes a reality, Jesus is the secret nature of God revealed in a way humans can understand.

Prophetically, the wise men were led by a star to give honour to the Christ in his infancy, and the gifts they brought told of royalty, priesthood and suffering. Prophetically, John the Baptist recognises in Jesus the fulfilment of Isaiah's words. He, too, was led by a sign – the sign of the Spirit settling almost physically on Jesus as he is baptised.

### Discussion starters

1 'Before they spring into being I announce them to you.' It is one of the hallmarks of God, this preparing of us in advance so that we are ready to cope with some truth he desires to share with us. Do we follow God's signs readily? How can we discern which signs are from God?

2 What does today's gospel teach us about John the Baptist, and how does John's behaviour challenge us?

### All stage talk

*Theme:* Follow that sign!
Beforehand make a number of signs that are familiar to everyone. For example:

Show each sign in turn, and ask people: Where might you be if you saw this? How would it affect your behaviour? Now show this sign . . .

. . . and have someone carrying it round the building. Who followed this? Where did it lead to? Have the star carried round to where the crib is, with everyone following, or a representative group. From the crib show the last sign:

Remind people of how this affected John the Baptist's whole ministry, and let the sign lead people round to the font. This is the place where God leads us to commit our lives to him, ready to follow Christ and allow him to take charge. You can now use the Baptismal affirmation of faith.

## Intercessions

We pray for all who spend their lives leading others to you, supporting and encouraging them on your journey; give them your ideas, your love for others, your joy and your humility.

*Silence for prayer*

Father, today and every day:
**lead us to yourself**

We pray for our leaders and advisers in politics, business, education and health; for good values, integrity and compassion,
for courage to stand up for what is right.

*Silence for prayer*

Father, today and every day:
**lead us to yourself**

We pray for our relationships with our friends, neighbours, colleagues and those in our family; for the grace to forgive readily, listen attentively and to be available whenever you need us.

*Silence for prayer*

Father, today and every day:
**lead us to yourself**

We pray for the frail and the wounded, the harrassed and the despairing;
for hope in the suffering, comfort in distress, and healing of body, mind and spirit.

*Silence for prayer*

Father, today and every day:
**lead us to yourself**

We pray for those who have died, and for those who mourn and miss their company; we pray for the grace to die a good death and live with you for ever in the joy of heaven.

*Silence for prayer*

Father, today and every day:
**lead us to yourself**

We thank you for all those who have helped and inspired us in our Christian journey;
for the experiences that have led us to know and love you more.

*Silence for prayer*

Father, today and every day:
**lead us to yourself**

## Other ideas

• During a hymn have a star or candle leading the wise men round the church to the crib. This may either be people dressed up, or the crib figures.

• Incorporate three flower arrangements in the main arrangement today, representing the gifts of the wise men. Use yellows, golds and orange for the gold, white, grey and blue for the frankincense and purple, magenta and red for the myrrh.

## In the crèche

*Aim:* For the children to understand that God leads us.

Have a follow-my-leader game, making a 'conga' type line and going wherever the leader takes them. Now give the leader a star to carry, and everyone follows the star, going over things, round things and through things on the way. Let it lead them to a crib scene, or a picture of Jesus and the wise men, so the children can see what presents have been brought.

## Children

*Aim:* For them to look at different ways God leads us in our spiritual journey. Beforehand set up the secret worship place, which is where the trail will end. It might be a large cupboard or under-stair area, a small vestry or even a tent. Whatever you decide it needs to be out of sight when the children start their trail. Set the children off in groups on a trail, either inside or out, depending on the weather. Each group follows their own colour of stars, which are placed far enough apart for there to be times when the direction is uncertain until they look more carefully (rather like cairns on mountains).

Every group's journey eventually leads to the same finishing point. This worship area is beautiful. It may have flowers placed on a mirror, lights or candles (great care!) an open bible and a cross. Have a rug or blanket down on the floor and quiet music playing, and make the entrance low, so that they have to stoop to go in. The idea is to make it a secret place of wonder which they are led to find. Have a SILENCE notice outside, and make sure the children come in quietly. When everyone is crowded in, tell them quietly and simply how God led the wise men to find him; how he led John the Baptist to recognise him, and he leads us to find him as well. But we don't all come by the same route. God uses all the different events of our lives, and the different people we meet; he can use sad times as well as happy times.

Sing a worship song together that the children know well, and then pray for people who are going through different bits of their journey at the moment. Have

music playing again as the children file out and colour this star prayer to hang up at home.

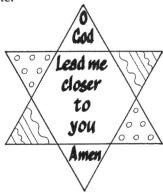

## Young people

*Aim:* For them to explore the link between God's guidance and our willingness to follow.

First have a number of star-shaped cards placed words down. In turn, people select a card and read what it says. They then choose whether to do what it says or not. They will find that these instructions lead them on to another, which again they can either choose whether to take on board or not. Here are some suggestions for the cards – you can add other particularly relevant ones for your group.

1  Ask Andrew to read you Luke 6:27
2  Work with Sam to find Jeremiah 17:7-8
3  Ask Jane to read you Matthew 18:1-4
4  Work with Ben to find John 6:35

Show a star, and talk about (or read in Matthew 2) how the wise men were not only shown the sign in the sky, but also chose to follow it. The star wasn't always visible; when it wasn't they had to wait expectantly for it, rather than rushing on in the wrong direction. Then read the gospel for today – what sign was John the Baptist given to guide him?

We are shown guidelines and instructions in our daily bible reading and prayer life, and also through conversations and events in our life. We decide with our wills whether or not to take notice of them or not.

# 1st Sunday after the Epiphany

## YEAR 1

*Thought for the day:*
*God gives us the grace necessary*
*to reveal his glory.*

### Readings
Psalms 46, 47
Isaiah 61
Ephesians 2:1-10

### Reflection

Double glazing firms, bedroom and kitchen designers are always on the look out for householders who will allow them to use their homes as showplaces. They are willing to cut their prices for anyone prepared to let potential customers see their excellence. They are assuming that their claims of good quality will be proved true by the actual quality of the work carried out.

Our readings this week are about God's workmanship in people's lives, which is bound to reveal his glory. No one who genuinely seeks God's company and is willing to yoke him/herself up with God as a working partnership, can fail to end up revealing God's glory. This is because we do not manufacture our own resources, which would be of variable and sometimes dubious quality, but receive all necessary grace directly from God. Since he knows and loves us inside out, we can trust him to make a personal delivery of whatever resources will best blend with our natural strengths, weaknesses and experiences, to create a life of beauty and love.

### Discussions starters

1  How do we sometimes prevent God from providing the grace we need, rather than want, in our lives?

2  Work through the Isaiah reading, noting the practical ways in which Jesus displayed God's grace and glory in his ministry.

### All stage talk

*Theme:* We need God's freely-given grace to show God's glory.

You will need a bowl, a potato and an efficient potato peeler, or several sets of these things if the congregation is large.

First arrange for people with bowls and potatoes (but no peelers yet) to stand at intervals around the building, so that everyone can see what's going on. The volunteers can be of any age – a mixture of ages is best.

Now tell everyone that these people have been given an important job to do; they have to peel a potato and they can start straight away. When they can't start because they have no peeler, tell them to use a coin or a key, a credit card or anything they happen to have brought with them. If they can't find anything at all to use they'll have to use their finger nails. After giving them a little time to struggle, point out how we often struggle to live as Christians relying on whatever we happen to have handy, and so we make heavy weather of loving our enemies, forgiving one another or accepting criticism. Actually God never asks us to work at anything without supplying us with the grace we need. Ask if a potato peeler would make this job easier and give out the peelers.

Now they can do a far more effective job, with far less struggle. We will all lead far more effective lives, which show God's glory, if we are open to God and take time to receive his grace, rather than rushing in to work in our own strength. Ask them to put the peeled potatoes in a bowl of water near the door, to remind us as we go out of church that we need God's grace if our lives are to shine with his glory.

## Intercessions

Father, we pray for the church on earth; wherever your vision is disturbing our assumptions, wherever your promptings are nudging us to action, we ask you to keep us attentive and obedient.

*Silence for prayer*

Give us your grace:
**and let your glory shine**

Father, we pray for our world; wherever self interest is blinding us to needs, wherever past evils are preventing peace, we ask you to renew us in love.

*Silence for prayer*

Give us your grace:
**and let your glory shine**

Father, we pray for our homes and our neighbourhood.
Wherever there is a breakdown in communication, wherever patience wears thin, or interests clash, we ask for your guidance and protection.

*Silence for prayer*

Give us your grace:
**and let your glory shine**

Father, we pray for those who are suffering. Wherever pain or terror is overwhelming, wherever lives are damaged and wounded, we ask you to bind up and make whole again.

*Silence for prayer*

Give us your grace:
**and let your glory shine**

Father, we pray for the dead and dying, and those who mourn.
Wherever souls are approaching your eternal kingdom, wherever loved ones grieve, we ask for your mercy and comfort.

*Silence for prayer*

Give us your grace:
**and let your glory shine**

Father, we pray for our hearts to be filled with thankfulness.
Wherever we see beauty and loveliness, wherever we experience compassion and forgiveness, we ask you to lift our hearts to give you glory.

*Silence for prayer*

Give us your grace:
**and let your glory shine**

## Other ideas

Have a small group of dancers to demonstrate this dance to the song: 'I declare the glory', and then invite groups all over the room to join in. It is only a simple folk dance, suitable for all ages and most constitutions!

I declare, the glory of the risen Saviour
*circle left*
is living in my life
*walk into centre and out*
I declare, he gives me victory
*circle right*
over every kind of strife
*walk into centre and out*
And if I feel I'm homeless
*right hand turn with partner*
and should I feel alone
*left hand turn with partner*
it's then I know, security
*dos-y-dos with partner*
is found in Christ alone
*swing partner*

(Sam Horner © Daybreak Music Ltd, Silverdale Road, Eastbourne)

## In the crèche

*Aim:* To enjoy watching hidden things being revealed.

You will need some kind of soft toy for hiding, some white candles, paper, brushes and ready-mixed water-colour paint.

Begin with a game of hiding the toy, getting the children to guess where it is or hunt for it.

Then help the children make some swirly lines all over the paper with the white candle. We've made lovely pictures, but we can't see them yet. Now the children can reveal their pictures by brushing a colour wash over the paper. No one can see God, but Jesus shows us what he is like.

## Children

*Aim:* To see how God's glory is revealed in Jesus and in our lives.

You will need a beanbag, some pages from a magic painting book, brushes and water.

Begin in a circle (or several if the group is large), throwing a beanbag to everyone in turn. Practise throwing and catching in a way that challenges each person's skill – both hands/one hand/under one leg etc. and work at improving individual performance. Then stop using the beanbag but pretend to carry on practising. Are we really getting anywhere now? No – we need the beanbag to practise beanbag skills! In the same way we need God's grace to practise loving; if we don't ask for that, or try to do the loving on our own, our Christian life will be just as empty as us pretending to catch and throw.

At this point have some prayer and a worship song such as 'Jesus, Jesus, can I tell you what I know' or 'I am a new creation'.

So when we do work in the grace of God, what happens? Give out the magic painting pages and watch the way all kinds of colours show up when we simply use water. In our lives, we will quite naturally show the colours of God's glory and the world will be a more caring, forgiving, happier place.

## Young people

*Aim:* To explore the way God's grace enables us to show God's glory.

First, talk about allergies, sharing the gory details of any they or their friends have when they eat or touch something they are allergic to. Point out that the people concerned don't work at making that rash or asthma attack – it happens naturally as a result of contact with a particular substance.

Now think about good automatic reactions, such as feeling less hungry through eating, less tired through sleeping, being able to get through a locked door if you use a key, or smelling good through dabbing on perfume or aftershave. Again, these things happen quite naturally as long as the right input is given.

Read the beginning of the Isaiah passage together. What happens as a result of the Spirit of the Lord being on him? (Jesus used this passage to refer to himself). There is both a commission and an enabling.

Read the Ephesians passage and see how God's grace enables us to work God's love in a natural way – we won't have to contort ourselves out of shape because God will work within us the way we are, using our gifts and talents, but also our weaknesses, whereas if we fight against accepting and using his grace we make life unnecessarily hard for ourselves.

# YEAR 2

*Thought for the day:*
*God gives us the grace necessary to*
*reveal his glory.*

## Readings

Psalm 46,47
Genesis 8:15-9:17
Acts 18:24-19:6

## Reflection

As the great flood recedes, Noah and his family walk freely into a new life, with the rainbow – a recurring memory aid – to remind them of God's covenant with them. The God who has power to destroy, promises life for his people. It is like an ancient baptism, where the old life is drowned and the new is full of God-given protection and hope. The whole unfolding of the bible story develops this theme to its fulfilment in the new life of the resurrection, and in every individual Christian baptism through the generations ever since.

Baptism is not only about the washing away of sin, as it was for John the Baptist's followers. Jesus brought a new significance to baptism, which needed explaining to some of the early Christians, who had not heard about the Pentecost experience. Jesus had promised that when he returned to heaven he would send the Holy Spirit to fill the disciples with enabling power – it would be the life of God actually living in them. Baptism in Jesus has ever since been baptism of both water and spirit, and the new life we are baptised into is God's gift to us.

## Discussion starters

1  As Prescilla and Aquila listened to Apollos, their visiting preacher, what do you think went through their minds? How can we learn from their way of dealing with the situation and Apollos' response?

2  Talk through the significance of the symbols of water and breath in the sacrament of baptism.

## All stage talk

*Theme:* Rainbows and promises.
Beforehand prepare this puzzle on an OHP acetate, or on a large display sheet of paper. Alternatively the puzzle can be reproduced on the handout and given to everyone as they come in.

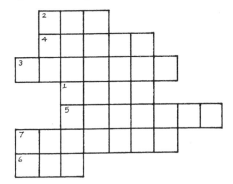

Today's talk will be interspersed with clues to the puzzle. The order of solving the clues is important.

1  (For a Brownie/Cub/Junior to answer.) Who did God tell to build a large boat?

   *As you write in the answer, remind everyone of the wickedness of the people, and God's decision to clean things up, keeping Noah and his family safe because Noah was not doing what everyone else did, but doing what he knew was right in God's eyes.*

2  (For a Mum/Dad/Uncle/Auntie to answer.) What was Noah's boat called?

   *As you write the answer, you can tell them that the other place this word is used is for the basket Moses was put in when he was a baby. The same people may be able to think of what these two events have in common.*

3  (For anyone under seven.) What did Noah take into the ark with him?

   *(They may well say particular sorts of animals. This is fine.) When you've had a few suggestions, and if no one has yet said animals, just gather the ideas together and write in animals to cover them all.*

4  (For Grandads/Grandmas/anyone eligible for a pension.) What did the ark float on?

   *Point out how the very water which destroyed everything evil kept Noah, his family and the animals safe.*

5  (For clever people to answer.) When else in the bible do we find water used as a sign that an old, bad life is being drowned, and yet through this drowning, a person's life is saved?

   *Explain that all baptisms used to involve getting totally wet, and that helps us understand the symbol of water. When we are baptised in the name of Jesus, all our previous sin is drowned and destroyed. As we come up out of the water, we are born to a completely new life in Jesus.*

6  (For anyone who ate toast for breakfast.) What was the word you said before 'life in Jesus'?

   *If no one get this first time, repeat the previous sentence about being born into a new life in Jesus. Obviously no one was listening the first time! Explain how this new life is a free gift to us, and we can't ever earn it. What we do have to do is receive it and use it.*

7  (For anyone who came to church on wheels.) When God makes one of these he always keeps it. What is it?

   *When Noah and the animals were safe, God made a promise that he would never destroy the earth. As a sign of this promise he used . . . (direct everyone's attention to the vertical word) . . . the rainbow. Whenever we see a rainbow we can remember God's promise to take care of us.*

## Intercessions

Father, we remember the church communities which are thriving and those which seem to be dying; we pray for all in both lay and ordained ministry, and ask you to breathe new life into us all.

*Silence for prayer*

God is with us:
**he will never let us down**

Father, we remember the world's leaders and all in local and national government; we pray for your wisdom, sensitivity and integrity.

*Silence for prayer*

God is with us:
**he will never let us down**

Father, we remember those we live, work and relax with; we pray for your loving to enrich all our relationships and your spirit of forgiveness to become second nature to us.

*Silence for prayer*

God is with us:
**he will never let us down**

Father, we remember those whose bodies ache, whose spirits shudder and whose memories terrify.
We pray for your healing and wholeness.

*Silence for prayer*

God is with us:
**he will never let us down**

Father, we remember with thankfulness the lives and examples of loved ones who have died. We commend the dead and dying to your merciful love.

*Silence for prayer*

God is with us:
**he will never let us down**

Father, we offer you our thanks
and praise for the many times
you have rescued us and the many
blessings you lavish on us each day.

*Silence for prayer*

God is with us:
**he will never let us down**

## Other ideas

• Have quiet music coming in as a background to the first reading, starting at verse 11 of chapter 9.
• Have one flower arrangement expressing the baptism of water and Spirit. Set the arrangement on a mirror, surrounded with pebbles and shells, and use fiery colours as well as white, with the flowers dipping down to touch the mirror.

## In the crèche

*Aim:* For the children to look at the story of Noah.

Have ready a bowl or baby bath, a toy boat and a container of water. As you tell the story of God wanting to save Noah and his family and the animals, involve the children in making appropriate sound effects. Then slowly pour water into the bowl so that they can see how the boat began to float safely on the flood. If the bath you are using has a soak away system you can even have the water receding and leaving the boat on dry land again for Noah and his family to start a new life.

## Children

*Aim:* For them to see the connection between Noah's story and baptism.

Start with a game which directs attention to the different characters of water. When you call WATER! everyone 'flows' around the room. At ICE! everyone 'freezes'; at RAIN! everyone jumps up and down on the spot, and at RAINBOW! everyone joins hands to make a semicircle.

Now tell the story of Noah, with children joining in various sound effects and actions. Go through the actions and sounds with the children first, so they can listen out for where they come in the story.

Then show some pictures of baptisms, including some of total immersion. Explain how everything unloving, bad and selfish is being 'drowned' and the person being baptised is being reborn to a new, fresh life in Jesus. This is what Jesus taught us to do. Talk together about people they know who have been baptised recently, and if possible show the children the font, with its lid off, and the things that are used in baptism.

Help the children to make this rainbow, which could perhaps be displayed in the baptistry:

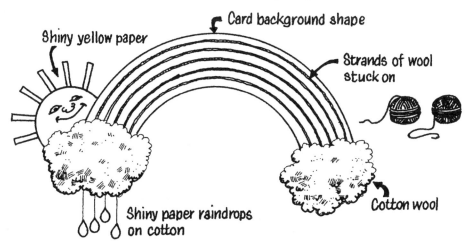

## Young people

*Aim:* For them to look at the difference between John's baptism and baptism in the name of Jesus.

First read the Noah passage of the end of the flood, and the rainbow's promise. Try the puzzle from the All stage talk or talk together about the way the water both destroyed evil and gave new life.

Then go on to read the passage from Acts, pausing at the point where Apollos says he has only known John's baptism. See if the group can work out the difference between this baptism and the sort Paul is talking about. When you have had a go at this, read on to find out what answer the bible gives. Make the connection between the sign of water and drowning here, and the Noah story.

Look at the baptismal promises and suggest ways that the church can ensure that people really know what they are taking on when they come to be baptised. Take note of any suggestions and put them before the next PCC.

# 2nd Sunday after the Epiphany

## YEAR 1

*Thought for the day:*
*God calls his disciples to spread the good news of the Kingdom, whether the people listen or not.*

### Readings
Psalm 15,16
Ezekiel 2:1-7;3:4-11
Matthew 10:1-22

### Reflection

This week's readings look at the way Ezekiel and the disciples are commissioned for ministry. In both cases the sending is preceded by availability and vision. Ezekiel, spending time in God's presence, is shown something of God's glory, and the experience is so powerful that it throws him to the ground. The disciples, having answered Jesus' call, have left everything and for some time now they have been walking close to the Master, seeing at first hand his grace and truth. God needs us to be in his company before he can show us the richness of the Kingdom, and unless we see this first, we will not be able to spread the good news with any conviction at all.

Notice, too, that the instructions given are clear and definite. We are awfully good at getting a rough idea and racing off to do things our way without waiting for those instructions! We need to be a little more patient, sometimes, wait on God expectantly and only move when he says 'Go now'. It concerns me that in some outreach programmes we try to take on the instruction part ourselves, judging who are the most likely ones to listen to us and concentrating our attention on them. Why does this happen? I suspect it is because once again we feel we have to work *for* God instead of *in* him. In fact, he has far more idea of who and where and when, so we might just as well recognise that and pray in listening mode before writing our lists.

### Discussion starters

1  Look at the two passages together and compare them; who are they to go to/who weren't they to go to/what were they to do if people didn't listen?

2  With a job description and career prospects like these, why on earth are the commissioned prepared to go? Would we be?

## All stage talk

*Theme:* Being obedient when we are commissioned.

First ask for five volunteers and choose people who have curly hair. Tell the congregation that you are going to commission them. Quietly tell the volunteers to go out into the congregation and each collect one person with curly hair and bring them back to you. When they arrive give each person one of these words, written large enough for everyone to read: I AM SENDING YOU OUT AS SHEEP AMONG HUNGRY WOLVES. Ask people in the congregation to unscramble the words and the people to arrange themselves in order. Point out that if the volunteers hadn't obeyed the instructions, the message you wanted to tell everyone would have been incomplete. Added to which they all look a bit like sheep because they all have curly hair!

The original volunteers heard you asking for help because they were paying attention and listening. When God chooses us and commissions us to do something in our life, we will only notice his call if we are paying attention to him and expecting him to communicate with us.

(Write on a flip chart/OHP: 1. Pay attention and listen.) Those volunteers stuck to their instructions, even though some people they asked didn't want to go with them. We are to stick to what God asks us to do even if it looks as though our own ideas might get quicker results. (Write down: 2. Stick to the instructions.)

Our message is a warning to everyone God sends to do his work – it may well be dangerous, hostile and frightening at times to be an active Christian. God very thoughtfully warns us first so that we aren't thrown by this when it happens. (Write down: 3. Be prepared for big trouble.)

Thank the helpers and display the message.

## Intercessions

Father, we want to pray for all who work to spread the good news of your love, for all who face insults and danger in the process.

*Silence for prayer*

In all things, loving God:
**let your will be done**

Father, we want to pray for our world's leaders, for all in positions of authority and influence.

*Silence for prayer*

In all things, loving God:
**let your will be done**

Father, we want to pray for the people we are fond of, and those we find it difficult to get on with.

*Silence for prayer*

In all things, loving God:
**let your will be done**

Father, we want to pray for those who feel trapped by illness, oppression, disability or guilt.

*Silence for prayer*

In all things, loving God:
**let your will be done**

Father, we want to pray for your mercy on those who have died and on those approaching death.

*Silence for prayer*

In all things, loving God:
**let your will be done**

Father, we want to offer you our thanks for the way you love us and look after us so patiently and courteously.

*Silence for prayer*

In all things, loving God:
**let your will be done**

## Other ideas

Have a time when anyone involved with outreach ministry (including children) can be prayed for by the rest of the church.

## In the crèche

*Aim:* To help the children understand that God gives us jobs to do.

Start by playing the singing game: 'Here we go round the mulberry bush', acting out all the jobs we have to do, like brushing our hair, washing our hands and so on. Some jobs are fun (like decorating the Christmas tree) but other jobs are not (like clearing up the bedroom). God wants us to help him by being friendly and kind.

## Children

*Aim:* To teach them about the instructions Jesus gave when he sent the disciples out. Prepare a few cards with instructions on, such as: 'walk round the circle and shake hands with everyone'; 'walk to the table and find the biscuits, then offer one to the people wearing blue'; 'hop round and offer a biscuit to everyone else'.

Now read or tell the children the story of Jesus sending his disciples out, counting up the number of disciples and writing each instruction on a board or flip chart. Talk together about why these instructions were given.

Make these drawstring purses with a prayer on the coins.

## Young people

*Aim:* To explore the way Ezekiel and the disciples were sent out and relate this to the way God commissions us.

Put the Ezekiel passage in its context of prayer and then read through it. Go straight on to the sending out of the disciples, and then ask people in small groups to fill in this chart:

| INSTRUCTIONS | EZEKIEL | MATTHEW |
|---|---|---|
|  |  |  |

Come together to discuss the results of the research, talk about why those instructions were given and how important it is for us to do things God's way rather than ours. Share ways of being attentive so that we are able to hear God's calling, not just at prayer times but as we walk about and when we are going to meet people.

# YEAR 2

*Thought for the day:*
*Our God is a God*
*of wonders, and*
*it shows.*

## Readings

Psalms 15,16
1 Kings 20:1-29
Matthew 13:44-end

## Reflection

Against all the odds in this series of assaults the comparatively puny kingdom of Israel emerges almost unscathed, while the superpowers of the day are beaten back and defeated. At intervals during the narrative, the man of God appears with the next piece of intelligence on which the next moves are based, and each time the reason given is clear: their victory will show others that God is real, active and powerful.

The parables from Matthew's gospel emphasise that God's Kingdom is not simply better, richer and more satisfying than any other, but is in an entirely different league – outdoing our wildest dreams.

Yet the local community at Nazareth, who had watched Jesus grow up and knew all the usual gossip about his family, were unable to see the Kingdom's beauty and liberating power. Sadly, when we convince ourselves that God must be human-sized in every way because we are, we effectively block his dynamic and powerful presence in our lives.

Rather pathetically we strain to make this impotent, boring Jesus seem relevant, when the real Jesus, full of astounding power and breathtakingly intimate relevance, is locked out. As soon as we begin to believe in the real God, remarkable things begin to happen.

## Discussion starters

1  Dare we believe in a God we cannot control?
2  What can we learn about God's Kingdom from the parables in this passage in Matthew?

## All stage talk

*Theme:* Our God is a God of wonders, and it shows.

Ask if anyone is brave enough to stand up on their own and say, 'I am a Christian'. Have a few people from different ages to do this and recognise that we don't find it easy to stand up on our own and admit our faith, even here among friends. No wonder we find it so hard to stand up and say what we believe when we are among people who disagree, sneer at God, or may think we're weird.

Ask three people to come and be the Israelites and stand out in front while everyone else suddenly stands up and points at them. We often feel like the Israelites – very small and vulnerable – when we find ourselves the only Christians around, or when we are feeling very strongly tempted to do wrong, and so we keep quiet when we could be speaking out against evil, or we try and avoid going where our faith will be challenged.

But what did the prophet say? (Display these words: 'I will deliver this vast army into your hands, and you will know that I am the Lord'.) Have all the people to be the prophet and whisper these words to the few in the front. Emphasise that these words are true; we are fighting against evil and the evil is certainly powerful, but we are fighting in the power of God, who is far more powerful and in his strength we can be brave.

## Intercessions

Father, we pray for all whose Christian
ministry brings hardship and persecution.

*Silence for prayer*

Keep us safe, O God:
**for in you we take refuge**


Father, we pray for all in positions of
power and responsibility,
and those negotiating for peace.

*Silence for prayer*

Keep us safe, O God:
**for in you we take refuge**


Father, we pray for those amongst whom
we live and work, for our friends
and all whom we value.

*Silence for prayer*

Keep us safe, O God:
**for in you we take refuge**


Father, we pray for all who feel
overwhelmed with troubles, and all who
are mentally or physically impaired.

*Silence for prayer*

Keep us safe, O God:
**for in you we take refuge**


Father, we pray for those who are fearful
or superstitious, and those who long to
believe in your reality.

*Silence for prayer*

Keep us safe, O God:
**for in you we take refuge**


Father, we thank you for all you have
taught us and all you are teaching us in
our lives at the moment.

*Silence for prayer*

Keep us safe, O God:
**for in you we take refuge**

## In the crèche

*Aim:* To encourage looking at unpromising
things expectantly and positively.

You will need all sorts of junk and some
ordinary household items, such as a
saucepan, wooden spoon, plastic containers and dried peas, and none of the usual
toys and books.

Explain that today we have only got
this stuff to play and work with, and then
encourage everyone to think of ways to
enjoy what we've got. You could make a
band, for instance, or build models, or
just enjoy putting small things into bigger
containers and emptying them out again.

## Children

*Aim:* To familiarise the children with the 1
Kings passage, relating it to their own
experience.

The narrative is excellent for telling and
understanding through acting out. Make
a mock up of a television for the narrator
to speak through, and direct the action
like a news, or documentary programme,
with the different groups of people frozen
in battle positions and moving whenever
their part of the action is referred to.

Then go through it again, with someone
ringing a bell whenever a learning point is
reached. The point is briefly discussed and
written up, and then the action continues. I
suggest the bell could be rung at the
following points, but of course you may
well be directed to notice other things.

- We sometimes find ourselves under
  attack, either from other people, or
  from nasty feelings inside us.
- We think if we give in a little, the
  temptations will go away.
- They don't.
- It's a good idea to ask some wise people
  for advice when we're in trouble.
- Sharing the trouble gives us courage.
- God is fighting our battles against evil,
  so we are strong in his strength.

- God doesn't always sort things out in the way we might expect.

## *Young people*

*Aim:* To explore the Ben-Hadad narrative and relate it to personal experience.

Read the 1 Kings passage together either from the dramatised bible, or with different people taking parts in the original version. As with the children, go through it twice – once to enjoy the story and the second time to stop it whenever there is something we can learn from it about fighting our own battles against evil in our lives, about trusting God even when things look pretty bleak, and about God's victory over evil.

It might help them in fighting temptation to recognise that when Satan seems to be attacking us it is really God he is trying to get at through us, and we are in a way like the battle ground. It's when we stop getting in God's way that he can act powerfully.

# *3rd Sunday after the Epiphany*

## YEAR 1

*Thought for the day:*
*God reveals himself through*
*signs and wonders.*

## *Readings*

Psalm 135 or 136
Isaiah 26:1-9
John 4:43-end

## *Reflection*

The impression we are given on reading this week's psalm and the Isaiah passage is that God is totally and joyfully in control. Everything he orders, happens, and all the signs point towards God's presence. Yet when we read and watch the daily news we see instead a world of disintegrating values, thriving greed and many innocent victims, all of which points people towards either no God at all, or a fickle, cruel one. Our faith begins to look like wishful thinking. And then we watch Jesus in this passage from John, deeply hurt by the crowd's usual shallow demands for ever more spectacular special effects, rather than the lasting inner peace they need. The self in us can blot out God's glory, prevent his kingdom from advancing and obstruct his work of love.

When we multiply this by the amount of selfishness there is world-wide, we can begin to see why the Kingdom advances so slowly. But advance it does and, bit by bit, wherever people offer their own personal territory for Christ to dwell in, wherever faith timidly begins to grow, there it is that healing can start and redemption can restore the years that the locusts have eaten.

## *Discussion starters*

1 We can't kid ourselves into faith, however much we strain ourselves, because faith is a gift, freely given. But how can we prepare the ground for faith to grow?

2 What signs did Jesus show in his life which led his disciples to believe that he was the promised one from God?

## *All stage talk*

*Theme:* Noticing the signs of God's glory.
Begin by talking about how first impressions are sometimes spot on, and sometimes disastrously wrong. We gradually get to know who someone really is by the clues their words and behaviour give us.

Ask a volunteer (of 12 years or over) to come and help. Secretly show them the picture of what they are and then hang the picture on their back so that no one can see it. Invite everyone to ask the volunteer questions to which s/he can only answer 'yes' or 'no'. Keep track of what is found out until eventually the identity is guessed correctly and the volunteer turns round to reveal that s/he is indeed who they thought.

What on earth has this to do with our theme?

The fact is that we get to know Jesus in exactly the same way – bit by bit we start to discover his character by seeing how he acts towards people in the Gospel. Bit by bit we learn that he is revealing God's nature to us, until eventually we can say for certain that he truly is the Son of God.

It's the same with our experience of the living God. Gradually as we keep in close touch with him we get to know him better and recognise wonders in our lives which are typically God's doing. Perhaps we've been praying and praying for God to sort out a problem, and then events start coming together in a way which is totally different from what we had in mind, but solves the problem in a better way than we could have hoped for. And we thank God very fondly and affectionately, because we recognise that it has been a typical God-response to our need, and we have got to know him better in the process.

But we must seek him; we would never have found out who the volunteer was unless we had asked and used our curiosity and imagination. If we walk through this week more alert, attentive and expectant, we shall notice the signs of glory we may have been missing.

## Intercessions

Father, wherever your church has become short-sighted, inattentive or inflexible, work in your healing love.

*Silence for prayer*

Lord, awaken us:
**to notice your glory**

Father, wherever our nations
have lost their way,
their sense of human worth
or their integrity,
nourish them with your love.

*Silence for prayer*

Lord, awaken us:
**to notice your glory**

Father, wherever our relationships are
fragmented, or shallow
or offensive to you,
challenge us with your love.

*Silence for prayer*

Lord, awaken us:
**to notice your glory**

Father, wherever people are suffering,
whether physically, mentally or
emotionally, comfort them with your love.

*Silence for prayer*

Lord, awaken us:
**to notice your glory**

Father, wherever people are fearful of
death, or anxious for the future,
reassure them with your love.

*Silence for prayer*

Lord, awaken us:
**to notice your glory**

Father, wherever your will is being fulfilled,
or hearts are learning to trust your love,
we join you in your joy.

*Silence for prayer*

Lord, awaken us:
**to notice your glory**

## In the crèche

*Aim:* To enjoy noticing 'secret' beauty around us.

You will need such toys as kaleidoscopes, a 'fly's eye' lens, Japanese unfolding flowers or magic trees, paints, brushes and paper, Russian dolls, polly pockets, transformers, and anything which looks quite plain but reveals lovely and exciting secrets when you really get into it.

Play with these toys, pointing out the fact that they look ordinary and dull, but aren't when you get to know them inside out. You could also make some splodge pictures which are then folded and opened to reveal a symmetrical design like a butterfly.

## Young people

*Aim:* To help them see how God reveals his glory in signs.

You will need a selection of optical illusions like those shown below.

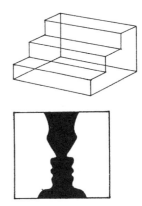

## Children

*Aim:* To help them recognise Jesus' glory through his signs.

You will need some ready-made icing mixture and a variety of fillings, such as chocolate drops, hundreds and thousands, or cherries.

First play the 'Who am I?' game as described in the All stage talk. An alternative version of this is to ask the children to guess by gradually adding dressing up clues to the volunteer, such as whiskers, tail and ears until the identity is revealed.

Now tell the story of healing when Jesus didn't even actually touch the man's son, and notice how the man is convinced when he realises the timing of the boy's recovery. Point out our need to look if we are to see God's glory at work in our lives and pray about this.

Help the children make these sweets which look quite ordinary but have a surprise in the centre.

Start by looking at pictures until you can see them in both forms; then work out a jigsaw together. Point out that as you get more clues, it gets easier to understand the picture. Think also of 'Blind Date' where, in a few questions, the aim is to reveal enough of the possibles' characters to judge their suitability for a date!

Since God is a person, we will need to get to know him as we do human people – through our conversations and quiet times together, through seeing the way he thinks and acts. Look together at John 1, where John claims that the Word of God came and walked about amongst us. His evidence is that they could see his glory, full of grace and truth. Explain how John then goes on to record a series of seven signs of the glory which support Jesus' claims, including today's healing. Take a whistle-stop tour through John to notice the other six: 2:1-12 (water into new wine); 4:43-54 (feeding the 5000, then walking on the water); 5 (healing of the lame man); 9 (blind man sees while sighted shut out the light); 11 (Lazarus is raised to life). Make a note of each as you go through, so that they can look at the overall picture.

If there is time, share evidence that members of the group have seen in their own lives which shows that God is living and active.

# YEAR 2

*Thought for the day:*
*God reveals himself through*
*signs and wonders.*

## Readings
Psalm 135 or 136
Nehemiah 13:15-22
John 5:1-21

## Reflections
The detailed system of rules had been drawn up with the very best of intentions. Having come through the time of exile, the people were determined to protect their precious faith and their national identity, and realised how necessary it was for them to live according to the commandments. In the same way a rule of life is important for us. Few of us would be able to keep up a learning programme without the support of a weekly class, and those hoping to lose weight find it much easier if they sign on at weight watchers! But rules have this dangerous habit of taking over. We so want to do things right that we reduce perfection to make it controllable,

and make ourselves tick-lists of rules that we can keep to and practise, while the spirit of the original vision is lost.

Jesus insisted that he had come to fulfil the Law, rather than abolishing it. And that included recognising the real priorities and not allowing real needs to be ignored through addiction to the rule system.

This man needed to be set free, both from physical paralysis and from sin, and nothing could be more in keeping with God's sabbath than giving him his freedom. The contrast between this generous attitude of God and the pettiness of the Jewish authorities fussing about him carrying his mat would be laughable if it weren't so serious.

We need to follow and worship the God who gives rules for our guidance, and not start worshipping the rules themselves.

## Discussion starters
1   To what extent were the Jewish authorities right in what they said to the healed man, and to what extent were they tragically wrong?

2   It is always difficult to get the balance right between becoming self-righteous on the one hand and self-indulgent on the other. How can we address this in our lives and in evangelism?

## All stage talk
*Theme:* God's glory shows in the way Jesus fulfils the Law.

Begin by reminding everyone of the ten commandments. Have them written up and uncover them one by one as people say them. Point out how they make for a stable, secure society, now as then, so they are very necessary and good.

Now show everyone a very delicate glass vase, which you want to send through the post. Can you just put it in an envelope? (Do so.) Or would tying string round the envelope help? When it is agreed that you will need to pad it to keep it safe, produce some appropriate packaging and ask a couple of people to pack the vase really carefully.

That's what had happened to God's law – because it was so precious to them, people wanted to keep it padded with all sorts of detailed rules, to avoid it getting broken, which is understandable.

But when it's all padded up like this we can't see it and forget what it really looks like. If, when this package arrives, we display it like this on the mantelpiece it isn't going to be much use as a vase any more, is it? The authorities were so fussy about the rule not to carry your mat on the sabbath that they couldn't see that God loves to set us free.

Jesus fulfilled the Law by unwrapping it (do this) so people could once again experience its beauty and use it. (Put some flowers in the vase.) So – we need to keep God's Law and not make excuses about that, but not wrap it up so tightly that we prevent God's glory from being revealed in our loving behaviour, our compassion and our delight in setting people free.

## Intercessions

Father, we ask for your encouragement and inspiration in all areas of ministry in the church; pour out your blessing on all who work for the spreading of the Kingdom.

*Silence for prayer*

Living Spirit of God:
**you give us life in abundance**

Father, we ask for your guidance and protection in all areas of conflict and confusion; pour out your wisdom on all who lead.

*Silence for prayer*

Living Spirit of God:
**you give us life in abundance**

Father, we ask for your faithful presence in our homes, and all the homes in this parish; pour out your spirit of patience and forgiveness wherever the sparks fly.

*Silence for prayer*

Living Spirit of God:
**you give us life in abundance**

Father, we ask for your reassurance and comfort wherever people are hurting or crying inside the brave face; pour out your welcoming love and give them the peace they crave.

*Silence for prayer*

Living Spirit of God:
**you give us life in abundance**

Father, we ask for your firm holding wherever our journey leads, and at the time of death, your mercy.

*Silence for prayer*

Living Spirit of God:
**you give us life in abundance**

Father, we ask you to accept with joy our thanks and praise for all you are, and all you accomplish.

*Silence for prayer*

Living Spirit of God:
**you give us life in abundance**

## Other ideas

In Psalm 136 have different people to call out the first half of each verse from all over the church, with everyone joining in the response: 'For his mercy endures for ever'.

Have everyone singing the summary of the Law to the tune of 'London's burning', using actions as shown.

You shall love the
  (*hands on heart*)
Lord your God with
  (*point up, hand open*)
all your heart and
  (*one hand on heart*)
all your mind and
  (*both hands hold head*)
all your strength!
  (*clench fists and show biceps*)
all your strength!
and love your neighbour
  (*one arm round shoulder of next person*)
and love your neighbour
  (*other arm round person on other side*)

This can be sung in a round, of course.


## In the crèche

*Aim:* To experience keeping to a route by following the rules.

You will need a play mat with roads marked on it and/or some chalked roads to walk or drive things along. Also a length of string or rope. First try following a leader round about the room, in and out of chairs and so on. Then practise keeping model vehicles to the roadways, walking along a twisting path which is drawn and carefully walking along the length of rope or string. God's guidelines for us are to love him and love one another.


## Children

*Aim:* To help the children see the difference between keeping God's Law and not getting bogged down in petty rules.

You will need two large cartons and some strips of card about as long as the boxes

are tall. Beforehand cover the boxes on one side and write out the summary of the Law on them: '*love God*', and '*love one another*'. On the long strips write things like: *Don't carry your mat on the sabbath; you must not walk more than a short way on the sabbath; you must do this; you must not do that.*

First sing the summary of the Law with actions as set out above. Have the boxes displayed, and then explain how all the other rules were added to the Law to protect it. The children can get these rules and lean them up against the Law, until we can't see it very well any more.

Now tell the story of Jesus healing the man on the sabbath and pause when he picks up his mat. What do they think the synagogue teachers will think about that? Point out how they had protected the Law so well that they had lost sight of its real meaning. Jesus swept away the clutter (let someone do this) to see the important part again.

Help the children make this model to remind them.

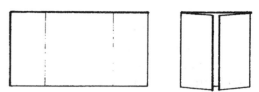

① Fold thin card like this

② Cut into the side flaps

(3) On the middle section write and decorate the law

(4) On the side flaps write 'Jesus shows us what is important.'

## Young people

*Aim:* To see how God's glory was revealed in his fulfilling of the Law.

First read the Old Testament passage and explain its historical context for the people of Israel. (This was after their exile, when they were trying to make a fresh start and were determined to keep themselves as a race set apart from the surrounding nations. Sabbath keeping and no mixed marriages were the clear signs of this.) See if they can also sense any spiritual dangers in having such exact rules.

Now read the New Testament passage, either miming it or with different people reading different parts, and explore the link between the Jewish rule system and the teachers' attitude to Jesus healing on the sabbath. Why didn't Jesus keep to the rules if he was supposed to be fulfilling the Law? How in fact was this truly a fulfilling of the Law? Are there any ways in which we prevent God's glory from radiating out because of complex rule systems which obscure the real truth?

# 4th Sunday after the Epiphany

## YEAR 1

*Thought for the day:*
*God reveals his glory in the way*
*he rebuilds and restores.*

### Readings
Psalm 34
Zechariah 8:1-7
Acts 15:1-21

### Reflection

What a lovely picture of tranquillity and an ordered society is suggested in this prophecy of Zechariah. All age groups are presented living their lives in a natural, relaxed way, without trauma or violence. It is probably the sort of world most of us would be happy to inhabit, and Zechariah sees it as the fulfilment of God's plan to restore his people.

You may know someone who enjoys restoring old cars, or furniture, or an old house. Think of the way they lovingly and painstakingly match up materials, work for hours on a small area and pay attention to detail. That's why the restored thing often ends up working more smoothly, or looking more beautiful than it did before!

When God restores us, whether as individuals, churches or nations, he does so with that same delight and attention to detail. It is a happy thought that he is restoring you at this moment.

If you are restoring an ancient cottage, you probably wouldn't restore the plumbing in its original form. The restoration would include modern plumbing, electricity and so on, to make the cottage even better to live in. In the same way God's restoration is never exactly the same as the original. What is essential and fundamental remains in all its glory, but, as the early church discovered, God is constantly making new as he restores. Gradually, both in us as individuals and in the church more of his truth is revealed and worked in. Provided we are happy to go along with this dynamic, and often surprising, state of affairs, God will be able to lead us with all the tenderness and sensitivity of the greatest restorer ever.

## Discussion starters

1 Imagine yourself into the position of these people of Israel, in exile from their own country. Think how Zechariah's words might have affected you.

2 Work through the different stages of the Jew/Gentile problem of the early church. What can we learn from the way the problem was tackled and solved?

## All stage talk

*Theme:* Restoration work.

You will need the help of someone who enjoys working on old cars, or antiques, or DIY and is willing to take part in a short interview. Begin by introducing the guest and asking them a little about their work

• What do they enjoy most about their work/hobby?

• What are they working on at the moment?

• What's the trickiest bit of restoration they've ever done?

Thank them for their help and write up the word 'RESTORATION' in the middle of a sheet of paper or on an OHP. Around it write the qualities people noticed about what restoration seems to need (such as patience, love, enthusiasm, concentration etc.)

Point out how God, speaking through the prophet Zechariah, promised to restore his people, and what a tatty, rusty state they were in: they had made such a mess of living God's way that they were now living in exile, far away from the country they loved. It may be that some of them thought they were beyond repair. It may be that we feel we've messed our lives up so much that they are beyond hope of restoration. God has other ideas! However awkward or difficult a situation is, God delights in putting things to rights – restoring us to the place where we belong. That place is safe within his Kingdom.

## Intercessions

Father, we remember all those who spend their lives proclaiming your truth and love; protect them from danger within and without, and refresh them in times of weariness.

*Silence for prayer*

God of tenderness:
**you restore our souls**

Father, we remember all heads of state, ambassadors and political advisers; let your will for our world be accomplished through the decisions they make.

*Silence for prayer*

God of tenderness:
**you restore our souls**

Father, we remember all families where relationships are strained;
let peace and understanding love find its way into every room.

*Silence for prayer*

God of tenderness:
**you restore our souls**

Father, we remember those whose bodies
do not function effectively,
and those whose bodies are abused;
bring some good from their suffering
and healing to their needs.

*Silence for prayer*

God of tenderness:
**you restore our souls**

Father, we remember those who have
died and also their families and friends;
let their sadness be comforted.

*Silence for prayer*

God of tenderness:
**you restore our souls**

Father, we remember all the ordinary,
everyday delights which make us smile
and lift our hearts.

*Silence for prayer*

God of tenderness:
**you restore our souls**

## Other ideas

Make an arrangement of all the tools and
materials you need for the car/house/
boat etc. restoration. Display them
imaginatively with this prayer, which
could be said by everyone.

'Lord, our God,
we believe in your power to restore
anything, anyone, anywhere;
and we open our hearts
to that miracle of your love. Amen.

## In the crèche

*Aim:* To help them experience God's
delight in putting things to rights.
You will need all kinds of slightly broken
and scruffy toys, a messy drawer or
cupboard and the necessary equipment
for putting them right.

First play this game, or something
similar. Get the children to stand in a space
and mark their place in some way so they
know that's 'home' for them. When the
music plays, they dance around all over
the place, but when it stops, they run back
to stand in their own special place.

Now have a look at the things you have
brought, let the children see what is wrong,
and then work together to put things right,
just like God does with all of us.

## Children

*Aim:* To help them understand God's
delight in restoration.
You will need something the parish needs
mending, sorting out or re-covering (such
as a notice board, an area of the
churchyard, a general tip which could be
a useful cupboard) and cleaning/
repairing materials.

Tell the children about the people of
Israel messing up their side of the
covenant with God and eventually
ending up as exiles. Link this with how
we feel when we've messed things up
and landed ourselves in trouble.
Introduce someone as the prophet, who
has a message for them all. (If this person
is a clear reader, s/he can read out a
simplified version of the prophecy
her/himself. God loves his people and
promises to restore them to their own
country. His message makes people
hopeful again. God doesn't enjoy
punishing us – what he enjoys is helping
us put things right.

Now tackle the restoration work
yourselves, singing as you do so and
enjoy working on it.

## Young people

*Aim:* To look at how the early church coped
with a difficult problem in the process of
God's development programme.

Split the group in two and have both groups working on the passage in Acts. In each case they need to read it together, one group sympathising with the Jewish viewpoint, the other as Gentiles. Then come together to have a short role discussion which identifies the problem and helps them see how feelings ran high.

Now work through the passage noting the order of events so as to see how the problem was tackled and resolved. (The willingness to listen to one another, to change where necessary, to pray together – all these are very noticeable). Beside the events, work out a possible model we could use in contemporary disputes in the church and pray expectantly about this.

# YEAR 2

*Thought for the day:*
*God reveals his glory in the way*
*he rebuilds and restores.*

## Readings
Psalm 34
1 Samuel 21:1-6
Matthew 12:1-21

## Reflection

We might moan at rules and even rebel against the silly ones from time to time, but at a deeper level there is for most of us a security in the 'rules' system. When the majority of people keep to an agreed set of rules we are freed from living in anarchic fear. The Pharisees had originally protected the integrity of the Jewish faith by reasserting its laws during a time of violent attack and subtle persecution.

Unfortunately, it is all too easy for the rule keeping to become more important than what it is designed to protect, and then we are left with a hardened shell.

Sometimes in our churches, traditions which began as a way of solving a particular difficulty become hardened into intractable rules, even though the original reason has long disappeared. We need to be very careful about what we set in stone, and why.

I sometimes wonder what Jesus was talking about in the temple that time he got left behind. Could he have been questioning the essence of the law so as to understand what it was really about? Certainly in his ministry he is often found bringing people back to the freshness of God's concern for his children, and their concern for one another. Rules are not ladders to God; the spirit of God's law may, on occasions, mean ignoring some of the detailed red tape that has tangled the issue. We are to tread a balanced path between treating our God so informally and casually that we insult him and peering so pedantically at rules that we cannot see where the living Jesus is going.

## Discussion starters

1  What do you think you would have done in Ahimelech's situation? He and his family paid a terrible price for helping David (1 Samuel 22.)

2  There is often conflict in Christian families when Sunday activities clash with church times and so on. Having read Jesus' teaching about the sabbath, how do you think we should organise our weekends?

## All stage talk

*Theme:* Making the meaning clear.
Have a large sign prepared which says:
LOVE GOD
LOVE YOUR NEIGHBOUR
AS YOURSELF
and have ready a number of smaller pieces of card and a marker pen. (Alternatively, you can write the main

message on an OHP acetate in one colour, and have another acetate placed over the message, with other colour pens at the ready for writing in subsequent messages.)

Ask two people to hold the sign so everyone can read it and invite everyone to do just this. Explain how this truth was shown to Moses, and through him to all the people of Israel. God wants this close relationship of love with his people, and that spills over into the way we treat one another.

Unfortunately, people being people, gradually lots of other details about the basic law of love crept in, partly to explain it in practical ways. Ask people to suggest some practical details arising from the basic rule, and write each one on another piece of card, inviting someone to hold it up, until the original message is hardly visible through all the fussy details. (Details might be such things as

- go to worship twice a week
- say your prayers at least twice a week
- don't do any work at all on Sundays.)

Explain that some of the teachers of the law in Jesus' time had got over-enthusiastic with their detailed rules, and some of them had lost sight (as we have) of the real meaning of God's law of love. So what Jesus did was to clear away all these extra bits (do so) and reveal the law again in all its beauty. It is a beautiful thing to live lovingly – responding to God's love for you, and passing on that love to others.

## Intercessions

Father, we call to mind all who teach the Christian faith, all those in training for ministry, and those preparing for baptism and confirmation; we ask for the Spirit to guide us into all truth.

*Silence for prayer*

Our God listens to his children:
**Our God answers prayer**

Father, we call to mind all those involved in education, those who report world events and comment on them; we ask for your wisdom and integrity, your discernment and values.

*Silence for prayer*

Our God listens to his children:
**Our God answers prayer**

Father, we call to mind those who have influenced our thinking this week, those we influence by our words and behaviour; we ask you to realign our priorities and give us courage to live your way.

*Silence for prayer*

Our God listens to his children:
**Our God answers prayer**

Father, we call to mind all who are suffering in hospitals, bedsits, huts and houses throughout the world. We ask you to restore each person to wholeness and joy.

*Silence for prayer*

Our God listens to his children:
**Our God answers prayer**

Father, we call to mind those who have reached the end of their earthly life and are meeting you face to face; we ask for your mercy on them, and on those who miss them.

*Silence for prayer*

Our God listens to his children:
**Our God answers prayer**

Father, we call to mind the many blessings in our lives, and the ways you reveal yourself to us; we ask you to deepen our understanding of you, so that we can love you more and more.

*Silence for prayer*

Our God listens to his children:
**Our God answers prayer**

## *Other ideas*

• Have the passage from Matthew acted out, with the actors reading or saying the different characters' words. This needs to be very simply and clearly done, and is effective when worked as a series of 'stills', with the actors turning to look at whoever is speaking, and freezing in that position, before moving into the next 'still' or tableau. The prophecy from Isaiah can be read chorally by all the actors.

• Have one flower arrangement placed inside an animal's cage with the door open. Beside the flowers is an inscription which reads: Is it against our law to heal on the sabbath?

## *In the crèche*

*Aim:* For the children to sense that Jesus shows us what God is like.

Have some magic painting books, brushes and water and also some things to make rubbings of with wax crayon. These can either be things like walls and trees, or you can make card pictures like these.

Build each layer of card up

As the children work talk together about how the shapes or the pictures were there already, and you are showing them up. God was always there, making the world, and loving his people; Jesus came and showed up the way God thinks and behaves.

## *Children*

*Aim:* Jesus shows up what the law really means.

Start with a picture which you have covered with lots of pieces of paper, labelled with letters. Taking it in turns, the children ask for a letter to be removed, and they see how quickly they can discover what the picture is. Only when all the bits are removed will the picture be clear to see.

Remind everyone of the ten commandments, either in full or in summary of the law, and then have a couple of leaders or helpers being Pharisees telling the children some bad gossip about Jesus disobeying the law in various ways. (Eating wheat and healing someone on the sabbath.) What do the children think? Are the Pharisees right? It's true that Jesus did these things. Was he being disobedient to God's law?

When they have had a chance to think about that, read how Jesus answered the Pharisees' complaints.

Then let the children do this puzzle.

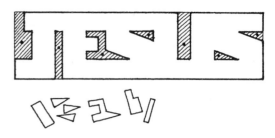

1. Colour in the dotted parts.
2. Cut these parts out.
3 Try to make them into Jesus' name on a plain sheet of paper.

## Young people

*Aim:* For them to look at what the law of God really means.

Start by reading together the passage from 1 Samuel 21. What do they think about what happened here? Was it right for David and his army to eat the sacred bread?

Now read the passage from Matthew 12 and then have small groups working on role plays, where two are Pharisees, and two are disciples discussing Jesus' behaviour.

Are there any rules in our own church which might sometimes get in the way of the real truth, instead of making it clearer? Take note of what is said, and act on it by praying together for guidance as to what should be done.

---

# 5th Sunday after the Epiphany

---

## YEARS 1 AND 2

*Thought for the day:*
*God's wisdom is that of a living,*
*powerful creator.*

## Readings

Psalm 119:121-136
Jeremiah 10:1-16
1 Timothy 3:14-4:10

## Reflection

I wonder if you have noticed how people often seem to resemble their dogs? I suppose the owners must choose a breed which suits them, reflecting their own personality, so that they can feel comfortable with one another.

If we try creating gods to suit us we may end up with something which expresses our inner fears and hopes, but it won't have any real power or life of its own since it has merely sprung from our own ideas. Following such gods will make us as empty and lifeless as they are. Now the making of idols doesn't necessarily involve gold leaf and beaten silver. It is quite possible to believe we are worshipping God when actually we are worshipping a false image of him – perhaps an image which distorts his true personality to fit in with what we want, or with what our damaging experiences have taught us.

There are many of these false images around, both outside and within the church, and you may recognise them. There is the meek and mild, rather wet, inoffensive and ineffectual image; the severe, demanding headmaster image; the spying on us, ready to pounce when we're just getting happy image; and the indulgent, anything goes image, to mention just a few.

None of these is anything but an idol and we should just smash them up if we find them forming in our hearts, because they won't help us. We will have created them in order to control God, but the living creator is not controllable. His wisdom and power and glory are those of a Being we can honour and love, but never cage. As we reach out to him, our lives will take on the colours of his glory.

## Discussion starters

1  Why do we humans try to manipulate the living God into a false image?

2  What marks out worshippers of the true God?

## All stage talk

*Theme:* Getting the right image.

Begin by asking three people to read the short sketch from today's Other ideas. We all have different images of the people we know and each person is actually all these and more. As we get to know a person better, we keep adjusting our image of them.

As we get to know God better we shall find the same thing – we will gradually be putting right any false images we have of him and be more able to love and worship him as he really is. Sometimes our false images of God have been handed down to us by how we were first introduced. There are empty seats here now because some people in our area have rejected what is in fact a false image of God and one of our main tasks is to show people the true God.

Let's look at some of these commonly held false images:

This god is always ready to condemn us and is very severe, very demanding and disapproving of us enjoying ourselves.

This god made the world a long time ago and then lost interest. He's actually rather lazy and lets us get on with destroying ourselves.

This god is rather pathetic; he smiles naively and doesn't understand the real world that we have to cope with. If you ask him for help he'd probably say he'd like to but it's all rather difficult with things as they are.

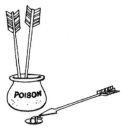

This god picks on people and makes life terrible for them.

This god is a little slave-magician, who runs round doing everything we ask but is somewhat deaf and forgetful.

Let's be quite clear about this: all these

gods are false images and are nothing at all like the true and living God. We need to destroy them. (Either cross them all out or, if you are using paper, tear them up and throw them away.) Thank goodness people who have these images often do reject them. How tragic that they think God is like that – no wonder people decide not to worship him.

So what is our God really like? Write 'The true God is . . .' in the centre and have people adding to the qualities they have discovered him to be.

## Intercessions

Father, renew and deepen the faith of
your people; enable us to spread your
good news by our words and our lives.
*Silence for prayer*
Living God:
**we worship you**

Father, breathe your peace into the
violence of our world;
we long for your kingdom to come.
*Silence for prayer*
Living God:
**we worship you**

Father, refresh and soothe
all our scratchy and worn relationships;
fill our homes with your love.
*Silence for prayer*
Living God:
**we worship you**

Father, comfort and reassure
all those who are suffering;
heal them to wholeness.
*Silence for prayer*
Living God:
**we worship you**

Father, have mercy on those
who draw close to death;
make us all aware of your abiding
presence.
*Silence for prayer*
Living God:
**we worship you**

Father, awaken us to see again
the wonder and delight of life;
fill us with thankfulness.
*Silence for prayer*
Living God:
**we worship you**

## Other ideas

• This sketch could lead on to the All stage talk, or to a reflective penitential time with music as a background, while people examine their own false images of God.

There are three parts.

Three chairs are arranged as for a parents' consultation evening at school. The teacher is already there and the parents come in.

| | |
|---|---|
| **Teacher** | Ah, good evening, Mr . . . Mrs . . . ? |
| **Dad** | Baker, Mr and Mrs Baker. |
| **Mum:** | We're Adam's Mum and Dad. |
| **Teacher** | Oh, yes, Adam. I can see the resemblance . . . (*confidentially*) He's got his father's nose, hasn't he! |
| **Dad** | Really? Can't say I'd noticed, as a matter of fact. |
| **Mum** | Now his Auntie Wendy, she had a nose like Adam's, didn't she, Kevin? She looked just like . . . |

**Teacher** How interesting, Mrs. Baker. Well, I know you'll be delighted to hear how well Adam has been going this year.

**Dad** How well he's been going?

**Mum** He's been doing well, has he?

**Teacher** Yes, I'm delighted with his progress. And he's always so polite, too.

**Dad** *(Surprised)* He is?

**Teacher** Yes, Adam is one of those lads you can always rely on, I find.

**Mum** *(Rather puzzled)* You do?

**Teacher** I certainly do. Only yesterday he tidied all the P.E. equipment for me and made a marvellous job of it.

**Dad** Did he really?

**Mum** I didn't realise he had a gift for tidying anything up.

**Teacher** And he always gets on with his work in class.

**Mum** *(Doubtful)* What about when he's with Mark Taylor?

**Teacher** Oh yes, they do work well together, don't they? If I have any concerns about Adam, it's just that . . .

**Mum and Dad** Yes?

**Teacher** He's a little bit too quiet.

**Dad** Well, I must say 'quiet' is not an adjective that immediately springs to mind for describing my son.

**Teacher** When he gets confident enough to speak out in discussions we'll all benefit, I think. And now if that's all . . ? *(Stands up)*

**Mum and Dad**: *(Standing up and shaking hands with teacher)*: Oh yes, thank you . . . Good-bye.

*(They walk away and look at one another)*

**Mum and Dad** Were we talking about the same boy?
*(They shrug and walk off.)*

• Use the sheet or acetate of the attributes of God which people have suggested. It might look like this:

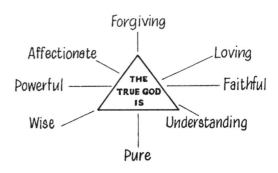

While the organ or music group plays a quiet hymn of worship, everyone reads through the sheet, as an act of praise and worship. Or, if the church is used to being more vocal, ask everyone to proclaim these truths aloud as they read them in any order.

## In the crèche

*Aim:* To help the children enjoy the truths about our God.

Have some joyful music on tape (such as Kids' Praise or the Ishmael Praise parties) and have a time of dancing. Now play this game – whenever you proclaim something about our God which is true, the music plays and everyone dances. Whenever you proclaim something about him which is not true, the music stops and everyone sits down and shakes their head, saying 'That's not true!'

Here are some examples of truths: God loves us; God is our friend; God will never let us down; God lives for ever; God forgives us.

And here are some examples of untruths: God is frightening; God is too busy to hear us; God only like us when we're good; God likes telling us off.

# 6th Sunday after the Epiphany

## Children

*Aim:* To help them understand the beauty and wonder of our God.

Have written out on cards the different truths about God, together with the false images people sometimes have about him. Throw the cards down on the floor and let the children sort them out according to what is true and what is not. Sing a song or hymn of praise together, such as 'O-O-O How good is the Lord', replacing the verses with the written truths about him.

Then help the children to make several banners to proclaim these truths, and display them in church.

## Young people

*Aim:* To help them discern the true and living God, rather than false images of him.

If the young people have not been in church for the sketch (see Other ideas) you can use it now. Afterwards look at the bible readings for today, comparing the images people worship with the power and beauty of the living God. Sing some songs of worship and praise, such as 'I will declare', 'Majesty', 'You are beautiful beyond description', 'Father, we love you' and 'Living Lord'. Get each person or small group to take one description of God and write it so that it expresses the meaning. These can be displayed through the year on the church notice board.

## YEARS 1 AND 2

*Thought for the day:*
*Jesus' glory is revealed in the parables*
*he tells.*

### Readings
Psalms 127,128,133
Isaiah 5:1-7(or 1-16)
John 15:1-11

### Reflection
We may not be aware of it, but most of us speak in pictures much of the time. Without thinking we talk of people 'getting stuck in', 'catching illnesses', 'making heavy weather of something', 'just touching on a subject' or 'bursting to tell you a piece of news'. Such metaphors enable us to communicate abstract ideas in a way that others can immediately respond to and understand. In a sense, parables are spiritual metaphors, since they enable us to comprehend deep spiritual truths through pictures and stories.

It's quite possible to enjoy a parable at its immediate, story level; it's also possible to be happily enjoying it at this level and suddenly find ourselves shaken and deeply disturbed by a new understanding of the truth about ourselves. Jesus' parables are dangerously powerful, beneath those innocent exteriors.

Today's picture of the fruiting vine helps us to see clearly the idiocy of trying to bear fruit independently of the vine. We are always so good at dictating outcomes to God and assuming he will agree with our way of doing things. But when we see this picture of the fruiting vine we are brought up with a start to recognise the real situation – twigs bear no fruit at all unless they are a continuation of the vine and have the life of the vine in them. And what and when they fruit is not for the twigs to decide, either; the fruiting will happen quite naturally, providing that twig stays firmly attached.

## Discussion starters

1  Look at some other parables of Jesus and discuss what their spiritual meanings are for you.
2  Sometimes Jesus wouldn't explain the stories he told until later. Why do you think he did this?

## All stage talk

*Theme:* Lifelines.
You will need a long piece of rope (such as a washing line), some shorter pieces of rope or string and a large pair of scissors.

Start with the rope coiled up and just hold one end. Explain that everyone is about to see a speeded up sequence of a grapevine growing. If the congregation enjoys joining in, they can make appropriate noises as the days and nights go by (such as snoring, 'wakey wakey', eating noises, yawning and snoring again, interspersed with rainstorms and singing 'The sun has got his hat on').

As the grapevine grows down the centre aisle, tie on branches (the shorter strings). When it gets to the time for fruiting, tie some volunteers on the end of the short strings. This should make it possible for the grapevine to stretch out quite firmly. Go up to one branch and cut it off or untie it from the vine. What will happen to these grapes that are just beginning to form? Explain that they will just wither and crumple (the volunteer

can do this); the branch can't make any more grapes because it's cut off from the life of the vine. Remind everyone of what Jesus said: 'I am the vine and you are the branches. Apart from me (show dead branch) you can do nothing.' We need to check that we really are fixed firmly on to the Jesus vine, so that his life can flow through us and make our lives fruitful.

## Intercessions

Father, we bring to mind all pastors and ministers in your holy, world-wide church; we thank you for them
and want to support them with our love.
*Silence for prayer*
The life we live:
**is your life within us**

Father, we call to mind the responsibilities we share in acting as stewards of your creation;
increase our love and respect for one another, regardless of nationality or colour.
*Silence for prayer*
The life we live:
**is your life within us**

Father, we call to mind those whom we love and those who love us; those we tend to criticise and those we admire.
*Silence for prayer*
The life we live:
**is your life within us**

Father, we call to mind all those who are feeling weak or vulnerable; all those struggling to make sense of their suffering.
*Silence for prayer*
The life we live:
**is your life within us**

Father, we call to mind those who grieve
for their loved ones who have died;
we remember those entering heaven.

*Silence for prayer*

The life we live:
**is your life within us**

Father, we call to mind your faithful love,
your patience and your mercy.

*Silence for prayer*

The life we live:
**is your life within us**

## In the crèche

*Aim:* To teach the importance of being
joined on to Jesus.
Try this action song, to the tune of
'Three Blind Mice':

Grow, grow, grow
*(Start very low and small, and get bigger)*
grow, grow, grow
see all my fruit
*(clench fists and open fingers one by one)*
see all my fruit
*(open fingers on other hand)*
I'm rooted in Jesus
*(point to feet firmly on the ground)*
as you can see
It's Jesus who puts
*(point upwards)*
all the loving in me
*(point to heart)*
It's Jesus who makes me
*(draw hands up from toes to head)*
a fruiting tree
*(and stretch out branches)*
I know, know, know
*(nod and bend in the wind.)*

Now stand in a line and pass a piece of
fruit along it to someone at the end. That
works; but if one person moves out of the
line, the fruit can't get through.

## Children

*Aim:* To explore the nature of a parable.
First talk about secrets and keeping
special things in secret places. Now tell
them a parable – a story which has a
secret hidden inside. (It's the story of the
vine growing grapes and the branches
that are cut off being unable to grow any.)
Tell the story with a plant and good root
system, either brought inside, or with the
children gathered round a plant outside.
Cut a branch off at the appropriate time.

Try and work out what the secret
meaning of the story is. They may be able
to think of the secrets in other parables
that they know, such as the lost sheep.

Now help the children make this
model of what a parable is which they
can use to keep their own secrets inside.

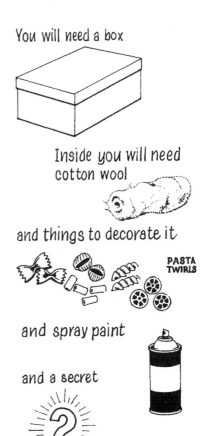

You will need a box

Inside you will need
cotton wool

and things to decorate it

PASTA TWIRLS

and spray paint

and a secret

## Young people

Aim: To look at parables in layers.

First read the Old Testament vineyard story and the New Testament vine and branches passage. Set up a chart like this:

and look for the different 'depths' or layers of meaning in the readings. Write them in.

Then in small groups, try making some composite pieces of writing which unlock the meaning of a parable. The word PARABLES is written down the side of the page and each letter becomes the beginning of a line. Here is an example to give you the idea:

> Parables
> Are a
> Really
> Amazing way of
> Bringing out a message.
> Listen and you will
> Eventually discover a
> Secret meaning.

The finished pieces of writing can be shared and later written up and decorated and put in the parish paper.

## BEFORE EASTER

# 9th Sunday before Easter

## YEAR 1

*Thought for the day:*
*Jesus teaches us by meeting us in our*
*present situation and guiding us*
*forwards from there.*

### Readings
Psalm 71
Deuteronomy 5:1-21
Luke 13:22-end

### Reflection

Although the ten commandments were written down so long ago, and the nomadic desert life of the people they were first addressed to has little in common with our own, we can still sense in them the holiness of God and his loving concern for us. Their teaching is as simple as it is profound: love and honour the God of creation, and let that love spill over into your relationships with everyone else. When the priorities are right the rest of our lives will become the secure and fulfilling span we can delight in.

When we read Jesus' teaching about the narrow gate straight after the reading of the ten commandments it is easy to assume the narrow way consists of following the commandments pedantically in the battle for seats in heaven, and of course it doesn't mean that at all.

Jesus is looking at any one person, loaded with bundles and parcels of material possessions, bitternesses and grudges, ambitions and pride. The entrance gate to full life is so narrow that all these bundles will have to be left outside before the person can walk unimpeded into God's kingdom. Instead of struggling so hard to get ourselves and our parcels through we need to shed all but the liberating truths of the good life – loving God and love one another. That way we shall hardly notice that the gate is narrow.

But it is one thing to know this and quite another to put it into practice. We know from experience that we find it easy to keep collecting parcels and have to make a deliberate, daily point of laying them down so that they don't accumulate. It happens particularly as a substitute for the real thing which takes up no space at all – knowing that we are loved and provided for.

This is what saddened (and still saddens) Jesus so much; that in spite of his reassurance of God's love and forgiveness, we turn our backs on the freedom such love offers and choose instead to collect our cumbersome bundles which actually block us off from self-fulfilment.

### All stage talk

*Theme:* Getting through a narrow gateway.

Beforehand prepare a narrow gateway. This may be a very narrow space between two pieces of card secured to chairs, two broom handles held close together by volunteers, or any other ingenious but simple method you think of. You will also need some big, bulky parcels, such as rolled sleeping bags, huge balloons, large cartons tied with string etc.

First remind everyone of the narrow gate mentioned in the reading from Luke and introduce your home produced model. Ask for a volunteer to help explain Jesus' teaching about how to get through narrow gates. Load the volunteer up with all the bundles and parcels, either mentioning what they are or actually sticking labels on them as people suggest the things we often carry through life with us (such as resentment, I've-got-to-be-better-than-anyone-else, a cool image, I-want-it-so-I'll-have-it, me-first, and so on.)

Now let the person demonstrate what happens when s/he gets to the narrow gate. Ask them to try doing the things you suggest: first we might try to push through with everything and then get stuck; or we might try going in sideways, but that doesn't work either; or we may even squeeze through on our own and try pulling the luggage through after us, but because we find this is impossible we prefer to go back out again, rather than leaving the luggage behind.

But there's only one way we can get through, and that's by accepting that what we are going to is better value than all the clobber we have collected. Once we realise this we can say good-bye to it and leave it there outside while we walk quite easily into the life God has prepared for us.

## Intercessions

Father, breathe your spirit of life
into all the members of your church;
keep us open to your word and
sensitive to your will.

*Silence for prayer*

All-knowing God:
**teach us your ways**

Father, breathe your spirit of counsel
into every debate and international
conference; alert us to act with
responsibility and integrity.

*Silence for prayer*

All-knowing God:
**teach us your ways**

Father, breathe your spirit of love into
every home and neighbourhood; make us
slow to criticise and quick to forgive.

*Silence for prayer*

All-knowing God:
**teach us your ways**

Father, breathe your spirit of healing
into all those who are weakened or
damaged, whether physically, mentally,
emotionally or spiritually; give them the
reassurance of your presence.

*Silence for prayer*

All-knowing God:
**teach us your ways**

Father, breathe your spirit of peace
into those who are approaching death
and those who have recently died.
Help us to trust in your infinite mercy.

*Silence for prayer*

All-knowing God:
**teach us your ways**

Father, breathe your spirit of thankfulness
into our hearts as we receive,
our minds as we notice,
and our lives as we journey.

*Silence for prayer*

All-knowing God:
**teach us your ways**

## Other ideas

• As today we are alerted to the need for discarding what is spiritually unhelpful to us, try having a reflective or penitential time in which you think of two things or areas in your life which have become unnecessary or spiritually damaging to you. Clench these things in your hands and recognise how much they mean to you. Then slowly open your hands and allow God to dissolve their importance to you.

- In order to sensitise ourselves to listen attentively, have everyone very quiet and trying to hear a pin drop. Then listen attentively to God's peace among us.

## In the crèche

*Aim:* To understand the need to let go of self in being a Christian.

You will need a fairly narrow mouthed jar of nuts and a small, hand sized container with sweets or dried fruit in for each of the children.

First tell the story of the racoon who put his hand into a hole in a tree to get some nuts, and act out the story with your jar of nuts. He took a big handful and then found he couldn't get his hand out. What could he do? (They may suggest that he lets go of the nuts). The trouble was, he wanted the nuts so much that he didn't want to let go. So there he stayed, without being able to move around and without being able to eat any nuts either, until he saw how silly he was being. Let the children fill their jars with sweets or dried fruit and go through the racoon story again with them all acting it out.

## Children

*Aim:* To look at the teaching aspect of Jesus' ministry.

Beforehand prepare two simple sock puppets tied with string to this script so that children will be able to read it

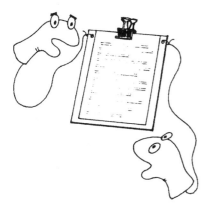

**Cathy**  Dad, you know the hose pipe?

**Dad**  Hang on, Cathy, I'm rather busy. I've got to get this garden watered before lunch.

**Cathy**  But Dad, that's what I mean, the hose pipe is . . .

**Dad**  Cathy I said I was busy. You run off and play.

**Cathy**  O.K. Dad, but I wish you would listen.

**Dad**  In a minute, love. Right, I'll just turn on and . . . AAAHHH! The hose is leaking and all the water is making me soaked!

**Cathy**  Yes, Dad, I knew it was going to do that. I could see the hole in the hose pipe.

**Dad**  Then why didn't you tell me, you rotter!

Ask two confident readers to make the puppets act out the sketch, and then talk about how Cathy's Dad could have avoided getting soaked. Sometimes we could all save ourselves a lot of trouble by listening to one another better. Jesus went around talking to people and listening to them and explaining how their lives could be freed from all the guilt and fear which worried them so much. Lots of people listened and learnt from what Jesus said. He helped them sort their lives out. But lots of others were too tied up with their own ideas to really hear what Jesus was saying – they listened with a bit of themselves, but didn't really listen deep down, so they missed out. At this point the children can read the gospel reading from Luke.

Help the children make this jigsaw (shown overleaf) to complete before a certain time is up (depending on the age and ability of the children).

1

Used birthday card

2

LISTEN TO GOD!

3

Cut

## *Young people*

*Aim:* To explore how Jesus taught the 'simple' way of love.

Look together at the ten commandments, noticing what the priorities are and linking them with Jesus' summary of them: love God and love your neighbour as yourself. Then read the teaching in Luke about the narrow gateway, emphasising that there is only room for us as we are, and no way we can get through while carrying all the clutter of possessions, bitterness, an inflated sense of our own importance and so on.

Have some large bulky bundles and discuss what labels they may have. Pray together for discernment to see what luggage we have collected which has become too important to us and is preventing us from living God's way.

Draw a poster for the church notice board which shows a narrow opening with a notice hung up beside it saying 'Please leave all luggage at the door'.

## YEAR 2

*Thought for the day:
Jesus teaches us by meeting us in our present situation and guiding us forwards from there.*

### *Readings*
Psalm 71
Job 28 (or 9-end)
Luke 6:20-38

### *Reflection*

Like many aged and sharp-witted people, my 89 year old uncle is very wise. His wisdom comes from having lived, quietly and observantly, over so many years and so many changes, so that he has an overall perspective which is of great value to the rest of us. In Job's case it is his suffering which opens him to a fresh understanding of how vast and incomprehensible God is.

Wisdom is closely linked to the quality St Francis would call humility – that earthiness borne of human experience which enables us to face things as they really are, both in the world around us and within ourselves and in our relationship with almighty God.

Jesus' direct teaching in Luke's version of the sermon on the mount addresses all his committed followers in every generation, recognising that, in our limited humanity, we are bound to be constantly yearning for a clearer, more comprehensive understanding of God, and daily made aware with sorrow of how far we fall short of loving him. But Jesus tells us to consider such a state blessed, because what it shows is that our relationship with God must then be honest and realistic; the time to worry is the moment we feel we have God sewn up and our lives comfortably in control.

For that is not the wisdom of truth but the folly of self-inflicted blindness.

So we can be happy to begin every morning at Jesus' feet, knowing ourselves ignorant and poor, but delighting in the way he will guide and teach us through each step of our day.

## All stage talk

*Theme:* Chips off the old block.

Beforehand prepare two chunks of wood, which should be quite different from each other. From each cut a small chip. Also prepare some cards stuck on pea sticks and have a thick felt tip pen at the ready to write in the signs.

First ask everyone what thing an ant might think of as huge. Then a cat. Then collect some ideas of what they themselves think of as huge. Remind everyone that all of these are contained in the mind of God and he is far greater than we can ever imagine. But let's have a go at imagining what God is like. Write the descriptions on the notices which people can hold up.

Now give out the two chips of wood and show everyone the blocks they came from. Ask a cluster of people round each chip to decide which block their chip came from. How can they tell? – By the way it feels; by its colour; by the grain etc.

Jesus says that we are to behave in the same way God does – we are to be chips off the old block, and by looking at us and the way we behave, people should be able to recognise that we are Christians. So how will that mean we are to behave? Look again at the notices and they may be able to help us. If God is prepared to love everyone, whether they deserve it or not, then that's how we ought to be. If God is forgiving, we need to be as well. If God is trustworthy, so should we be to one another.

Look at the chips of wood again. If we're honest, we know we don't always

behave like God. Jesus suggests that we recognise we are only chips and don't get carried away into thinking we're the block of wood. So long as we don't pretend we know all the answers he will be able to teach us through our lives to become more and more like him.

## Intercessions

Father, we call to mind all those in Christian ministry
and all whom they serve in your strength.

*Silence for prayer*

Father, we need you:
**we depend on you for everything**

We call to mind all those who make decisions which affect our lives and the life of our planet.

*Silence for prayer*

Father, we need you:
**we depend on you for everything**

We call to mind the members of our families and also our neighbours
and friends.

*Silence for prayer*

Father, we need you:
**we depend on you for everything**

We call to mind those who are ill
and those who cannot be physically independent.

*Silence for prayer*

Father, we need you:
**we depend on you for everything**

We call to mind all who are celebrating and rejoicing today. With them we lift our hearts in thankfulness.

*Silence for prayer*

Father, we need you:
**we depend on you for everything**

## Other ideas

• Use the qualities of God written on posters and have them carried, one by one, up the centre of the building. In turn the carriers of the posters call out what God is like and the whole congregation responds, like this:

Leader   Our God is loving and forgiving.

All        Oh God, make us loving
            and forgiving.

• With the main flower arrangements, have them paired with a tiny posy in the same style and using the same colour of flowers. Have the little arrangements carried up by the arrangers at the offertory, to be placed beside their 'parent' arrangement.

## In the crèche

*Aim:* To notice that offspring look like their parents. When we are loving we are like God the Father.

Play some of the parent/offspring matching games with cards of different animals and their parents. Sort out a heap of plastic farm animals into families and play with them. If the toddlers are old enough explain that when their parents are looking after them lovingly they are being like God because God looks after us lovingly.

## Children

*Aim:* To recognise what God is like and see that behaviour reflected in people who love him.

First play a game. Work out the number of pairs of children there are, and mix up that number of pairs of animals – a parent and baby. Show each person the name or picture of one animal. Without using any animal noises the children have to act out their animal until they find their pairs. They carry on miming their animals until everyone is paired up. Suitable animals

for this game are: rabbits, elephants, birds, kangaroos, snakes, lions and horses.

Explain how people should be able to recognise us as God's children by the way we behave. What do they think God is like? Write all the suggestions down in bright colours on a poster. (This is one of those times when you may end up learning more than you expected to!)

Have a lively praise song to celebrate God being as he is and follow it with a short 'sorry' time of quietness, remembering when we haven't behaved like God our Father.

Help them make a zigzag book by sticking a different quality of God's nature on each page. If there is time they can add others of their own.

## Young people

*Aim:* To celebrate the qualities of God's nature and face the challenge this gives us.

First play this game. One person thinks of someone in the group and everyone asks questions to try and guess who the mystery person is. They can be quite straightforward questions (i.e. has she got black hair?) or for an older group the questions can be more subtle (i.e. what might his favourite car be?; where might she choose to go for a honeymoon?). In the game we are working out someone's identity and character.

We can find out about God's character by reading about him, seeing him revealed in Jesus and through living in his company. Read the Old Testament passage together and then go straight on to the passage from Luke.

Make a list together of what God seems to be like, noting his righteousness and high expectations of our behaviour as well as his love and mercy. Discuss how easy it is to pick up on the parts we want to hear and disregard the truths about loving enemies and not being complacent.

Help them to use the challenge of today's reading in tackling one particular area in their lives and bringing it under God's government.

# 8th Sunday before Easter

## YEAR 1

*Thought for the day:
God knows us inside out.*

### Readings

Psalm 139:1-8
2 Kings 4:8-37
Mark 1:21-end

### Reflection

Psalm 139 expresses the wonder of God's intimate knowledge of us at every stage of our life. He has known you with perfect and complete understanding up to and including this moment now, recognising your happiness and your pain and loving you through it all. God's close friends learn to love others with that same nourishing love.

In today's reading we hear the heartrending story of the Shunamite woman being granted great, unasked for blessing in the form of her son, and then being faced with the bewildering situation of God taking that blessing away. Through his friend, Elisha, God was able to pour out his healing on the limp body of her dead child, and turn the agony of grief into joy and deepened faith.

In Capernaum Jesus' authority in preaching went hand in hand with his capacity to heal. In his healing, the God of love was taking authority and searching out the depth of each person's being, bringing about harmony, wholeness and peace.

### Discussion starters

1 Make a note of everything the Shunamite woman does and everything Elisha does. What can we learn from this about faith?
2 What do you notice about Jesus' prayer/work balance? Check your own input/output against this model.

### All stage talk

*Theme:* Loving people better.
You will need a copy of Yellow Pages, a sock with hole and mending eqipment, a broken mechanical thing (such as a plug with loose connections) and the equipment to put it right.

Talk about what most of us do when the washing machine breaks down – we may kick it and then look for an expert in the Yellow Pages. (Ask someone to find a list of such experts.) They can put it right because they know how the machine works, so they understand it.

With illness research goes on because once we understand the nature of the disease we have some chance of healing it. Show everyone the things you have brought which need mending and ask for people who understand about darning and mechanical things to put them right.

While they do so, explain how God knows us inside out because he made us. He knows our bodies and what they are capable of, their weaknesses and their particular oddities. And he loves them. That's why Jesus could heal all those people – it wasn't a magic trick, it was love which gave him the understanding of them and the power to mend them, just as these people can mend things they understand.

## Intercessions

Father we bring to your healing love
our shallowness of faith,
our need for your grace and power
in the church throughout the world.

*Silence for prayer*

You know us completely:
**and love us for ever**

We bring to your healing love
our need for your serenity and wisdom
in the governments of all the nations.

*Silence for prayer*
You know us completely:
**and love us for ever**

We bring to your healing love
our need of patience, mutual affection
and forgiveness
in our homes and families.

*Silence for prayer*

You know us completely:
**and love us for ever**

We bring to your healing love
the injured and broken-hearted,
the weak and the frightened.

*Silence for prayer*

You know us completely:
**and love us for ever**

We bring to your healing love those
whom death has released from pain, and
those in great sorrow at losing loved ones.

*Silence for prayer*

You know us completely:
**and love us for ever**

We bring you our thanks and praise for
all that is good and hopeful and positive,
all that is redeemed from suffering.

*Silence for prayer*

You know us completely:
**and love us for ever**

## Other ideas

Cradle one hand in the other. Love that hand and its owner as Jesus does, with understanding and affection. Use those same hands to reach out in the sharing of the Peace with everyone around.

## In the crèche

*Aim:* To teach that Jesus made people better.

Using puppets or teddies tell the story of Jesus healing Peter's mother-in-law.

## Children

*Aim:* To teach the story of Elisha healing the Shunamite boy.

Start with a game in pairs. The idea is that one of the pair tries to be a mirror image of the other – by really concentrating on the other person you start to reflect them.

That's like us with God; when friends of God stick really close to him they start to reflect him and begin to behave like him. Elisha was a very close friend of God so he was able to let God's love work through him to heal this boy.

Now tell the story with the children acting out the different parts as you direct them.

Together make a cartoon strip of the story, with different children working on the main events:

1  The boy saying, 'My head, my head!'
2  The boy sitting on his Mum's lap.
3  Mum laying him on the bed.
4  Mum meeting Elisha and begging him to help.

5 Elisha breathing life into the boy.
6 The boy sneezing and feeling better.
Collect the sections and photocopy them into booklets to give the children next week.

## Young people

*Aim:* To look at Jesus' healing/prayer ministry. First go through the gospel reading with these questions written on a chart: Who? Where? When? What? How? So? and fill the chart in as you find the information.

Notice how Jesus undergirds all his ministry with long times of prayer. Discuss our own prayer commitments in the light of Jesus' example, being practical and encouraging.

# YEAR 2

*Thought for the day:*
*Christ can heal us to wholeness,*
*but only if we let him.*

## Readings

Psalm 139:1-18
Numbers 21:4-9
John 9 (or 9:1-25)

## Reflection

Bronze snakes may sound to us a somewhat bizarre form of alternative medicine. Immediately we start getting into the 'How could it possibly work?' mode, which isn't really the point.

More helpful is to notice how Moses never takes his eyes off God when he's under attack, and his obedience enables God to heal those who choose to cooperate. We see the same element of choice in Jesus' healing of the man born blind.

There are never any restrictions on eligibility as far as God is concerned, and no one needs to remain spiritually blind.

But we do have to choose – we can either pretend we can see, and in so doing stay blind, or we can admit our blindness and our need of healing, which always involves swallowing our pride.

We may, for instance, have an image of ourselves as a carer, and find it very hard to suddenly accept that we need to be on the receiving end of someone else's caring. Or our qualifications and experience may make it difficult for us to admit that occasionally we are in the wrong.

Christ asks us to respond and cooperate with him so that he can make us whole. And wholeness may or may not involve physical healing; wholeness heals us in a way that will last for ever.

## Discussion starters

1 The bronze snake was like the biting snakes but without the poisonous bite. Can you see the connection between this and the Son of Man being 'lifted up' on the cross?
2 Why do you think the blind man's parents, the religious leaders and the man himself all reacted as they did?

## All stage talk

*Theme:* Being healed from different kinds of blindness.
You will need a blindfold, either a jacket with parka-type hood or a length of bendy cardboard with tie-ups, and an optician's chart with the letters arranged like this:

J
ESUSCA
NHELPY
OUSEE

Talk about the different kinds of blindness we have met in the gospel today. First there is the man who had been born blind. Ask someone to help you by being blindfolded. (If there is a blind person in your congregation you could ask them beforehand if they would mind being interviewed at this point.) Ask the blind/blindfolded person how it feels not to be able to see, which things they find particularly difficult and so on. If you are working with a blindfolded person, take the blindfold and ask them how it feels to see again. Jesus enabled the blind man to see.

What about the Pharisees – the religious leaders? Were they blind or not? Ask for a volunteer and put on them the sight-restricting hood. What can they see and what can't they see? Explain how this can happen to any of us – we can be so rigid and concerned about a particular way of looking at things that we are effectively blind to anything outside our range of vision. Prejudice is like this hood; so is having a 'hobby horse about something' so that every conversation always comes round somehow to fishing, or the incompetence of a particular political party, or the trouble with young people today, or bad health.

Sometimes this tunnelled vision completely blocks people from seeing the good news of God's love. If they ask, Jesus can take those hoods off and enable them to enjoy full sight. But if they insist that they can see perfectly well already, then Jesus will be unable to help them and their narrowness is condemned.

## Intercessions

Father, we bring to you
our desire to see you more clearly.

*Silence for prayer*

Open our eyes, Lord:
**heal us from blindness**

Father, we grieve with the oppressed and downtrodden, and long for your governing of the nations.

*Silence for prayer*

Open our eyes, Lord:
**heal us from blindness**

Father, we lay before you all our relationships, both the fulfilling and the challenging.

*Silence for prayer*

Open our eyes, Lord:
**heal us from blindness**

Father, we remember with affection and love all those who are in pain or distress, offering our availability for you to use.

*Silence for prayer*

Open our eyes, Lord:
**heal us from blindness**

Father, we call to mind those whom death has hidden from our eyes, but whom we continue to love and cherish, knowing they are safe in your care.

*Silence for prayer*

Open our eyes, Lord:
**heal us from blindness**

Father, we thank you
for the gift of physical sight
and the richness of spiritual insight.

*Silence for prayer*

Open our eyes, Lord:
**heal us from blindness**

## Other ideas

Have people miming or acting out the gospel as it is read, and then have someone interviewing the characters about the events and their own attitudes.

## In the crèche

*Aim:* To experience what it feels like to be without sight. Take turns to be blindfold and try walking about with someone or doing tasks which are easy when you can see, such as pouring water from one container into another, or building a brick tower. Younger children can play 'peep-bo' types of games. Thank God for our eyesight.

## Children

*Aim:* To teach the story of the blind man being healed. Begin with a game using your eyes, such as pinning the tail on the donkey or 'squeak, piggy, squeak'.

Talk together about how difficult it is when you can't see, and then tell the story from today's gospel, either using the floortiles method, or acting the story out as you tell it, with everyone moving to different parts of the room for the different parts of the story.

Then help the children make this model with moving eyes to remind them of the passage they have been hearing about.

Cut slits

Cut out eyes and nose

## Young people

*Aim:* To look at both physical and spiritual blindness. First read John 9 with people taking different parts. If the group enjoys acting, you could act the passage as you read it. Then have a role-play involving the man himself, his parents and two friends he hasn't seen for a while and who want to know what has happened to him. Follow this with a role play of some Pharisees talking to one of their friends who was visiting his brother when all this took place.

Talk together about the different kinds of blindness in the story and use the episode to challenge the state of our own 'sight'.

---

# 7th Sunday before Easter

---

## YEAR 1

*Thought for the day:*
*If you are a sinner,*
*then Jesus considers*
*you a friend.*

## Readings
Psalms 56, 57
Jeremiah 33:1-11
Luke 7:36-8:3

## Reflection

As we get older we all find there are things in our past which we would love not to be there; things we wish we had managed differently; things we still blush with shame to remember. It may go even deeper than that. Perhaps we have hurt or damaged another person so much that we feel we can never forgive ourselves, and yet there is no replay button to put things right.

Sometimes it is far easier to forgive others than to forgive ourselves. We may work through our guilt and accept forgiveness, and then find these ghosts from our past still haunting us. Jesus understands that – he knows what we go through and why we react as we do. He is not a condemning God but a God who likes us as well as loving us; a God who is patient with us and doesn't mind us taking ages for the penny to drop. It isn't the ones who keep messing things up that God finds hard to work with – it's those who think they know it all already.

So don't get too disheartened by your sin; it isn't long, drawn-out guilt-wallowing that will take the sin away, but simply the grace of a loving and merciful God. Come to him in real sorrow of course, but let him ease that sin and guilt out of you by his forgiveness, and then enjoy getting on with your life freed from its burden.

## Discussion starters

1   How does Jesus' attitude to sinners suggest we ought to behave towards those whose behaviour we disapprove of?

2   Do we let God completely forgive us, or do we tend to punish ourselves as if this will help?

## All stage talk

*Theme:* Accepting God's forgiveness. Begin with the sketch set out below in Other ideas. After the sketch ask people to say what they thought the sketch was about. Ideas may well come from this which you and I haven't thought of. That is excellent; they may be issues which people in your congregation need to hear. Draw the ideas together – unless we accept our need of help, God can't help us. All the time we reckon there's nothing wrong with us we don't go to a doctor; it's only when we recognise our need of spiritual healing that we start valuing Jesus and listening attentively to what he says.

## Intercessions

Father, we remember all those who are insulted or despised for their faith in you.
*Silence for prayer*
Lord, we take refuge:
**in the shadow of your wings**

We remember those caught up in conflict, and those who strive for peace.
*Silence for prayer*
Lord, we take refuge:
**in the shadow of your wings**

We remember those who irritate and annoy us, and those we irritate and annoy.
*Silence for prayer*
Lord, we take refuge:
**in the shadow of your wings**

We remember those whose bodies are trapped in pain,
and those whose minds are trapped in confusion.
*Silence for prayer*
Lord, we take refuge:
**in the shadow of your wings**

We remember those who have died and those who ache with mourning.
*Silence for prayer*
Lord, we take refuge:
**in the shadow of your wings**

We thank and praise you, O God, for your parenting and special love for each of us.

*Silence for prayer*

Lord, we take refuge:
**in the shadow of your wings**

## Other ideas

*Drama sketch:* At the doctor's.

Have a sign up with the doctor's name on it and the doctor wearing a stethoscope. A patient walks in with wads of cotton wool plastered over his eyes so that he can barely see. He gropes around, bumping into the wall, and finds his way to the chair, with the doctor guiding him, something like this:

**Doc**    Ah, good morning, Mr Henning! Do take a seat . . . no, that's the table . . . the seat's over to the right a bit.

**Patient**    Alright, alright, I know where I'm going. What do you think I am . . . blind or something?

**Doc**    Now how can I help you?

**Patient**    Help me? How on earth would you be able to help me? Anyone would think there was something wrong with me!

**Doc**    Er . . . Perhaps I could examine your eyes?

**Patient**    *(jumping up)* Oh no you don't! I've heard about people like you. As if I'd trust my eyes to your interfering fingers. They're my own eyes, aren't they?

**Doc**    Well yes, of course, but . . .

**Patient**    There you are then, my eyes are my own private business, thanks very much. Now why don't you get a move on and stamp these library books. *(He puts some books on the table.)*

**Doc**    But Mr Henning . . .

**Patient**    *(getting up and groping round walls to the door)* I don't know . . . the library system isn't what it used to be . . .

**Doc**    *(shrugs his shoulders and shakes his head. Outside there is the sound of a horn blaring, a screech of brakes and a loud cry.)* There's no helping some people!

## In the crèche

*Aim:* To enjoy friendship.

Have some teddies and other soft toys acting out different facets of friendship. For instance, one can be feeling lonely and another comes round to play; one has just got a new toy and shares it with a friend; one is finding it hard to do something and her friend helps; one feels left out so the others make sure he can join in, etc.

Play together in twos, threes and fours and tell them how Jesus is our friend.

## Children

*Aim:* To think about what makes a good friend.

Use puppets to act out different situations where the children decide whether there's a good friend or not. Make some of these very obvious, such as comforting and sharing situations, but make some more subtle, such as a disagreement where the puppets argue and end up laughing. It is important that children realise we are talking about the real world and not some cloud cuckoo land. They need to know they can trust Jesus with their grumpy and angry times as well as with the times they are feeling good.

Make a list of all their ideas about what makes a good friend and point out how Jesus is all of these and more so: he is the best friend we could ever wish to have.

## Young people

*Aim:* To explore the quality of God's friendship.

Read the Old Testament passage together and think about how God was befriending Jeremiah here. Then read the New Testament passage, if possible from the dramatised bible.

Go through the different characters in turn, looking at what each was thinking. When you get to Jesus, think about how he felt towards each of the other characters – bearing in mind his love and affection for each of them.

Now try looking with Jesus' eyes at various people in different situations where there is conflict or misunderstanding. Look at one international situation, one national and one very local. How will Jesus' personal and forgiving love, coupled with perfect knowledge and understanding of backgrounds affect the way we respond to the people in these situations?

# YEAR 2

*Thought for the day:*
*If you are a sinner,*
*then Jesus considers you a friend.*

## Readings

Psalm 56,57
Jeremiah 30:1-3,10-22
Luke 13:1-17

## Reflection

The psalmists and prophets had spoken with wonder of God's being completely righteous and yet at the same time completely merciful. In a sense these two qualities seem impossible to balance up. Surely if God is utterly pure and perfect he will not be able to stand the presence of evil?

But Jesus shows by his behaviour how righteousness and mercy are blended; he never baulks from the truth and never excuses, yet with his whole being he longs for people to be freed and happy. The overwhelming love Jesus feels for the sinner allows him to cope with the terrible pain of their sin and still reach out to their need for rescue. It is a little like parents who might drag their child from a burning house, even when the flames are burning them.

And we find that whenever Jesus comes into contact with evil spirits, it is not he who cries out in agony but them. Only the one who is totally in control can deal with evil, and Jesus is in control because his righteousness is more powerful than the power of evil.

## Discussion starters

1  To what extent should we be understanding, and when should we speak out against sin?

2  Why didn't Jesus just keep strictly within the expected rules?

## All stage talk

*Theme:* Jesus loves setting people free.

You will need some lengths of rope, chain or thick string, a blindfold and a bicycle lock with padlock.

Talk about how we often tie our lives up in knots. They may remember having done something wrong and then having told a few lies to cover up. Or there may be some who have once had a row with someone and now dread bumping into that person ever again. Those kinds of experiences are rather like pieces of rope tying us up and preventing us from moving freely. (Ask for a volunteer who will help by allowing you to tie them up here and there.)

There are other things which chain us as well. Pick out a really strong rope or chain and explain how selfishness ties us up and restricts our movement dreadfully – we're so busy thinking about ourselves, our own needs and wants, our own rights and so on that we can't reach out to other people at all. (Tie up the arms firmly.)

Arrogance and vanity make us think we're so wonderful that they stop us seeing the truth about ourselves (put on the blindfold) and fear and guilt can make us too terrified to move forward (tie up the legs).

So we end up spiritually trussed up, living a compromise and never living life as fully as we could.

Jesus loves us and hates seeing us like this; he yearns to set us free, and the good news is that he can. When we hesitantly let him into our lives he will start untying our ropes of selfishness, taking off our blindfolds of arrogance and vanity, unchaining our fear and guilt (do this with the ropes etc.) until he has set us free to live happily and love others. (The volunteer can caper around a bit to demonstrate).

## Intercessions

Father, wherever people's faith is stunted or withered we plead for your breath of life.

*Silence for prayer*

Lord of power:
**you can transform our lives**

Wherever people are trapped by oppression or weakened by complacency we plead for your kingdom to come.

*Silence for prayer*

Lord of power:
**you can transform our lives**

Wherever people live out their daily lives in stress and disappointment we plead for your restoring love.

*Silence for prayer*

Lord of power:
**you can transform our lives**

Wherever people's lives are restricted by physical weakness or hunger or poverty we plead for your healing love.

*Silence for prayer*

Lord of power:
**you can transform our lives**

Wherever people are dying we plead for your mercy and comfort.

*Silence for prayer*

Lord of power:
**you can transform our lives**

Wherever there is loveliness and serenity, integrity and wisdom we praise you for your glory.

*Silence for prayer*

Lord of power:
**you can transform our lives**

## Other ideas

*Dance:* to express the truth of God setting lives free.

A group of mixed ages begins by moving around slowly, each restricted in some way. One may wander blindly with hands over eyes, one has legs twisted and is only able to slide, one has twisted arms behind their back and moves awkwardly. Think through the ways we are restricted (as in the All stage talk) and use the group's ideas as well. One person represents Jesus and walks quietly amongst the group, sitting or moving slowly with each in turn, reaching out to them but unable to heal while s/he is ignored and rejected. Then one person turns slightly towards him/her and as s/he lays hands over the affected part the person is released and able to move freely.

Now this person can work with Jesus until the group is fully set free and able to dance, giving God the glory.

## *In the crèche*

*Aim:* To explore the idea of setting free.

Have some wild creatures in a suitable container to look at with the children (snails, worms, beetles and ants are usually the easiest to find!) and enjoy them, teaching respect and kindness for all creation. Then explain that the creatures are not able to live freely if we keep them caged like this, so we must set them free to enjoy living their lives outside again. All go out and set the creatures free.

## *Children*

*Aim:* To explore how Jesus gives us freedom.

Tell the story of the crippled lady being healed on the Sabbath in the synagogue. You could do this acting out the crowd watching, the Pharisees watching and Jesus calling out to the woman – she wasn't standing next to him. Look closely at the details in the account so that you get the real atmosphere rather than a clinical 'Jesus trick'.

If the children have not been involved in the All stage talk, then try the tying up and releasing of one of them in the way described above.

If they have already been involved with this in church, play this game:

Divide the children into teams. One child from each team is caged in with chairs and can only be released by a special combination lock which the rest of the team have to solve. Whoever solves the combination code first and releases their team member, wins.

Here is the muddled message:

SET IN LET YOU AND LOVE FREE HIS
WILL JESUS
which they must unravel to say:
LET JESUS IN AND HIS LOVE WILL
SET YOU FREE.

## *Young people*

*Aim:* To explore the blend of righteousness and mercy in God's nature.

First read the passage from Jeremiah and pick out from it both justice and mercy. Now read the passage from Luke and identify the same qualities in Jesus during this situation. Give out some newspaper stories for people to discuss in twos or threes and try to discover what happens when there is an imbalance or a misunderstanding of these qualities. How can Jesus' behaviour (both here and in other parts of the gospels) help us to tread the right path in delicate and difficult situations?

Stick the pictures and headlines on a chart and have a time of intercession for those involved in the situations. Provide stationery so that if it would help to write letters of protest or encouragement you can do so straight away.

**LENT**

# *1st Sunday in Lent*

## YEAR 1

*Thought for the day:*
*We need to build up our defences*
*against temptation.*

### Readings
Psalm 119.9-24
1 Samuel 26
Luke 22.1-23

### Reflection

We have two poignantly human stories this week. We can imagine David and his companion daringly creeping right into Saul's camp at night and finding themselves in this position of power over the king. We can only wonder at the thoughts which might have been going through David's mind as he stood there with Saul sleeping soundly at his feet. Perhaps some of you will have been on the receiving end of violent hatred or jealousy; David knew this to the point of his life being always in danger, and removing Saul would remove all that.

But David's love for God is stronger than any other human feelings he might have, and that love for God erupts in honour for God's chosen king, however insane and desperate his behaviour has been.

For Judas, the hopes and dreams of his expectations for Jesus could not cope with the actual Jesus he discovers. Had Judas already developed an open commitment to God, then this would surely have overwhelmed the disappointment and confusion he felt about Jesus; but as it was, the temptations were allowed to race forward into sin.

If we are ever to cope with the temptations we are bound to get, it is vital that we build strong defences. And the only strong and effective defence is a deep relationship with God, so that he fights the battles in and through us.

### Discussion starters

1   How does the night visit in 1 Samuel affect the spiritual growth of a) Saul and b) David?

2   Where does temptation turn into sin and how can we stop that happening?

### All stage talk

*Theme:* Temptation.

You will need a tennis racket, a number of soft, sponge balls or balls of screwed up paper and a large cardboard carton.

First go through the passage from Samuel, bringing it to life. Ask people what David might have been thinking as he stood there over Saul. What might he have been tempted to do?

Temptations are bound to fly at us from all directions all through our lives. Ask someone to help you to explain this by standing there as a group of people pelts them with balls. Sometimes the temptation is only slight (one ball) such as when you are tempted to kill your sister or brother. You know deep down that though she irritates you you wouldn't really want to do her any serious injury, so your fondness for her acts like a screen (they hold racquet up) and stops the temptation from getting any closer. (Throw ball so that the racquet screens the person.)

Sometimes the temptations fly at us so powerfully and urgently that even with the screen it is difficult to stop them getting to you. (Try this with lots of balls at once.)

What God provides for us is all-round protection. (Let the volunteer crawl into the large carton). If we make a habit of crawling into God's protection every day, then we will be better equipped to say `NO!' to temptation. Don't try and fight off temptation on your own.

## Intercessions

Father, we pray for all who are going through a time of temptation at the moment. Strengthen and protect them all.
*Silence for prayer*
Your commands, O Lord:
**are our delight**

We pray that your church may always hold true to your truth and love
with your love.
*Silence for prayer*
Your commands, O Lord:
**are our delight**

We pray for those in positions of power that they may not give way to corruption but work with integrity.
*Silence for prayer*
Your commands, O Lord:
**are our delight**

We pray for those in our families
and those who live in our neighbourhood,
that we may live in harmony together.
*Silence for prayer*
Your commands, O Lord:
**are our delight**

We pray for those in prison
and those imprisoned by guilt.
*Silence for prayer*
Your commands, O Lord:
**are our delight**

We pray for those who have died through neglect, mismanagement of resources, violence and oppression.
*Silence for prayer*
Your commands, O Lord:
**are our delight**

Father, we thank you for the way
you protect and enfold us every moment
of every day.
*Silence for prayer*
Your commands, O Lord:
**are our delight**

## Other ideas

The atmosphere of the Old Testament reading is brought out well with music in the background and people miming the actions as it is read.

## In the crèche

*Aim:* To help the children learn to recognise the difference between good and bad things.
Have two buckets, one labelled GOOD and the other labelled BAD. Give the children some cardboard happy and sad faces. Toys or puppets act out various actions and after each one the children run and put a sad face in the bad bucket or a happy face in the good bucket as appropriate. Here are some ideas for the actions, to get you started:

BAD: hitting, kicking, ignoring, saying unkind things, snatching.

GOOD: cuddling, sharing, giving, admiring, thanking, being obedient.

## Children

*Aim:* To help them to deal with temptation.
Have ready a sword and a mug of water, and introduce the story by looking at these two objects.
Tell the story of Saul and David, either

acting it out or using moving figures on a floor story mat.

Talk about the very strong temptation most of us have to get our own back on someone who has been nasty to us. Think together about how David managed to resist the temptation to kill Saul. Link his love for God with his determination to honour and respect Saul.

Help them make this sword and cup to remind them.

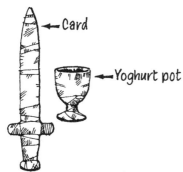

Cover the sword and cup with aluminium foil.

## Young people

*Aim:* To look at the similarities and differences between the Old Testament and New Testament passages, so as to explore the nature of temptation and sin. Have a chart drawn up like this:

| DIFFERENCES | | SIMILARITIES | |
|---|---|---|---|
| 1 Sam 26 | Luke 22 | 1 Sam 26 | Luke 22 |
| | | | |
| | | | |
| | | | |
| | | | |
| | | | |

Read both passages, either together or in two different groups, and then work through them, writing in all that is similar and all that is different in them. Discuss what enables people to resist temptation in their lives, bringing out how important our relationship with God is in dealing effectively with temptation.

# YEAR 2

*Thought for the day:*
*We need to build up our defences*
*against temptation.*

## Readings
Psalm 119:9-24
Exodus 17:1-13
Matthew 26:1-30

## Reflection

We are all familiar with the usual kind of temptations, where we find ourselves wanting to do or say what we know we shouldn't. But the temptation we are looking at today is rather different – it is temptation in the sense of putting God to the test.

Not that it's anything new, of course; Adam and Eve tested God's integrity when Satan hinted that God's command to steer clear of the fruit from the tree of the knowledge of good and evil was based on defence of his power, rather than concern for their well-being.

Such testing often happens when, for some reason, we feel disappointed with God. Perhaps we have been praying fervently for someone to be healed and instead they die; or we may have been following God closely and suddenly some catastrophe knocks our life to bits. Or we see a wonderful, loving person struck down with disease while a selfish slob survives. We can feel quite powerful anger against God, disappointed that he should allow such things to happen.

The people of Israel knew their very survival depended on finding water, but there was none. Judas was convinced that the Messiah was going to rise in physical power but Jesus seemed to be letting him down and smashing his hopes and dreams. With the people of Israel, with Judas and with us, the bitter disappointment is based on two things: a misunderstanding of the nature of God and an unwillingness to surrender our survival to his safe keeping. And both take a lifetime to change.

## Discussion starters

1 How do we know for certain that God is concerned for our eternal well-being?

2 If we really trust God's goodness, how will that affect our response to suffering?

## All stage talk

*Theme:* Putting God to the test.

Begin by asking different people to test things for you, such as a felt tip pen, a battery (put it in a torch), a cake and a well-made paper aeroplane. Point out that people tested the things by trying them out. Why didn't they test the aeroplane by putting it in the torch? Or the felt tip pen by eating it? Because they already knew what each thing was like and they expected them to behave in keeping with their nature.

Ask people to raise their hands if they have ever been disappointed with God. Reassure people that practically everyone does at some time, because we have high expectations of God, and when he doesn't answer our prayers the way we want him to we are likely to feel disappointed. We might feel quite upset, or angry with him. Or we might wonder if he really is as powerful and loving as we have been told. Many aren't Christians because they reckon that if there was a good, loving God he wouldn't allow all the suffering we see around us and, as the suffering does go on, there can't be a God.

But that's like saying that because the paper aeroplane doesn't make the torch work it must be a useless paper aeroplane. In fact it's a very good aeroplane, but its nature is to fly, not make torches work.

The trouble is that we don't always understand the nature of God very well. If it was his nature to stop everything bad from happening by force, then he would never have given us free will. Nor would he have hung and suffered on the cross – he'd have just climbed down and walked away. God's nature is to work alongside us, suffering with us and using his power of love to bring some lasting good out of the pain. We only see a tiny section of our whole life while we're alive here; lots more awaits us in eternity. There is certainly terrible evil here, but God will struggle against the evil in our situation and save every drop of goodness and love that he can rescue in each person's life.

## Intercessions

Father, we pray for the church
and all Christians in their various callings;
we remember the conflicts and divisions,
and the movement towards unity.

*Silence for prayer*

Lord, we believe:
**that in all things you work for our good**

We pray for those who have been given great responsibility in this world.

*Silence for prayer*

Lord, we believe:
**that in all things you work for our good**

We pray for our parents and all who have influenced our thinking.

*Silence for prayer*

Lord, we believe:
**that in all things you work for our good**

We pray for those in great need,
financially, emotionally or physically.

*Silence for prayer*

Lord, we believe:
**that in all things you work for our good**

We pray for those whose earthly journey
has come to an end; and we pray for
those who feel empty without their
physical company.

*Silence for prayer*

Lord, we believe:
**that in all things you work for our good**

We praise and thank you, Father,
that we can trust you with our lives.

*Silence for prayer*

Lord, we believe:
**that in all things you work for our good**

## In the crèche

*Aim:* To enjoy water and thank God for it.
Have large plastic groundsheets over the
area and washing up bowls of water with
different containers to play with, chatting
together as you play about the way God
provides the water we need. Have a jug
of water and some cups so as to drink
some too.

## Children

*Aim:* To familiarise the children with the
Old Testament reading – water from the
rock.

Begin with any group of songs which
involve a lot of dancing about and aerobic
actions (such as 'I've got that Joy' and
'Zip Bam Boo') so that everyone gets hot
and thirsty. Have everyone sitting down
and pour out some water for them all to
drink, noticing how good it feels to drink
water when you are really thirsty.

Now tell the story of the grumbling
people of Israel in the desert and how
Moses didn't grumble but went to God
with the problem instead. That showed
how much he trusted God, and God was
able to help.

Talk together about the story and what
it can teach us about talking to God about
our worries instead of just getting angry
and grumbling about things.

Help the children make this model of
water coming out of the rock:

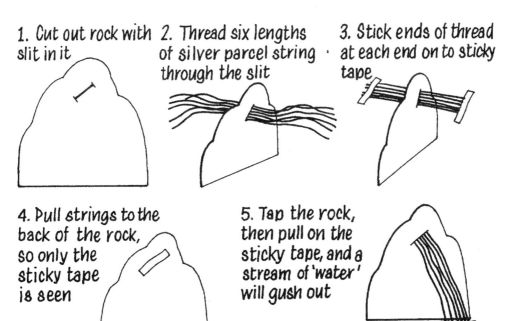

1. Cut out rock with slit in it

2. Thread six lengths of silver parcel string through the slit

3. Stick ends of thread at each end on to sticky tape

4. Pull strings to the back of the rock, so only the sticky tape is seen

5. Tap the rock, then pull on the sticky tape, and a stream of 'water' will gush out

## Young people

*Aim:* To tackle the area of our (sometimes false) assumptions about God.

Begin by drawing attention to some of the tragedies which make people think there can't be a loving God, or he wouldn't allow such suffering. Then read the first part of the Old Testament passage, where the people feel in real danger of dying out there in the desert with no water. Now read on to see how Moses reacts instead of being disillusioned. Break off to discuss the importance of doing this in our times of panic and suffering, even when there seems no hope at all. Finally look at the outcome of God responding to Moses' correct assumption that God cares and will provide.

Make a chart headed: 'How do we know God is concerned with the welfare of his world?' Discuss this, jotting down the thoughts that are raised. Think about how we might help someone who is at the 'grumbling' stage to understand God better.

---

# 2nd Sunday in Lent

## YEAR 1

*Thought for the day:
Following Christ is not always a comfortable place to be.*

### Readings

Psalm 119:73-88
Genesis 37:1-28
Luke 22:24-53 (or 39-53)

### Reflection

We might think that to live loving lives would normally result in an ordered, peaceful existence, where we were well-liked and appreciated. In fact that is often what non-Christians expect Christians to be. Yet although the loving may make committed Christ-followers warm, encouraging people, it also sharpens their eyesight to see injustice, evil and corruption more clearly. This in turn creates a thirst for righteousness and before long you find conflict as people battle to uphold what is right and disturb complacency.

Jesus warned his followers about this and even suggested they should be happy about it. Certainly, in Christian terms, being highly thought of by everyone is a dangerous place to be.

Apart from the more obvious conflict as the authorities arrest Jesus, there is also the inner conflict of Jesus in Gethsemane. He longs to do his Father's will and yet his humanity screams against the inevitable horror of pain and rejection. Our lives are in constant conflict as to whether God's will or ours will win. Sometimes we can only honestly say that we'd like to desire God's will, rather than desiring it already. Often we aim to avoid the conflict and talk about something else.

But we know that at those times when we are acutely aware of the conflicts our faith is getting us into, we shall be in good company, and we shall never be tempted more than we are able; an escape route of some kind will be made available just before things get impossible, or we will be revived and comforted.

### Discussion starters

1   Judas betrayed Jesus with a gesture of friendship, which must have been particularly hurtful. Does the church (or do we, as individual Christians) sometimes betray Jesus under cover of being his friends?

2 Families are often full of feuds and jealousies. Sometimes it is our following of Christ that causes division. Is there any way to avoid this, or do we just have to accept it?

## All stage talk

*Theme:* Conflict.

Explain that living the Christian life can sometimes feel rather like coping with an assault course. Ask for some volunteers to help you set up some obstacles in a central aisle. There may be a heavy groundsheet for crawling under, chairs or a small stepladder to climb over, a dustbin sack to jump in and some thick gloves to put on before using a knife and fork with which to eat a mini mars or a few smarties.

You will also need someone to run the course during the talk.

Remind everyone of how Joseph was treated by his brothers. Could he have avoided that? Perhaps he could have been more tactful earlier on, but now he couldn't really avoid the conflict and had to just go through it. (The volunteer goes under the groundsheet.)

What about Jesus; could he have avoided the conflict and pain of being crucified? What did he pray for in Gethsemane?

He certainly asked if he needn't go through with it (the volunteer goes round the climbing obstacle) but he didn't get a 'yes' answer to that prayer. Going through that agony and carrying on loving those who were killing him was the only way Jesus could save the world. So he did it. (The volunteer goes over the obstacle).

What about us? Suppose there's a fight going on in the playground or on the underground. Can we avoid the conflict or do we have to get involved? It's probably wisest to avoid it (the volunteer walks round the dustbin bag) because it could make matters worse and we might get badly hurt. But suppose you are living in a country where you will be imprisoned unless you deny your faith in Christ. Can you avoid the conflict? (Ask the volunteer to put on the gloves and try eating with the knife and fork.) Answering this question honestly is as difficult as what the volunteer is doing – we need to pray urgently for those who are in this position, that they might be given the strength and courage to do God's will even when it is full of danger.

## Intercessions

We call to mind all who are insulted or persecuted for their faith; all who speak out and those who are afraid to.

*Silence for prayer*

Help us, O Lord:
**we put our trust in you**

We call to mind those working for peace, justice and hope in an aching world.

*Silence for prayer*

Help us, O Lord:
**we put our trust in you**

We call to mind those whose lives
are bound up with ours;
we remember all the families and streets
represented here.

*Silence for prayer*

Help us, O Lord:
**we put our trust in you**

We call to mind those whose bodies
battle against disease or pain;
those whose minds battle against
confusion and depression.

*Silence for prayer*

Help us, O Lord:
**we put our trust in you**

*Continued overleaf*

We call to mind those who are dying in fear or loneliness; those who have recently passed into eternity.

*Silence for prayer*

Help us, O Lord:
**we put our trust in you**

We call to mind the ways we have been helped through difficult times, and have grown to understand more of your loving care. And we commend the rest of our life to your keeping.

*Silence for prayer*

Help us, O Lord:
**we put our trust in you**

## Other ideas

Have some music from 'Joseph and the amazing technicolour dreamcoat' being played as people come in, or as part of the first reading.

## In the crèche

*Aim:* To help the children get the feel of meeting obstacles and getting round, over or through them.
You will need lots of pillows and cushions, a blanket and some cardboard cartons. Anything which is safe and exciting to climb on or crawl through will be excellent.

Arrange these on the floor to make a kind of obstacle course and help the children to get round it.

## Children

*Aim:* To teach them the story of Joseph.
Tell the story of Joseph and his brothers, either with cut-out figures on the floor story mat, or, if you don't mind anyone seeing your awful drawing, draw quick sketches of the different parts of the story as you tell it. Simple figures like this are all you need.

Either draw on a long frieze or on different pages of a sketch book. Talk together about why the brothers hated Joseph, how Joseph might have felt as he was thrown down into the cistern, and when he was sold to the Ishmaelites. Look at how Reuben behaved differently from the rest of the brothers.

Now help them make this model of Joseph in his splendid coat.

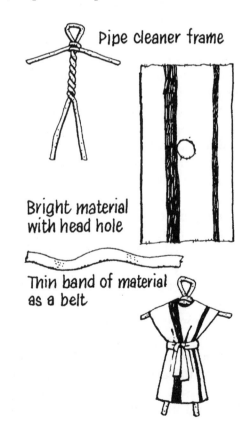

Pipe cleaner frame

Bright material with head hole

Thin band of material as a belt

## Young people

*Aim:* To look at some of the conflicts and dangers which Christians face.

You will need a selection of books and information about Christians who risk extreme hardship, persecution or other danger for practising their Christian faith. Some examples are: Brother Damien, Martin Luther King, William Wilberforce, Sister Emanuel, Desmond Tutu, Terry Waite, Mother Theresa, St Clare, Florence Nightingale and any local unsung heroes and heroines at your church.

Read the passage from Luke together, noticing how Jesus prays so deeply for the agony to be avoided, but recognises that he must go through with it.

Discuss the areas in our own lives where being a Christian makes for unavoidable conflict, and encourage one another by praying for these difficult situations and all the people involved.

# YEAR 2

*Thought for the day:*
*Following Christ is not always a comfortable place to be.*

## Readings

Psalm 119:73-88
Amos 3
Matthew 26:31-56

## Reflection

Amos was writing at a time of national security and wealth, and he is horrified at the complacency and ethical corruption which is rife among the chosen people whom God has cherished and led. They may be keeping all the rules about the Sabbath and tithing and so on, but their hearts are very far from the God they claim to worship. Such behaviour is abhorrent to God, whose mercy is stretched to the limit. Their corruption cannot go unpunished; as the chosen people they have a special responsibility.

Speaking out against complacency and corruption landed Amos in big trouble and we, too, are likely to meet opposition and insult if we stand up for what is right and good.

Jesus himself, after all the healing and affirming, ends up being arrested furtively at night, betrayed by one of his friends. Yet in all this ugly conflict, he never alters his courteous, loving behaviour. He excuses the disciples' inability to keep him company when he really needs them by accepting that although their spirits are willing, their bodies are weak; he looks Judas in the eye and addresses him as 'friend'; he refuses to allow the use of swords and spears. There is no accounting for such extraordinary behaviour without the presence of a love so deep and tender that it overcomes all the expected anger and indignation.

It is this God with whom we can trust our lives – not just the well-prepared, well-groomed parts we are pleased with, but all the messy, half-finished, badly-managed parts we are ashamed of. We can face him with the very worst of this, knowing that in his love for us he will still greet us as 'friend'.

## Discussion starters

1 What do you think Amos might thunder against in our church and society?

2 Are there any areas in our lives where we hang back from acting as Christians for fear of the consequences?

## All stage talk

*Theme:* Who dares?

Begin by daring some volunteers to do various things, such as singing a nursery rhyme on their own, walking round the church blindfold, or putting their hands into a bowl of custard.

Ask how many who are at school may be laughed at or teased for coming to church. (This is very common in many areas.) Encourage these people by recognising that they have been daring to come here today. Anyone who is teased or insulted at home or school or work for being a Christian is being brave, and Jesus knows all about their courage.

The truth is that if we are not being ridiculed, or meeting any conflict, it probably means we aren't living dangerously enough. Perhaps we've only got other Christians as our friends; perhaps we have arranged our hobbies and work so as to enjoy a peaceful life well away from anything challenging.

If so, we need to look at Amos and, most importantly, at Jesus, and be prepared to make friends with someone who could do with some friendship but isn't well liked; or perhaps we need to check that our nice peaceful life isn't making us complacent – perhaps it needs shaking up a bit.

## Intercessions

In the muddle of our ecclesiastical arguments, our narrow self-interest and our embarrassment, teach us to fix our eyes on you.

*Silence for prayer*

Lord, wherever you lead us:
**we will go**

In our defensiveness and nationalism, and our fear of being considered weak, teach us true courage to speak out for what is right.

*Silence for prayer*

Lord, wherever you lead us:
**we will go**

In the comfort of our homes and families, teach us the grace to be hospitable and welcoming.

*Silence for prayer*

Lord, wherever you lead us:
**we will go**

In the needs of those who are ill and injured teach us to see your face.

*Silence for prayer*

Lord, wherever you lead us:
**we will go**

In the sorrow of dying teach us to see also the gateway to heaven.

*Silence for prayer*

Lord, wherever you lead us:
**we will go**

In all the beauty of your creation, teach us to see the beauty of your holiness, and sing your praise with joy.

*Silence for prayer*

Lord, wherever you lead us:
**we will go**

## Other ideas

• Have a slow, ominous drum beat playing softly as a background to the Amos reading.

• Today's readings are very challenging to our lifestyles. Have the words: COMPLACENCY, CORRUPTION, INJUSTICE, INEQUALITY, IMMORALITY written up on large posters on the walls spread around the church. While music is played (possibly some Taizé or some African or Indian hymns) people can either walk around to the posters or sit and look around at them, asking God to enlighten them about any changes needed in their own lives, or any action to be taken to make a stand against evil.

## In the crèche

*Aim:* To make them aware of what is right.

Play snakes and ladders, using one of the original versions which the Victorians devised. Pictures of goodness have ladders to climb up and bad behaviour pictures are at the top of the snakes. If you can't get hold of a suitable version you can make one by sticking these pictures on to card.

## Children

*Aim:* To introduce them to the challenging nature of being a Christian.

If the children haven't been involved with the All stage talk, begin with some dares (see above). If they have, play the 'What would you do?' game. Have a number of cards with situations on them. The children take turns in picking a card and saying what they would do in the circumstances. The others decide whether they think the person acted in the best way or not. No doubt you would like some ideas to start you off before you think of brilliant ones yourselves, so here they are:

1 You are playing ball with some friends and the new ball rolls into the road. You don't want the ball to be squashed by a car. What do you do?

2 You keep finding the person who sits next to you is copying your work. What do you do?

3 Your swimming training is booked for a Sunday morning. There is no reason why it shouldn't be later in the day. What do you do?

4 Your group of friends is teasing you because you are being friendly to a child they don't like. What do you do?

Now tell them how Jesus made himself unpopular by pointing out ways in which the religious leaders were misunderstanding God's Law. The leaders didn't like the way Jesus was friends with bad people, either, and they thought he was being very rude to call God his Father. So although he hadn't done anything wrong, but had stood up for what was right, they came to arrest him in the night.

We are followers of Jesus, and Jesus warns us that we won't always be very comfortable if we follow him. Do we dare follow him?

Help them make this secret agent identity card to carry around with them.

**If the 'top secret' is in black ink they can draw themselves in pencil and it will still show**

## Young people

*Aim:* To help them be aware of the unhealthy state of society and its expectations.

First explain the background to Amos, so that they can hear the prophecy in context. Then read it together, explaining the meaning where necessary as you go.

Make a list of some of the situations which Amos might speak out against in our society, our era and our church. Put a star by any they feel could be changed by popular opinion.

Put a circle by any they reckon most people go along with because they want to stay out of trouble.

Put a triangle by any that people have protested about and ended up getting into trouble.

Now have a look at any conclusions the markings suggest.

Pray together for the courage to stand out even when at risk.

# 3rd Sunday in Lent

## YEAR 1

*Thought for the day:
Christ had to suffer in order
to rescue us.*

### Readings
Psalm 119:105-120
Exodus 5:1-6
Luke 22:54-end

### Reflection

As we read the passages from Exodus and Luke we find ourselves looking at a valuable parallel situation. In Exodus, Moses is on the brink of rescuing the people of Israel from slavery in Egypt, and has reluctantly agreed to approach Pharoah with his bold request to let his people go. Naturally, Pharoah is possessive of this abundant source of slave labour, and considers that the best way to put a stop to such ideas is to work them impossibly hard, making their lives worse than ever. The effect on the people of Israel is to ridicule and alienate Moses whom they feel has landed them in a bigger mess than ever.

Jesus, too, is on the brink of rescuing his people, and his life-giving truth has made the religious leaders react possessively. The result for Jesus is that even his friends alienate him.

We can sense the appalling isolation and sorrow both of Moses and Jesus at this point of their ministries; it makes me wonder if one of the reasons for the transfiguration was Jesus' comfort and preparation which only Moses and Elijah would be able to give, since both had experienced the aching weariness of rejection. In his humanity Jesus would have been heartened by talking over this impossibly terrible task before him with others who understood.

## Discussion starters

1 If a prayerfully planned innovation at church or in the locality starts meeting violent opposition, can we assume that it is against God's will, or could there be other factors at work?

2 What do you think was in the look that Jesus gave Peter when the cock crew?

## All stage talk

*Theme:* Making life difficult.

Beforehand prepare sufficient brick jigsaws for there to be one per six people. The jigsaws look like this

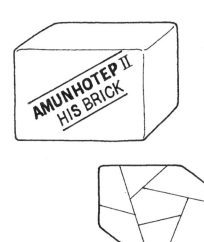

Have the jigsaw pieces given out to each row before the service.

First remind everyone how Pharoah used his immigrant population for work in the building industry. It got his favourite buildings finished and it kept the people out of mischief. (He was not heavily into good race relations.)

We are all members of that nation of slaves, and we have to make bricks. We'll see which side of the church completes their quota of bricks quickest. Time how long it takes for each section of the church to have all their bricks 'made'.

Now emphasise the impossibility of Pharoah's command by giving the same task, except that this time the pieces of jigsaw are taken to different parts of the church before everyone begins, so they need to be collected before any brick making can start. Stop everyone at the time they completed the task the first time. They will be able to imagine the frustration the people felt, being punished for failing where they couldn't possibly achieve. Some of us feel life is like that quite often and it makes people angry and resentful.

The people of Israel take their anger out on Moses, who talked about rescue from slavery but has, in the short term, made life harder for them.

This seems to be a pattern of rescue, right through to Jesus having the pain of being abandoned by his friends and crucified so as to rescue us. So if we find that after being led to a deeper and closer walk with God, life starts getting extremely difficult, that's not a signal to give up, but to hang on, as it could well be the darkest hour that comes before the dawn.

## Intercessions

Father, we lean on your love as we pray
for your church – collectively
and as a mixed bag of individuals,
with needs, disappointments and fears.

*Silence for prayer*

In all things, Father:
**we pray your kingdom in**

*Continued overleaf*

We lean on your wisdom as we pray for local, national and international leaders, subject to pressures and conflicting values.

*Silence for prayer*

In all things, Father:
**we pray your kingdom in**

We lean on your affectionate understanding as we pray for our homes and all homes in this area, with their expectations and misunderstandings, their security and insecurity.

*Silence for prayer*

In all things, Father:
**we pray your kingdom in**

We lean on your compassion as we pray for all who are hurting in body, mind or spirit.

*Silence for prayer*

In all things, Father:
**we pray your kingdom in**

We lean on your faithfulness as we pray for those who have died, and those who mourn.

*Silence for prayer*

In all things, Father:
**we pray your kingdom in**

We lean on your accepting love as we pray in thankfulness for all you are doing in our lives, and all you have in mind for us in the future.

*Silence for prayer*

In all things, Father:
**we pray your kingdom in**

## Other ideas

Many people battle with feelings of anger and resentment, striving to overcome them, when actually they need to allow God's grace to sort out the situation for them. The readings this week may well bring such situations to the surface in people, so it is a good time to tackle them.

Briefly outline the truth – that gritted teeth and determination won't cure the resentment and anger but God will. Ask everyone to clench their fists, as in anger, and notice the person or people who immediately come to mind when they do this. If no one does, that's fine. Now ask everyone to open their fists so their hands are palm upwards. Those who have been led to recognise anger, hurt or resentment inside them hold the situation open to God in their hands without trying to do anything about it; the others hold themselves open to be channels of God's healing love. (Of course no one will be able to see who is holding what.)

In silence, or with quiet music playing, ask those who are holding their anger and resentment to do nothing, while everyone else prays for God to deal with the situations, heal the wounds and dissolve the resentment away. Then everyone can sing 'O Lord, your tenderness' together.

## In the crèche

*Aim:* To help them understand how being rescued often involves being uncomfortable.

On a doll (or a real baby) go through the business of changing a nappy, with the children making the crying noises where appropriate. Often the baby doesn't enjoy being sorted out (crying noises), but he does like it when he feels comfortable and clean again (gurgling noises).

## Children

*Aim:* To teach them this section of the Moses story, helping them to understand what was going on.

If the children have not been involved with the All stage talk you can start with making the brick jigsaws. Otherwise give out beanbags and divide the children into equal groups. First they stand in circles with one person in the middle who throws the beanbag to each group member in turn. Next they have to take the same amount of time to do the same thing, except that they first have to find the hidden beanbag.

Now tell the story of Moses, Pharoah and the bricks without straw. Have some words describing feelings printed on card and scattered on the floor. Have three hoops (or lengths of string) labelled MOSES, PHAROAH, and THE PEOPLE OF ISRAEL. Discuss how each might have felt, putting the word cards in the appropriate hoops. Some may overlap, like a Venn diagram.

Here are some suggested words to describe their feelings:
angry, depressed, lonely, irritated, threatened, selfish, determined, embarrassed, sad, cheated, puzzled.

## Young people

*Aim:* To help them understand the implications of the readings in our own lives.

Read the passage from Exodus with different people taking various parts and everyone reading the parts spoken by the people of Israel. As with the children, have a Venn diagram drawn on a chart like this:

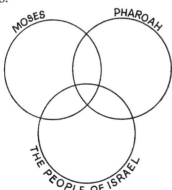

and a selection of words to describe their feelings. They can discuss where to place the words, and they can add other ideas of their own. Here are some suggestions to start you off: angry, bitter, resentful, defensive, cunning, greedy, disillusioned, confused, doubting, isolated, embarrassed, ridiculed.

Now read the gospel passage and try another Venn diagram, this time looking at Jesus, Peter and Judas.

Remind them of how Moses went on to lead his people to freedom, and Jesus went on to save us from the slavery of our sin and give us full life. Help them to see how the dark patches in our lives may well be the way forward to something far better than we could dream of. Pray together for trust and courage in the dark times.

# YEAR 2

*Thought for the day:*
*Christ had to suffer in order*
*to rescue us.*

## Readings
Psalm 119:105-120
Job 2
Matthew 26:57-end

## Reflection

Satan is no fool and he reads us pretty well, homing in on the areas of our weakness and the cracks in our spiritual armour. In the drama of the Job story, Satan reckons that if he can inflict real physical pain then ideals and honour will fly out of the window. Every torturer thinks in the same way. Job's wife is tempted to despair, but Job continues to be faithful to God during this testing.

If we look now at Jesus, we are aware of his silence as, one after another, the false witnesses come forward. The humiliation and degradation are appalling for anyone, but particularly for one who has divine authority and is now despised and rejected by those he came to save.

It is only when the leaders call on him to speak the truth in the name of the living God that he is bound to respond. As the living God of truth himself, he cannot do other than admit the truth – that he is indeed the Son of God. The terrible tragedy is that the leaders are so blinded by their expectation of what the Christ should be like that they interpret Jesus' reply as blasphemy.

## Discussion starters

1   There are many reasons why Jesus was not received when he came to live among us, in spite of all the love he showed. Why do people not receive him – now as well as then?
2   What similarities can you see between the Job story and this episode in Peter's life?

## All stage talk

*Theme:* Great expectations.

Arrange beforehand for two people to help you. They will need to have strong voices, and one needs to be either a stranger to the congregation or someone who is known and accepted as someone who will speak their mind.

When you go to stand in the usual place for giving the talk, the first person stands up just where they are and starts to preach in the way you usually would. (It is a good idea if they are sitting towards the back.) Hopefully this will take people by surprise and before the speaker has got very far the second person (sitting some distance away) starts to protest loudly. They might protest that the speaker can't possibly be the preacher if s/he's just standing there, and anyway s/he isn't qualified and these all age services have really gone too far etc.

Then the two speakers walk slowly up to the front and stand with their backs to the people. The second speaker holds the first in a (pretend) half Nelson as you say: 'I charge you under oath by the living God: tell us if you are the Christ, the Son of God.' The first speaker replies, 'Yes, it is as you say.' The second speaker turns to the people and starts protesting – 'this can't possibly be true; so this person is guilty of blasphemy!' Then they walk back to their seats.

Explain how people were so sure about what the Christ would be like that when he turned out to be different they couldn't believe he was really the Son of God, but just pretending. Ask them to think of a time when they haven't been believed, and how unpleasant that is. That gives us a hint of what it felt like to be God, coming to his own people and being rejected by them.

God is a God of surprises, so keep open-minded about where and how you can meet him – it may not be the way you expect.

## Intercessions

Father, we pray for the church, your body on earth, with its richness of variety and its poverty of splits and schisms.

*Silence for prayer*

You hold our lives:
**safe in the palm of your hand**

Father, we pray for the world you have created, with its struggles for peace and its cravings for fulfilment.

*Silence for prayer*

You hold our lives:
**safe in the palm of your hand**

Father, we pray for this neighbourhood
in which you have placed us,
with its visible activity
and its hidden problems.
*Silence for prayer*
You hold our lives:
**safe in the palm of your hand**

Father, we pray for those who are ill
at home or in hospital,
with their longing for health
and their struggle with pain.
*Silence for prayer*
You hold our lives:
**safe in the palm of your hand**

We pray for the dead and dying,
with their need for mercy and their hope
of heaven.
*Silence for prayer*
You hold our lives:
**safe in the palm of your hand**

We pray with thankfulness and love
for the Spirit transforming our lives.
*Silence for prayer*
You hold our lives:
**safe in the palm of your hand**

## Other ideas

The Job reading works well as a mystery play. Either use the dramatised bible or enjoy working out who says what with a small group. You can have stylised costumes for God and Satan, or just have ordinary clothes but with tabards over the top for God, Satan and Job.

## In the crèche

*Aim:* To encourage them to persevere at a task and enjoy accomplishing it.
Have some tasks which individual children or groups can do. The tasks should be ones they find quite hard but which are not beyond their capability,
such as getting a number of toy cars from one end of the room to the other, or collecting a number of bricks and then building with them. The actual tasks will depend on the age level and ability of those in the group. Enjoy working on the tasks together and encouraging them to carry on until they have completed the challenge.

## Children

*Aim:* To look at Jesus' arrest and persecution, addressing the question of why such a good person was treated so badly.
First show the children these messages and ask them to read them.

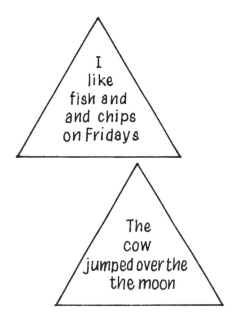

They will probably read them without noticing the repetition because they are not expecting it. We tend to see what we expect to see, and many faithful Jews expected Christ to be like another King David, leading his people to fight against the Romans so that they were free from Roman rule. Jesus wasn't like that, and talked about his kingdom in a very different way, so many people didn't recognise him as the Christ.

Now give out Happy Family cards and play a round of this game, where you can ask one person if they have a particular card and they have to answer honestly. Warn the children that in the story, Jesus will be asked a question, and you want them to listen out for what he replied.

Now tell or read the passage from Matthew, using pictures from a children's bible. Or a few of the young people could come and act it out in a simple way. Afterwards talk about the question Jesus was asked. He was under oath of the living God so he had to tell the truth. But they thought he was only pretending.

Now help them to make this three dimensional scene of the court and Jesus looking at Peter.

Jesus and
the soldiers

Peter

Folds

## Young people

*Aim:* To look at the reasons for Jesus' suffering.

Begin with this game. Explain that you and your accomplice have a code and they are going to try and crack it. If they think they understand it, then they can have a go at decoding the next message. Carry on till everyone has sussed out the code. This is the code: for each letter of the word you say something beginning with the letter (such as 'Could we put it here? . . . At the corner, I think . . . That's it' which turns out to be CAT.) The misleading part is that at the same time you are carefully placing a knife and fork in various ways, so that people expect this to be the code, rather than the things you are saying. In fact, the knife and fork are of no significance at all.

Now read the gospel passage together, with a small group acting it out if that method suits them.

Talk about how our expectations in the code put us off understanding for a while, and how the religious leaders' expectations of the way the Messiah would behave effectively blocked their acceptance of him when he came.

# 4th Sunday in Lent

(For suitable Mothering Sunday readings, see Pentecost 17)

## YEAR 1

*Thought for the day:*
*In the glory of God's presence the covenant of the law is sealed between God and his people; Jesus himself becomes the sacrifice binding them in the new covenant.*

## Readings
Psalm 119:161-176
Exodus 24
Luke 23:1-25

## Reflection

The Exodus reading is a combination of three different traditions, so that we get a kind of hologram effect of the radiance of God's glory, the deep significance of this holy moment, and a sense of a new beginning for God's people as this covenant with God is sealed through the blood of sacrifice. It is one of those breathtaking moments where we feel drawn in to share a glimpse of God's glory, realising that 'only the splendour of light hideth thee'.

And then we are taken off roughly to another glimpse of God – Jesus at his most vulnerable and weak, falsely accused and eagerly despised by the very people whom God had trusted with that solemn covenant; by all of us who promise our faithfulness and then let him down, again and again.

Notice how Jesus redeems every situation, even this one: the longstanding feud between Pilate and Herod is healed. The Christ goes forward to the time of sacrifice, when the old covenant is fulfilled.

## Discussion starters

1 Try reading the Exodus passage in its separate strands, noticing which points are emphasised in each case and then reading the complete passage again, hearing this 3D effect more clearly.

(J tradition: v.1,2,9-11; E tradition: v.3-8,12-15a,18b; and P tradition: v.15b-18a)

2 What do we learn about Pilate and Herod from the Luke reading?

## All stage talk

*Theme:* Glimpses of glory.

Prepare beforehand a large card with the word COVENANT written on it. Cut the card into two sections along the middle.

Talk about when we go to see plays or films and find we're sitting right behind someone tall, or the row we're in is so far back that we can't see very much at all. We bend our necks to see through the gaps and, just as we catch a glimpse of all the action, someone in front bends over to talk to their friend so that all we see is the back of their heads!

Today we heard about Moses and the people of Israel catching just a glimpse of God's glory on the mountain at this time of God giving the Law and making a covenant with his people. Give out the two pieces of card to two people and ask them to stand one on either side of you, so that everyone can see the cards. Explain what a covenant is by showing how both parties promise something to the other and so both parts need to be kept. When both sides promise (the card pieces are brought together) it makes a covenant; if one party breaks their side of the promise (one person takes their section away) then they are breaking the covenant.

God promised to protect and look after his chosen people, and the people promised to keep God's Law.

Although God always keeps his promise because he is always faithful, people aren't as good at keeping their promise. Sometimes we get so many things in our lives between us and God that they block us off from seeing him clearly. We need to clear away some of those things in our lives so that we get more than a glimpse of God's glory – we need to seek him out so that we get to know him really well and can enjoy his company, as Moses did.

## Intercessions

When following you brings danger, Lord,
or weariness or discomfort,
we long for your help.

*Silence for prayer*

In the shadow of your wings:
**we shall be in safety**

When we watch the violence and selfishness of this world, its bewilderment and fear, we long for your peace.

*Silence for prayer*

In the shadow of your wings:
**we shall be in safety**

When we work through our relationships and feel for those we love,
we long for your guidance.

*Silence for prayer*

In the shadow of your wings:
**we shall be in safety**

When our hearts touch those who suffer, and know their pain and distress,
we long for your healing love.

*Silence for prayer*

In the shadow of your wings:
**we shall be in safety**

When those we love meet death
and we must let them go,
we long for your mercy and welcome.

*Silence for prayer*

In the shadow of your wings:
**we shall be in safety**

When we see the beauty and wonder of your glorious creation and of your holiness, we long for an eternity to praise you.

*Silence for prayer*

In the shadow of your wings:
**we shall be in safety**

## Other ideas

• Many churches have posies of flowers for children to give to their mothers today. Make this a time of affection which leads on to a sharing of the peace, so that no one is left out, and all are shown God's love.

• Have two or three generations of one family to bring the offering to the altar and to lead people in the intercessions.

• Have one of the flower arrangements incorporating a lego house, and use bright, primary colours.

• As it is unlikely that children and young people would be having separate teaching today, give out this activity sheet for them to work on in church during the adult-centred times.

Mothering Sunday

My Mum likes to eat [    ] for tea
When I [    ] she's pleased with me
My Mum watches [    ] on T.V.
I love her and she loves [    ]!

Draw your Mum, or the
person who looks after you

Fill in the blanks to
make a poem

# YEAR 2

*Thought for the day:*
*In the glory of God's presence the covenant of the law is sealed between God and his people; Jesus himself becomes the sacrifice binding them in the new covenant.*

## Readings

Psalm 119:161-176
Isaiah 52:13-53:6
Matthew 27:1-32

## Reflection

The readings for this week are heavy with pain and take us to look into the heart of suffering. The tortured man in the Isaiah reading is described with great compassion, but also with the intensity and detail which can only come from real experience. It is as if all the grief, torment and alienation of the exiled chosen people is focused in this prophetic image of the suffering servant.

And we, who live after the coming of Christ, can recognise in it the costly nature of our salvation; by his self sacrifice Jesus buys us back when we have been sold as slaves to sin. When God forgives us and eradicates our guilt and sin, it is no casual affair like using the tippex while his mind is on something else, or loading us into the 'heavily soiled' programme overnight. It is an expensive business, costing him death by crucifixion, but since that is the only way, he allows it to happen. Such is his amazing love for us.

## Discussion starters

1 Why do you think God bothered to get involved with humans in the first place if he could see how things would go so wrong?
2 How does Jesus' death help us now?

## All stage talk

*Theme:* Counting the cost.
You will need a bucket, a ball of string, two full bags from the local supermarket, a pair of child's trainers, a cheque book and credit card.

Talk about what things cost, asking the prices of such things as Sonic, a Mars, a 5 litre pot of emulsion etc. Point out how the cost is known by those who have wanted or needed these things; our want or need pushes us to find out the cost so that we can work out whether we can afford it or not.

What about the cost of bringing up a child for a year? Let's check that out. It's something like 52 trips to Safeways (dump the shopping bags down) a couple of pairs of trainers, a chequebook full of club subscriptions, school uniform, birthday presents and a holiday, and a credit card bill of petrol for the chauffeur service. But that's not all - it also costs an enormous length of patience (unravel the string up the whole length of the aisle) and 365 buckets of love, a fresh bucket for every day of the year.

If we look around, we'll find quite a few parents who are more than happy to pay that cost for the privilege of a year's worth of son or daughter! That's how God feels about us – he is glad to pay what it costs to set us free from our guilt and sin and worry and fear, even though the cost is incredibly high – rejection and ridicule, pain and death by crucifixion. That's a huge number of buckets of love.

## Intercessions

Father, you know us better than we know ourselves,
and are well aware of the needs and pains in your church.
We lift them now to your healing love.

*Silence for prayer*

Father, we love you:
**we love you and we trust you**


In our world there are decisions to be made, countries to be governed and people to be honoured.
We lift them now to your grace and wisdom.

*Silence for prayer*

Father, we love you:
**we love you and we trust you**


In our neighbourhood and in our homes there are celebrations and tragedies, times of hope, of weariness and tenderness.
We lift them now to your parenting.

*Silence for prayer*

Father, we love you:
**we love you and we trust you**


In our hospitals and clinics there are many in pain, many who are fearful, and many who have lost hope. We lift them now to your comfort and protection.

*Silence for prayer*

Father, we love you:
**we love you and we trust you**


As each day others die and enter your presence, we ask for your mercy
and commend them to your safe keeping.

*Silence for prayer*

Father, we love you:
**we love you and we trust you**

As we walk through our lives in your company, we rejoice in your friendship and delight in your love for us.

*Silence for prayer*

Father, we love you:
**we love you and we trust you**


## Other ideas

• As this is Mothering Sunday and it is usual for all ages to worship together, give out this card to the children as they come in and lend out small packs of crayons, so that they can colour them during any adult-centred parts of the service and give them to their mothers:

Photocopy both sides of full-page design onto thin card and fold in on the dotted lines.

• It is important that singles don't feel left out of the worship today. Mothers are something we all have, regardless of age or marital status, and it may be helpful to have a time to remember our own mothers, forgiving where that is needed, and thanking God for them where that is a joy. Have some music playing as a background to the thoughts and prayers.

A MOTHER IS VERY SPECIAL TO ME

# WHAT IS A MOTHER?

# 5th Sunday in Lent

## YEAR 1

*Thought for the day:*
*Jesus could only buy us full life by*
*submitting to full death.*

### Readings

Psalm 66
Lamentations 3:19-33
Luke 23:26-49

### Reflection

Although we are thinking about the victory of the cross today, we are actually plunged into the middle of the battle. As we hear the sneering, cynical voices advising Jesus to save himself, we are aware of them echoing that tempting voice of Satan at the start of Jesus' ministry – 'If you are the Son of God, throw yourself down and the angels will make sure you're not hurt.'

How agonising it must have been for Jesus to have these taunts thrown at him. Of course his suffering was madness to many of the onlookers; if Jesus really was God's Son then they would consider it ridiculous for his life to end in this ghastly way, so since he wasn't doing anything about it, didn't that prove that his claims must be false? No God worth his incense would allow his Son to die in this ridicule and failure under the gibbet's curse. What could possibly be gained from it?

In the blur of physical torture, emotional misery and spiritual loneliness, Jesus knows that although they do not understand, this is still the only way to express God's total love for them. His self giving can be no more complete than this and, through this dying, all will have access to the glorious fullness of life which is God's desire for us.

### Discussion starters

1  What has Jesus' attitude to suffering got to help us as we struggle to make sense of apparently pointless suffering in our own lives?

2  Look at the different attitudes of the criminals crucified with Jesus, and at Jesus' response to them.

### All stage talk

*Theme:* Why on earth . . ?

Begin by asking various people 'Why?' questions to which they have probably got logical answers. (For instance, 'Why are you wearing scout uniform?'; 'Why do you wear glasses?'; 'Why are you sitting down?') Young children are always asking 'Why?' (Why?) Because as humans we want to make sense of the life we find ourselves in. When we understand why something happens we feel more comfortable with it – more in control.

But some questions are much harder to answer. (Like 'Why does the sky look blue?) Only clever, knowledgeable people can answer those kinds of questions. Some questions we can't even answer from research in the library or years at college, because they aren't head knowledge but heart knowledge. (For instance, 'Why do you love someone?' and 'Why did that young person have to die?')

There must have been people at the crucifixion who were asking 'Why?'. Those who had known Jesus healing people and loving them may well have been those who were most disappointed to see him refusing to save himself. Perhaps they felt frustrated that he wasn't doing anything to get out of the pain.

It may be that we can't see the point of some dreadful tragedy in our own or someone else's life, and our hurt makes us sneer at God: 'If you were really a God of love you'd prevent this or sort it out.'

Jesus on the cross shows us that he stays with us in the agony of the hurt, and will in some way, which we don't yet understand, bring good and new life from it.

## Intercessions

Father, we pray for all who follow Christ,
for those whose faith is being tested,
and for those who have drifted away.

*Silence for prayer*

Into your hands, O Lord:
**we place our lives**

We pray for all leaders and advisers,
all meetings and councils,
that right decisions may be made.

*Silence for prayer*

Into your hands, O Lord:
**we place our lives**

We pray for all those we love and those we find it difficult to love; for those whose loving is damaged and those who have no one who cares about them.

*Silence for prayer*

Into your hands, O Lord:
**we place our lives**

We pray for those who are persecuted or imprisoned, for those locked in fear or hatred and all who are in need of healing.

*Silence for prayer*

Into your hands, O Lord:
**we place our lives**

We pray for those who have died alone or in fear, for those who are finding it hard to accept another's death.

*Silence for prayer*

Into your hands, O Lord:
**we place our lives**

We give you thanks and praise
for bringing us safely to this moment,
and offer you the future, with all that it holds.

*Silence for prayer*

Into your hands, O Lord:
**we place our lives**

## In the crèche

*Aim:* To help the children see that often things need to be broken before they can be used.

You will need some cooking chocolate, some shredded wheat, bowls and spoons for mixing and cake cases. You will also need some hot water for melting the chocolate.

You are going to make chocolate nests for Easter. Pretend to try making these by stirring the unopened packets together, then, as you all share in the breaking of the chocolate and the wheat, talk about how this has to happen so that we can make them into something even nicer. Watch the chocolate softening and melting and then share round the stirring of the wheat into the chocolate. Keep these nests in a cool, airtight tin until next week.

## Children

*Aim:* To help them understand how brokenness and dying are necessary for new life.

You will need some jam jars, blotting paper, beans and water, and a jar showing a bean which has already germinated.

Read to the children the story of the crucifixion from a children's bible, *The Road to the cross* (published by Kevin Mayhew) or use one of the children's video versions. (Think carefully about what you use, as it is important that you have something which is suitable for your particular age group and experience – some of the excellent adult film versions are very disturbing for young or sheltered children.)

All the violence and pain directed towards Jesus is difficult to cope with, and it may help the children to see how beans have to break apart to allow germination and new growth.

Arrange the beans in the jars like this, and keep the blotting paper very damp.

Damp blotting paper

Water

After the beans have germinated they can be transplanted into the garden.

## *Young people*

*Aim:* To look at the crucifixion through the eyes of those present.

First read the account of the crucifixion in Luke, with people reading the different parts.

Have a chart divided into three columns.

Make a list together of the people mentioned. Put them in one column and beside each name jot down how they behaved towards Jesus and what may have been the underlying reason for their behaviour. This close study will help to build a realistic picture of the events, and will highlight attitudes and behaviour in our own faith journey which can be acknowledged and better understood.

# *YEAR 2*

*Thought for the day:
Jesus could only buy us full life by
submitting to full death.*

## *Readings*
Psalm 66
Isaiah 53:7-end
Matthew 27:33-54

## *Reflection*

It is no mistake that the psalm for today is full of joy, even though the other readings are filled with sorrow and suffering. The psalm is there like a whisper of the promise of resurrection – the promise that this terrible time of pain and rejection is not the end but the beginning, rather like the ache of labour before a baby is born. I remember being so enveloped in the hip-cracking stage of labour that as our first child slithered into the world I was momentarily taken by surprise that she was a baby! All the effort had a purpose after all.

As the Christ, the anointed one of God, hangs in agony on the cross, he is jeered at and coaxed to use God's power to come down and save himself. To the human mind, seeing only the small area surrounding the present, that is a logical and sensible thing to do. We are forever coaxing God to be sensible. And God's refusal to do things our sensible way often makes us angry, hurt and confused. But God sees the whole picture, from eternity to eternity; this terrible suffering and death is a necessary part of our rescue, and Jesus loves us far too much to throw our chance of rescue away.

## *Discussion starters*

1 What can we learn from the crucifixion that will help us when faced with the problem of suffering?

2  People often say, 'If only . . . then I'd
   believe.' What is misguided about this
   way of thinking?

## All stage talk

*Theme:* Through death to glory.

Ask two people to come out and stand at
least three metres apart. Ask one of the
people to walk down to reach the other.
Was there any problem in that?
(Hopefully not.) Now ask both people to
get to you, only this time with one
condition – they mustn't move. Can they
do it? (No, it's impossible.) If they want to
get across to reach you they will have to
go on a journey to do it. Is the journey
easy or difficult? (They can try it to find
out.) They probably did that with no
trouble at all.

But suppose the journey is made very
difficult? (Tie all four ankles together
with a scarf and walk away from them.)
Can they get to me now? (Let them try.)
As they are moving along explain that
they can certainly do it, but only by using
a lot more effort, and with quite a
struggle. Stop them halfway and explain
how being crucified was like a terrible
journey that Jesus had to make to rescue
us. In the middle of his journey people
shouted at him to come down from the
cross and save himself from the suffering.
Ask the people if they would be capable
of untying the scarf and walking free. So
could Jesus have come down from the
cross, so why didn't he? He did it because
there wasn't any other way to rescue us
apart from accepting all the chains of our
sin and carrying them for us, even though
it made his journey so difficult. So instead
of opting out, he carried on (the people
can carry on too) until the journey was
finished so we can all be set free (untie
the legs of the volunteers).

## Intercessions

Father, we pray for all in your church
whose journey through life
is hard, dangerous, exhausting or
confused.

*Silence for prayer*

Lord of love:
**live and work in us all**

We pray for those whose lives are disrupted
by war, famine or political unrest.

*Silence for prayer*

Lord of love:
**live and work in us all**

We pray for our families, friends and
neighbours, all who cause us concern and
all in need of your peace.

*Silence for prayer*

Lord of love:
**live and work in us all**

We pray for all whose lives are filled
with pain, resentment or hatred,
all trapped in addiction or despair.

*Silence for prayer*

Lord of love:
**live and work in us all**

We pray for those who have died,
and those who miss them.

*Silence for prayer*

Lord of love:
**live and work in us all**

We give you thanks for the gift of life,
for every moment of every day.

*Silence for prayer*

Lord of love:
**live and work in us all**

## Other ideas

- Have the gospel read with different voices, using the whole congregation to say 'Come down from the cross'.
- Play the slow section from Mozart's clarinet concerto as a background to the Isaiah reading.

## In the crèche

*Aim:* To understand that grain dies to provide food.

Let the children sift their fingers through a bag of grain (barley is fine) and then show them some stalks of wheat and a bag of flour. Then teach them this action song (see overleaf for words and music):

Push Little Seed

1. Push one finger up through other hand.
2. Open hands for sky.

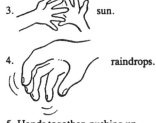

3.         sun.

4.         raindrops.

5. Hands together, pushing up.

6. Hands form a ball for the world.

7. Rub tummy 'may be fed'.

## Children

*Aim:* To help them understand how Jesus' death brought life.

You will need some packets of jelly, water and enough little pots for each child to have one.

Tell the story of the crucifixion using a suitable source for the age and experience of the children in your group. Talk together about it, being sensitive to reactions, as this can be a very disturbing time for some children. It is very important that the children see it in the context of the resurrection, and are not left after one session with the starkness and pain of the crucifixion.

Explain how often things need to be broken before they are transformed to something new, and let them all help making jellies, breaking up the cubes and melting them, so that they can be made into all sorts of shapes. If the jellies can be popped in a freezer for a while they will be solid before the children go home; for most of us, though, it will be a question of transporting them in liquid form!

## Young people

*Aim:* To understand the link between the crucifixion and the Isaiah passage of the suffering servant.

Read the passage from Isaiah first, asking them to think about who it reminds them of. Then read the gospel passage, involving as many readers as possible and follow it with a worship chorus such as 'Such love, pure as the whitest snow', or 'You laid aside your majesty'.

Try to put yourselves in that time before the resurrection and think about whether you might have got angry at Jesus not saving himself, and doubted his claim to be the Son of God. You could use the role-play technique here, with a group of onlookers under the cross, talking about the man who hangs, dying, above their heads. End with a time of quietness and prayer.

**HOLY WEEK**

# *Palm Sunday*

## YEARS 1 AND 2

*Thought for the day:
The King of glory rides on a donkey
into Jerusalem.*

### Readings
Psalms 61, 62
Jeremiah 7:1-11 or Exodus 11
Luke 19:29-end or Mark 14

### Reflection

Palm Sunday is a whirlwind of moods and emotions, expectations and disappointments, fresh insights and determined blindness. The psalms for this week are like a quiet, steady pulse at the centre; like our prayer life pulsing quietly in us while all the urgency of action and reaction sweep us along in our daily living. 'Nevertheless my soul waits in silence for God: for from him comes my hope.'

We see Jesus rejoicing with the ecstatic crowds as he enters the city; weeping with distress over Jerusalem because she has failed to recognise what she has been waiting generations to see; furious with the money changers abusing the sanctity of God's house of prayer; and accepting the inevitability of betrayal, arrest and death. These are violent, passionate times.

However violent, passionate or chaotic our own lives are, we can always anchor ourselves in to the bedrock of God's utter faithfulness and stillness. That never changes, and is always secure.

### Discussion starters

1  Our society believes in allowing everyone the freedom to do more or less what feels right for them, so long as it doesn't interfere with others. Where does this view start to clash with Christian values and beliefs?

2  Why did Jesus feel so angry with the money changers in the temple, and why do you think he decided to deal so forcibly with them?

### Intercessions

We pray for the church, the body of Christ, longing for its healing, strengthening and openness to your will.

*Silence for prayer*

The Lord is among us:
**his Spirit prays through ours**

We pray for the world and all the nations, longing for peace and tranquillity, justice, mercy and forgiveness.

*Silence for prayer*

The Lord is among us:
**his Spirit prays through ours**

We pray for all our relatives and the family life of our country, longing for the grace to love and honour one another, to trust and to persevere.

*Silence for prayer*

The Lord is among us:
**his Spirit prays through ours**

We pray for those who are ill or in distress, longing for your comfort, healing and refreshment.

*Silence for prayer*

The Lord is among us:
**his Spirit prays through ours**

*Continued overleaf*

We pray for those who are passing
through the gate of death,
longing for your merciful love.

*Silence for prayer*

The Lord is among us:
**his Spirit prays through ours**

We praise you and worship you
for all your blessings,
but especially for your generous saving
love and faithful presence with us.

*Silence for prayer*

The Lord is among us:
**his Spirit prays through ours**

## Other ideas

If you are having a Palm Sunday
procession, let it express the joy and
exuberance of that journey into
Jerusalem. Children can wave prunings
from trees, or these pom-poms which are
quite easy to make.

1. Cut a handful of lengths of different coloured crepe paper

2. Fold it in the middle

3. Put two rubber bands on it like this

Make sure that everyone knows the songs
to be sung in procession – onlookers
should see a group of joyful Christians,
not a slow supermarket shopping queue.
Try singing 'Hosanna, hosanna', 'You are
the king of glory', 'Sing hosanna' or
'Blessed be the name of the Lord' among
the traditional favourites.

## In the crèche

*Aim:* To enjoy praising God as Jesus rides
on a donkey into Jerusalem.

Tell them the story very simply, using
fuzzy felt pictures, and then play some
children's praise tapes, dancing and
singing along to them, and waving pom-
poms or streamers. Some songs are
particularly suitable for dancing to, such
as 'Be bold, be strong and sing' (Spring
Harvest Kid's Praise 93), 'Brand new
song', 'Let's praise God together' and
'Zip bam boo' (Spring Harvest Kid's
Praise 92).

## Children

*Aim:* To see the contrast between the joy
of the entry into Jerusalem and the anger
of Jesus at the abuse of the temple.

First make the pom-poms as shown
above in Other ideas. Then use them
either in an all age procession, or in a
time of singing and dancing on their own.

Then tell the story of Jesus chucking
out the money changers, acting it as you
tell it, explaining how the temple was
being misused and then literally
overturning a few tables and spilling
everything on to the floor. The shock of
seeing and hearing this really helps them
realise the depth of Jesus' concern to put
things right.

## Young people

*Aim:* To bring the events of the readings
to life for them.

If you have access to one of the videos
about Jesus' life, show them the section of
the entry into Jerusalem and the cleaning
up of the temple. Or they can act this out,
with everyone involved, either as
vendors or crowd members. Afterwards
talk together about how different people
felt when Jesus came in and started
protesting, overturning tables and so on.

If possible, join in with an all age procession, leading the singing or dancing for one or two of the songs.

# Holy Week

## YEARS 1 AND 2

### Ideas for all age activities

Many churches plan days for children during this week, to enable them to follow the events of this week in ways they can relate to. But there is also a place for all age events, particularly where the parents of the children involved are not regular church goers. Here are a few suggestions to set you thinking:

• Invite everyone, of all ages, to an Easter trail, and organise hot soup or a barbecue at the end of it. Choose a place to walk which is easily accessible, and be prepared to borrow wheelchairs if necessary. It may be a pleasant country area you choose, or a city walk that takes in some of the most depressed areas near you, or a combination of both.

Plan it rather like a nature trail, with things to look out for along the way, and points to stop at. Draw out the route with these places numbered on it, and give these out at the start of the trail. Ask different groups of people in the parish to be responsible for what happens at each stop. This may be a brief sketch, a song, pictures of a symbolic activity or anything they feel will help people reflect on the events of the week and their relevance to our lives today. Each stop ends with prayer.

For instance, the local tip may be a suitable place to reflect on repentance and God's forgiveness; a building site, or an area of growing trees may be suitable for reflecting on building our lives on Christ, and so on.

Make sure that leaders walk the trail in advance, to check that it works and is not too long. Six to ten stops is about right, depending very much on ages, and places. Finish with a hot picnic and some singing.

• Have an all age vigil of three hours, during which people can come and go, and different age groups are responsible for planning half hour sessions. You may end up with a mixture of quietness, craft activities, Taizé worship, a worship band, action songs and so on.

• Make the children's day a family day, with activities for parents and children to do together, and other times when an adults' programme is run alongside the children's teaching. Begin and end with a short time of all age worship, and meet up together at a break to share hot cross buns and a drink.

• If your church has an Easter Vigil on the night before Easter Day, consider changing the time to very early morning, so that dawn comes during the service, and you can finish with a shared breakfast and egg hunt. Involve the children and young people in the drama of the readings, have a bonfire, and think about holding this event (weather permitting) on a beach or a local hill.

## EASTER

---
# *Easter Day*
---

## YEARS 1 AND 2

*Thought for the day:*
*Death cannot hold the Lord of life.*
*New life for him means new life for all*
*who believe in Christ.*

### Readings
Psalms 113, 114, 117
Isaiah 12
Romans 6:3-14

### Reflection

Today the whole world-wide church rejoices in celebration of God's victory over sin and death. Having submitted to the complete, punishing result of all sin, and having continued loving and sinless throughout, Jesus cannot be held in by death, but is transformed into new life which will never end. He has enabled us to have a new and full relationship with God which was not previously possible.

The joy of Easter only makes sense when we have travelled with Jesus through the agony of Good Friday and seen there the terrible effect of sin. When we are baptised we pledge our allegiance to Christ, showing by our 'immersion' in water that we share his death, dying to our sin and desiring it to be killed off in us. Then as we rise up from the water we show that we are sharing in the new Resurrection life, living now not for ourselves but in the power and spirit of Jesus.

### Discussion starters

1   What does Paul mean when he says, 'You are not under law, but under grace'?
2   What about Christians who have been brought up in the faith and can't remember a time before they were baptised?

### All stage talk

*Theme:* Old life, new life.

Beforehand cut a rough circle shape from a very large carton (such as will hide a small child). Also cut a number of teardrop shapes out of paper and leave one of these on each row before the service. Just before the talk secrete a small child behind the card gravestone, holding a bunch of spring flowers.

(There may well be people in church today who have not been during Lent, Palm Sunday or Good Friday, so it is a good idea to take everyone through the disappointment of Good Friday before leading on to the joy of Easter Day – otherwise it is rather an empty celebration.)

First talk about times when we have been disappointed with a present or a treat, and how let down and rather flat we feel. The disciples must have felt like that on Good Friday when Jesus, their master and friend had been killed.

Sometimes we feel disappointed with God, too. Perhaps he doesn't answer our prayer for someone we love to get better, or perhaps things aren't working out for us in the way we hoped they would. Ask people to find the teardrop on their row and, as they pass it along to the aisle, to look at it and think of their own personal disappointments or regrets. Have a couple of people to collect the teardrops in a basket and walk up in silence to lay them at the foot of the cross. In a way, that's what was happening as Jesus hung dying there.

But Jesus couldn't be bound in death, and on the third day the cave entrance was found rolled away and Jesus was alive. At this point, roll the card stone away and the small child jumps up, holding a bunch of flowers, which s/he gives out to people all over the church.

## Intercessions

We think of the church celebrating in clusters and crowds all over the world, and pray for a deepening of love and faith.

*Silence for prayer*

Lord of life:
**you do all things well**

We remember the areas of the world where there is conflict and confusion; and we pray that all may come to know God's love.

*Silence for prayer*

Lord of life:
**you do all things well**

We remember those we have met and talked with during the week, and pray for God's blessing on their lives.

*Silence for prayer*

Lord of life:
**you do all things well**

We remember those waiting for surgery, and those in long-term care, and pray that God's will may be beautifully accomplished in their lives.

*Silence for prayer*

Lord of life:
**you do all things well**

We remember those who have died very young, and those who are finding this hard to accept, and we pray for God's grace and reassurance.

*Silence for prayer*

Lord of life:
**you do all things well**

We remember the wonder and generosity of God, his faithfulness and his mercy.

*Silence for prayer*

Lord of life:
**you do all things well**

## Other ideas

• If you are not doing the all stage talk, use the teardrop section as part of the time of penitence.

• Ask everyone to bring bells and ring them in a burst of praise with the organ or music group just before the Easter anthems.

• If you have a suitable spot, create an outside Easter garden for passers-by to see.

• Decorate the door with greenery, flowers and ribbons, and hang banners from the pillars which show various kinds of new life.

## In the crèche

*Aim:* To enjoy celebrating that Jesus is alive.

You will need some marzipan, some of which you have coloured.

If it is Year 1, remind the children of the chocolate nests they made (Lent 5). If it is Year 2, use cake cases with cellophane straw inside. Now you can all roll some little egg shapes to go in the nests. As you work, explain why we are making eggs and why they are all getting chocolate eggs today – they are a sign of new life.

## Children

*Aim:* To teach them about the first Easter.

You will need a collection of those yoghurt pots which have two sections, some potting compost, pebbles and little flowers, small pieces of white cloth, and cardboard.

Tell or read the children the story of Easter, either using pictures, or moving everyone around to act out the story. Aim to get across the sadness which was suddenly changed into excitement and joy.

Now help them to make a tiny Easter garden. If there is an area of garden round the church you can go and gather the pebbles, earth and flowers, of course.

Fold up here

Card stuck on to the yoghurt pot

## Young people

*Aim:* To celebrate the good news of Easter.

You will need some balloons, acetate pens (or others that work on balloons) and, if possible, a helium balloon filler. Failing this, strong lungs will do nicely.

Most churches would provide for young people to be in church today, but in case yours aren't, read the Easter events from one of the gospels, rather than using the Romans passage. Then ask them to write 'Jesus is alive' on the balloons and decorate them so they can blow them up and give them out to people at the end of the service.

---

# 1st Sunday after Easter

## YEAR 1

*Thought for the day:*
*In Jesus we see the face of God, and his risen life enables him to live in us.*

### Readings
Psalms 30,48
Deuteronomy 11:1-15
2 Corinthians 4:5-end

### Reflection

As we continue to rejoice in the resurrection, the emphasis this week is on personal encounter with Jesus. First the Deuteronomy reading reminds the people of Israel that their faith in God is based on their personal experience of his power and guidance in their lives, as they were carefully led out of slavery and through the desert. It is that real knowledge which will strengthen their courage in the difficult times ahead, as they approach the promised land.

Then Paul's letter reminds the Corinthians that Jesus, the Son of God, was dead and is alive. The implication of this is that the One who shows us God's nature in person is freely available and accessible to ordinary people in every age. The astounding truth of this privilege and joy sparkles inside them and us like treasure inside clay pots, and inspires us all to live God's way of love.

This is where Christianity is so different from a moral code or set of ethics; so different even from following the teaching and example of a good man in history. Jesus' living presence among us means that we can talk things over with him, sit quietly and listen to him, be comforted and nudged into action by him, feed from him in our hearts and be nurtured in his love. He is our teacher, companion, lover and Lord, and as we allow Jesus more and more into our lives, we shall increasingly reflect the wise and loving nature of God.

## Discussion starter

1 How can we get to know Jesus in this personal way?
2 What about the dark or foggy times when we aren't aware of Jesus' presence?

## All stage talk

*Theme:* See for yourself.
You will need a supermarket bag and two or three things in it which have distinctive shapes (such as a squash/wine bottle, a banana and a saucepan).

Show everyone the bag and ask them what they think might be inside. It might be all sorts of things, but we don't know because we can't see them. That's what a lot of people think about God – he might be there but they don't know because they haven't seen him.

Suppose I let someone come and feel the things in the bag. (Invite someone to do so). Now they are getting some experience of what the things feel like, and that gives them a much better idea of what they are. All through the Old Testament people groped their way to understanding what God was like, and they felt his presence with them as they were led out of slavery in Egypt.

Suppose I show you the things in this bag? (Take the objects out and display them so everyone can see.) A couple of thousand years ago, God came physically into our world and walked around as a human person. His name was Jesus and at last everyone could see exactly what God was like.

Suppose I put the things back out of sight again. Do you still know what they are and what they are like? Yes, we know for certain because we have seen them. When we say that we believe Jesus is alive, it doesn't mean that we think he might be – it means we know for certain that he is because we have seen him in the gospels, we've seen him in the way his close friends live, and we've met him in our own lives and felt his closeness to us. Our faith is not about a list of rules, but about a real, living person who can completely transform our lives.

## Intercessions

We pray for all whose faith is shaky, those who hesitate to trust you and those who are just beginning to believe.

*Silence for prayer*

Open our eyes, Lord:
**to know and love you more**

*Continued overleaf*

We pray for the areas of fighting and bitterness, for the downtrodden and despised, for those with authority to improve conditions.

*Silence for prayer*

Open our eyes, Lord:
**to know and love you more**

We pray for the very young and the very old, for mothers, fathers and children and all the homes in this parish.

*Silence for prayer*

Open our eyes, Lord:
**to know and love you more**

We pray for the ill and injured,
those who live fearful,
anxious lives and those who are
disillusioned with life.

*Silence for prayer*

Open our eyes, Lord:
**to know and love you more**

We pray for those who are approaching death, those who have died recently and all who fear death.

*Silence for prayer*

Open our eyes, Lord:
**to know and love you more**

We pray for a deeper sense of thankfulness for all you have given us and for all you are in us.

*Silence for prayer*

Open our eyes, Lord:
**to know and love you more**

## Other ideas

- Take the collection in clay flowerpots.
- Put night lights inside a number of different shaped clay pots and use these as a focus for prayer.

- Have some flower arrangements – some large and some small and simple – made in flowerpots.

## In the crèche

*Aim:* To experience knowing something is there when you can't see it.

Play some of the 'peep-bo' type of games, and also use a 'feeling bag' to pass round. The children try and guess what's inside and they are only shown when everyone has had a go.

## Children

*Aim:* To help them grow in awareness that Jesus really is alive today.

In your worship time, pray that the children will be made aware of Jesus' presence among us. Remind them of how excited Jesus' friends were when they found out that he was alive again, and talk about how he could suddenly be with them now, without even having to open doors.

Explain how we can get in touch with Jesus at any time of the day or night and he's always pleased to enjoy our company, whether we're happy or sad, muddy or clean.

To help them remember this at home, make these clocks.

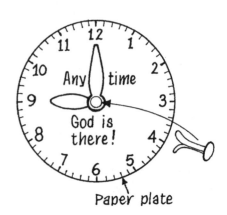

Paper plate

## Young people

*Aim:* To help them see examples of how faith in the living Jesus changes people's lives.

If you have some new Christians in the church, invite them along to tell their story; not that older Christians couldn't do it too, of course, but often new Christians are still excited about it all. Or you can use excerpts from auto-biographies, such as Nick Cruz's story in *Run baby, run.*

Let it also be a question time to air their concerns about their own faith or lack of it, or difficulties their non-Christian friends have with believing in a real, living Jesus. End with a time of expectant prayer.

# YEAR 2

*Thought for the day:
Whatever may happen to us,
ultimately we shall be safe in the
hands of the living God.*

## Readings

Psalms 30, 48
Deuteronomy 4:25-40
Revelation 2:1-11

## Reflection

There is all the difference in the world between doing something because you have been told to and know that you will get punished in some way if you don't do it, and doing something out of love for someone. In the second case the whole business is lighter and even the really unpleasant or revolting jobs can seem reasonable.

In this Deuteronomy passage the people are reminded of God's remark-able, intimate love and affection for them,

his power and his glory. As they remember all that he is and does they will be encouraged to walk in his ways, even though this is going to be difficult – almost impossible for them.

Similarly in the prophecies to the churches in Revelation, it is God's love for his people and their responsive love to him that will support them during the times of persecution ahead.

We can go on for just so long in the habits of church going, following rules out of a dull sense of duty, but sooner or later we shall start to rebel, either secretly or openly, and God sees both with no trouble at all.

What God desires is not a rather bleak following of rules, but a warm and vibrant love and longing for him which responds to his love for us. Out of this will pour a delight in living even dangerously, if that is what he has in mind for us.

## Discussion starters

1  Since we all find it impossible to walk without sin all the time, how can we ensure that we don't stray too far, and how can we find our way back?

2  For what might the churches today be praised and criticised? What in them do you think pleases God and what saddens him?

## All stage talk

*Theme:* Living dangerously.

You will need a climbing rope and a life jacket, or some other equipment which protects you from danger in dangerous hobbies. Also a DANGER sign.

First show the equipment, talking about what mad things climbers and slalom canoeists get up to. Ask for a show of hands as to who reckons each is a dangerous hobby. Those who do such things rely on their equipment to protect them, even when they are in acute danger. (If you have any free-fallers, white water enthusiasts etc. you could interview them briefly about their most scary moment.)

God is our life-line. He is our sure protection when we are living dangerously in his service, and whatever happens to us (even death), we know that we shall be safe in his hands.

What if we roped up together and then walked down the high street, or put on life jackets and then proceeded to do the washing up? It would be ridiculous, wouldn't it! But sometimes we behave like that - we come to church and offer our whole life to God, sing his praise and pray for the world, then go home and live as safely as we can, keeping our faith as quiet as possible and not getting involved with any evangelism if we can help it.

Let's think again: God promises his protection and we love him, so let's take our courage in both hands and really make ourselves available for him to use in whatever ugly situations he may need us to be.

## Intercessions

When we want to hide from serving you;
when we doubt your promise to be with us,

*Silence for prayer*

Lord, teach us:
**how to be faithful**

When we find ourselves standing
against worldly values

*Silence for prayer*

Lord, teach us:
**how to be faithful**

When we meet with selfishness,
laziness and criticism in ourselves
and others around us,

*Silence for prayer*

Lord, teach us:
**how to be faithful**

When we hear of the ill and lonely who
would welcome some friendly contact,

*Silence for prayer*

Lord, teach us:
**how to be faithful**

When we see others die
and remember that this life will pass,

*Silence for prayer*

Lord, teach us:
**how to be faithful**

When we grumble and complain
instead of living thankfully,

*Silence for prayer*

Lord, teach us:
**how to be faithful**

## Other ideas

• Have DANGER notices around the church or 'government health warnings' such as 'Being a Christian can make you unpopular'.

• Pray for people imprisoned for their belief – Amnesty International has information and if you supply cards and pens, letters can be written and sent in protest. Or you could have an exhibition highlighting such problems with prayers written amongst the information and suggested response.

## In the crèche

*Aim:* To make the children aware of how people who love us make sure we are safe.

With puppets or toys act out some situations like a little one running into the road and being pulled back by a big one. The little one is cross until the big one explains that s/he wanted the little one to be safe.

Then look at things which keep us safe – car seat belts, zebra crossings, railings etc.

## Children

*Aim:* To show how God loves us through the good and bad times.

You will need two chalked lines to make a very narrow path which is hard to walk along, or one of those twisted wire contraptions from your May Fair which buzz or ring when you accidentally touch the wire.

Begin with everyone having a go at keeping on the straight and narrow and finding it impossible to do without a few slips.

Talk together about how it's just as hard for us all to keep to everything that is good and loving and generous and trustworthy and kind all the time. There may be some things which people find particularly hard, and it is worth talking through these honestly and lovingly.

The good news about God is that he doesn't give up on us or turn away in disgust whenever we do these things. He knows about them alright, and they make him sad, but as soon as we begin to say we're sorry, he forgives us. We are safe with the living God.

## Young people

*Aim:* To recognise God's love which challenges and keeps us safe.

Read the Deuteronomy passage together and look at a biblical atlas to see where the people of Israel had come from, reminding one another of what happened where. All these events gave them a powerful experience of God so that they knew they could rely on him.

Have a browse through some literature about ways to serve God in challenging situations, such as V.S.O., Action Aid, Christians Aware, Feet First, Operation Gideon and Time for God, just to get them thinking for the future. If there is anyone in the community who has recently been involved with such a venture, invite them in to join the discussion, so that questions and doubts can be raised and talked through.

Pray together for God to govern our lives in the future, wherever that may lead. Exciting, isn't it!

---

# 2nd Sunday after Easter

---

## YEAR 1

*Thought for the day:*
'I bring life'

### Readings
Psalm 49:1-16
Exodus 32:1-14
Luke 7:11-17

### Reflection

Like Midas turning all he touched to gold, God's touch turns all to life and hope. Even the deadest, most impossible bits of our lives, and the lives of those who turn our hair prematurely grey, can be transformed if we let God touch them. So often a situation of worry or conflict drags on and on and we begin to wonder if it will ever be happily resolved; today's readings point us to real hope when the going is hard and our energy drained.

Hope is not wishful thinking – that is about as useful as a couple of whiskies, a trip to the hairdresser, or whatever else you indulge in to buck you up when you want to forget about things. Hope looks problems straight in the eye with the compassion Jesus had for the widow, and the power of transforming life we see in the resurrection. Hope looks at the impossible and says, in effect, 'Yes, that's ghastly and destructive; God has both the power and the desire to transform it for good'.

It follows that we worshippers of such a God need to plead, extensively and expensively for our world. We need to pray with the love and compassion in our hearts that Moses felt for the wayward people of Israel, because when we do this we are behaving like chips off the old block – like genuine children of our compassionate and forgiving heavenly Father.

## Discussion starters

1  Why did the people of Israel go astray so quickly? What can we learn about our outreach programme – do we provide sufficient nurture for people when they first join the community?

2  What do we learn about the character of God from Jesus' behaviour in the passage from Luke?

## All stage talk

*Theme:* God brings life and hope.
Bring in some plants in pots, some of which are wilting pretty badly for need of a good soaking. Choose the kind of plants which respond quickly to kind treatment. You will also need a watering can. Place some of the plants in awkward, hidden places in the building.

Begin by displaying your good, healthy plants, and contrast them with the sad– looking ones. Explain how we sometimes feel spiritually dry and thirsty, sometimes wilting in the stress of a deep worry, or something sad happening in our lives.

God is like a gardener who loves his plants – he sees us wilting and comes to pour his love and hope into our lives again. (Water the plants.) Some plants are easy to water, but others, like us, get themselves in really awkward places, miles from the water and difficult to get at. But God doesn't leave them to go on wilting, he goes out to find them and takes lots of trouble to get at them because he loves them, and wants them to be full of life. (Go around watering the other plants.

There is no area of your life or our world which is beyond the refreshing touch of the loving, powerful God. (Stand all the plants where they can be seen through the service, so that by the end they can be seen to have brightened up.)

## Intercessions

Wherever Christians are spiritually dry or brittle, wherever the loving has lost its freshness, we pray for refreshment.
*Silence for prayer*
Father, touch our lives:
**and give them new life**

Wherever the nations scramble for power and revenge, wherever materialism dulls the spirit, we pray for realigned priorities and values.
*Silence for prayer*
Father, touch our lives:
**and give them new life**

Wherever homes are disturbed by financial problems, difficult relationships and long-term illness, we pray for guidance and support.
*Silence for prayer*
Father, touch our lives:
**and give them new life**

Wherever slow recovery makes time hang heavily, wherever hope and joy are fading, we pray for encouragement and delight.
*Silence for prayer*
Father, touch our lives:
**and give them new life**

Wherever people are dying to this world, wherever lives are cut short by accidents, war or famine, we pray for your mercy and words of comfort.

*Silence for prayer*

Father, touch our lives:
**and give them new life**

Whether our hearts are light or heavy, whether the day goes well or not, we give you praise and proclaim your love.

*Silence for prayer*

Father, touch our lives:
**and give them new life**

## Other ideas

• Incorporate a watering can in one of the flower arrangements, to remind everyone of how God brings freshness, life and hope.

• Have people carrying the painted flags and names of various countries in particular need of prayer and standing at different parts of the building. Ask everyone to gather round the flag nearest to them and pray in silent clusters for the people and their problems. Music can be played as a background to the prayer, or everyone can sing the chorus of 'Shine, Jesus, shine', praying in this for the country they are thinking about.

## In the crèche

*Aim:* To experience God's delight in bringing order out of confusion and refreshment to the wilting.

Have some plants that need watering, pencils that need sharpening, wool that needs untangling and toys that need organising. As you sort everything out, talk together about how God enjoys sorting out and putting right.

## Children

*Aim:* To teach them the stories of the golden calf and of the widow of Nain.

Split the group in two, and help each prepare a presentation of one of the stories. They can act, mime or work with puppets. Then let each group show their presentation to the other.

Have a time to pray for the world – for anywhere they have seen on the news and want to pray for. It is helpful to have some pictures from the week's newspapers cut out and spread on the floor to help focus the prayer.

## Young people

*Aim:* To raise awareness of the need to feel compassion as we plead for our world.

Read the passage from Luke together, and talk about Jesus' compassion for the widow which made him respond in action.

Focus today on a particular need. There may be something which the parish is particularly involved with; there may be an area which God leads you to look at as you prepare the session. Whatever it is – drug abuse, homelessness, famine, local unemployment, families in stress – come prepared with information, pictures and articles, case studies and so on. Have a time of sharing all the material around, and perhaps invite someone personally involved to talk informally and discuss the problem.

The aim is to take the problem out of the general into the particular, so that we can pray with love and sympathy, standing alongside those who suffer.

# YEAR 2

*Thought for the day:*
*'I bring life'*

## Readings

Psalm 49:1-16
Ezra 1:1-8
Revelation 2:12-end

## Reflection

Any restoration programme must start with a candid look at the present state of affairs, recognising what is strong and can be built on, and acknowledging what is in a dangerous state of repair so that these areas can be demolished, and rebuilt on firm foundations. When Jesus brings life to our lives and our world it is just the same. We can't just casually shrug our shoulders and expect him to get on with building a grand edifice in our lives on a rotten or cracked foundation.

In Ezra, we watch the preparations for the rebuilding of the temple at Jerusalem, as Cyrus, King of Persia, allows ethnic groups to return to their homelands. The gathering of sufficient resources is vital for the work to be carried out, and everyone needs to contribute towards expenses and materials. Then, in Revelation, we hear the Spirit's message to the churches, preparing them for the great and terrible times ahead. All that is good and praiseworthy is recognised and valued; all that is less good and needs attention is also noticed so that it can be put right.

That is how it must be in our lives, too. It is important to incorporate into our individual prayer life a regular, candid review of where we are, where we are heading, where God is beginning to work in us and where we need to sort out sin or redirect our attitudes and priorities. Whether we do this together with a wise spiritual companion, a group of praying Christians or on our own with God will probably depend on our characters and background, but the important thing is to do it regularly, so that the transforming love of Jesus is not prevented from working in any area of our lives.

## Discussion starters

1  When is criticism constructive, and when is it destructive?

2  What holds people back from the prospect of being transformed, however gently or dynamically?

## All stage talk

*Theme:* Assessing the damage before the repairs can begin.

Bring in a bike in unroadworthy condition and ask a couple of people who have recently passed their cycling proficiency test (or some other well qualified person) to take a look at the bike and say what's good about it and what's in need of attention. As the items are mentioned, write them up on a chart or OHP in two columns.

Now we are in a much better position to put the bike right. We are quite happy to accept this as a sensible way of going on for a machine, but start getting very upset if the same sort of things are pointed out in us. Instead of welcoming fair criticism as a useful guide to help us put things rights, most of us find criticism hurtful, and get upset about it. Yet we probably know the criticism is correct – we just didn't want anyone to notice!

And we do want people to accept us and think well of us.

So let's try a double-ended approach; to think of criticism as a positive thing and welcome it as a means to put things right; and to make sure that whenever we need to criticise someone, we do it sensitively and lovingly, talking to them about it, not about them to someone else.

## Intercessions

We remember the bickering and petty-mindedness that goes on in all areas of church life, and ask for your healing love.
*Silence for prayer*
Show up our darkness:
**and cancel it with your light**

We remember the bitterness and greed which tears our world apart,
and ask for your peace.
*Silence for prayer*
Show up our darkness:
**and cancel it with your light**

We remember our families, and the homes in this parish, with their laughter and crying, anger and frustration,
and ask for your caring love.
*Silence for prayer*
Show up our darkness:
**and cancel it with your light**

We remember those who suffer and find life hard to cope with, and ask for your comfort and encouragement.
*Silence for prayer*
Show up our darkness:
**and cancel it with your light**

We remember those who are moving from this life into eternity, and those heartbroken at their going.
We ask for greater trust in you.
*Silence for prayer*
Show up our darkness:
**and cancel it with your light**

We thank you and give you glory
for all you are doing in our lives
and all you have in mind for the future.
*Silence for prayer*
Show up our darkness:
**and cancel it with your light**

## Other ideas

Have a time to reflect on where people are in their spiritual growing, and where they need to recognise areas that need attention. This can be done in silence or with background music, leading in to everyone singing 'Purify my heart'.

## In the crèche

*Aim:* Spotting the mistakes.
Recognising what is wrong and what is right is a skill that can be developed. With young children, play a game of spotting what's wrong. While they hide their eyes put something wrong, such as a pencil in a candlestick, a glove on a foot, or a pair of glasses on the handle of a cup. Then let them search around to find the mistake and put it right.

## Children

*Aim:* To help them see the importance of being honest with God.
You will need a ball or beanbag, and a dressing-up outfit of some kind. First play a game of deceit, such as 'Queenie, queenie, who's got the ball?' (This is one the wrinklies in the church will remember!) Then dress one child up to disguise him/her as something different. Are they taken in by the disguise?

Talk together about how hard it is to deceive someone who knows us really well. God knows us better than we know ourselves, which can sometimes be a good thing, and sometimes not, depending on whether we're proud or ashamed of the way we're thinking and behaving. It's not worth bothering to pretend we're something different when we're talking to God because he's in on the secret of what we're really like. That means that we can be natural and honest with God, trusting him with what we are really feeling and thinking. Then, when we're open about the things we don't like in our way of living, God will be able to sort us out.

Help them make this model to remind them that we don't need to wear a mask when we're with God.

GOD
L ♡VES
O ME O
JUST AS I AM

Cut out eyes and nose

Tape, to make a hinge

Elastic tape knotted at back

## Young people

*Aim:* To help them understand that they are precious to God just as they are.

You will need a selection of magazine pictures which show the kind of images people crave – sexy, rich, rebellious, cool, efficient, powerful etc. First take time to look at the images and jot down words to describe them.

Compare notes, and discuss any images they are aware of cultivating. Talk over some cases when they have found a person's real character doesn't match up with the image they wear. It is when people let you see behind the image that you get closer to one another, and the relationship can grow.

Now read the Revelation passage and notice how in this relationship there is both praise and criticism which can only take place in an atmosphere of trust. Discuss whether there is anyone from whom they are willing to receive constructive criticism (possibly sports/ dance teachers) and work out why this is. It may well have something to do with feeling accepted as they are. Point out how God is always constructive and sensitive to our fears when he works on the areas which need developing or changing or healing. We can trust him because he loves us already, and will give us encouragement as well.

# 3rd Sunday after Easter

## YEAR 1

*Thought for the day:*
*Even if people don't believe in God,*
*he never for a moment stops*
*believing in them.*

### Readings
Psalms 121, 126
Numbers 22:1-35 (or 1-20)
Acts 17:16-end

### Reflection

The strange story of Balaam and his talking ass shows how the people of Israel are protected as they move into the promised land. Even an alien wizard cannot curse them but, much to the Moabite king's consternation, ends up blessing them instead. Don't be put off by the way God appears to be turning fickle (verse 22). Two versions of the story have simply become intermingled here, and as they vary in certain points there are apparent contradictions.

The important thing to notice is that God does not exist only in the minds of his followers – he is the source of everybody's life, whether they acknowledge it or not. Paul picks up on this as he talks to the Athenians; he explains God to them in terms of their own religious ideas. But there is a problem.

If we invent a god to worship we can choose its characteristics to fit in with what we want for ourselves; we can make sure it doesn't interfere with our own desires and comforts, and use it to back up our social policies and war initiatives.

In contrast, the one, true God is not dependent for his survival on our daydreams, and we are in no position to manoeuvre him into the places we dictate. Acknowledging this was hard for the Athenians and is hard for many people today. Sadly, many prefer to stay with the tinpot gods of their own making, popping into their inventions the odd characteristic of the true God which happen to appeal to them, and very dangerous this can be.

### Discussion starters

1  What sort of mishmash religions, posing as 'C of E' on hospital forms have you noticed in our society?
2  Having seen Paul's approach to evangelising the Athenians, and its effect, how would you set about preaching the truth of the Gospel to unchurched people in our own society?

### All stage talk

*Theme:* Designer gods.
As people come into church, give them all a pipe cleaner and a piece of string. Begin the talk by asking everyone to design an animal of some kind using the pipe cleaner and string provided. Everyone can hold up their masterpieces for general admiration.

Point out that everyone's creation is different because we all had our own ideas. We might have picked up on certain qualities of real animals, but even the best of our creations is not much like any real animal we might know.

People invent gods to worship rather as we made our animals. Sometimes there are aspects in these gods which are like the real God, but they are not really anything like the one true God who loved us all into being and is the beginning and end of all things.

We cannot pick and choose with God, making him as we feel on any particular day; we cannot make him at all, because he is there already and always has been. What we can do is enjoy him as he is, enjoy him loving us, and enjoy getting to know him better and better.

## Intercessions

Lord of glory, we ask you to show us more of yourself, to inspire all ministers and teachers of your word, freshen our faith and cultivate our love.

*Silence for prayer*

Our help comes from the Lord:
**who has made heaven and earth**

Lord of glory, we ask your help in the governing of our planet, in all national and international decisions and in the organisation of our resources.

*Silence for prayer*

Our help comes from the Lord:
**who has made heaven and earth**

Lord of glory, we ask you to bring healing and reassurance,
comfort and wholeness to all who suffer.

*Silence for prayer*

Our help comes from the Lord:
**who has made heaven and earth**

Lord of glory, we ask you to welcome into your presence those who have reached the point of physical death.

*Silence for prayer*

Our help comes from the Lord:
**who has made heaven and earth**

Lord of glory, we give you thanks and praise for all that is good and lovely, honest and pure.

*Silence for prayer*

Our help comes from the Lord:
**who has made heaven and earth**

## Other ideas

As a statement of faith, try using the baptism responses, and encourage people to say 'This is our faith – we believe and trust in one God, Father, Son and Holy Spirit' as if they really *do* believe it!

## In the crèche

Aim: For the children to understand that God likes them and looks after them.
Have some pictures of Jesus being kind and natural, healing and teaching. Some of the older bibles have excellent glossy pictures in, and you can also have a selection of the lovely bible stories available now. Enjoy a 'snuggle and read' session and sing an action song such as 'God is good to me' or 'I've got that joy, down in my heart'.

## Children

*Aim:* For them to learn to accept God as he is.
Begin by playing monster consequences. (Everyone draws a monster head, folds the paper down and passes it on. Now everyone draws a monster body, and so on.) Display the finished monsters and enjoy them.

There are also books available from libraries which have the pages split into three, and you can make your own combination picture of an animal or person. You could use this kind of book, or make your own by drawing three pictures, cutting each into three and letting the children make them up into different pictures.

Explain how people invent gods, and tell them the story of Paul walking through Athens and noticing the altar to an unknown god, then using this as a starting point to tell them the good news of the one true God.

Then help the children to make their own 'photo fit' kit. However they assemble it, the caption will always read the same: 'our God never changes'.

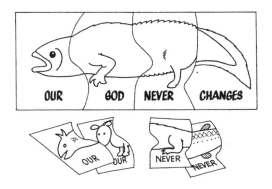

## Young people

*Aim:* For them to understand that God continues to believe in those who do not believe in him.

Begin by reading Acts 17, acting it out as a radio play if you like, with sound effects of crowd noises and so on. Have available some reference books with pictures of Athens so that they can see where it all happened.

Look at pictures of some of the Greek gods and goddesses and explain how the people of Athens always enjoyed talking about new philosophical and religious ideas. Look at how Paul uses the existing situation to preach the gospel. Discuss why the resurrection made the listeners start losing interest or scoffing.

Now think about some of the weird and wonderful ideas people have about God today, and discuss what point of contact we can make to start telling them about the real God. This could either be discussed in the whole group, or given as a role play exercise in small clusters, where some people are acting out the part of those with confused or misguided ideas about God.

# YEAR 2

*Thought for the day:*
*No matter how ruined or damaged our lives are, God has plans for a full restoration programme and is ready to start work straight away.*

## Readings
Psalms 121, 126
Ezra 3
Revelation 3:1-13

## Reflection

It is worth looking carefully at the order of events in the passage from the book of Ezra. When our reading begins, the exiles have returned to Jerusalem, seen the temple ruins, donated money towards the rebuilding fund and then spent several months settling back into the towns. Now they are ready to do something about the temple, but the first thing they do is to gather for worship, rebuilding the altar so that sacrifices can resume straight away, even before the temple is rebuilt.

That is the right order in every rebuilding programme, whether we are talking about dead churches, crushed personalities, decayed morals or broken lives. The temptation in such situations is to look with hopelessness on the rubble all around us, the enormity of the problems, and the danger of opposition. Perhaps the last thing we feel like doing at this point is offering praise and thanks to God. But if only we can bring ourselves to God's presence we shall be offering a real sacrifice of praise, proclaiming by our act of worship that we want Christ to come first in our lives. With this as the foundation, the rebuilding programme will have the soundest leadership and advice that anyone could wish for.

## *Discussion starters*

1  Notice that some of those who remembered the previous temple building were not grumbling and critical of the new model, but weeping. What does that suggest about their spiritual state of health?

2  How seriously do we take the priority of prayerful preparation in our own projects, our church events, and our country's policies and legislation? Make a note of any positive recommendations so that your discussion is fruitful.

## *All stage talk*

*Theme:* First things first.

Begin by having pre-arranged people to set up a fitness training course in the centre aisle. This needs to be done quickly and efficiently, as if it is all part of the training session. It only needs to be very simple – perhaps a skipping rope in one place, a step or box at another, and a small mat somewhere else. Have three volunteers, of mixed ages, and ask each to jog to one of the positions. They are going to do circuit training, skipping with the rope, stepping on and off the box and doing sit-ups on the mat. Start the stopwatch and move them on to the next activity after 20 seconds so that they have all completed the circuit in one minute.

Why do people do things like this? To get fit/have healthy bodies. What might happen if you weren't fit and rushed straight into a game of squash or football? You may get an injury, or even have a heart attack. We need to train to be fit before the big match, not after it.

We know that so well, and yet we sometimes expect to cope with very difficult and challenging problems in our lives without bothering to get spiritually fit first. What might our training circuit look like for getting spiritually fit?

Incorporate the ideas people suggest, which will no doubt include reading the bible, praying/listening and serving others. Put a small group of people reading a bible and commentaries suitable for different ages at one place, someone praying at another place, someone with a towel, jug of water and a basin at another.

If we get cracking on this daily circuit training, we will be making sure we're spiritually fitter and better equipped to face whatever the day throws at us.

## *Intercessions*

There are places where the church is weak and complacent; where we are deaf and blind to where and how you are leading us. Open our hearts to hear and see you more clearly.

*Silence for prayer*

Father, let our lives:
**be strongly built on your love**

There are places where brutal force and corruption seem to have the upper hand; Quieten our lives and give space to all leaders to hear your wisdom.

*Silence for prayer*

Father, let our lives:
**be strongly built on your love**

There are homes where arguments flare up all the time, and people are sad and lonely. Fill each home in this parish with peace and love.

*Silence for prayer*

Father, let our lives:
**be strongly built on your love**

There are people with raging temperatures and bodies full of pain. Keep them safe and bring them to wholeness.

*Silence for prayer*

Father, let our lives:
**be strongly built on your love**

There are people from every country
who have recently died.
Welcome them into your kingdom
and comfort those who miss them.

*Silence for prayer*

Father, let our lives:
**be strongly built on your love**

The world you have given us to live in is
full of beauty.
We thank you for all that fills us with joy.

*Silence for prayer*

Father, let our lives:
**be strongly built on your love**

## Other ideas

• Take this sentence: 'God is good – his
love for us lasts for ever!' and have it
proclaimed first by one single voice, then
by two voices from somewhere else in the
church, then shouted by four children,
then boomed by five men, then chorused
by six ladies and finally by everybody so
that we can participate in the sense of
building a people of praise.

• Have the main flower arrangement
designed to include some oasis and a pair
of secateurs, and a picture of a building
or landscape which has inspired the
colours in the arrangement. The whole
thing will then give a sense of planning,
and working carefully through stages to
reach the end result.

## In the crèche

*Aim:* To experience rebuilding from ruins.
Have plenty of building materials
available. Empty cartons are just as good
as purpose-built blocks, and they have
the advantage of coming in a great
assortment of sizes. Enjoy building with
them, knocking them down and then
rebuilding them, and as you all build
telling them the story of how the temple
was all in ruins, and Ezra and the people
of Israel built it up again.

## Children

*Aim:* To tell the story of rebuilding the
temple and look at spiritual rebuilding.
Start with a lively fitness training session,
taking pulses before and after, and having
a workout of such activities as running on
the spot, stretching, stepping, skipping,
sit ups, and jumping. Have a tape of
children's praise music on as you work.
Then have some quiet music as you talk
together about building our bodies up to
be strong.

Now read or tell the children the story
from Ezra, about another kind of building
and, as you mention the rubble and ruins
of the temple, scatter on the floor the
different pieces of the temple jigsaw (as
shown above). As you come to the part
where the first thing the people did was
to offer their sacrifices of praise to God,
offer God some praise yourselves by
singing something the children know
well and enjoy singing enthusiastically.
Also have a time of prayer for people
who are scared of different things, as Ezra
and the people were scared of their
enemies if they started rebuilding the

temple. (Children will often be very honest about this and can pray for one another.) As the rebuilding programme in the story gets under way, let groups of children work on the jigsaw puzzle – prepare enough jigsaws for there to be one between every four children. Sing with praise and thanksgiving as the people of Israel did when the foundation is complete.

Buildings eventually fall down, and bodies eventually die, but we can build our spiritual lives which will last for ever. How? The children may well have some good ideas which can be noted down. Then the children can make a spiritual building from junk to take home. It might look something like this:

## Young people

*Aim:* To look at rebuilding costs for individuals, and for the churches.
Start by reading Ezra 3, and then study the passage to discover:
a) which bit they rebuilt first
b) how they paid for the rebuilding materials

c) what the people were frightened of
d) how old the supervisors were
e) what happened when the foundations were laid
f) why some of the older people were weeping.

You could either do this as one group or in smaller groups of two or three.

Now read the passage from Revelation 3 and talk together about what makes for strong churches, and what kind of things make them weakened.

What things do these words to the churches in Sardis and Philadelphia alert us to that we need to address in our own churches and in ourselves?

# 4th Sunday after Easter

## YEAR 1

*Thought for the day:*
*Prophets say what we need to hear –*
*not what we want to hear.*

### Readings
Psalms 57, 63:1-9
Numbers 22:36-23:12
Luke 16:19-end

### Reflection
We are always trying to organise or bargain with God in various shades of subtlety. There are times, for instance, when our desperate prayers are suspiciously like rubbing the oil lamp, and telling the genie what to do next. Or we go ahead with our brilliant plans and only when we have got everything organised

do we approach God and ask for his stamp of approval. Or, since we can only see the immediate problem, we badger God to act in a particular way. Yet God's orchestration is superb, and his way of accomplishing things is not only beautiful, but also remarkably economical, since he will bring blessing to many from one event. He surprises us, and opens us up to possibilities we never imagined.

We can rest assured that, while he lovingly serves, he is not our slave, and if we pray for what would harm us he will not give it to us, for he knows how to give good gifts to his children.

Sometimes what God says to us is uncomfortable because it battles against our selfishness or pride. No wonder Balak was cross; no wonder Dives was frustrated – they suddenly realised that their power and influence were not comparable with God's, and that his power sometimes blesses those we would condemn.

We need to listen to God's voice through the daily events and words and through daily reading and reflection of scripture so that we get to be attuned to his wide-scale will, where we are just one bit in the whole scheme of things.

## Discussion starters

1 What similarities can you find between Balak and Dives?

2 Are we prepared to let God in to do the organising and planning with us in our lives/parish?

## All stage talk

*Theme:* More input, less output.

If possible, beg or borrow a radio controlled car for today. If you don't know anyone who owns such a thing devise one using a willing child, and a carton which she holds round her middle like this:

Tell the controlled car (in either version) which way you want it to go and see how it does exactly what you tell it. Balak thought he could do this with all his subjects. Parents wish they could do it to their children! Children wish they could do it to their teachers! And sometimes that's the way we treat God – we might say, 'Well, I don't believe in God any more because I asked him to get me a bike and he didn't'. That doesn't prove that God isn't there – it proves that God isn't a radio controlled car or a slot machine or a magic lamp! And that's true. He isn't.

God certainly comes among us as one who serves, but we mustn't presume to take him out of a matchbox at Christmas and in emergencies. Dives wanted to organise God as he did his money, but he discovered in the end that God was the one in charge. God is not our slave, and his way of doing things is much better than ours anyway, because he understands the whole situation and all the people involved. He's rather like a conductor or composer, bringing all the different parts of the orchestra together to make a beautiful harmony.

So what have we learnt from Balak and Dives?

- that we can't control God
- that God is in control
- but that God never makes us do what he wants; we are free to choose.

## Intercessions

When we are teased or laughed at for what we believe;
when we find it hard to be faithful;

*Silence for prayer*

Then we take refuge:
**in the shadow of your wings**

When we are confronted with violence, homelessness and war and stand alongside the victims and outcasts,

*Silence for prayer*

Then we take refuge:
**in the shadow of your wings**

When we remember our homes, and those we live near, and plead for those who do not know what it is to be loved,

*Silence for prayer*

Then we take refuge:
**in the shadow of your wings**

When we are ill or in pain, anxious or fearful,

*Silence for prayer*

Then we take refuge:
**in the shadow of your wings**

When we approach death;
when we mourn the loss of loved ones,

*Silence for prayer*

Then we take refuge:
**in the shadow of your wings**

When we delight in the freshness of creation; when we feel your joy uplifting us,

*Silence for prayer*

Then we take refuge:
**in the shadow of your wings**

## Other ideas

While everyone reflects on the way God harmonises and orchestrates the events in our lives so as to redeem and bless us, play some music which weaves several different strands together into harmony. Some suggestions – music by Thomas Tallis, Pachelbel's Canon, or some chamber music by Vivaldi, Bach or Handel.

## In the crèche

*Aim:* To help them feel the difference between being 'clockwork toys' and thinking children.

First show the children some clockwork toys and enjoy playing with them. As they play, help them notice how a clockwork toy goes on doing the same thing whatever you tell it, until it stops. Play now at being clockwork toys, with the children being wound up before setting off. (Remind them that they have to run down after a while!) God could have made us like that, but instead he made us free to choose and make up own minds.

Let them all move around to some children's praise music, first as clockwork toys and then as themselves, dancing any way they feel like.

## Children

*Aim:* To help them learn to work with God at the helm of their lives.

First play 'traffic lights', where a caller shouts out either RED, AMBER or GREEN. If RED, they stop and sit down, if AMBER they crouch, and if GREEN they run about. Change the caller several times. Then talk about who was in charge during the game – was it the group leader, the ones who called out the colours or the children? (In a way it was all of these, because the group leader was in charge of the whole activity, the callers were in charge of what order to do things and the children were in charge of themselves in keeping the rules.)

Now read or tell the story of Dives, with the children helping you act it out. Dives was in charge of all his riches when he was alive; he thought he was in charge, anyway. Lazarus didn't feel in charge of anything. But they found out when they died that God was in charge. Dives wished and wished he had known that while he was still alive, because then he might have done things differently. Well, we *do* know that God is in charge, so we can make sure we spend time in God's company so we know what he'd like us to do in our lives. He won't push and shove; God hopes we will choose what is right, because he knows that will make us happy for ever, but he leaves us free to make our own choices between good and evil. Whichever we choose, God is still in charge.

Offer the children a choice of media to use to express the Dives story – perhaps crayons, paint or modelling clay.

## Young people

Aim: To explore the nature of God's authority compared with ours.

Bring a few national newspapers and give them out to small groups, asking everyone to pick out stories which show someone acting in authority. Give each group a chart with two columns. In one column they name the person acting in authority, and in the other a comment on their decision or action, such as 'wise', 'foolish', 'thoughtless' or 'evil'.

Join into one group to share the findings. They will no doubt have found a considerable number of instances which highlight human weakness and make us thankful that we are not ultimately in charge of creation.

Now read the Dives story, and talk together about the way Dives still half expected to organise God and then bargain with him, even after death. There may be an alarming amount of evil in this world, but through dying and being raised from death, Jesus' love has won the final victory over all that is thoughtless, unwise, destructive, cruel and hopeless.

# YEAR 2

*Thought for the day:*
*God not only shows us the route, but*
*walks with us each step of the way.*

## Readings
Psalms 57, 63:1-9
Nehemiah 1
1 Corinthians 15:1-28

## Reflection

We can learn a lot from Nehemiah as he puts his faith into practice when faced with a problem. When things are jogging along nicely it is fairly easy to feel good and noble. But we Christians will be noticed if our gentleness and loving spirit extends to the trying or devastating times. How we react in these circumstances will be the real witness to what we believe, and will set others wondering what the secret is. I'm not talking about a set, determined smile, nor a laid back casual assumption of forgiveness here. I mean real hurt knocking real people sideways, and struggling through their suffering in God's company.

How we react at those crucial moments will be largely determined by the way we have been living the rest of our lives. For Nehemiah that meant rushing into the arms of God with his grief, opening his heart to the possibility of being wrong and yearning to put things right and live once more in harmony with God.

Just as good trees cannot help producing good fruit, so Nehemiah's pattern of living makes it natural for him to think and do the right thing. In the same way it is a natural progression for those who believe in Christ to live their lives out in love and service, and come with Christ through physical death into eternal life. We can only start where we are, and God is happy for that to be so. Perhaps we have become slack in our daily prayer life, for instance. Now is the very best time to start placing God at the centre, rather than fitting him in the spaces left over after all the other demands.

## Discussion starters

1  Work through Nehemiah's prayer to see the pattern and content, and learn from it some good ideas about how to pray.

2  If we really believe that there is life after death, and that heaven will be an endless time of joy and beauty in God's presence, what difference will that make to the way we live our lives?

## All stage talk

*Theme:* We use what we trust.

Show everyone three things: a colander, a calculator and a calendar. Ask a volunteer to tell you which of the three things they choose to find the answer to 637x314. Ask them why they made that choice. Try to persuade them that the others might work. Try the sum on the thing they chose (which I am assuming was the calculator – if it wasn't, try someone else!) Are we surprised? No. Why not? Because we know that calculators do sums – we can trust them.

Why did Nehemiah go to God rather than anyone or anything else? He knew

from experience that God would organise things the best way for his will to be done. Do we trust God like that or not quite, yet? Think of who or what you go to first when there's a problem; *that* is what or who you trust most.

## Intercessions

Trusting in your love we pray for all arguments and conflicts in the church; for all who feel confused about their faith.

*Silence for prayer*

Father, you hold our lives:
**safe in your hands**

Trusting in your authority we pray for all international discussions and negotiations; for all who give orders to others.

*Silence for prayer*

Father, you hold our lives:
**safe in your hands**

Trusting in your gentleness we pray for new-born children and their parents; for all families in crisis.

*Silence for prayer*

Father, you hold our lives:
**safe in your hands**

Trusting in your wisdom we pray for those who labour to find cures and protection from disease; for all who suffer in body, mind or spirit.

*Silence for prayer*

Father, you hold our lives:
**safe in your hands**

Trusting in your mercy we pray for those who have reached physical death; for those who miss them or feel guilty about them.

*Silence for prayer*

Father, you hold our lives:
**safe in your hands**

Trusting in your goodness we pray with thankfulness for all we have received and been enabled to share.

*Silence for prayer*

Father, you hold our lives:
**safe in your hands**

## Other ideas

• Use part of today's reading from Corinthians as the statement of faith, written out for everyone to join in either on sheets on an OHP.

• Have two or three 'stations' of prayer concerns where action has been requested, such as an Amnesty prisoner of conscience, a political debate where Christians need to make their opinions known, or a local issue where support is needed for those who are being neglected or dismissed.

While music is playing, invite people to walk round and look at the displays, adding their names to letters provided, or writing letters or cards to those in authority.

## In the crèche

*Aim:* To help the children know that they can talk to Jesus whenever they feel sad, happy or frightened.

Play a game of 'What's the time, Mr. Wolf?', so that they sense the idea of running to safety. Talk with the children about the things that make them sad and frightened, and where they feel nice and safe. Jesus loves them and is a safe place to be. Pray with the children in simple, natural language, so that they can talk to Jesus whenever they want.

Then spend the session helping the children make something they wouldn't be able to do on their own, talking as you work about the way we can help one another, and Jesus will always help us to do difficult things like being kind when we don't want to be, or making friends when we are lonely.

## Children

*Aim:* To help them get used to the order of prayer first, action second.

First play a game of placing a series of pictures in order. (To prepare this game cut up some comic strips and stick each frame on card.) Talk about how important it is to get things in the right order; what a mess there would be, for instance, if I poured out the milk before getting my bowl of cornflakes, or tipped out the paint pots before going to the sink.

Now tell the children about Nehemiah, explaining how dangerous it could be for him to go and ask the king to let him go to Jerusalem. (They may understand this fear if they think of how they feel when they've got to ask permission for something from a very strict person who scares them.)

Nehemiah got things in the right order: 1) PRAYER 2) ACTION. Then God helped him say the best things, prepared the situation and everything worked out well.

You could also read to them a short piece from Corrie Ten Boom to see the same thing happening.

They can make this emergency card to carry in a purse or wallet.

EMERGENCY CARD
✦ STEP 1: PRAYER
✦ STEP 2: ACTION
...GET THE ORDER RIGHT...GET THE OR

## Young people

*Aim:* To put into practice the head knowledge of prayer first, action second. First ask them to put in order a list of stages for washing an elephant, or making a honey and marmite sandwich. (My daughter actually chooses to make and eat these!) Or you could write the stages beforehand and let them sort them.

Read the passage from Nehemiah, explaining the background enough for them to understand his reason for panic. Then look at the order of his actions, noting that prayer comes first.

Next look at Paul's letter to the church in Corinth. Try to think what might have been going on that caused Paul to write all this. He must have already been through the horror and sadness stage and the praying, so that this letter was his resulting action.

Show them some issues which cause us distress (such as those mentioned in Other ideas). Together pray openly and expectantly, and then put into practice the plan of action that seems right. Bear in mind that the ideas may not come in your short session; ask everyone to continue praying and discuss ideas next time. It may well be that other events will happen which link up and lead you forward in a particular way.

# 5th Sunday after Easter

## YEAR 1

*Thought for the day:*
*God is far more ready to lavish his blessings on us than we are to receive them.*

### Readings
Psalms 65, 67
Deuteronomy 28:1-14
Luke 10:38–11:13

### Reflection

The Deuteronomy reading describes the kind of life our society might enjoy if we were all living in accordance with God's values and laws. History has borne out the terrible truth that corruption and widespread destructive violence results in misery and widespread suffering for many. In contrast, a community living with care and respect for one another enables the individuals within it to enjoy peaceful and ordered lives. Naturally the personal tragedies and disappointments remain, but even disasters and family worries are helped to healing in the context of a genuinely loving, caring community.

Such is the community which the church should be, with its priorities right and its morality reflecting the qualities of God. Blessings are bound to spring up as a result of God's people living in harmony with their creator and saviour. It is all a question of using things in the way they are designed to work. I used my daughter's stroller as a wheelbarrow on a number of occasions until the wheels couldn't cope and the whole thing collapsed. That wasn't the stroller's or the designer's fault – it was the direct result of my using it in a way it wasn't designed to be used. We are designed to work within a moral code, and basic integrity, goodwill and mutual respect needs to permeate the way we live if we are to experience any degree of freedom from fear and danger. That is living God's way. If we turn our backs on this we will not be able to benefit from God's freely-given forgiveness, and all his blessings which he so enjoys lavishing on us.

## Discussion starters

1  In what ways does corruption in our society make for misery and fear in people's lives?

2  How can we learn to ask for what is in harmony with God's will?

## All stage talk

*Theme:* Living as God designed us.

Have an example or two of using something for what it was designed (such as a bicycle being carefully ridden or a sleeping bag to snuggle up in). Have volunteers to demonstrate the correct use of these things.

Now ask people to suggest to the person sitting near them what might happen if we used the bike to iron a shirt or the sleeping bag to skip with. Ask some stalwart volunteers to demonstrate, using a fairly old shirt and tatty sleeping bag in case of accidents.

Explain how God has designed us for living in a certain way – with God at the centre of our lives, caring for one another, being unselfish and respecting each other and one another's property – and it doesn't work very well if we live spiteful, greedy or selfish lives instead. We need to pray every day, keeping closely in touch with God who made us and knows us

well, so that we can live out our lives the way he designed us to. That way we'll feel right and our lives will be a lot more useful and cause a lot less damage.

## Intercessions

We remember all the Christians worshipping all over the world; especially those who are feeling discouraged or inadequate.

*Silence for prayer*

In all your people, Father:
**let your will be done**

We remember the leaders of the nations, all in charge of making important decisions and all who have sidled into corruption.

*Silence for prayer*

In all your people, Father:
**let your will be done**

We remember the members of our families and those who make life easy or difficult for us.

*Silence for prayer*

In all your people, Father:
**let your will be done**

We remember those dependent on drugs or alcohol; all whose bodies don't work properly and all who have been damaged by violence.

*Silence for prayer*

In all your people, Father:
**let your will be done**

We remember those who have died and those who miss their company.

*Silence for prayer*

In all your people, Father:
**let your will be done**

*Continued overleaf*

As we delight in the rich variety of your creation,
we offer our lives for you to use in whatever way you want.

*Silence for prayer*

In all your people, Father:
**let your will be done**

## Other ideas

• Have a group to act out the New Testament reading, with the three sections being taken by different groups of people. The first section covers Mary and Martha, and can be a straightforward narration and mime. For the Lord's Prayer try having quiet music playing in the background and simple, stylised movements to express the meaning of each 'heading'. The section about persisting in prayer can be mimed, or acted with different parts being spoken, either using a script or their own words.

• Have the different sections of the Lord's Prayer written out separately on pillars or walls. Ask people to turn towards each section and read it together, with time left for reflection and prayer before turning to the next section.

## In the crèche

*Aim:* To learn that asking is acceptable. Bullying or demanding is not.

Play a game such as 'Happy Families' which involves asking other people if they have a particular card. Or hide one of the toys behind your back and the children have to ask questions about it until they can guess what it is. Another game with the same idea is 'Queenie, Queenie, who's got the ball?' Provide them with paper and glue and have an assortment of things like milk bottle tops, short lengths or coloured wool, pasta etc, so that they can practise asking for the things they want for their picture.

## Children

*Aim:* For the children to become familiar with the Luke scripture and deepen their understanding of prayer.

Pin pictures or names of animals/people to the children's backs and set them off to find out who they are by asking other children questions about themselves. (No one is allowed to cheat by giving the answers away!) After a suitable time gather the children and ask each one what they think they are. Unpin them so they can see the full truth.

Talk about the way praying and reading the bible help us get to know what God is like and we'll end up knowing more about ourselves as well. Read the way Jesus taught his friends to pray, and go through the Lord's Prayer simply and clearly so that they know what it means. Use whichever version is most helpful to the children in your group.

Let the children draw round their hands and stick one section of the prayer on each finger, so that they can use their fingers to help them pray. Try this out together, with spaces between the sections to give everyone time to think about what they are saying. Emphasise the truth that they are talking to someone who already knows them well and loves them very much.

1  Our Father in heaven
     hallowed be your name.
2  Let your kingdom come,
3  let your will be done
     on earth as it is in heaven.
4  Give us this day our daily bread,
5  and forgive us our tresspasses
6  as we forgive those who tresspass
     against us.
7  And lead us not into temptation
8  but deliver us from evil.
9  For the kingdom, the power
     and the glory are yours
10 for ever and ever. Amen.

## Young people

*Aim:* For them to learn more about the different aspect of prayer as expressed in the Lord's Prayer – praise and thanksgiving, intercession and petition, penitence and commitment.

First read together Psalm 65 and then the reading from Luke. Discuss some of these points:

Is Jesus praising Mary for being lazy?

What does 'listening' mean if we can't hear Jesus answering us?

In what ways does Jesus speak to us?

What is the Lord's Prayer teaching us about praying?

Go through the Lord's Prayer section by section so that it challenges our present level of prayer and encourages us to pray with more confidence. Suggest that they keep a prayer diary and check it often to see for themselves how God does indeed answer prayer. This session may open up some disappointments, doubts and misunderstandings. Deal honestly and lovingly with each point so that young people who are learning to explore and question their faith can do so in an atmosphere of safety and mutual respect.

# YEAR 2

*Thought for the day:*
*God knows best.*

## Readings
Psalms 65, 67
Nehemiah 2
Matthew 13:24-43

## Reflection

In the parable of the wheat and tares, the servants were all ready to pull up the weeds. It must have seemed the sensible thing to do, especially when they were full of righteous anger at what their enemy had done. Their instinct was to get rid of the evil as quickly as possible The owner's wise decision to let the weeds grow along with the wheat until harvest ensured the protection of the crop, even though there was a risk of the wheat being weakened by the weeds.

Sometimes in our world we look at all the evil and maybe wonder why God doesn't *do* something about it. Why doesn't he tear it away and clean it up so we wouldn't have to fight against it all the time? We learn from this parable that God's ways are not necessarily our ways, and his special care for each person means that he will go to tremendous lengths to save them, even if he gets accused of weakness in the process.

When is it right for us to go charging in with righteous vacuum cleaners or gardening forks and when is it right to leave God to sort things out in his own good time? The only way we can be sure about this is by keeping in close contact with God himself, through times of prayer and quietness, with our hearts adjusted to obedience, whether we agree with his decisions or not.

This is the way Jeremiah lives, with a constant undercurrent of prayer going on beneath his tricky conversations and challenging circumstances. Since he is in touch with God and ready to go along with what God suggests, remarkable good comes out of all kinds of dangerous and discouraging situations. So often we tend to use prayer as a last resort; when prayer comes naturally as the first, middle and last thing we do, we shall start to see dramatic answers to our prayers, and a gradual transformation taking place in our lives.

## Discussion starters

1 When people say such things as 'Well, all we can do now is pray', what does this reveal about their attitude to, and opinion of, God?

2 Why is it that so often our own ideas, plans and solutions seem to differ from the way God wants things done? What can we learn from this that will help us develop as Christians?

## All stage talk

*Theme:* It's good sense to follow God closely because he is in the best position to guide us.

First ask for an intrepid explorer and blindfold the valiant person who volunteers. Now set out an obstacle course which ends with building a tower of three cartons. The course might have chairs to block the way, something to go under or over and the three cartons at the far end, which are to be brought through the obstacles one by one.

Ask for three other volunteers and explain to the explorer that s/he can choose any one of these guides to help them build the tower by going through the obstacle course. The first guide is blindfold and has his legs tied together. The second guide can see but can only see the place where the carton tower will be built. The third guide can see and is able

to move around wherever she likes. The big question is. . . *which guide will the explorer choose?*

Before the explorer chooses, let everyone tell someone near them which guide they would choose and why. Then ask the explorer to decide, and set them off, timing their task to create urgency.

Afterwards explain how God is like the guide who can see and move anywhere he likes. This makes him by far the wisest choice in our lives, because he can see the whole situation, he knows where we are and what our limitations and weaknesses are. He can come alongside us and help us through even the most frightening, or difficult times in our lives.

## Intercessions

Father, we pray for the excited new Christians and the mellow, experienced ones; for the doubting, cynical ones and the hesitant believers.

*Silence for prayer*

In every situation:
**God knows best**

Father, we pray for the responsible and peacemakers in our world, and for the defensive, arrogant and ambitious.

*Silence for prayer*

In every situation:
**God knows best**

Father, we pray for the contented, thriving families and for those struggling to survive each day.

*Silence for prayer*

In every situation:
**God knows best**

Father, we pray for those recovering from surgery and for all those in great pain.

*Silence for prayer*

In every situation:
**God knows best**

Father, we pray for those who have recently died and for those dying now.

*Silence for prayer*

In every situation:
**God knows best**

Father, we thank you and praise you for all the blessings you shower on our lives, and ask you to keep us in closer touch with you from now on.

*Silence for prayer*

In every situation:
**God knows best**

## Other ideas

• Ask two or three people of different age groups and lifestyles to come out and tell quite a simple account of how God has answered their prayer. This doesn't need to be a whole life witness, but rather examples of how the living, active God breaks into our ordinary daily lives. Afterwards everyone can join in an act of thanks and praise, such as the 'Glory be . . .' or a song of praise.

• Three of the flower arrangements can express the parables of the wheat and tares, the yeast in the dough and the tiny mustard seed which grows tall.

## In the crèche

*Aim:* For the children to know that they can pray anywhere at all and God always hears.

Play a game which involves the safety of a home base, such as 'What's the time, Mr Wolf?' Show pictures of baby lambs and chickens which scuttle back to Mum to be safe when there is danger. We can know we are kept safe in God's care.

Help them make a communal book called 'Where I can pray'. Each page has a different place which the children suggest, such as 'I can pray in the bath' or 'I can pray on the swings'.

## Children

*Aim:* To increase the children's understanding of prayer as a valuable thing to do.

Start with a game which involves listening, talking and answering, such as the signature collecting game. Each child is given a sheet with a list of people whose signatures are needed – such as 'someone with red hair' and 'someone who has a green Ford car'.

Now read them the Nehemiah passage, asking them to stand up whenever it mentions that Nehemiah prays. Draw their attention to how Nehemiah is often praying inside while a conversation is going on, and we can do this too whenever we are in a tricky situation. Take a situation like facing a bully in the playground and act it out with two different characters, asking them to freeze every so often while everyone suggests the prayer that might be going on silently. Remind them that God can act to bring good out of the situation if we keep the channels open through prayer.

Now help them make this prayer tree, (shown overleaf) writing their prayer concerns on one side of the leaves. Keep the tree going each week, filling in the date and outcome on the back of the leaves as the answers become apparent. Gradually the children will come to see how God answers prayer, and recognise that some answers take longer than others, and the answer is sometimes 'No' or 'Not yet' or 'This way is better', rather than always what or how we want it to be.

our prayer Tree

# Ascension and Sunday after Ascension

## YEAR 1

*Thought for the day:*
*Having paid for our freedom with his*
*life, Jesus our Saviour enters into the*
*full glory to which he is entitled.*

### Readings
Psalms 108, 110
Isaiah 65:17-end
Revelation 5

### Reflection

Today we are celebrating the moment of Jesus bringing humanity triumphantly into heaven, highlighting the ushering in of a whole new order of things. Isaiah had foreseen the image of creation totally at one with its creator, and when God became humankind at the incarnation the impossible was enabled to happen. As old Simeon could see as he held the baby Jesus in his arms, such an act on the part of God was bound to lead to rejection and suffering and, sure enough, at the crucifixion God's yearning for his people to be reconciled to their maker poured out in the blood of Jesus onto the earth beneath the cross.

So it was that through entering into humanity, God had enabled humanity to enter into the divine in the person of Jesus.

As happens so often in the bible, prophecies are both fulfilled and awaiting fulfilment. Jesus entered into glory at a specific time in history but ever since, up to and including our own time, God continues to draw all things to a glorious

## Young people

*Aim:* To deepen their understanding of payer and the value of living prayerfully.
Beg or borrow the use of a walkie-talkie for today and set up beforehand an Anneka Rice-style treasure hunt within the range of your walkie-talkie. Have two people setting off and the others back at base, keeping in contact with them and helping them to find each clue in turn. Make sure the clues can only be solved with the help of information back at base – perhaps using bible references and codes.

Now discuss what it felt like to be outside, waiting for help from base, and how necessary the contact was between them and base. Talk about how prayer is the vital link between us and God, and how all kinds of coincidences start happening when we keep the channels open and allow our lives to be used for the furthering of God's kingdom.

conclusion through Jesus. The world as we know it will not last for ever; our particular hardships, tragedies and joys will not last for ever either. But we will last. We are part of God's scheduled plan and the way we live our lives will affect the way that plan is carried out.

## Discussion starters

1  Can we hasten the coming of the kingdom? How?

2  Does our world show any indications that the kingdom of God is advancing?

## All stage talk

*Theme:* Only Jesus could do it. And he did.

First ask everyone to imagine that someone has just staggered into church and they've been shot. (You could have a pre-warned accomplice to act this out.) Assure everyone that this is only pretend, but if it happened, what could we do? He might be begging us to help him and get the bullet out (he begs for help) but we know that if Mrs. Eastoe or Mark or David Stowe tried to put things right our poor injured person would probably die (loud moans and more begging for help). Can anyone think of someone who would be able to help him? It would have to be a surgeon at the hospital. So we would get the ambulance, and they would get him into the operating theatre. Now if the surgeon can't be bothered because he's having his lunch and reading the newspaper, our friend will definitely die (feeble moans). But it's much more likely that the surgeon cuts him open very carefully, sews up the bits that need sewing up, and soon our friend is fine again and can go home. (The patient thanks everyone, enthusing over what the surgeon has done for him, and walks out of church waving cheerfully.)

We are all damaged and injured by our selfishness, our guilt, our vanity, bad temper and so on. The only person who can save our lives and set us free to live in harmony with God is someone who is both God and human. Is there anyone who fits that description? Jesus does. Will he want to bother with us lot, though? Yes, he certainly does. Because he loves us, he came to live among us and he died for us. After he came to life again he went back to heaven, and we are joining with all the angels and saints in heaven today in saying, 'Thank you, Jesus – we think what you did was wonderful, and we think you're brilliant, and we love you.' (Or words to that effect.)

## Intercessions

Loving Father, give encouragement, vision and deeper faith to all your followers, so that the church truly expresses your love.

*Silence for prayer*

You are our God:
**with you, nothing is impossible**

Dissolve away all fear, suspicion and greed which lead to corruption in our world.

*Silence for prayer*

You are our God:
**with you, nothing is impossible**

Be present in every home, so that the love increases and each person is given respect and value.

*Silence for prayer*

You are our God:
**with you, nothing is impossible**

Guide those in medical research and bring wholeness to all who are in any way distressed.

*Silence for prayer*

You are our God:
**with you, nothing is impossible**

*Continued overleaf*

Welcome into your heaven all those at the stage of death, and give consolation to their loved ones.

*Silence for prayer*

You are our God:
**with you, nothing is impossible**

Give us a greater sense of your glory so that we can worship you with our whole being.

*Silence for prayer*

You are our God:
**with you, nothing is impossible**

## Other ideas

• The Isaiah passage lends itself well to being read chorally with either a very small group of voices, or by the choir. It needs to be written out with lines allocated to SATB and conducted just like singing. If you've never tried this before, do have a go; it's fun to work at and can bring out the beauty of a passage like this.

• Flower arrangements this week can work on expressing the sense of splendour and glory as Jesus receives the honour due to him. Make them grand and majestic, perhaps incorporating a cross.

• Include a time of 'worshipping in the beauty of holiness'. Gentle worship songs or quiet organ music can lead people down into a time of stillness and silence. It may help to have a focus, such as flowers, candles, water or the ordinary human quality of their own hands as they reverence Jesus and worship him.

## In the crèche

*Aim:* To help them realise that Jesus is there even though they can't see him. Play a peep-bo game with some soft toys, and then with people, pointing out the fact that they are still there, even when they can't be seen. Explain how Jesus is close enough

to talk to all the time, wherever they are, even though we can't see him.

## Children

*Aim:* To help the children understand why Jesus had to go away.

Show the children what looks like a blank sheet of paper, but is in fact invisible writing. (You can use lemon juice for this or an invisible writing pen, widely available from toy shops.) Explain that there is a hidden message on the paper, but they won't be able to receive the message unless something happens first.

Now make the message visible, either by using the other part of the invisible writing pen, or by warming the sheet of paper with a hair drier if it is written in lemon juice. The word that emerges is POWER.

Go over the resurrection appearances and how the disciples saw Jesus going away from them so that he was no longer visible to them. We couldn't receive our message until something happened to the paper. The disciples couldn't receive God's power – the power of his Spirit – unless Jesus left them in that particular time and place. Now he would be available to every person in every country in every age, including us!

Let them experiment with writing secret messages and making them visible again. Then give them a fresh sheet of paper on which they write in invisible ink: JESUS IS HERE. This is one for their family to discover at home.

## Young people

*Aim:* To help them understand what the Ascension was and what it means. Start by having a whistle-stop tour through all the accounts of the Ascension, noting what features are similar in each and what different details each supply.

Try to glean from the accounts the important things which are being said – that Jesus is victorious; he has won the battle against sin and death and is given authority to reign. Then look at these discussion starters:

Why didn't Jesus go straight up to heaven when he rose from the dead?

Why didn't he make sure everybody saw him?

I suggest that rather than working as a whole group for this part, you have people in small groups of two or three, so as to enable everyone to join in. Share some of the discussion points in the whole group afterwards.

# YEAR 2

*Thought for the day:*
*Christ's amazing humility is to be our perfect example.*
### Readings
Psalms 108, 110
Jeremiah 31:1-13
Philippians 2:1-8

## Reflection

In the Old Testament Jeremiah describes the lovely serenity of living in harmony with God. Instead of their religion being an empty ritual with overmuch importance invested in outward signs, the exile will leave the people of Israel spiritually leaner and fitter. They will be able to enjoy life as God intended as they live in obedience to him, delighting to do things his way.

With the coming of Christ, this prophecy takes on new significance for the new people of God. Christ's breathtaking journey of humility has brought him to the point of jeering rejection and a cursed death. Yet through it all his love continues to flood outwards, taking him through all this to the complete and glorious life which we are invited to share.

No wonder he is exalted to the highest place, worthy of all our honour, worship and love. Even as we marvel at such humility, we realise that Christ is calling us to live out our lives in the same way.

## Discussion starters

1 Do we dare to put aside all the credibility, popularity or status we crave in order to follow Christ in such a total, self-emptying way? Do we even want to?

2 Look at each area of your life and tackle any weeds of self-deception, self-seeking or ambition you find. In God's presence, with your eyes fixed on Christ, lay them aside and ask God to fill the emptied areas with love.

## All stage talk

*Theme:* Through suffering to glory – dangerous journeys.

First ask for a couple of volunteers to start balloons off from the back of the church and ask everyone to try to pass these balloons up across the seats to the front without letting them drop to the floor or go backwards.

Then talk about how it feels to start at the bottom again when you change schools, go to a different area or have to change your job after being made redundant. Rather like the balloons, you feel a bit wobbly and vulnerable, and are not sure if you'll be able to manage.

Jesus, the Word, or expression of God, had been present when our universe first began. He knew all about the excitement of stars bursting into being, planets being formed and all the ideas of creation taking shape. But so as to put us right and give us life that wouldn't end, he was quite prepared to put all that aside and become a human baby, starting at the weakest level. God was willing to become one of the creatures he had made.

It was bound to be a very dangerous journey, because he was depending on people, and people can let you down. People can be dangerous, people can kill. (Pop the balloons.) God knew the risk he was taking, but because he loved us he reckoned we were worth the risk. The worst happened, and some people hated the goodness and love they saw in Jesus. Jesus allowed himself to be killed, but death couldn't hold the God of life. He came to life again having won the terrible battle against evil for us. He will be alive now for ever, reigning over us, loving us and living both in heaven and in our lives when we let him in.

## Intercessions

In every church, in every Christian, we long for God's love to blossom.
*Silence for prayer*
Amen:
**let your glorious will be done**

In every country, in everyone who has influence and authority,
we long for God's wisdom to prevail.
*Silence for prayer*
Amen:
**let your glorious will be done**

In every home, in every neighbourhood, we long for God's forgiveness to flourish.
*Silence for prayer*
Amen:
**let your glorious will be done**

In every hospital, in every suffering person, we long for God's healing to comfort and restore.
*Silence for prayer*
Amen:
**let your glorious will be done**

In everyone who mourns; in all who are dying, we long for God's peace to come.
*Silence for prayer*
Amen:
**let your glorious will be done**

In all our joys, our sorrows and our choices, we rejoice that God is indeed in control.
*Silence for prayer*
Amen:
**let your glorious will be done**

## Other ideas

• In the second reading, have one person to read verses 1-5, one half of the congregation to read together verses 6-8, and the other half of the congregation to read verses 9-11. The reading could either end here, or be finished by the first reader.

## In the crèche

*Aim:* To help them understand that God is here even though we can't see him. And to give God thanks and praise.
Play some peep-bo games with younger children, where they can enjoy the excitement and reassurance of things and people disappearing and appearing again. Talk to somebody who is out of view so that everyone knows they are still

there. Tell them that Jesus is here, even though we can't see him, and have a lively thanks and praise time with instruments and dancing.

## Children

*Aim:* For them to learn how Jesus persevered right to the bitter end so as to win the victory over evil.

Begin by playing a game such as crab football or wastepaper basket-ball, in which one team is aiming to get through to the goal while the other team are trying to stop them.

Point out how games like this are like our life as Christians, when we are aiming to do what is God's will but it isn't always easy, and sometimes evil seems to be winning. Also, they may notice how the team members help one another, which is what happens to us - Christians and all the saints help and encourage one another along the way.

Now read the passage from Philippians, and point out how Jesus was not going to give up, however difficult or dangerous things got.

Help them to make this game to play at home to remind them.

## Young people

*Aim:* Help them to understand that Jesus is in glory and his kingdom is spreading.

First read the Jeremiah passage and talk about how it can sometimes be good for us to have to put up with hardship and discomfort from time to time. Make a list of what good can come out of such situations.

Now look at the Philippians passage, reading it in two parts as suggested in the Other ideas section. Have some world maps which are marked to show how Christianity has spread outwards from Jerusalem. Talk about how God's kingdom is still spreading, and if possible show some pictures of worship in areas where Christianity is growing fast at the moment. What aspects of our society have been changed for good through the influence of Christians? What prevents more being done?

Pray for all Christians who are deeply involved with peace-making, justice, aid and so on, and write letters or postcards of encouragement to them.

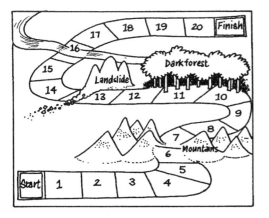

# PENTECOST

# *YEARS 1 AND 2*

*Thought for the day:*
*When God's Spirit is poured out on*
*his people, it shows.*

## *Readings*
Psalm 68:1-20
Joel 2:21-end
Romans 8:1-17

## *Reflection*

Most of us live with a sneaking suspicion that if we tried a bit harder we would be able to conquer all our bad habits. What is really happening is that we don't like to admit to ourselves that we are not completely in control, and prefer to think of ourselves as comfortably lazy instead. Sometimes we decide to make that extra effort, and there are plenty of DIY books just waiting to tell us how to make the most of ourselves, how to improve our memories, or how to organise our housework and our finances. Gradually the rather depressing truth dawns on us that however good the rules and advice, we still end up bound by our weaknesses, habits and sins.

So what's the answer? Do we go back to self-deception, or melt into despair at facing the truth? Happily we need do neither of these things. God already knows exactly what our faults and failings are and he also knows that by ourselves we are never going to be able to unlock the prison we are in. That is why he came alongside us in the Incarnation, and bought our freedom at the expense of his life. The thing that we can't do, he does for us; with God's Spirit inhabiting us the whole set-up changes.

Whereas, left to ourselves and our own resources, we fail with depressing regularity to change our deep-seated habits and weaknesses, God's indwelling Spirit actually uses our weaknesses for good, and enables us to tackle the impossible successfully. A lot of this happens through changed attitudes - through the confidence of knowing we are completely accepted and forgiven. As we experience the love God has for us we become healed of all that started those habits in the first place.

## *Discussion starters*

1 Jesus doesn't invade or gag our characters when he lives in us. He sets us free to be more fully ourselves. What might this mean for those who are bossy?/gossip-mongers?/addicts?

2 Does receiving God's Spirit mean that we shall never sin again? How will those filled with God's Spirit cope with sin in their lives?

## *All stage talk*

*Theme:* 'I will pour out my Spirit on all people'.

Protect the demonstration area with a ground sheet before starting the talk, just in case of spills. Have lots of buckets, jugs and mugs available, some empty and some with water in them.

Begin by explaining that all these represent people who go to church and are Christians. Sometimes, sadly, people may know all about Jesus, when he lived and what was and wasn't written about him, what everything in church is called and so on, but they are empty inside (tip the jug up). If anyone goes to them for a drink of God's love (try it), the person needing the drink will go away thirsty – they won't be able to get refreshed or comforted or healed or loved because the person they thought could help them is all dried up inside.

Let's try another Christian. (Try another container.) That's much better – this Christian is full of the loving Spirit of God so the thirsty person will come into close contact with God's love through them.

Look at all the different shapes of containers. We don't have to be a special shape of Christian to qualify. We may be simple or dramatic (choose containers to emphasise this), tall or short, Evangelical or Catholic. God is delighted to pour his Spirit into all of these, but one thing is necessary for all of us: we need to go to the source to be filled. We need to tell God that we want him to fill us with his living Spirit, and when he starts to, we need to keep ourselves open so that he can. He may fill us full in a rush, or he may gently fill us bit by bit; however he chooses to do it will be the very best way for us.

## Intercessions

As we still our bodies and open ourselves to God we think of the church leaders, preachers and all who minister to God's people. With them and for them we pray. . .

*Silence for prayer*

Spirit of the living God:
**fall afresh on us**

We think of all the world's nations, the problems, quarrels, misunderstandings and mistakes. With them and for them we pray . . .

*Silence for prayer*

Spirit of the living God:
**fall afresh on us**

We think of those in our family, those we like and those we seem to annoy. With them and for them we pray . . .

*Silence for prayer*

Spirit of the living God:
**fall afresh on us**

We think of those in hospitals and hospices, outpatients at the local accident centre and those ill at home. With them and for them we pray . . .

*Silence for prayer*

Spirit of the living God:
**fall afresh on us**

We think of those who are close to death, those who have recently died and those who miss them. With them and for them we pray . . .

*Silence for prayer*

Spirit of the living God:
**fall afresh on us**

We think of all your amazing creation, from the microscopic to the cosmic, and remember with thankfulness that we are part of this glory you have made.

*Silence for prayer*

Spirit of the living God:
**fall afresh on us**

## Other ideas

Use the medium of dance and music to show the way God's Spirit spreads out amongst his people as they live in the power of his love.

Have six to eight people in their ordinary clothes, and representative of different age groups, genders and personalities. One other dancer wears white and represents the person of Christ. This dancer goes to stand next to a cross in the church. The others begin from different places all over the church, some on their own and others in small groups. It is particularly effective to have them simply getting up from wherever they are sitting, and making their way towards a central, visible place where they move into a tableau of praying Christians. Have someone standing with arms raised, someone kneeling with head bowed, someone sitting with palms upturned and so on, so that many different Christian traditions are represented. Play a reflective hymn or song either live or on tape as the dancers hold their positions and the dancer representing the person of Christ walks slowly down to the praying group. As this dancer approaches, the others become aware of his/her presence and greet him/her and then each other with a sign of peace. They then turn outwards and walk out to the different parts of the church, passing on the greeting of peace and indicating that these people can pass the peace to others in their row.

## In the crèche

*Aim:* To celebrate the joy of God being with us.

Help the children to make or decorate some shakers and jangly instruments and then have some lively songs and dances, using taped music and live percussion if you can stand noisy rejoicing.

## Children

*Aim:* To understand and celebrate what happened at Pentecost.

First help the children to make these streamers and then read or tell the Pentecost story, with the children using their streamers at the appropriate places.

Then have a lively time of singing and dancing, using their streamers and some of these songs:

Jesus is greater than the greatest heroes

The Holy Spirit sets my feet a-dancing
I am a new creation
We are one in the Spirit
(and there are lots of others).

Move from the lively praise into a time of worship, settling down and singing something like:

Jesus, Jesus let me tell you what I know
Father, we love you
All of my heart

Peg to fix crepe paper together. Tie string round peg, hold string and swing streamer.

Two lengths of crepe paper or ribbon

## Young people

*Aim:* To see how Joel's prophecy is fulfilled.

First look at the reading from Joel, and then go straight on to the Pentecost story, taking note of the way they link up. Look at the signs of God's Spirit among his people in Acts, and in God's people today. Be careful that they do not get so stuck into the specific signs that they miss the all-important sign of love.

# Trinity Sunday

## YEARS 1 AND 2

*Thought for the day:*
*God is creator, redeemer and life-giver*
*all at once, in every situation.*

## Readings

Psalms 29, 33
Exodus 34:1-10
Acts 2:22-36

## Reflection

It is no mistake that Pentecost is followed by Trinity Sunday. An outpouring of God's Spirit works in us to create a desire to seek God so as to understand and love him more deeply. There are plenty of clues in his behaviour and his creation, his words and his followers. Following such clues we find God to be utterly faithful to his promises, compassionate to all in need, completely just and completely merciful.

We can express all this as God who is Father, Son and Holy Spirit, but in a sense this is shorthand for describing a God so great that he is indescribable. The Trinity helps us to remember that our God encompasses more than any human 'one' can. We are always in danger of over-emphasising one particular aspect of God and under-emphasising the others. The Trinity enables us to hold to a more balanced view of God.

But we must never lose sight of the fact that we cannot button up God's existence by anything we say about him, however profound; for the more we come to know about him, the more we will realise there is to discover.

## Discussion starters

1 The Exodus reading makes it clear that Moses had a remarkable under-standing of God. What can we learn from Moses' life which might give us some advice for ways in which we could grow closer to the God we worship?

2 Think of church architecture through the centuries and see how this has expressed in solid form the aspects of God which have been emphasised at different times. What are the dangers of highlighting aspects of God?

## All stage talk

Begin by asking a couple of volunteers to take part in a guessing game. Give one person a note with the name of an animal written on it. This person tries to describe the animal to the other person, who has to guess what the animal is. If you have access to an OHP or flip chart you could get the second person to draw what they hear being described. You could have two or three goes at this, or you could ask everyone in the congregation to pair up and play the game. The way you do it will depend on the expectations and nature of the congregation!

Now fix a cardboard pair of rabbit ears on a volunteer and explain how we all tend to describe things in terms of what we know already. We would probably describe a rabbit as being furry with long ears because our own ears are short, and we are generally lacking in fur. Ask for suggestions as to how a rabbit might describe a human? (It might be something like a bald rabbit with very short ears.)

It's even harder trying to describe someone we have never seen, like God. It's difficult, but we do our best by looking at the world he has created and picking up clues from this. What can we tell about God by (a) looking at his creation? (Write these qualities up for everyone to see.) (b) Looking at Jesus? (Write these qualities too.) (c) Looking at the working of the Holy Spirit? (Add these qualities.)

When we worship the Trinity we are remembering all these qualities in the God we love.

## Intercessions

Holy God, we come to plead for the church in its weakness and lack of unity; may we be one as you are one.

*Silence for prayer*

Holy God:
**we trust in your goodness**

Holy God, we come to plead for our world in its confusion and injustices.

*Silence for prayer*

Holy God:
**we trust in your goodness**

Holy God, we come to plead for our families and friends
in their needs and difficulties.

*Silence for prayer*

Holy God:
**we trust in your goodness**
Holy God, we come to plead for those who suffer in their pain and weariness.

*Silence for prayer*

Holy God:
**we trust in your goodness**

Holy God, we come to plead for the dying and the bereaved
in their grief and loneliness.

*Silence for prayer*

Holy God:
**we trust in your goodness**

Holy God, we come to plead for the coming of your kingdom
in every place and in every person.

*Silence for prayer*

Holy God:
**we trust in your goodness**

## Other ideas

Use the qualities of God explored during the All stage talk and invite everyone to savour those qualities with thankfulness as they say them aloud together. Everyone will be proclaiming different qualities at different times, so there will be a general murmur or shout of praise which will die away into silent adoration.

## In the crèche

*Aim:* To help them understand what God is like through looking at his creation. Have lots of lovely pictures and books available, and if possible take the children around outside to look at the sky, plants and flowers. As you enjoy all these things, talk about how lovely they are and how lovely God must be who thought of them and made them happen.

## Children

*Aim:* To help them understand more about God's nature.

Have a large sheet of paper entitled: 'What we know about God'. A long strip of lining or wall paper is ideal, and the larger the paper, the larger their writing can be. Sit all along both sides of the paper, with a variety of felt tip pens available. Talk together about what God is like, and have every right idea written down colourfully on the paper. If they need some help, see what they can work out from the way the universe is created, the way we are created, the way Jesus behaved and the way God's friends behave.

Have some quiet music playing as all the characteristics of God are read out in turn. Compare these with what Peter says in his post-Pentecost sermon and with what Moses knew of God. Phrases from the psalms can be used instead.

Using felt tips, stickers, or paints and photos, fill in the areas between the words, so that the whole sheet of paper is a blaze of colour expressing the character of God.

## Young people

*Aim:* To explore how the Trinity came to be expressed as such.

Begin by having a juggling session, using light scarves, juggling balls, rolled up socks or anything else 'jugglable'. Make sure there are enough for everyone to have a go, and see if anyone can manage to keep three balls going at once. Enjoy their performance.

Have the doxology written up so everyone can see it. They may well have come across this during worship; say it together now. Look into the meaning to discover how many people are being worshipped in this prayer. Encourage discussion about what the Trinity explains, and point out that in a way this is like trying to juggle with ideas about God. We are attempting to hold all our knowledge of God at once, so as to keep as close to the truth as possible

Look at Peter's sermon after the coming of the Holy Spirit, to see how the idea is expressed of God being three persons yet one God.

Work out together what you believe about God the Father, God the Son and God the Holy Spirit, and form this into a chant, rap or set of responses that could be used in worship as a statement of faith.

# 2nd Sunday after Pentecost

## YEAR 1

*Thought for the day:*
*There's no better feeling than being restored to the God who loves you and to whom you belong.*

## Readings

Psalms 85,133
Deuteronomy 30:1-10
Matthew 18:10-22

## Reflection

The passage from Deuteronomy looks longingly towards a time when external laws and punishments will no longer be needed, because people will have God's law within them. Alongside that longing, which we all share, is the messy, sordid, bickering and vengeful world we all inhabit. In Matthew 18 we can sympathise with Peter as he asks the obvious human question and Jesus answers with the impossible answer – we are to go on forgiving and forgiving just as long as there is something and someone to forgive.

We know from the lost sheep's perspective how lovely it is to be found. We are used to seeing Jesus the good shepherd searching until the straying sheep is retrieved.

But Matthew follows this parable with Jesus' teaching on how we are to do a spot of good shepherding ourselves. Sometimes in our enthusiasm for preaching the gospel we can end up driving lost sheep scuttling down ravines instead of approaching them with understanding, noticing where the brambles have caught them and carefully untangling them. Sometimes we must expect to get cut and bruised as we scramble over sharp rocks to reach out and catch hold of lost sheep. And if all else fails, and the lost sheep refuse to be brought back, Jesus advises treating them as pagans or tax collectors. Does this mean reject them? I think not, for how, according to Jesus, are we to treat tax collectors and sinners? Surely as those who are sick and need a doctor; they are to be prayed for and loved. The forgiving goes on and on.

## Discussion starters

1  Are we able to forgive others better than we are able to forgive ourselves?

2  Do we put into practice Jesus' guidelines for dealing with people who sin against us – both as individuals and within our local church community? Have we any systematic strategy or do we fight shy of tackling the problems through embarrassment? Is there any way we could improve matters?

## All stage talk

*Theme:* Belonging.

Pick out two people of any age who belong to the same family and look alike or are wearing similar clothes. Tell everyone that they are from the same family. How can we tell? (Looks/mannerisms/clothes etc.)

Now ask someone to pick out a scout/rainbow. How can we tell? (Uniform.) If I wore a scout uniform would I be a scout? What else is needed? I need to make my promise. As Christian we do that.

Could I be one of the Smith family? (No.) What if I made a promise? That's still not enough. For me to be one of the Smith family Mr and Mrs Smith would have to adopt me, and then I would be.

That's what God does. What is his son's name? (Jesus.) And God has adopted us as his sons and daughters, which makes us all brothers and sisters of one another and of Jesus, which makes us feel secure and comfortable and loved. That makes us want to behave lovingly to one another, because we're all 'family'. So we look after one another and forgive one another like Father does.

## Intercessions

Father, we lay before you our longing for many to know the joy and freedom of your service, and we remember the needs of all who minister your love and teaching.

*Silence for prayer*

The Lord will indeed:
**give what is good**

We lay before you our loathing of corruption and injustice, and remember the needs of all peace makers, negotiators, leaders and advisers.

*Silence for prayer*

The Lord will indeed:
**give what is good**

We lay before you our concern for all broken families, all children being raised in turmoil, and we remember the needs of all parents.

*Silence for prayer*

The Lord will indeed:
**give what is good**

We lay before you our desire to help those whose lives or bodies are broken through war or abuse and we remember the needs of all victims.

*Silence for prayer*

The Lord will indeed:
**give what is good**

We lay before you our memories
of those we love who have died,
and entrust them to your everlasting care.

*Silence for prayer*

The Lord will indeed:
**give what is good**

We lay before you our thankfulness
for the way you come to search for us
whenever we are lost.

*Silence for prayer*

The Lord will indeed:
**give what is good**

## Other ideas

As the summary of the Law, sing these words as a round, to the tune of 'London's burning':

> You shall love the Lord your God with
> all your heart and all your mind and
> all your strength! All your strength!
> And love your neighbour,
> and love your neighbour.

This is even more exciting when sung with actions, and the round can be split four ways if you're feeling brave, so the whole church ends up full of each section of the law all at once, with a visual, as well as an aural round.

## In the crèche

*Aim:* To enjoy the sense of belonging.

Have two or three hoops (or lengths of string) and sort all the toys and pencils into sets – perhaps soft and hard, or blue and red. Make sure there is something that doesn't fit in and ends up feeling the odd one out. Talk about how horrid this feels when it happens to us.

Make a new category so that everything is included and belongs. Jesus's love is like a big cuddle around us, and no one is left outside. Have a friendly, joining in song, such as the 'Hokey Cokey'.

## Children

*Aim:* For them to understand Jesus' teaching on forgiveness.

Take the disciples' question – 'How many times should we forgive someone when they have sinned against us?' Work out Jesus' answer as a sum, and explain that this means every time.

Ask if any of them can remember having to forgive someone for something. It is important that children are allowed to talk seriously about such things, because forgiving is hard whatever our age, especially if the wounding is deep. If we are not careful, and talk too glibly about forgiving, they may assume it's easy for adults and feel guilty for struggling and failing. They need their leaders to be quite frank about how difficult it can be, and how we sometimes have to keep working at it. They also need to know that we can all ask God to help us – giving us the grace we need to enable us to forgive others.

Look at the guidelines Jesus gave us about forgiving in the lost sheep story by telling the story with some props or felt shapes on the story mat, and making a note of what we have to do if we're good shepherds. (e.g. Wanting things to be put right, making the effort to go after them or make the first move in patching up a quarrel, being prepared to spend time on them, and being prepared to get a bit bruised and muddy.)

Then the children can make a sheep each to remind them, using card and cotton wool.

## Young people

*Aim:* For them to understand Jesus' teaching on forgiveness.

Start by reading Deuteronomy, and then go straight on to the Matthew passage, noticing how in the real world we don't seem to have God's law in our hearts fully, so there is a desperate need to know what to do when we are sinned against. Jesus' teaching on forgiveness is backed up by his previous story of the lost sheep, and goes in for sensitivity, understanding and compassion, rather than condemnation. For us all, this is easier said than done!

Talk together about the difficulties we have in forgiving and look at some of the world's current problems to see if sinning against and/or lack of forgiveness are the cause. They nearly always are.

Using Jesus' parable and his direct teaching, sort out some practical ways in which we could work at our reactions to being insulted, ignored, gossiped about or otherwise sinned against.

# YEAR 2

*Thought for the day:*
*In Christ we can all belong – he has broken the barriers down.*

## Readings

Psalms 85,133
Ezekiel 37:15-end
Ephesians 2:11-end

## Reflection

Most of us have been left out or rejected at one time or another. For some this may have been a brief sense of isolation, while for others there may have been a harrowing experience of not being acceptable, which has dominated relationships and damaged our ability to trust. And that is a hard road to travel on.

Our need to belong somewhere, our need to be at one with others, is deep and instinctive. So we can feel an almost physical yearning with the broken, desolate people of Israel as we read such phrases as 'I will be their God and they will be my people'.

Ezekiel, speaking in the language of pictures, shows by the sticks how the split nations will be restored. A hand holds both sticks together and makes them one. The hand held a special significance of strength and authority, and it is as God takes these separate nations quite literally 'in hand' that they become one through his power and authority.

The Ephesians reading picks up the same idea, as it is 'in Christ' that both Jews and Gentiles can become one. Wherever there are barriers which cause differences, wherever there are wounds of rejection, in Christ's power and authority they can be healed. It is the healing power of love which unites us and enables a very motley bunch to be built into one body.

## Discussion starters

1   Look at a chart of events in the Old Testament to see what had happened to the people of Israel to make them two separate sticks and where they are when this prophecy was written.

2   How can your church ensure that visitors sense the truth of Ephesians 2?

## All stage talk

*Theme:* We are made one in Christ.

Have ready some pieces of card with these diagrams on them:

Explain that we often spend time looking at what is supposed to happen in life. Today we are going to look at what actually happens, more often than not. Ask six volunteers to make up the first diagram. Here are all these nice friends, and before long they start getting cross with one another and having arguments and upsetting one another. (Ask them each to find an adversary from within the group.)

Give one of each couple a red team band to wear, and give the others blue bands. Explain that all this blue-banded lot get together and feel at one because they have a common enemy – all those other horrors with red bands. (They move into diagram 2.) Then the isolated people with red bands find they have grievances in common and move together. (Form diagram 3.) Within their own groups they can feel really acceptable by being different from and superior to the other group – and can we think of some real life examples of this? (Such things as racial prejudice, gangs, exclusive sects and tribes.)

What happens when a strong outsider arrives on the scene, trying to make peace? (Ask one to join in.) What often happens is that now the two groups join up so as to fight the common enemy. (Move into diagram 4.) They have become united and put aside their differences, emphasising now what they have in common against the new enemy – they all have bands and she doesn't. Can we think of some real life examples of this? (A coalition government during war, or civil rights campaigns.) It's a very human way to behave, and it means a lot of people spend their lives fighting.

Jesus can help. He draws us all together so that no one is left out, and we all have a common enemy which is evil. At our baptism we are asked, 'Do you renounce evil?' and we reply, 'We renounce evil!' (Try this now.) Together in Christ's love and power, we are made one.

## Intercessions

We remember all the clusters of Christians in our area, and pray that we may truly be one in Christ.

*Silence for prayer*

Hear, O Lord:
**and answer our prayer**

We remember all the areas of violence and hostility in our world, and pray for peace between nations and individual people.

*Silence for prayer*

Hear, O Lord:
**and answer our prayer**

We remember all families struggling against poverty, inadequate accommodation or illness, and pray that you will show us how best to help them.

*Silence for prayer*

Hear, O Lord:
**and answer our prayer**

We remember the vulnerable and the ignored, the outcasts and the oppressed and pray that we may open our hearts to loving involvement.

*Silence for prayer*

Hear, O Lord:
**and answer our prayer**

We remember those who have died and their loved ones, and pray that you will comfort all sorrow.

*Silence for prayer*

Hear, O Lord:
**and answer our prayer**

We remember with joy your constant loving and forgiveness, and pray that we may show our praise
not only with our lips but in our lives.

*Silence for prayer*

Hear, O Lord:
**and answer our prayer**

## Other ideas

Ask everyone to come to church with one flower or piece of foliage. (It's as well to have some spares available for those who forget.) During the singing of something like 'Bind us together', 'We are one in the Spirit', 'Lord, you have my heart' or 'When I look into your holiness', have a slow procession of God's people bringing their flowers to the front and placing them in a bucket of water. Then one or two of the noble tribe of flower arrangers set to work making a work of beauty out of this varied collection.

## In the crèche

*Aim:* For them to understand that Jesus breaks down the barriers between us. Using a blackboard and chalk or OHP, draw the children a story about barriers making people miserable. Here is one basic idea, but do make it your own by adding to it appropriately for your children.

Two very different characters live next door to one another. As they are so different they build a high wall between them. Now they feel sad and lonely; (change their expressions). They both pray about being sad and lonely, and ask Jesus to give them a friend. Jesus gives them an idea – they think of each other! So they work together to break down the wall and make it into a beautiful rockery where flowers grow. Now they have a friend and are happy again.

## Children

*Aim:* For them to understand the meaning of Jew, Gentile and Christian, and look at who can be what.

First talk about the different surnames in the group, listing them as you do so, with all the different Christian names under the surname headings, so one family name may have several names listed.

Play a game where everyone is moving about until you call a family name. Only the members of that family carry on moving, the others must freeze.

Explain that we are members of that family because we were born or adopted into it, and that when we read about the Jews in the bible, it means people who were born as members of the Jewish race which could be traced right back to Abraham. No one else could be a Jew, and God chose this people to work through. Through them all the other nations of the world would eventually be saved.

Have two hoops labelled 'Jews' and 'Gentiles' and explain that the Jews were God's people of Israel and the Gentiles were everyone else. Have some names written on small cards, and ask the children to work out where they should go. Suggestions for names: Abraham, Goliath, Joseph, Moses, Pharaoh, Jesus, Mary, Peter, Paul, St. Francis and the names of the children.

Now take the hoops and names away and replace them with one hoop labelled 'Christian – a follower of Christ'. Scatter around the hoop these labels; men, women, boys, girls, people with black skin, people with pink skin, people who go to (West Leigh) school, people who support (an approved) football club, people who support (a rival) football club, Jews, Arabs, Indian people. Ask them to put into the hoop those they think can be Christians, and leave outside those who can't. (This may be interesting.) Draw them to the realisation that *everybody* can be a Christian, whether they are born as Jews or Gentiles. Now stick all the names in place inside a large circle painted on a sheet of paper and label the poster:

EVERYBODY CAN BE A CHRISTIAN
IF THEY CHOOSE – NO ONE
IS LEFT OUT.

Pray together for the different peoples of our earth, using a globe or globe/beachball and passing it round as you sing, 'He's got the whole world in his hands'.

## Young people

*Aim:* To help them understand the reasons for splits in God's people, both then and now.

Beforehand search out some clear maps of Old Testament events. I have found these particularly helpful:

> *The Atlas of the Bible* – Readers' Digest
> *Atlas of Bible History* – Lion
> *The New Bible Atlas* – Lion

Begin by having a short anecdotal discussion of times when they and you have been in the kind of awful situation that doesn't seem to have any hope of a solution.

Using the maps and information books explain how the kingdom came to be split, and take the story as far as the exile. At this point read together the passage from Ezekiel, so that they will be better able to appreciate how the people would have felt as they heard this prophecy. Follow this with the New Testament reading to see how the prophecy came true.

What about now? Collect a list of all the different Christian denominations they can think of and talk together about the sadness of disunity in the church and the need for unity, rather than uniformity. Make note of ideas which come out of discussion as you think prayerfully about what we can do to draw Christians together, and look at what is already happening. If it seems appropriate, plan the outline of an interdenominational activity and worship which could be used in the not too distant future.

# 3rd Sunday after Pentecost

# YEAR 1

*Thought for the day:*
*New life means revolution, and it can only happen through God's freely given power.*

## Readings

Psalms 11,20
Micah 3:5-end
Matthew 5:27-end

## Reflection

As we read these passages we sense how slippery the ground is under our feet once God's values and standards are disregarded. No one knows where they are any more; trust is eroded and community structure breaks down. It is, sadly, a familiar picture and we can see this happening all around us today. It seems to carry its own momentum, and we look on with a feeling of helplessness as we find accepted behaviour careering further and further away from God's values; where nothing is fixed and all is relative, and based on self. More and more laws, externally imposed, are manifestly not the solution, and today's readings point us towards the real and only effective answer.

They all talk of change at the level of the heart, rather than rule-keeping; they involve an inner revolution which replaces 'self' at the centre with 'God', so that increasingly we can live our lives in the way God does – as 'chips off the old block'.

No one is suggesting that this will happen easily, or all at once. No one is pretending that we won't make blunders or bad decisions, even after we have committed ourselves to following Christ and renouncing evil. But it will be a question of grazing our knees rather than falling headlong, because when our hearts are centred on God we will not be able to continue in sin – it will hurt us and distress us too much. Living God's way will certainly put us in the front line before long, because our values and personal ethics will not necessarily tone in with the accepted behaviour of our society. This may either result in a kind of persecution, or involve us in a personal struggle to do things God's way when temptation is severe. We could never cope with this on our own, and happily we don't have to. God provides us with the necessary strength, and will always lead us beside still waters when our drooping spirits need reviving.

## Discussion starters

1   In the Micah passage, what made God especially disturbed by the prophets, leaders and judges?

2   Do you find that Jesus' teaching on how we should live seems excessively strict? How on earth does he expect us to keep to his rulings?

## All stage talk

*Theme:* Holding on for dear life.

Beforehand, beg or borrow a ballet student or two from a local dance school and ask them to work out a short routine of exercises at the barre.

Begin by introducing the students, and starting the exercise routine at the barre. Then interview them, to find out about why they need the barre there.

Point out that we have been hearing about all sorts of difficult rules to live up to in our lives, and if we try them on our own we'll probably wobble all over the place and fall right over.

But Jesus is saying that he understands that; he knows we will need something to hold on to for support, and he isn't expecting us to be out there on our own.

New life in Christ means having Christ and his strength to hang on to during the difficult times each day when it's very hard to do what is right.

Ask the dancers to do one of the barre exercises again as everyone thinks of something they find hard to do in God's way – like always telling the truth, talking about people behind their backs without being critical, noticing jobs that need doing or spending money wisely – and remembers to use the 'barre' of God's love and firm support next time.

## Intercessions

Father, in our Christian ministry to one another we need more discernment and less defensiveness, more stillness and less rush.

*Silence for prayer*

Father, teach us:
**to live life your way**

Father, in our national and international affairs we need more listening and less bullying, more giving and less taking, more co-operation and less thirst for revenge.

*Silence for prayer*

Father, teach us:
**to live life your way**

Father, in our relationships we need more understanding and less intolerance, more encouragement and less condemnation.

*Silence for prayer*

Father, teach us:
**to live life your way**

Father, in our pain we need your comfort,
in our brokenness your forgiveness,
in our anguish the assurance of your love.

*Silence for prayer*

Father, teach us:
**to live life your way**

Father, at the hour of our death
we need your presence and your mercy.

*Silence for prayer*

Father, teach us:
**to live life your way**

Father, in you our every need is met and
satisfied, and we thank you for the
personal love you have for each one of us.

*Silence for prayer*

Father, teach us:
**to live life your way**

## Other ideas

Use the dance students (or your home
grown produce) to do these actions to a
sung Lord's Prayer.

Our Father
who art in heaven
Hallowed be thy name
Thy kingdom come
Thy will be done
as it is in heaven

(Look down)
(Look up)

Give us this day our daily bread
and forgive us our trespasses
as we forgive those
who trespass against us
and lead us not into temptation
but deliver us from evil
For thine is the Kingdom,
the power and the glory
for ever and ever.

Amen

(Cup hands)

(Move arms slowly upwards
and raise heads at the same
time)

## In the crèche

*Aim:* For them to understand that Jesus
helps us to do what is right and loving.
Try drawing a picture of an animal which
keeps going wrong, so you scrumple up
the paper and throw it away several
times. Get fed up about it – you don't
think you'll ever be able to get it right.

Someone offers you a template or a
stencil and then you can't help getting it
right because the edges guide your
crayon. Let the children know that when
they find it really hard to be kind or share
their toys or stop sulking, they can ask
Jesus to help and he will guide them to
live lovingly, just as the template guided
your drawing.

Have lots of stencils or templates and
a variety of coloured papers and crayons
to make pictures with.

## Children

*Aim:* To look at how Jesus' teaching to love
your enemies turns things inside out.
Show a quick clip of Tom and Jerry from a
video, or some pictures from a comic strip.
Why is Tom Jerry's enemy? How can they
tell? Talk about other enemies they know
about and/or have, and how that can be
seen by the resulting behaviour.

Explain what the Jews had been
taught about how to treat their enemies
(hate them).

Now read the passage from Matthew
about loving your enemies as well as your
friends, which really turns our normal
behaviour inside out. Jesus doesn't say we
mustn't have enemies; but he does tell us
to love them if we have them!

Give the children these bags to make, which turn inside out to show God's way of living.

Plain material   Bright material

A. Cut with pinking shears

B. Sew together with dull fabric on outside

C. Turn inside out to show bright fabric

## Young people

*Aim:* To explore the teaching in Matthew 5 with reference to their own lives and decisions.

Start by reading the passage from Matthew 5, looking up the Old Testament references as you go. (They are: v.27 – Exodus 20:14; v.31 – Deuteronomy 24:1; v.33 – Leviticus 19:12; v.38 – Exodus 21:24, Leviticus 24:20, Deuteronomy 19:21; and v.43 – Leviticus 19:18.)

Make it clear that Jesus was not smashing the old law, but explaining its true meaning; he was helping his listeners to get at the spirit, rather than the letter of the law, as the Pharisees' teaching tended to do.

Go through the sections one by one, jotting down their ideas about what the spirit of these laws might be in our own lives.

# YEAR 2

*Thought for the day:*
*The kingdom of God is righteousness taking root in individuals and so affecting the whole of society for good.*

## Readings

Psalms 11,20
Isaiah 32:1-8
Mark 4:21-end

## Reflection

Ours is not at present a society where people feel secure. It is a place where the elderly are fearful to open their front doors in the evening, where unlocked cars and bicycles are said to be courting theft, where many students lock away their food (or hang their cheese out of their windows!). Many people have a deep sense of unease at the increasing violence and disrespect for lives and property. It seems so vast and widespread a problem, in which we feel powerless to change things, and can easily lead to apathy and despair.

Is 'righteousness' a forlorn hope as the world appears to lurch out of control? Today's readings direct us to the only way widespread right can prevail: it is a question of individuals being trained in right living, thinking and choosing. As more people are rooted in righteousness these values will spread, working like yeast in dough.

But before that can begin to happen, individuals are needed who are prepared to be taken over by God's living Spirit; people who are willing to have God reigning in their lives.

## Discussion starters

1 What are the differences and similarities between following good rules and being truly righteous?

2 In the parable of the growing seed the kingdom of God is shown to grow naturally. To what extent must we work for the kingdom to grow, and to what extent does it happen through grace?

## All stage talk

*Theme:* Doing what comes naturally.

First of all give some examples of how things happen naturally. Put some sugar in a drink and it can't help tasting sweet; have a brace clamped to your teeth and they can't help growing straight. Mix blue and yellow and you can't help making green. (All these can be actually watched if you wish – all those with braces can come out together and flash a silver smile.)

This principle works for bad things as well as good. If you drink 16 pints of lager you can't help getting drunk; if you put on skunk perfume you can't help smelling of skunk.

Today's readings are saying that since this is so, we will need to be loving people in order to behave in a loving way; we will have to be dedicated to serving God and others if we are to be able to act with God's character. Whatever kind of people we are on the inside will naturally show in the way we behave on the outside, so rather than working on doing things we think will impress people, God is inviting us to work with him in a transforming process from the inside – he can make us the kind of people who naturally think and love unselfishly, and enjoy our lives all the more for it.

## Intercessions

We pray that your church will have courage to speak up for what is right and loving; we pray for those who are persecuted or imprisoned because of their faith.

*Silence for prayer*

Father, fill us up:
**with goodness and with love**

We pray for integrity and wisdom in all who advise and lead in our world; we pray for the areas where law and order has broken down.

*Silence for prayer*

Father, fill us up:
**with goodness and with love**

We pray that our homes may be places of welcome, comfort and friendship; we pray for all who will walk in and out of our homes this week.

*Silence for prayer*

Father, fill us up:
**with goodness and with love**

We pray for all who are victims of greed, cruelty and revenge; we pray for those who hate, and all who are finding it difficult to forgive.

*Silence for prayer*

Father, fill us up:
**with goodness and with love**

We pray for those who have come to the end of their earthly life and those who mourn.

*Silence for prayer*

Father, fill us up:
**with goodness and with love**

We praise and bless you for every scrap of tenderness, every spark of joy, and every glimpse of your glory.

*Silence for prayer*

Father, fill us up:
**with goodness and with love**

## Other ideas

• Incorporate seed and seed heads in one of the flower arrangements today.

• Have someone mixing yeast in dough at the beginning of the service and have a look to see how it has affected the dough by the end.

• Have everyone acting out the calming of the waves, with the storm getting louder and the boat rocking. When Jesus' puts his hand out over the water (the congregation), they all calm down. They will experience the sensation of being calmed. Now ask them to allow Jesus to stretch out his hand over their lives – over the storms of stress/anger/guilt/ emotional turmoil or pain. Allow him to bring his peace. You could have quiet music playing during this, a song such as 'Be still' or 'O Lord, your tenderness', or simply silence.

## In the crèche

*Aim:* For the children to hear the story of Jesus calming the waves.

Tell the story with the children acting it out. You could have the adults forming the boat and crowd the children inside it.

## Children

*Aim:* To introduce them to the idea of our lives being under God's authority.

Begin by playing any ball/beanbag game where the rules are explained and kept to. Then talk together about why the rules were useful for everyone's enjoyment, and what might have happened if there weren't any rules. Tell them how good and well-disciplined they were to keep to the rules in the game, even when they wanted to cheat.

We have to train ourselves in self-control over little things so that we'll be able to stand up against temptation in bigger things (like drugs, alcohol or stealing). What are God's rules? Sing the summary of the Law together in a round. (see p.199.) We won't always want to do what is right. But Jesus will always strengthen us to be able to resist temptation.

## Young people

*Aim:* To explore the difficulties and rewards of living a 'righteous' life.

Play this giant game of Snakes and Ladders, using a carton for the dice and a grid chalked or marked on the floor for the board.

Here are some suggestions for snakes:

1   Accept a smoke of dodgy substance.

2   Someone asks you to hand round sandwiches for the elderly people's tea, and you pretend you've got too much homework.

3   You exchange the peace with your brother in church and then tease him mercilessly when you get home.

4 When your Auntie complains she hasn't had a thank-you letter you insist it must have got lost in the post.

5 You dish out the scrambled egg and give the portion with egg shell to someone else.

6 You wind up your best friend and then get offended when s/he thumps you.

Some suggestions for ladders:

1 You find school assemblies really boring, so go with some practical, exciting improvements to see the Head.

2 You offer to make posters for the church notice board instead of just whinging about how sad it looks.

3 You admit you've noticed that the washing up needs doing and actually start on it.

4 You attack the burnt-on casserole dish with a brillo, rather than pretending it needs a week-long soak.

5 When your friend gets blamed you admit it was really your fault.

6 When you reach for the volume control you remember the others in your home with different tastes.

# 4th Sunday after Pentecost

## YEAR 1

*Thought for the day:*
*True freedom neither means doing what you like, nor being trapped by someone else's sin.*

## Readings
Psalms 42,43
Ezekiel 18:1-4,19-end
Romans 14:1-15:3

## Reflection

If ever you thought the Old Testament was not showing the loving God of the gospels, the Ezekiel passage is certainly one to read. It is clear-sighted with eyes of love, freeing those who live enchained with others' guilt and challenging the spiritually complacent. It delights in the individual, recognising both privilege and responsibility. And listen to those lovely words which are so in touch with Jesus' image of the good shepherd: 'Do you think I enjoy you being lost? I hate it!' – or words to that effect.

So any of us who feel that the skeletons in our family cupboard somehow condemn us before we start can relax in the freedom of knowing that in God's eyes they make no difference at all.

In his letter to the Romans Paul unpacks the implications of living in God's freedom. No longer are we bound in detailed, complex, legalistic rules. Yet our very freedom implies that we will be sensitive to others and not enchain them or knowingly make life in any way difficult for them.

The result will be less of an emphasis on whether those around us are wearing the right depth of dog collar, singing modern or traditional music, and so on. Instead the emphasis will be on encouraging one another along our journey of faith – we will be less critical and judgemental and more understanding and sensitive about what might help or hinder people in getting to know and love the God who can save them and transform their lives.

## Discussion starters

1  Religious wars are often what put peace-loving people off organised religion. What has gone wrong to bring about a religious war?

2  If we seriously decide to pray 'Thy kingdom come, thy will be done' what attitudes and behaviour might we need to change a) in ourselves; b) in our local worshipping community; c) in our particular church tradition?

## All stage talk

*Theme:* What does God mean by freedom? Beforehand organise some prison bars. This might be a large oven shelf or anything similar.

First ask for a volunteer, who holds the bars in front of their face so that they look imprisoned. Sometimes we feel imprisoned by our family background. It may be that there is a history of cancer in our family, or suicide; perhaps there has been an alcoholic, or someone with mental illness; perhaps, however old we are now, we still remember a childhood experience of being intensely disliked, ignored or abused in some way. These things can imprison us and make us feel frightened and sad – as if we are partly to blame for their poor health, their sin or their weakness, and however sensibly we try to shake that off, it keeps hold of us.

The wonderful news of our God is that he holds no one of us guilty for what happened to our ancestors; Jesus can set you free from all that sadness and fear, (take the bars away) so that you can live again and enjoy the life God has given you.

Now once you are out, you are free.

So if this person feels like killing me, does that mean he can? (No!) Why no? As God behaves to him – respecting and loving him – he needs to behave to others, so as to preserve their freedom as well. We can't delight in God forgiving us and then rush out and criticise someone else!

We might hear this and think we know all about this teaching already. But think again – what about when we discuss the service afterwards; do we only mention the boring bits, laugh over the organist's mistakes and huddle with our own friends? And when those around us are using God's name as a swear word, what do we do? (A hint – if you have got into the habit of swearing like this yourself, start turning it into a prayer as you say it.)

God sets us free; let's enjoy that to the full – remember to pass it on.

## Intercessions

Father, we pray for all church leaders, and all who minister to others through their teaching of the faith.
Keep us available to encourage them and help them wherever we can.
*Silence for prayer*

My soul is thirsty for God:
**thirsty for the living God**

We pray for those who influence the thinking and general behaviour of people all over the world; for clear guidance in what is right and true.

*Silence for prayer*

My soul is thirsty for God:
**thirsty for the living God**

We pray for all those entrusted with the responsibility of bringing up children; and for all those who are finding adolescence difficult.

*Silence for prayer*

My soul is thirsty for God:
**thirsty for the living God**

We pray for all whose lives are restricted through illness, disability or frailty; we pray for all imprisoned by addiction.

*Silence for prayer*

My soul is thirsty for God:
**thirsty for the living God**

We pray for those who have died and for those who are finding life bleak without them.

*Silence for prayer*

My soul is thirsty for God:
**thirsty for the living God**

We pray with thankfulness for every reconciliation, every flame of love and tenderness, every word of forgiveness and every act of loving care.

*Silence for prayer*

My soul is thirsty for God:
**thirsty for the living God**

## Other ideas

• Remember that the exchange of peace needs to be a real effort to make peace with one another, recognising your differences and offering your willingness to accept others with love.

Make today's peace take this seriously; give time for people to move about to enable those who need to make peace with one another to do so under cover of the general moving around. Let one another out of whatever prisons they are in.

• Have a flower arrangement like a living card, so that it looks something like this:

## In the crèche

*Aim:* To help them understand what it feels like to be set free.

Squash all the group into a tiny space at one corner of the room. Have a stopwatch going and pretend you can only escape into the open when the bell rings. When it does, enjoy moving around the whole room, stretching your bodies and feeling the sense of freedom.

If possible have a caged pet with you for the session, and talk together about how we need to make sure our pets don't feel trapped in their cages; plenty of interesting things to do and chew are very important to keep our pets happy, and plenty of exercise.

## Children

*Aim:* For them to understand that God wants us to be saved and not lost.

Begin by playing this team game. At the front of each team is a bowl of water and various small plastic containers, enough for each team member to have one. Some distance away is an empty bowl. The team have to transfer the water from one bowl to the other, using the containers. (This could well be an outdoors activity!)

Afterwards remind the children of how they tried to carry the water carefully because they didn't want even a drop to spill. That's how God feels about us, his people. He knows that if we choose to do what is evil in our lives we won't be able to enjoy everlasting life with God in heaven, and he knows how easy it is for us to choose what is wrong, instead of what is right. So God does everything he possibly can to stop us falling, because he loves us, and hates the thought of even one person being lost.

Explain how the people of Israel reckoned that children should be punished for what their parents did wrong, and then read them the passage from Ezekiel. Now help the children create this banner to explain the way God cherishes us. Have the hands drawn already, and then the children can draw themselves and place these drawings safe in God's hands.

## Young people

*Aim:* To explore the ways in which the Romans passage challenges our own behaviour.

Begin by explaining how the old Jewish laws had said there were some foods which Jews shouldn't eat. Some Christian Jews did not understand that as Christians they were now free to eat all foods. Now read the passage from Paul's letter to the Christians in Rome, noticing how he reacts to their problems.

Give out a questionnaire something like this (see below), but making sure it is relevant to your group's experience, and ask them to work on this in small groups. Afterwards, have a discussion on the answers chosen and pray together about any challenges or needs which have arisen.

## Questionnaire

Answer each question: yes, perhaps or no.

1 Would you buy something from a shop which sells a lot of New Age things and/or anti-Christian material?

2 You are a vegetarian and get invited out to a meal which turns out to contain meat. Do you eat it out of politeness, refuse to eat anything and grumble at your host, or eat the vegetables and leave the meat?

3 Some people at your church refuse to clap along to a song in church and you catch their disapproving look. Do you clap louder than ever through every hymn to show how freed in the Spirit you are, clap discreetly and feel guilty, or continue as you are but make a point of being friendly to them after the service?

4  At camp another Christian kneels to pray at night and gets teased. You are used to praying in bed, so no one knows you are praying. The following night, do you pray in bed as usual, kneel down as the other person is or join in the teasing?

5  You give up chocolate for Lent and your Baptist friend thinks the idea is medieval. Do you have a heated argument in front of non-Christian friends, go back to eating chocolate for a quiet life whenever your friend is around, or recognise that you hold the important things in common and it isn't worth arguing about such matters?

# YEAR 2

*Thought for the day:*
*God tells each of us our own story and loves us into his kingdom.*

## Readings

Psalms 42,43
1 Kings 10:1-13
John 4:1-26 or 1-42

## Reflection

Reports of Solomon's wisdom and wealth were what prompted the Queen of Sheba to visit Jerusalem. But it was when she experienced the splendour and marvel of Solomon's court firsthand that she was really impressed, to the extent that her heart was touched to praise a foreign God.

In the New Testament reading we find another woman being impressed by firsthand experience of the wonder of God. The story of the Samaritan woman at the well gives us such a photographic picture of the way Jesus works. Though God, he is also human, so he listens to people's spirits as they speak, allowing the real needs and fears to unfold. The woman's reaction to Jesus' shocking request for a drink gradually reveals her resentment about Samaritan treatment by Jews, her defensiveness about Samaritan worship, and her own personal needs. Jesus responds to her hurt and bitterness, her sense of injustice and her longing for personal acceptance and fulfilment. He leads her to understand something of God's truth, and only when she melts (I know the Messiah is coming) does he reveal his identity.

## Discussion starters

1  Go through the passage from John, covering up Jesus' replies as you go and thinking what you might expect them to be. What do Jesus' unexpected replies teach the woman, and what do they teach us?

2  Do we question Jesus in our prayer and during our lives? Perhaps we don't often become aware of his voice because we censor what we consider unsuitable things to talk over with him.

## All stage talk

*Theme:* Jesus speaks our language.
Beforehand ask a couple of computer crazy people to work out a very short conversation using as much jargon as they can fit in. If you have any Latin or Greek scholars, ask them to work out a brief conversation in that language, and if you have a couple of teachers, ask them to do a short discussion using all the technical attainment targets jargon. Of course you may have different skills and interests among your congregation, so home in on any kind of language which means everything to those in the know and nothing whatever to anyone else.

Begin by introducing the two or three conversations as if they are really going to help people. Then admit that you haven't actually understood very much yourself, and no doubt they haven't either. Language can sometimes block our understanding; church language can sometimes make visitors feel like aliens visiting a strange planet, if it is too different from ordinary language that we use every day. Some of the older translations of the bible, though beautiful to those who have grown up with them, can make a new reader suppose that Jesus has nothing in common with their own time, and only speaks in a language they don't understand.

But of course that isn't true. Jesus spoke to the woman at the well in a way that she understood so clearly that she shot off and dragged all her friends along to meet him.

When God makes himself known to you it will be in a way that you, personally, understand, because he knows you and loves you. He knows what makes you tick, what you are afraid of, what you hate doing and what you enjoy. He knows what you've been through in your life, what you can cope with easily and what you find very hard. So as he walks with you through each moment of each day right through death and beyond, he will explain things to you, comfort you and give you a nudge in ways which exactly suit your character and situation. All we have to do is live each day expecting him to be in touch, so that we recognise his voice.

He may speak during your prayer time by ideas that suddenly come and will solve a problem in a way you hadn't thought of before. He may speak by something from your bible reading suddenly hitting you with fresh and very personal meaning. He may speak through events that happen through the day, so that you understand them as picture language which God uses to teach you something he wanted you to learn or understand. He may speak through a conversation you have, or even overhear.

So often, though, God takes us by surprise, and we need to be prepared for that in case we think it can't be God because he's not following our rules. God made this whole universe, so nothing at all is unusable. Keep your eyes skinned, then, and be ready to listen whenever your God speaks.

## Intercessions

Father, the church has its areas of
weakness and pain; we long to be truly
and faithfully the body of Christ.
*Silence for prayer*
Father, we thank you:
**for hearing our needs**

Father, the nations bicker and fight;
we long for a world where love
and peace prevail.
*Silence for prayer*
Father, we thank you:
**for hearing our needs**

Father, our homes and families have
tensions and misunderstandings; we long
for your wise parenting in every home.
*Silence for prayer*
Father, we thank you:
**for hearing our needs**

Father, many are sad, stressed, in pain or
in need; we long for your healing
presence to comfort and renew.
*Silence for prayer*
Father, we thank you:
**for hearing our needs**

Father, some die destitute and unnoticed;
some die violently and many grieve for
their loved ones; we long for your
reassuring love and hope.
*Silence for prayer*
Father, we thank you:
**for hearing our needs**

Father, our lives are so rich with blessings; we long to show our thanks in our lives.

*Silence for prayer*

Father, we thank you:
**for hearing our needs**

## Other ideas

• Have the reading from John acted, using either your own dramatisation or the dramatised bible. Or have the reading mimed, using a narrator and dressed-up characters in a series of 'stills' or tableaux. Costumes from the nativity play come in handy here.

## In the crèche

*Aim:* For the children to know that in Jesus' eyes each one is special.

Start with a guessing game. Sit in a circle, so that everyone can see everyone else. Say 'Jesus loves someone who's got red ladybirds on their jumper/has curly hair and a blue shirt'. The children will have to guess who it is. When they have guessed, everyone says 'Jesus loves Carl/Lorrina'. Make certain that every child is described, and finish by telling the children how Jesus knows everyone very well indeed, and loves each person to bits.

## Children

*Aim:* For them to know that in Jesus' eyes each one is special.

Start by playing the countdown game. Everyone stands up, and you say you're thinking of someone and they can find out who it is by asking questions. You can only answer 'yes' or 'no', and the one thing they can't ask is whether it's a particular person. The game is really a process of elimination, so if someone asks 'Is this person wearing glasses?' and the answer is 'Yes', then everyone who isn't wearing glasses sits down. Finally there is only one person standing, and that should be the one you were thinking of.

Talk with the children about how God knows all the details about us and understands us really well. That makes him the very best person to trust with our worries and secrets, our successes and struggles.

Give the children this chart to fill in, which they don't have to show to anyone at all; in fact one way of doing this is by asking them to go and find a place of their choice, either indoors or, if possible, outside. Tell them that when you want them back you will ring a bell. When you are all together again, ask them to hold their charts, containing their own special information, as you all pray in silence for one another, knowing that at the same time each is being prayed for by someone else.

My best colour is [    ]
My best food is [    ]
What makes me scared
[    ]
What makes me happy
[    ]
What I like best about me
[    ]
What I don't like about me
[    ]

## Young people

*Aim:* For them to know that they are specifically and personally known and loved.

Start with two people reading this short sketch:

**Sentry**  Halt! Who goes there?

**Fred**  It's me – Fred.

**Sentry**  Fred with the pony tail or bald Fred?

**Fred**  Fred with the pony tail. Can I come in?

**Sentry**  That depends.

**Fred**  Depends on what?

**Sentry**  Well, what type of trainers you're wearing, for a start.

**Fred**  Is NIKE any good?

**Sentry**  Yes, NIKE's OK.

**Fred**  Well, they're not NIKE.

**Sentry**  What are they, then?

**Fred**  They were on special offer at Payless. Hang on, it says something on the sole . . . 'made in Hong Kong'.

**Sentry**  Well that's it, then. You can't come in if you're wearing those.

**Fred**  But my Mum made me get these.

**Sentry**  Then you'd better make sure you get the right sort next time. Go and make yourself a bit more acceptable, for goodness sake.

Talk together about how there are those who are only willing to be friends if we're wearing the right clothes, or have the right amount of intelligence or skill. And there are those who we wouldn't trust with our personal ideas or worries because we know they might use the information against us. But if we know someone loves us, then we can trust them even with things we are ashamed of, because we know they will try to understand, and our mistakes won't mean rejection.

Now read the passage from John, looking at how the woman might have felt about Jesus 'seeing right through her'. Bring out the point that Jesus knows us completely, and nothing at all is hidden from him. But he is also the God of love, so that knowledge is in safe hands, and he will always use it in the way that is best for us.

---

# 5th Sunday after Pentecost

## YEAR 1

*Thought for the day:*
*If we really understood God's law it would drive us weeping to his feet.*

### Readings
Psalm 119:41-56
Nehemiah 8:1-12
Luke 11:37-end

## Reflection

It is not normally fashionable in our society to obey rules. Perhaps this stems from a fear of blind, unthinking obedience which has led to inhuman behaviour; certainly since World War Two there has been a definite trend towards encouraging people to question and think for themselves. Valuable as this is, there is then another danger. It is now considered so important to be a self-assertive individual that it is often generally thought weak and wet to obey any rules at all. Yet we have discovered to our cost how freedom dwindles instead of grows in such a climate.

The psalmist obviously finds God's statutes really full of comfort and very liberating. The people listening with new understanding to God's law are cut to the quick, realising with sorrow how far they have wandered, and how they long for the freedom of peace which comes from living in harmony with their creator. Jesus hates to see people wandering away to misery, and takes this opportunity of a dinner party invitation to open the Pharisees' eyes. He does this by first making them surprised, shocked and disdainful, and then turning the tables so that they realise they are on the receiving end of their own judgement.

## Discussion starters

1  How can we make sure that people really understand God's word in a way which guides them to realise God's love for them?

2  The Pharisees had begun by zealously protecting the true faith, and upholding it against dangerous outside influences. Can you see how this might have turned into the false piety we see here? And are there any danger signs for the church today?

## All stage talk

*Theme:* Getting our priorities right.
Beforehand arrange for a willing volunteer to come ready to do a quick hair or make-up demo on someone; someone else to give themselves a nice shave in public; someone else to sit and read their bible and someone else to pray.

Ask these groups of people to arrange themselves where they can be seen, and start them off. After a while get everyone to think about which one is getting all smart and clean. The answer is that all of them are – the shaver and make-up person on the outside, and the bible reader and prayer on the inside. We tend to bother more with the outside than the inside, but both are important; let's try

spending the same amount of time on each! Then we won't be in danger of being all nice and clean on the outside and all selfish and unloving on the inside.

## Intercessions

We ask you to fill us with delight at doing your will, and at bringing others to know you. Refresh those whose faith is dry and stiff.

*Silence for prayer*

Father, take us over:
**both inside and out**

We ask for integrity in our own parish, in local and world decisions.

*Silence for prayer*

Father, take us over:
**both inside and out**

We ask for clear guidance in medical ethics, and the courage to stand up for your values.

*Silence for prayer*

Father, take us over:
**both inside and out**

We ask that you will welcome into your kingdom all those who have recently died, and we ask you to prepare us on earth to live with you in heaven.

*Silence for prayer*

Father, take us over:
**both inside and out**

We ask for the grace to live joyfully as we travel with you through our lives, and remember now all that you have done for us.

*Silence for prayer*

Father, take us over:
**both inside and out**

## *Other ideas*

- Have people to mime the Luke reading.
- Today is a good time to have a more thorough time of penitence and re-commitment to Christ.

Either read through the ten commandments as in the Book of Common Prayer, or use the summary of the Law like this:

YOU SHALL LOVE THE LORD YOUR GOD WITH ALL YOUR HEART AND MIND AND STRENGTH . . .

Does God come first in your thinking and planning? . . .

first in how you spend your time? . . .

and how you spend your money?. . .

Does God come first in your priorities?

Lord, have mercy; we have failed to keep your law.

YOU SHALL LOVE YOUR NEIGHBOUR AS YOURSELF . . .

Do you always give people your complete attention? . . .

Do you put yourself out for them, whether you like them or not? . . .

Are you being faithful in friendship and marriage? . . .

Do you respect other people's property and ideas? . . .

Are you content with what you have, and happy for someone else to get what you are wanting? . . .

Do you keep promises and confidences to yourself? . . .

Lord, have mercy; we have failed to keep your law.

## *In the crèche*

*Aim:* For them to learn that God wants them to love one another.
Use Punch and Judy, or any other puppets of your own, to act out situations where they hit one another, or steal something because the other puppet had done something nasty to them. Talk together about how everyone gets hurt if we live like this, and then play the situation through again, based on the children's suggestions for Jesus' way of doing it.

Another situation suitable for this, and familiar to the children, is where one puppet keeps winding the other up and then cries when s/he gets hurt when the patience wears thin. Who is really to blame? Loving is not always easy, but it works much better because God made us to love one another.

## *Children*

*Aim:* For them to hear Jesus' teaching to the Pharisees and look at real goodness. Beforehand gather a collection of some real jewellery and some pretend. Display them carefully so that they look precious, and ask a couple of children to take them round and show everyone. If there are a lot of you, sing a quiet worship song while the jewels are doing the rounds.

Talk with the children about which they thought were worth most, and why. Then let them in on the secret that some things were in the 50p range, though some of them may well have been taken in by them. It would only be when they broke easily or scratched that you'd realise with disappointment that they weren't as good as you'd thought. Some people are like this too.

Now tell or read the story from Luke, getting the children to help you tell it by acting out the parts as you come to them. Explain first (and have them acting out) how fussy the Pharisees were about all the ceremonial washing; then they will notice how Jesus was far more bothered about the really important things than the rituals which were mainly just for show.

Then provide a number of different media so that they can choose how they want to express the story and teaching to the people in church. Some could act out the story in their own way, using the props from the teaching, some may wish to make a poster encouraging genuine Christianity.

## Young people

*Aim:* To explore the growth of false piety and ways to avoid hypocrisy.

First explain how the Pharisees had originally formed to protect the Jewish faith from corruption at a time when where was a very deal danger of this happening. By Jesus' time they had got somewhat carried away with what they were preserving, and were now more concerned with the outer rituals and signs than the real thing.

Now read the passage from Luke together and think how the Pharisees, who still considered themselves guardians of the faith, would have felt about Jesus. List the things that might anger them, and the things that concerned Jesus as he tried to break through the hard crust of tradition and free the living faith that was trapped inside.

In twos or threes talk as Pharisees about Jesus when he's out of earshot. (Incidentally, Paul was a Pharisee, and we can see there what happened once he realised that Jesus was the key person in the very faith he was determined to guard.)

Take a look at your own faith and parish, checking areas where a 'back to basics' session may be needed.

# YEAR 2

*Thought for the day:*
*God's saving news of love is not for a few, but for every person in every nation.*

## Readings
Psalm 119:41-56
Jonah 3 and 4
Acts 13:1-13

## Reflection

One of the lovely things about reading the bible is discovering how human the characters are in it. We have the full range of people, from the petty minded to the pompous, the gentle to the wet and the courageous to the arrogant. No attempt is made to try and justify the dismal failures or gloss over the weaknesses, and so the story of Jonah is typical. Jonah had never liked the idea of his enemies being brought to repentance, and his response to God's call is to travel as far as possible in the opposite direction, which many of us might ruefully agree is a very human thing to do.

When he eventually gets to Ninevah and the people repent so that God spares them, Jonah is outraged. He has to be put in God's position – delighting in something and not wanting its destruction – before he can begin to understand God's way of thinking. We often find it difficult to grasp that God loves people we don't, and is happy to expend tremendous energy saving people we might prefer to ignore.

In the reading from Acts, notice how the disciples in the early church took mission very seriously, and had caught Jesus' enthusiasm for bringing people the good news, regardless of the possible consequences and dangers. How many of our missionary or evangelistic programmes begin with prayer and fasting, waiting on God's ideas for who should lead the team, and so on?

We do need to take God seriously. If we are prepared to make ourselves available for his service even before we know the agenda, then he will use us and we shall find ourselves working for the spread of the kingdom with all kinds of unlikely people. The Christian's life is nothing if not full of surprises.

## Discussion starters

1 Why did Jonah get so angry? Do you see his point? Do you think he was justified?

2 As we can see from this passage from Acts, the spread of the gospel is bound to lead us into contact with evil, and we need to be prepared. Look at how Paul and Barnabas and the church prepared and draw up a possible preparation plan for use in your own area.

## All stage talk

*Theme:* What – them as well?
Begin by talking about those times in games at school when the captains are choosing teams. Some people are always the ones left at the end which neither captain wants on their side. Others are fought over, because they're so skilled. Now, without mentioning what the team is for, ask a sporty-looking type from the congregation to choose a side, and have

them all lined up holding a football, as in a team photograph.

Next tell them that they aren't actually a football team, but a washing and ironing team. Commiserate with the captain, asking if s/he's still happy with the people s/he chose, and giving the opportunity to change some members of his/her team if s/he wishes. (It will be interesting to see who is chosen now!) On a flip chart or OHP record how we go about choosing people for a job:

1 Know the people.

2 Know the job.

That way we can match up the needs with those who can best provide for the needs. And God does this all the time; because he knows us so well and knows people's needs so well, he can mix and match better than any of us. The trouble is, we often go rushing on to choose our own teams without really knowing what they will be needed to do.

If we look at the early church we find them taking time out to listen to God's ideas. They fasted – went without food – and spent a lot of time praying – spending time in God's company – and God chose two people to start the new mission who he know would be best for the job. They were Paul and Barnabas. When you next have to make a choice or a decision, talk it over with God, and be prepared for him to then put into your mind the name of someone you might never have even considered.

## Intercessions

Father, set your church on fire with your love for everyone, without exception.
*Silence for prayer*
Take us, Lord:
**and use us wherever you need us**

Father, let the greed and selfishness
which tear our world apart,
be overcome with generosity of spirit
and concern for one another's good.

*Silence for prayer*

Take us, Lord:
**and use us wherever you need us**

Father, let every home become a place of
comfort; safe, happy and welcoming.

*Silence for prayer*

Take us, Lord:
**and use us wherever you need us**

Father, let those who are distressed
and diseased find healing, refreshment
and meaning for their lives.

*Silence for prayer*

Take us, Lord:
**and use us wherever you need us**

Father, let those who have died spend
their eternity with you,
at peace and in joy for ever;
and may their loved ones be comforted in
their sorrow.

*Silence for prayer*

Take us, Lord:
**and use us wherever you need us**

Father, may we shine as lights
as you draw all people
to fulfilment in you.

*Silence for prayer*

Take us, Lord:
**and use us wherever you need us**

## Other ideas

• For one of the flower arrangements
today, import a large plant with big shady
leaves, and have a small arrangement
under its shade. You could arrange leafy
branches for the same effect.

• Have the psalm read with the two
halves of the congregation taking not
alternate verses, but alternate halves of
each verse, so as to bring out the
reflective echo of the Hebrew poetry.

i.e. 1   Let your loving mercy come
to me, O Lord:
2   and your salvation according to
your word.

## In the crèche

*Aim:* To help the children understand that
God made us able to choose, and he is the
best chooser of all.
Play a game where the children take
turns to choose a way to move (such as
hopping, clapping, blinking etc.) When
they have chosen, everyone does the
same movement.

Then have some painting, cutting or
collage work, where the children are
choosing what they want to put on their
picture. As you work talk about how
lovely it is to be able to choose, and thank
God for making us that way. God chooses
too. Who did he choose to be Jesus'
mother? . . . some of his friends? . . . as a
helper in this group? . . . a 3 year old at St
Aiden's? etc.

## Children

*Aim:* To look at some of God's surprising
choices.
Start with a fast and furious game of
choices. Label the corners of the room
Tarshish, Ninevah, home and big weed.
The children take it in turn to shout out
one of these words and then everyone
races over to that place.

Then sit down and retell the Jonah
story with their help. Whenever you
mention:

Jonah, they say: What me, Lord?

Ninevah, they say: DisGUSting!

Sailors, they get up and do 4 seconds
of a hornpipe,

Big Fish, they open and close their
mouths, fish-like,

and they make the appropriate noises when you say Wind and Sea.

Point out how Jonah was surprised and angry that God has chosen to save a place like Ninevah. We may be surprised at the jobs God chooses us for. He may need to use us at the shops, in the kitchen at home, down at the tip, in the middle of dinner or in the middle of a maths lesson.

Help them to make this moving model of Jonah and the big fish.

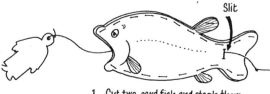

Slit

1. Cut two card fish and staple them together as shown
2. Cut a slit in the fish
3. Attach string to Jonah and thread through fish

## Young people

*Aim:* To look at some of God's surprising choices.

Begin with a game of choice such as Pairs or Pontoon, so that they are made aware of the way we are always making choices, and these are often 'blind' choices, where we don't know enough information to do much more than guess. Introduce the Jonah story, filling in all the first part, before reading together chapters 3 and 4.

Discuss why Jonah felt so angry, and how God helped him understand. Then look at the first part of the Acts reading, where Paul and Barnabas were chosen. If they had chosen without fasting and prayer, it would have been a blind choice, because they had no way of knowing what kind of situations these two would meet on the new mission. Asking God was, in a way like being able to use inside information and so get the best people for the job.

If we ask him, God will always help us like this.

# 6th Sunday after Pentecost

## YEAR 1

*Thought for the day:*
*In Jesus we are not just patched up but made new.*

## Readings
Psalm 77
Isaiah 43:14-44:5
Mark 2:18-36

## Reflection

Many of us are wary of change. What we are and the habits we have may not be perfect, but at least we know them well and have got used to them. The prospect of being changed can actually seem very threatening, even if we know the change will be for the better.

Yesterday as I walked home from the shops in the pouring rain I got a stone in my shoe. I decided that getting it out would be too much hassle, and I couldn't be bothered with all the inconvenience. So instead I hobbled along with the stone making my walk home a grind, rather than a delight. (I usually love walking in the rain.) At last I could bear it no longer, and sorted myself out. The relief and pleasure of walking stone-less was luxury!

We may be hobbling through life with spiritual stones in our shoes; we may keep asking God for crutches, or softer pavements, when what he longs to do is take the stones out and set us free to walk comfortably again. Jesus felt both anger and sadness at the attitude of the Pharisees to the sabbath, because their narrow legalism was preventing them from seeing the basic truth of God. The danger is there for all of us, and we are bound to get our priorities wrong from time to time, but so long as we stay humble enough to admit we may be wrong, then Jesus can work with power and make us new in our thinking, feeling and living.

## Discussion starters

1 In what sense does Jesus teach according to the law of Moses, and in what sense does he make all things new?

2 Are there any of our traditions or habits which need renewing, discarding and/or fulfilling?

## All stage talk

*Theme:* The importance of being made new.

Beforehand prepare a card stencil shape of a circle. Draw the circle outline properly, but when you cut out the centre, make sure it has some very obvious misshapen parts, so that it looks something like this:

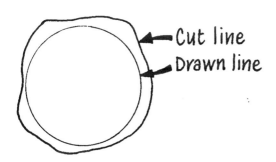

Have a flip chart or several large sheets of paper and a thick felt tip pen ready. Start by explaining that as part of a visual aid today you need to draw a circle, so you've made a stencil to make that easier. Proceed to draw round the stencil and then express your disappointment that the circle isn't any good. Nevermind, you can start again and do it properly on a fresh sheet of paper. Unfortunately, this shape goes wrong as well. Ask someone to try using the stencil and see if they can make it work.

When they can't, get people to explain why the circle keeps going wrong. (The stencil is the wrong shape; every time it's used, the misshapes will go on happening.) We sometimes feel rather like this – however hard we try, we find we go on making the same mistakes, messing things up in our lives again and again. We can't seem to help it. However hard I try, I shall always mess up this circle if I go on using this stencil. We need to make a new stencil for it to work properly, and in our lives we need to be made new so that we can't help but live loving, beautiful lives.

Ask a good cutter-outer to put things right, then try again. (Hopefully, this will be successful!) Admire the results of using a stencil which has been made new. In the same way, our lives will start to show good results when we allow God to sort us out. He works on us gradually, every day throughout our lifetime, and as he works on us and renews us, we start emerging as the person God intended us to be.

## Intercessions

(Note that here the silences come after the response.)

In the chapels, churches and cathedrals, and in every gathering of Christians, God all-knowing, God all-loving:
**come, make us new**
*Silence for prayer*

*Continued overleaf*

Where faith is frayed, where prayer is
casual, where God is patronised and the
harvest is ignored,
God all-knowing, God all-loving:
**come, make us new**
*Silence for prayer*

In the homes, shops, schools and meeting
places of our town,
in the conversations we have this week,
God all-knowing, God all-loving:
**come, make us new**
*Silence for prayer*

Where people are sad or burdened with
guilt,
where illness and frailty are hard to bear
cheerfully,
God all-knowing, God all-loving:
**come, make us new**
*Silence for prayer*

As those we have known and love
journey from this life into eternity, and
we call to mind that heaven is our home,
God all-knowing, God all-loving:
**come, make us new**
*Silence for prayer*

In our moments and days, our sorrows
and our joys,
God all-knowing, God all-loving:
**come, make us new**
*Silence for prayer*

## Other ideas

As an alternative form of confession and
reconciliation with God, try having this
sung by a single voice, or small group of
voices, preferably unaccompanied with a
space for reflection between each section:

Come, Spirit, come, prise open my heart.

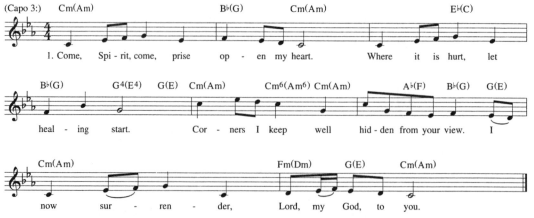

2. Come, Spirit, come take charge of my mind.
   Show me the darkness that you find.
   Help me to trust you, even with my shame,
   till freely acknowledge where I am to blame.

3. Come, Spirit, come, bring life to my soul.
   Your forgiveness makes me whole.
   Then from the pain and stress of sin set free
   I am dazed by the awesome love you have for me.

## In the crèche

*Aim:* For the children to understand that God's nature is to put things right.

Bring along a selection of things that need putting right, such as a pencil which needs sharpening, a plant which is flopping and needs a support, a (shortish) length of wool which needs untangling, and a clock which has stopped and needs winding up.

Show the children each item in turn, getting them to work out what is wrong and how it could be put right. Let the children help with the putting right, until you have a whole show of mended things to feel pleased about.

Explain that we like putting things right because God made us like himself, and he loves putting things right in people's lives. So we know that if ever we do anything wrong, we can go to God with our sadness, and he will help us put things right again.

## Children

*Aim:* For the children to know that God doesn't just patch up, but makes new. Take the children on a journey, using different parts of the building and/or churchyard, doing different sections of the story and teaching in different areas.

Begin in Egypt, and get them to tell you the familiar story of the people of Israel as slaves. When you get to the crossing of the sea, lead them out through two lines of chairs to the other side, where you can all rejoice that you are free. Lead them on to the Promised Land, where you tell them about how the people didn't stay faithful to God, but messed things up time after time, until at last they were overcome and taken off to exile in Babylon. Move off to another area at this point. The people know that although God had kept his promise they hadn't kept theirs and they knew they

had messed things up. Now read excerpts from the prophet Isaiah to see what God said to his people and how he gave them hope. Then take the children on a whistle stop tour over the same journey, explaining it in terms of a person: we get stuck in a bad habit like being lazy or selfish or telling lies a lot, and God leads us out of it, but gradually we find we're messing things up again until our bad habits hold us again like exiles. So God's words of hope are for us, too; in Jesus we can be gradually made new. He will sort out and heal the things that make us behave badly.

Give the children balls of clay and let them model something good emerging from a shapeless lump. Display the models with a sign: LOOK AT THE NEW THING I AM GOING TO DO. IT IS HAPPENING ALREADY – YOU CAN SEE IT NOW!

## Young people

*Aim:* For them to see how lives are changed and made new in Christ.

Briefly explain how the people of Israel were in exile, have broken faith with God time and again. Now God speaks to them through his prophet, Isaiah.

Read this passage together, and then go to Mark. Talk about how Jesus was fulfilling the promise the people had received in exile, and yet he wasn't easily accepted by his own people. List some of their ideas as to why his behaviour seems to have been angering them.

Now either watch a short clip from a video, or browse through information books in small groups so as to make a display of people whose lives have been completely turned around and made new through getting involved with Jesus.

There are lots of people to choose from, and you may have people in your congregation with stories to tell. Or look at some of these: Francis and Clare,

Father Damian, Jacquie Pullinger, Nicky Cruz, Mother Theresa, Corrie Ten Boom.

# YEAR 2

*Thought for the day:*
*In Jesus we are not just patched up*
*but made new.*

## Readings
Psalm 77
2 Samuel 12:1-18a (or-23)
Acts 9:1-22

## Reflection

We have two very powerful stories today, which give us a dramatic insight into the way God works in us to cope with our failures and wanderings and puts things right.

Both David and Paul are deeply religious people, devoting their lives to serve God, and fight against what they perceive as evil. Yet both are very human, and in spite of their religious fervour (or even because of it) become drawn to the point of murder. Paul was so concerned to protect the true faith from heretics that he was inadvertently persecuting the faithful; once God had shown him that Jesus was the one with the great 'I Am', the shocking truth dawned on him with blinding light, and he was changed for life. David, too ashamed for his sin of adultery to come to light, tried hiding it and then, when the honourable Uriah wouldn't play ball, David resorted to getting Uriah out of the way by having him killed at war. He was trying to scratch out the sin with more sin. Once Nathan confronted him with the appalling truth of what he had done, David immediately repented and was forgiven.

When we sin, a complete restoration programme is needed - no amount of worrying, extra good deeds or extra bad deeds will get rid of it. It may be painful, but we have to let God's light shine on it and show it up for the evil it is. Then, before we rush to cover it up from that searing light, we have to ask God to get rid of it for us. In my experience, the next bit is not nearly as awful as I expect. God immediately takes charge, and works very gently to put it away and heal the raw wound that is left. His forgiveness comes in a rush of love without a trace of condemnation.

Once God has dealt with your sin, he's standing there, ready packed and waiting for you to go with him on the next stage of your journey. Sometimes God has to wait like this for ages because we're so busy condemning ourselves that we haven't noticed that it's all over, as far as God's concerned! If you are still whipping yourself for something you did or didn't do years ago, let God sort it out and then get up straight away, stretch your legs and enjoy living again.

## Discussion starters

1  David understood that there would be consequences of his sin, although he had been forgiven. How does God show his mercy even here?

2  What can we learn in Acts 9 of the urgency of being constantly attentive to God?

## All stage talk

*Theme:* God does things thoroughly and expertly.

Beforehand contact a local builder/decorator and ask if they would be willing to bring their tools and take part in a short interview during a service. (Well, why not – live dangerously!) Also bring with you a roll of wallpaper and a bag of paste. Start by introducing your guest, and say you've got problems with wallpaper peeling off and going mouldy, so would it be okay if you paste some of this new wallpaper over it?

As he goes through the stages of preparation and repair necessary ask him to show the specialist tools required, then ask him to tell you about the most difficult case he's ever tackled.

After this interview explain how we all have problems in our lives from time to time which are a direct result of sin. Like damp walls, sin needs sorting out thoroughly, not just covering over; if we try to cover over, as David was, the sin and guilt don't go away, but make more problems. God is the only One able to sort our sin out by getting rid of it completely and making good afterwards, just as the experts do with walls.

First God  S . . .    Shows us our sin,
then he     I . . .    Invites us back to him;
but he      N . . .    Never condemns us.

## Intercessions

Thank you, Father, for the patient love you show in teaching and guiding us, challenging and coaxing us.
We ask you to bless each person on their journey of faith.
*Silence for prayer*
Your ways are holy, Lord:
**and your ways are best**

Thank you, Father, for every peace initiative, each act of goodness, each victory over evil.
Bless and guide the nations of our world.
*Silence for prayer*
Your ways are holy, Lord:
**and your ways are best**

Thank you, Father, for the friendships we cherish, for the members of our families, and for our neighbours.
Bless each home with your presence.
*Silence for prayer*
Your ways are holy, Lord:
**and your ways are best**

Thank you, Father, for all who care for the sick, the very young and the very old.
Bless all who suffer with the comfort of your love.
*Silence for prayer*
Your ways are holy, Lord:
**and your ways are best**

Thank you, Father, for the example of lives well lived and death honestly and bravely faced. Welcome into your kingdom all who have died in faith, and those whose faith is known only to you.
*Silence for prayer*
Your ways are holy, Lord:
**and your ways are best**

Thank you, Father, for all the abundance of life you provide for us.
*Silence for prayer*
Your ways are holy, Lord:
**and your ways are best**

## Other ideas

Have the first reading acted out, with parts being read or spoken by the actors. The dramatised bible could be used, or you could make your own version, keeping closely to the text.

## In the crèche

*Aim:* For the children to know that God is very good at sorting us out when our lives get in a mess.

You may be able to get hold of some jigsaws with all the pieces the same shape. If not, make some from old Christmas and birthday cards, like this:

First have the puzzles arranged all wrong and let the children help to sort them out. Explain that when we are unfriendly, unkind or bad-tempered we feel in a muddle, like a picture. If we ask Jesus, he will always help us sort things out again.

## Children

Aim: For them to see how God sorted out King David's sin and can sort ours out too.

Start by holding hands in small groups and getting into a real muddle. Then, still holding hands, try to straighten things out. We're going to think about how God sorts our lives out when we get in a muddle.

Explain simply and clearly what David had done – many of them will be familiar with such events through watching the soaps. Then read or tell Nathan's story. What do they think of the way the man behaved? Tell them what David thought, and then how Nathan showed David that he was the man in the story. See if the children can work out why this was so, before going on to Nathan's words from God. Point out how David was forgiven as soon as he had said 'I have sinned'. Whatever we do wrong, however badly we mess things up, God will always forgive us.

Then help them to make this card with instructions for what to do in case of sin.

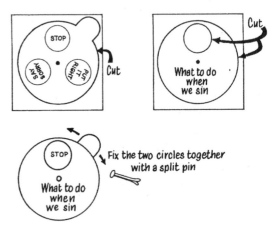

Fix the two circles together with a split pin

## Young people

Aim: To help them know about the dangers and consequences of sin, but above all of God's total forgiveness.

Read together the whole series of events which led to Uriah's killing, and Nathan's story. At this point stop to discuss David's situation, the way things had gone from bad to worse, and why he had given into temptation in the first place. (Was it something to do with staying behind instead of going out with his army? Or was he too used to getting his own way as king? etc.)

Now go on to read the next section, looking at David's violent reaction to the man in the story and his subsequent confession and immediate forgiveness. What does David's attitude to the baby suggest about his relationship with Bathsheba? In what way does God manage to retrieve every scrap of goodness in the situation and use it?

Explore some of these issues in a role

play, having each character in order giving their version of the story and how they felt about it. Characters: David, Uriah, Bathsheba, Nathan and one of the courtiers. What can all this teach us about dealing with temptation and sin in our own lives?

# 7th Sunday after Pentecost

## YEAR 1

*Thought for the day:*
*Since we are made in God's likeness,*
*the only real and fulfilling way to live*
*is in a loving, Godlike way.*

### Readings
Psalm 81
Genesis 50:15-end
1 John 2:1-17

### Reflection

It is tempting to take on God's unique job of judgement, rather than his characteristic of selfless love. On reading this passage from Genesis 50 we might have found it understandable for Joseph's brothers to fear judgmental reprisals once their father had died. But for Joseph, living closely and attentively in God's company, there is no question of holding grudges or taking the law into his own hands. Instead, Joseph thinks naturally in terms of forgiveness; through the insight and wisdom gained from all the experiences God has given him Joseph can see that God works in all things for good, and can turn even destructiveness on its head and make it fruitful.

We can probably all think of occasions where God has managed to bring some good out of a terrible situation.

The John passage takes this a step further. If we say we love God but don't act with God's style of practical, transforming love, then we must be liars. And there are plenty of self-professed followers of Christ whose destructive, critical, hypocritical lives prove them to be just that. As a result of such lives the church is weakened, and many who seek are put off. It is not comfortable to face the fact that our own behaviour may already have prevented someone from drawing closer to God.

As the same time, there are many whose generous, well-rooted lives work God's transforming love in the places they go to, the people they meet and the troubles they experience. As a result, our world is daily being refreshed, healed and restored. It could well be that in our better moments we ourselves have inadvertently helped someone on their journey of faith.

### Discussion starters

1 What does Joseph's reply to his brothers show us about his character and his relationship with God?

2 There is always the need to keep a balance between fully accepting God's forgiveness and living life to the full on the one hand, and presuming on God's forgiveness and living carelessly on the other. How do both Joseph and John help us to tackle this issue?

### All stage talk

*Theme:* Living the loving way, not just talking about it.

Start by showing everyone how you have spoilt something by using it to do what it wasn't designed for – such as a knife for a screwdriver, or scissors as wire cutters.

As we are made like God, and God is loving, we only feel that deep-down sense of peace and rightness when we are using our bodies, minds and spirits in the way they were designed to be used.

Now arrange two teams of three people (mixed in age and character) rather like a quiz show. Have each team holding their team name: THE GOD SQUAD and THE SELF SET. Ask a volunteer to be a Christian in the street, on his journey through life. He walks from the back to the front, and every so often you tell him to stop to sort out a problem. Have the first problem read out clearly, then ask each team what their advice would be. The Christian then decides which to accept, and the congregation can express their approval or not by clapping or groaning. Then he continues on his journey until the next problem and so on. It will be best if you think up situations pertinent to your congregation, but here are some suggestions to get you going:

1   The T.V. news shows a famine and you have just received your pay packet.
2   Your brother/sister has messed up your favourite tape.
3   The grass needs cutting but your friends are round.
4   You're gasping for a drink, and find a purse lying on the pavement.

In conclusion, make the point that if we say we're Christians it must affect the way be behave, but that even if we choose wrongly sometimes, God can still bring some good from the resulting situation.

## Intercessions

Father, we call to mind the world church; we acknowledge our divisions and mistakes and thank you for transforming them even as we pray.

*Silence for prayer*

Teach us, Lord:
**to walk in your light**

Father, we call to mind the wounds of our world born of collective greed and terrible blunders throughout history; and we praise you as you work to bring wholeness.

*Silence for prayer*

Teach us, Lord:
**to walk in your light**

Father, we call to mind the nurturing of children and the responsibility of parenthood and community; we need your guidance and grace, your protection and courage.

*Silence for prayer*

Teach us, Lord:
**to walk in your light**

Father, we call to mind those trapped in addictions, imprisoned by guilt, and drained through grief; on their behalf, we plead for rescue.

*Silence for prayer*

Teach us, Lord:
**to walk in your light**

Father, we call to mind those who have died, and those who are dying now, unnoticed and unloved.

*Silence for prayer*

Teach us, Lord:
**to walk in your light**

Father, we call to mind the way you have dealt with us so lovingly in the past, and we commit our future into your keeping.

*Silence for prayer*

Teach us, Lord:
**to walk in your light**

## Other ideas

• At the time of confession and reconciliation, have the qualities of love read out slowly (1 Cor 13) so that people can hear from the positives where they need to change things in their own lives.

• Have an exhibition of a project of practical, caring love which the parish is already involved with. Have symbols from this project offered for blessing with the collection, and have lists available for people to sign where they would be able to help.

### In the crèche

*Aim:* To help the children understand that whenever they're kind and loving they are working with God and behaving like him.

Have ready some lively Christian music on tape, and call out different ways of behaving, one by one. If it fits in with God's loving way of living, then the music goes on and everybody has a good dance. If it doesn't, everyone stands still and does the thumbs down sign.

Here are some ideas for things to say:
Sharing your toys.
Not letting your friend have a go on your trike.
Helping Dad.
Not doing what Mum tells you to.
Doing what you're told.
Hurting someone because you don't like them.

During the free play time, encourage all the kind, loving behaviour and remind them of the game.

### Children

*Aim:* To help them look at choosing God's way of behaving.

Start by playing a quick game, such as crab football where you all move around like this:

Talk together about the way we keep having to make choices in a game, and we sometimes know we've made bad decisions and messed things up. That's also true in life. Have a joint telling of the Joseph story – the part where the brothers had decided to get rid of Joseph. So the brothers had really messed things up for Joseph. Or had they? Explain how God always works to bring some good out of our mistakes. Can they think of any good that came out of what the brothers had done? Make a list of these, then tell or read what happened when their father had died, pausing to let them guess how Joseph will react to the brothers' story. (They may well recognise the temptation to twist the truth to get out of trouble!) Then go on to see what Joseph actually said.

Help them make this choosing chart and try it out on their friends and family.

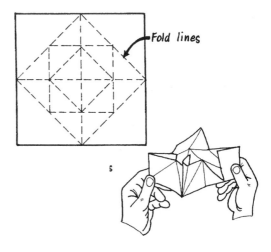

## Young people

*Aim:* To look at living Christianity in the real world.

As with the children, begin with a ball team game appropriate to the surroundings, and talk over the need to make quick, good decisions so as to enable the whole team to do well. In life we are always having to make decisions about the way we act, and some of those choices we make have lasting effects and can change or threaten to ruin our lives. Read the Genesis passage, and discuss how Joseph's brothers might have felt. What good had God managed to bring out of their wrong behaviour?

Read the John passage and lead them to see the importance of acting on what we believe, rather than just talking about it. Have a selection of leaflets about organisations which need support (either financial, practical or prayer support) and decide together on something that you could take on as individuals or in a group to put your faith into action.

# YEAR 2

*Thought for the day:*
*We are to love others in the way God loves us – completely.*

## Readings

Psalm 81
Deuteronomy 24:10-end
1 John 3:13-end

## Reflection

Long before Paul started taking the good news to the Gentiles, Israel's ancient laws had grasped the truth that God's love is outgoing, not restricted to those of our own clan or cluster. Remembering their history as aliens and outcasts in Egypt, they are to respond to people's needs whatever their position or ethnic origin.

To our shame, the Christian church has many times ignored or 'edited' such guidance and there still remain many terrible injustices actually committed in the name of our religion which cause misery and unnecessary suffering. If we are too used to them we don't even notice that they go directly against God's will for his people. Part of growing in Christ is getting a clearer vision of where such wrongs need righting, both in our personal lives and in the wider community.

Some people suffer from the opposite extreme – their conscience is hyper-sensitive and they find it very hard to believe that God finds them loveable and forgivable, knowing how far they fall short of perfect loving. John's advice is sensible and affectionate (V.19-20). He reminds us that God's loving heart is a lot more roomy than we suppose, and he knows all the mitigating circumstances. It is a life which is characterised by loving obedience to God's will which John is talking of, rather than the impossible – a totally sin-free life.

## Discussion starters

1  Are there any laws/acceptable behaviour in our society which exploit the vulnerable and poor? What would be a more Godly way of doing things?

2  It has been said that your wallet is the last part of you to get converted. How far do you think this is true?

## All stage talk

*Theme:* Don't just say it, do it!
Beforehand arrange two small tables to be available during the talk, each with a mixing bowl and spoon, bag of peanuts, bag of raisins and bag of chocolate chips. Also arrange for someone to read out the

recipe, one step at a time. Stand at one of the tables, and ask for a couple of volunteers to stand at the other table. Explain that you're fond of nutritious snacks, and are really keen to make one this morning. Introduce the person who will read out the recipe so that we all know what to do. As the steps are read out, encourage the volunteers to do what is said, but don't actually do them yourself – just keep babbling on about how good the recipe is, and how clear, and how you understand just what it means etc., etc.

When the snack is complete, let the volunteers show what it looks like and taste it. Now show your bowl, and let some of the younger children tell you that you haven't made anything at all. Protest that you must have done, because you had all the ingredients, and you listened to the recipe, and really agreed with it all. So what went wrong? The others heard what to do and did something about it; you didn't act on what you heard, so it really wasn't much good to anyone.

If we say we love God, but don't put that faith into action, our lives will end up as empty as that bowl.

## *Intercessions*

Father, we pray that all Christians may grow more loving, more active and more faithful, starting now.

*Silence for prayer*

God is greater than our hearts:
**and he knows everything**

Father, we pray for all world leaders and those who advise them, that they may make good decisions and act wisely.

*Silence for prayer*

God is greater than our hearts:
**and he knows everything**

Father, we pray for single parent families, families under stress and all who are separated from loved ones.

*Silence for prayer*

God is greater than our hearts:
**and he knows everything**

Father, we pray for the mentally ill, the physically damaged,
for the lonely and the fearful.

*Silence for prayer*

God is greater than our hearts:
**and he knows everything**

Father, we pray for those who have come to the end of their earthly life, and for those who miss them, or never had the opportunity to put things right with them.

*Silence for prayer*

God is greater than our hearts:
**and he knows everything**

Father, we bring to you our secret hopes and longings and our gratitude.

*Silence for prayer*

God is greater than our hearts:
**and he knows everything**

## *Other ideas*

For the Deuteronomy passage, have different voices to read the different laws, with everyone joining in v.13b, 18, and 22.

## *In the crèche*

*Aim:* For them to see that God's way is love in action.

First play a game of acting on orders, so that if you call out 'Run!' everyone does it. Possible commands are: run, squirm, roll, bounce, crawl; or move like a mouse/elephant/cat/goldfish.

Have a story time of any gospel story where Jesus acted out God's healing love.

## Children

*Aim:* For them to see that God's way is love in action.

Start by having a game of Simon Says, so that they make sure they only follow out the actions which Simon has told them to. Explain that in our lives we will probably hear all kinds of ideas about how to act, but if we listen out we'll be able to know which instructions come from God's will, and which don't. Give them some examples to practise on; if they think a suggestion comes from God they stand up – if not they stay sitting down. Some possible examples to start you making your own up:

Take that sweet – the shopkeeper isn't looking.

Give Mum a hand – she looks tired.

Wait for your friend to catch up.

Pretend you weren't involved in the fight. Own up.

Then make some sweets or cakes, following the instructions. Hand them round afterwards on paper plates which have this written on them:

TRUE LOVE SHOWS IN ACTION.

## Young people

*Aim:* To help them see how love can be translated into practical caring.

Read the Deuteronomy passage, explaining how compassionate and caring these laws were in comparison to the other ancient laws of neighbouring cultures. Then look at the John reading, to see what he considers real loving to involve. Look at the expense of love, and the necessity of acting it out, rather than just waffling on about it.

Either in small groups or all together, work out a composite 'recipe' for living God's loving way, which can then be published in the magazine or on next week's handout.

Here is one recipe to give you all the idea:

1  Take one family aching with hunger, home destroyed, eyes full of fear.
2  Gather some consciences from well fed Christians and prick them thoroughly.
3  When hearts are softened, wait for action to start.
4  Fill needs to the brim and hold carefully to avoid smashing hopes and lives.

---

# 8th Sunday after Pentecost

---

## YEAR 1

*Thought for the day:*
*What we are determines how we fruit.*

### Readings
Psalm 73
Numbers 11:16-17,24-29
Acts 8:4-25

### Reflection

Through the contrasts in these readings we can learn a great deal about how our deeply held values become second nature to us, and show up clearly when we are in a testing situation.

First we see Moses – the spiritually gifted leader of God's people. Notice how God is not providing extra power, but withdrawing power from Moses in order to empower the seventy men. It is all in a very good cause – to ease Moses' burden. But if Moses had become in the least possessive of his exclusive, charismatic leadership, he could have been a bit peeved, or even downright angry, as Joshua was on his behalf. As it was, his reaction shows the beauty of his spirit; he is delighted for others to receive gifts he has, and only wishes it could happen to everyone!

Then, in total contrast, we see Simon the Magus, fascinated by the power Philip shows, and even taking it all on board himself. So far, so good. Yet in fact he is still enchained by his old desire for personal power; as soon as he sees the signs of the Spirit coming through the laying on of hands, he wants to be the person in charge, and thinks of it as a commodity which we can control. He has completely misunderstood the message of God's lordship in our lives, and his abundant free giving.

## Discussion starters

1 How do you think we can train ourselves to be less possessive of our status, our ideas or our 'territory'?

2 Sometimes we put people on pedestals because we admire them. Having read the passage from Numbers, what dangers do you think there are in doing this? Is there anything we could do to protect young heroes and heroines from such dangers?

## All stage talk

*Theme:* A change of heart.

Beforehand, arrange with some prominent church person (such as the organist, or the guide captain) for them to come and interrupt you at the right place. Start by showing everyone an attractive tin of biscuits or sweets, which you tell them has been given to you by Mrs Boyton. Tell everyone how pleased you are to have it, and how much you especially love the custard creams etc., etc . . . As you are drooling over the biscuits Mrs Boyton herself interrupts, and says she has decided to take some of the biscuits she

gave you, so that she can give them to seven other people. That way you won't be burdened with a weight problem. As she reaches over to the tin, freeze the action, and ask people to think whether they would be pleased or grumpy if that happened to them. It happened to Moses, who had been given God's Spirit and then God withdrew some to give to seventy others. Who remembers how Moses felt?

Now carry on the action, Moses-style; be delighted, thank Mrs. Boyton for her idea and let her give seven biscuits away to other people.

So what have we learnt about Moses?

- He was not possessive of the gifts God had given him.
- He genuinely wanted the best for people.
- His life was well-rooted in God.

## Intercessions

In your presence we bring to mind all Christians; those recently baptised or recently returned to the faith, all church leaders and those whose faith is hesitant.

*Silence for prayer*

From eternity to eternity:
**you are God**

In your presence we call to mind the areas of conflict, righteous anger and hardened attitudes, and we pray for your lasting peace.

*Silence for prayer*

From eternity to eternity:
**you are God**

In your presence we bring to mind those who have influenced our faith development, those we love, and those who love us.

*Silence for prayer*

From eternity to eternity:
**you are God**

*Continued overleaf*

In your presence we call to mind those who are enchained by guilt, or bad and frightening memories which need to be released.

*Silence for prayer*

From eternity to eternity:
**you are God**

In your presence we call to mind those who have died and moved from time into eternity; their families and all who miss them.

*Silence for prayer*

From eternity to eternity:
**you are God**

In your presence we bring to mind the beauty, love and peace which surround us and bubble up even inside pain and grief.

*Silence for prayer*

From eternity to eternity:
**you are God**

## Other ideas

• Have the second reading mimed, or read by different characters.

## In the crèche

*Aim:* To help them understand that a tree can be seen by looking at its fruit.

Have a number of trees drawn like this:

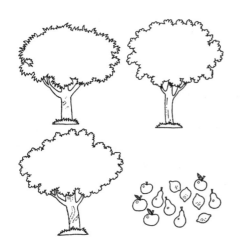

Cut out a number of fruits for each tree, made from coloured paper with sticky putty on the back. Tell the children that one of the trees is an apple tree, one a lemon tree and one a pear tree. But which is which? We don't know until the tree starts to grow fruit. (Stick one fruit on each tree.) Now we can tell what kind of tree each one is. Let the children sort out the fruits, sticking the right fruits on the right trees.

## Children

*Aim:* For them to get to know the story of Simon the Magus.

Get the children in a huddle in the centre of the room to tell them about how the early church met together and worshipped in Jerusalem. Explain that people started to persecute the Christians, especially the Greek speaking ones, so they scattered away from Jerusalem to be safe. (Some children are sent off in different directions.) One of these people was a man called Philip, and he went to Samara.

How do you think God brought good out of these persecutions? All the Christians who scattered, went and told people about Jesus wherever they went, so the good news spread and spread.

Now take everyone over to Samaria, to watch what Philip is up to. Let the children act out the story as you tell them how Philip was gathering groups and telling them about God's love for them, healing the sick and giving the blind their sight in Jesus's name. Many believed, and Philip baptised them in the rivers. Among those being baptised was a person called Simon, who was a clever magician and was very impressed with what Philip was doing.

Now the Christians at Jerusalem sent Peter and John to find out what was going on. (Have two people coming over from Jerusalem.) They were very pleased to find all these new Christians in the land which was the traditional Jews' enemy, and they laid hands on them so they could receive the Holy Spirit. The new Christians started speaking in different tongues and dancing around full of the Spirit. Simon the magician wanted to buy this power, so he could do it to people and have control over them. The apostles were furious that he should think such a thing, and had to pray over Simon for him to be freed from wanting power all the time. God's power is always freely given, and can never be bought, either by money, or even by good deeds.

Help the children to express some part of this story in paints, crayons, collage or clay.

## Young people

*Aim:* For them to explore the way our deeply held values show in how we act. First read the passage from Numbers and pick out the qualities of Moses' character which are shown up clearly by his reaction to Joshua's righteous indignation. Then look at the account of Philip's ministry in Samaria and the way Simon reacted to the coming of the Holy Spirit. What does his reaction show us about his values, in spite of the fact that he has listened to Philip's teaching and been baptised?

Work on the two accounts using role plays in small groups, either to be a chat in the wilderness involving Joshua, one of the seventy men, and an onlooker; or a chat in Samaria involving a recently baptised Christian, Simon and Philip.

# YEAR 2

*Thought for the day:*
*What we are determines how we fruit.*

## Readings
Psalm 73
Proverbs 8:1-17
Luke 6:39-end

## Reflection

Much of this week's readings are to do with consequences. Whenever there is a cross-roads or junction we choose which direction to go, and where we end up is a direct result of our choice, even if we don't actually reach anywhere for several miles. It's the same spiritually; there will be consequences of the choices we make which will eventually become apparent, whether we like it or not.

It is impossible to choose in a habitually selfish and demanding way, for instance, without sooner or later turning into a crabby old bully! It's impossible for a bad tree not to bear bad fruit. The Proverbs reading advises us to choose wisely, and the house builders on rock and sand point out the sense of this. But where do we get the good advice and guidance we need? Obviously we need God's guidance through prayer, but that may well come through good human advice – people who through being attentive to God can be used as channels of his wisdom and love. King Reheboam (1 Kings 12:9-11) followed the rash, greedy advice of his contemporaries and was led disastrously in the wrong direction. Jesus speaks with passionate anger against those whom others trust to lead them well, but are in fact blind guides, leading people into ditches.

God forbid that we should lead others to stumble, or even lead them away from the God who loves them. All teachers, preachers, church leaders and evangelists, all with power to influence anyone (and that covers most of us), need to make sure that our eyes are regularly and ruthlessly cleared of planks and specks of sawdust, so that we can help others, who trust us, to walk safely in the right direction and choose what is good.

## Discussion starters

1  In what way were the religious teachers of Jesus' time being blind guides? In what ways are religious people sometimes blind guides today?

2  To what extent do we have free choice, bearing in mind the factors of upbringing, genes, circumstances etc.?

## All stage talk

*Theme:* Consequences.

Begin by asking a couple of volunteers to run up and down, or jog on the spot, and as they do so, point out that if we choose to run fast like this there will be consequences. Stop the runners and demonstrate the way their breathing is much deeper and faster, and their pulse rate higher. They are probably warmer, too. All these things are natural consequences of the action they have been involved in.

If we choose to do something wise, like looking and listening carefully as we cross the road, the consequence will be that we have a far better chance of being safe. If you choose something foolish, like standing on your head when you haven't done that for forty years, the likely consequence is that you will probably damage your neck. We make these decisions all the time and how we choose will actually change the shape of our characters.

If we choose the selfish, unkind, greedy, or cruel way we will become selfish, unkind, greedy or cruel people. If, on the other hand, we choose the friendly, encouraging, honest or loving way, we will become friendly, encouraging, honest or loving people. What we become will be a consequence of what we choose.

## Intercessions

Father, you know our motives as well as our actions; bless our decision-making, so that we do not make wrong choices in our lives.

*Silence for prayer*

Teach us your ways:
**and help us to live them**

Father, you know the strengths and weaknesses of our church;
we do not want to hide anything away, but long for your advice and guidance.

*Silence for prayer*

Teach us your ways:
**and help us to live them**

Father, you know us, and those we live and work with; you understand the real reasons for our quarrels and upsets; we long for you to work your healing in those hidden areas.

*Silence for prayer*

Teach us your ways:
**and help us to live them**

Father, you know the individual history behind each person's revenge and each country's difficulties; we long for peace and tranquillity in our world.

*Silence for prayer*

Teach us your ways:
**and help us to live them**

Father, you watch with the sick and the dying; you feel their pain and know their fear; we long for them to know your loving presence with them.

*Silence for prayer*

Teach us your ways:
**and help us to live them**

Father, your creation is indeed very good, and we praise and thank you for all you provide.

*Silence for prayer*

Teach us your ways:
**and help us to live them**

## Other ideas

• Have a basket of fruit combined with the flowers in our arrangement today.

• Have a group of people to act out the second reading of the house building.

## In the crèche

*Aim:* For the children to understand the sense of building their lives on Jesus. Have a grand building session, using either building blocks (but not the interlocking sort) or a large number of cartons and shoe boxes. I have found that so long as they are asked in advance, shoe shops are only too happy to let you collect their boxes on a Saturday afternoon, ready for Sunday morning.

Try building first on a very wobbly surface, so that the construction keeps collapsing. Then build on a good strong base and see the difference. As you build you can sing about building your lives on Jesus to the tune of 'Three blind mice':

Here's my life, here's my life,
Strong and good, strong and good,
It's built on Jesus so you can see
My life is strong as strong can be
'Cos I love him and he loves me
Right through my life.

## Children

*Aim:* For the children to understand the sense of building their lives on Jesus. Begin by talking about earthquakes, floods and have some pictures of what happens to houses that are built on a place where these things happen. Pray together for the people whose lives and property are destroyed or ruined in such disasters. Why do people live in such dangerous areas? Usually because they can't live anywhere else. There's no way anyone would choose to build in an unsafe place. Then explain how Jesus said that anyone who hears God's word and instead of following it, turns his back on it, is as barmy as this: someone actually choosing to build their house on sand, knowing that it won't survive the storms and floods.

Get the children to act out the story, with their bodies becoming the houses and the floods, and their voices the sound effects.

Give each child a small box to make into a house called 'Marion/Julian's Life' built on Jesus. They can use the box at home to keep treasures in:

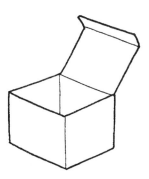

# 9th Sunday after Pentecost

## YEAR 1

*Thought for the day:*
*God's protection against evil will*
*enable us to get on with his work.*

## Readings
Psalm 90
Nehemiah 4:7-end
Matthew 6:1-18

## Reflection

Nehemiah is one of those practical, efficient and wise leaders who knows the importance of prayer being linked with action. ('We prayed . . . and set a guard . . .'; 'Remember the Lord . . . and fight.') The people were thus arming themselves not only physically, but spiritually as well.

It can sometimes be that we need to do a spot of building or rebuilding in our own lives, working with one hand and with a sword against evil in our other hand. Such times are exhausting and treacherous, but also immeasurably valuable and constructive. Addicts who have clawed their way through the withdrawal symptoms; adulterers who have struggled back to a right relationship; haters who have tackled the arduous journey to forgiveness – all these will understand exactly what I mean. And if you are involved with such building at the moment, let Nehemiah's rebuilding programme give you comfort; with God, nothing is impossible.

When we pray, we put ourselves available so that God can work his wonders through our lives. Through

## Young people

*Aim:* For them to understand the sense of building their lives on Jesus.

Start by giving out playing cards to everyone, and letting them make card houses, some on smooth, firm bases and some on rough wobbly ones. Whose can withstand most blowing?

Now read the passage from Luke together and look at why Jesus was so angry with the 'blind guides'. Talk about what it means to them to have their lives built on the foundation of faith in God, including the difficulties this may cause as well as the blessings. Plan a youth event which will reach their contemporaries who do not yet know Jesus as a living person.

Nehemiah's prayer, God could place his people where they were most valuable, and be ready when they were needed, and that is still what happens each day when we pray.

In the passage from Matthew we have Jesus' teaching about giving, praying and fasting. We have just seen how it is a natural and simple way of life to pray and then act. Jesus' words reveal what a complex, egocentric ritual it had all become, with the power base taken over for self aggrandisement instead of humble self offering. Out of these mistakes comes the simple, practical pattern of the Lord's Prayer, which reminds us at every phrase of our dependence on our loving parent God, and our need to check our own attitudes as well as praying for others.

## Discussion starters

1  You often hear people saying, 'Well, I've done everything I can; all there is left to do now is pray'. Why do we so often go for the action first, rather than the prayer? What does it suggest about our faith?

2  We are the body of Christ. How can we make sure that we are helping and supporting one another properly during the difficult, perilous parts of our spiritual journey?

## All stage talk

*Theme:* Prayer is armour.
Bring along various items of protective clothing: marigold gloves, a cycle helmet, wellington boots, a surgeon's mask and some earplugs. Demonstrate these items with volunteers, and explain how prayer is a protection against evil.

Nehemiah and everyone needed protection against invaders while they rebuilt the walls of the city of Jerusalem. As we are involved with the building of God's kingdom we shall find those who scoff and ridicule what we are doing, those who deliberately break down where we are building up, and others who can take us by surprise and discourage or destroy. Praying keeps the channels open between us and God, so that he can supply us with all the protective spiritual clothing we need.

## Intercessions

Father, we pray for the building up of your church; for each individual member as we struggle with doubts,
fears and weariness, with scorn or persecution.

*Silence for prayer*

From eternity to eternity:
**you are our God**

Father, we pray for the building of peace between nations, the building of honour and respect between people as we work through deep hurts from the past.

*Silence for prayer*

From eternity to eternity:
**you are our God**

Father, we pray for the building up of communities in areas where people feel lost and like strangers; for a sense of trust and mutual support.

*Silence for prayer*

From eternity to eternity:
**you are our God**

Father, we pray for those recovering from surgery and illness;
for those who lack energy and vitality;
for those who cannot face the future.

*Silence for prayer*

From eternity to eternity:
**you are our God**

*Continued overleaf*

Father, we pray for those who have
finished their earthly life
and now enter eternity;
and we pray for those who badly miss
their physical presence.

*Silence for prayer*

From eternity to eternity:
**you are our God**

Father, we pray that we may increasingly
notice your glory, delight in your care of
us and rest in your peace.

*Silence for prayer*

From eternity to eternity:
 **you are our God**

## Other ideas

• The last verse of Psalm 90 is a lovely
blessing which you could use at the end
of the service.
• Have one of today's flower
arrangements set in a wooden or metal
'treasure chest', so that the flowers spill
out of it, and the key is incorporated into
the arrangement.

## In the crèche

*Aim:* For the children to know that God
keeps them safe.

Have some protective clothing for them
to dress up in, such as rain or snow wear,
painting shirts, builders' hard hats and so
on. Play out some of the situations when
they would be needed. Tell the children
how God keeps them safe, and sing a
song such as 'God has put his angels'.

## Children

*Aim:* To hear the story of Nehemiah and
the people rebuilding the city walls.

This is a good story to act out, with a
group of children to be the builders, and
others to be the scoffers and invaders. If
you feel this may get too realistic with
your group, go for a less direct telling,
such as puppets, or using carpet tiles
with cut outs of the builders and
invaders. Bring out the important fact
that all action was preceded by prayer, so
that the whole plan was much more
effective.

Then help them make this building
game to play at home, so as to remind
them. To play the game they will need a
dice, and gradually the walls are rebuilt
according to the numbers thrown. If a 6 is
thrown, invaders are attacking at your
part of the wall, and you must miss a turn
while you cope with them.

Enough for one per player          15 bricks of card per player

## Young people

*Aim:* To explore the nature of prayer as
armour.

Begin by reading the first passage,
making a note of how they protected the
building programme from attack. It may
help to have the ground plan drawn, and
have two different colours of counters to
represent the builders and the attackers.
The counters are moved about as the
action develops, rather like a ministry of
defence map. Talk about how important it
was for everyone to be protected and

prepared.

Now look at the passage from Matthew, and notice the difference between the natural prayer of Nehemiah and the empty ritual of the Pharisees in Jesus' time. They may well have already been aware that 'saying prayer' is not necessarily the same thing as praying. Work through Jesus' advice and teaching on prayer in the light of their own experience, and discuss any difficulties in prayer they are having, either in private or in public worship. Enable this to be a constructive time, using any ideas that come out of it for positive action in the church.

# YEAR 2

*Thought for the day:*
*God's protection against evil will*
*enable us to get on with his work.*

## Readings
Psalm 90
2 Samuel 1:1-12, 17-end
1 Timothy 6:6-end

## Reflection
God always empowers us for the next job he has in mind for us, so that gradually, bit by bit, the kingdom advances. In a way it's rather like being in the cast of a repertory theatre, where we are always performing one play while being prepared for the next one. Following the same image, it would be ludicrous to go all through the preparation and not turn up for the performance. There is an urgency about working for the coming of the kingdom which we need to take seriously, opening ourselves to receive all the emotional, mental or physical preparation God provides, even if we can't at the time see where it is leading.

(It's rare for God to allow us to peek, and it's often just as well we can't, or we'd run off and hide!)

The more attentive we are, the better God will be able to prepare us. Humans are so argumentative by nature, and we tend to keep pestering God during a training session involving hardship or suffering, and complaining every inch of the way. Then later, we may eventually come to realise how important that time was in training us for a future task we were asked to do.

In this week's reading we watch David coping with the death of Saul and Jonathan, working through his grief at their loss before he is made king. And we see Timothy being prepared through Paul, for the difficulties and problems he will meet in his ministry.

In our Christian work, we never know when God is going to use us – that's one of the things that makes life so exciting! What that means, though, is that we must take on board all the training which comes our way, so that we are properly equipped for each task God asks us to be involved with.

## Discussion starters
1 How do you account for David's reaction to Saul's death when you remember the way Saul had treated David in his life? What can we learn from this?

2 What can we learn about Paul from his letter to Timothy? Which of his teachings do you think is particularly valuable today?

## All stage talk
*Theme:* Use God's gifts to do God's work.
Have ready a musical instrument, such as a violin or trumpet – it needs to be quite a bulky one; a set of football gear, including a football; a large basket of fruit; six

envelopes, three of which are labelled GOD'S WAY and the others MY OWN WAY. I will explain what messages are in which envelopes as we go along.

Introduce three volunteers who will be helping with this week's teaching, and explain that God always equips us for any job he wants us to do, but somehow, we often get it wrong.

Perhaps God gives us a musical gift (give the first person the musical instrument). Then we have a choice – are we going to do things God's way or our own way? The person can choose either envelope to open, and whichever one isn't chosen is opened afterwards so that both possibilities are seen.

GOD'S WAY: Use your musical gift to cheer people up and lead them in worship.

MY OWN WAY: Not bother to practise and never play for anyone.

One way gives a blessing to many, the other wastes the gift.

Now provide the second person with all the football equipment, saying as you do so that God may train us for quite a specialised job – perhaps for helping drug addicts through living with an addict in our family. When the person is all set up, choose which way to go.

GOD'S WAY: Play football for the school.

MY OWN WAY: Go swimming.

We sometimes decide to go our own way, completely ignore the gifts God has given us, and rush off instead to do something for which we are not equipped at all. Then we wonder why it all fails.

Give the last person a large basket of fruit, showing everyone how delicious all the fruit looks. Which envelope will be chosen?

GOD'S WAY: Give some fruit to people in St Clement's church who would really like some.

MY OWN WAY: Eat so much that you get tummy ache and let the rest go mouldy.

Sometimes God give us gifts which feel very nice, and instead of using them as he intends – to share with others – we get greedy and hang on to them.

Finally, let the last person do things God's way, and share out the fruit among the congregation.

## Intercessions

Father, we commend to your love
all church leaders and those in their care;
all who need encouragement and
reassurance.

*Silence for prayer*

May the favour of the Lord:
**rest upon us**

Father, we commend to your mercy
all the areas of violence in our world;
the hopes and disillusions, the potential
good and evil.

*Silence for prayer*

May the favour of the Lord:
**rest upon us**

Father, we commend to your tenderness
our relatives and friends, both those who
bring joy and those who cause us
great concern.

*Silence for prayer*

May the favour of the Lord:
**rest upon us**

Father, we commend to your loving care
all whose lives are caged by guilt or
terror; all who are coming to terms with a
disability; all who suffer through
another's cruelty.

*Silence for prayer*

May the favour of the Lord:
**rest upon us**

Father, we commend to your welcoming arms those who have arrived at the point of death, especially the unnoticed and uncared for.

*Silence for prayer*

May the favour of the Lord:
**rest upon us**

Father, we commend to you our thanks and praise for all that is good and beautiful, responsive and true.

*Silence for prayer*

May the favour of the Lord:
**rest upon us**

## Other ideas

Act out the first reading and involve everyone in reading the dirge; or have a slow drum beat and sorrowful quiet music in the background.

## In the crèche

*Aim:* To experience being prepared to do something.

Tell the children that you are preparing them all for a secret. First produce the overalls/shirts/aprons. Then some paper, then brushes and finally paint. See if they can guess what they're prepared for at each stage, and when everything is ready, tell them that you would like them to spend this morning making a special picture about the good and bad that is in the world. Let them now make a collage picture, and tell them as you work how God gets us ready if he asks us to work with him.

## Children

*Aim:* To experience being prepared to do something.

Start by playing 'What's the secret?' You have a child at the front and give them items, one by one. The other children have to guess what the child is being prepared for.

For instance, Jane might be given a leotard, some grease paint, a script, a ghastly costume and some ballet shoes. Her secret: she's going to be in a show. Alexander is given a lunch pack, a torch, a rucksack, a pair of thick socks, a map and a pair of boots. (Nothing needs to fit, as the children won't be dressing up.) Alexander's secret: He's going on a night hike.
Sam is given a bag of flour and a bowl, some cheese and a grater, a tin of tomatoes, an onion and some oven gloves. His secret: he's going to make a pizza.

Now explain to the children how God prepares us in our lives and equips us for what he need us to do. When Paul knew that his young friend Timothy was going to be a church worker, he wrote a letter full of advice. Read them a little of that letter, so they can hear it as a personal one. Have another child in the front to be Timothy. This time we work backwards – we already know what he is being prepared for; we're going to work out what he might need for the job.

If you have a blackboard or flip chart you can write or draw what they suggest, which will probably be extremely practical!

## Young people

*Aim:* For them to be aware that God prepares and equips us for the work he has in mind for us.

First read the passage from Samuel. Notice the grief and honour David has for Saul and Jonathan in spite of the way he has been treated during Saul's life. How did all these early experiences of David help to prepare him for his role as king? Jot down their ideas; they can remember themselves when times seem particularly hard in their own lives.

Now, in small groups of two or three, write down the sort of things parents say before leaving you to look after yourself for the day, or when you are going off on holiday.

Share and enjoy these lists, and then read Paul's letter to Timothy – preparing him for the difficulties and stressing the important things for him to remember. Finally, work out together what advice you might give to a Christian who is coming to work with the people at your school.

# 10th Sunday after Pentecost

## YEAR 1

*Thought for the day:*
*God's wisdom turns our priorities upside down.*

## Readings
Psalm 19
1 Samuel 18:1-16
Mark 9:30-end

## Reflection

The key to this week's readings is in Psalm 19, where we see the Law of the Lord praised as a thing of enormous beauty. It might seem strange to go ecstatic over a law, which we immediately associate more with speed limits and prisons than anything particularly beautiful, but what is meant here is the beauty of God's ways, the ways he has chosen and designed for us to walk in. In this sense, God's laws do indeed have power to refresh and revive, and to give us fulfilment and joy which lasts.

David, living according to God's Law, and attentive to him, is protected against Saul's fits of madness. God knows the dangers of David being in Saul's presence, but it is in his mind to have David there in preparation for becoming Israel's king, and he will keep David safe as he works in conjunction with God's will. We can read of the same kind of protection in lives like Brother Andrew, the bible smuggler, or Corrie Ten Boom in the concentration camps.

In the passage from Mark, Jesus can see the terrible dangers ahead, and knows that there can be no escape from them if perfect love is to overcome evil. But as yet that painful truth is hidden from the disciples; even when Jesus spells it out to them they don't understand. It is natural and human that they don't; their minds are still full of earthly values, where death shuts the gates on hope and further action.

It is this blinkering of eternal vision by immediate, material concerns which is tackled by Jesus' teaching about cutting off hands and gouging eyes out. It certainly looks pretty drastic! Jesus is using the very effective teaching method of exaggeration here, much as we might talk of being snowed under with work, or flying round with the hoover before guests arrive. It's while we are shocked or amused by the image that the truth of its meaning dawns on us, and in this passage Jesus is explaining that self fulfilment can go too far, to the point of wrecking our chances of real, lasting fulfilment. It challenges us to check our priorities and our values before it is too late.

## Discussion starters

1  Read through Psalm 19, especially verses 7-11. Link this with Mark 9:35. How do you think such a way of life can lead to fulfilment and joy?

2  In our society, our church, and our individual lives, what areas would we do better to reject or cut away in order to live God's way?

## All stage talk

*Theme:* God's mind: God minds.

Beforehand make three large card signs on which are written: GOD  MIND  S.
First ask three volunteers to hold the signs up in this order: GODS MIND and explain that this morning we are going to think about the way God's mind works: how God thinks.

Ask if anyone knows what you are thinking. They might be able to guess, but really our thoughts are very secret, unless we choose to give people clues to how we're thinking. Act out being angry about the choice of one of today's hymns, and see if anyone can then work out from this what is in your mind. Then act out something which shows you are pleased or surprised. (These could all be linked with the hymn numbers if you wish.)

Explain that God does want us to understand what's in his mind, so he gives us clues which we see in the things he has made. We know from the way the universe works, for instance, that God must be very careful and imaginative, enjoy lots of variety, like order and harmony, and consider everything important, from the largest to the tiniest item.

Ask the volunteers to rearrange themselves so that the message now reads: GOD MINDS. God cares about us and all his creation; he bothers about how we are feeling and what we are doing. He hurts when we hurt and aches when we mess our lives up for ourselves and those close to us. He is overjoyed when we find real happiness and delight with him in the way things are designed to be. If we want people to be really clear about what is in our mind, we talk, and explain how we are feeling and what we are thinking. And God does that, too. Jesus is often called the Word of God, and through Jesus' words we can find out clearly what is in God's mind. All through the gospel we get the message that God minds. He knows everything we think and say and do, and minds about it.

## Intercessions

Father, let your light stream into every Christian life to show up anything that needs cutting out, healing, renewing, softening or purifying.

*Silence for prayer*

Help us to think with your mind:
**and love with your heart**

*Continued overleaf*

Father, let your wisdom take control
in all decisions and advice,
all legislation and negotiation.

*Silence for prayer*

Help us to think with your mind:
**and love with your heart**

Father, let the warmth of your love be
present in every home and in every
relationship, in our celebrations and
our struggles.

*Silence for prayer*

Help us to think with your mind:
**and love with your heart**

Father, let the power of your healing
bring to wholeness those who are
disturbed and agitated, suffering in body
or mind or spirit.

*Silence for prayer*

Help us to think with your mind:
**and love with your heart**

Father, let your loving mercy bring
the dead and dying safely home
to heaven, and give comfort to
those who mourn.

*Silence for prayer*

Help us to think with your mind:
**and love with your heart**

Father, let your joy fill our lives
as we delight in living according
to your ways.

*Silence for prayer*

Help us to think with your mind:
**and love with your heart**

## Other ideas

Either have one arrangement of very
simple wild flowers, or ask a group of
children to make a number of small
arrangements to be placed at the front or
on window ledges.

## In the crèche

*Aim:* For the children to understand that
God thinks and acts lovingly.

Have some fruit such as apples,
peaches and tomatoes, and in turn show
each one, enjoy its look and smell, and
talk about how God makes all this
growing happen. God already knows
what this fruit looks like on the inside,
and if we cut it, we'll be the first people
to be in on the secret. Cut the fruit in half,
and enjoy all the detail of the inside. God
thought of it and likes us enjoying his
world. Now share the fruits and eat them.

## Children

*Aim:* For them to understand that God's
nature is to be loving and merciful.

Have a selection of shapes for the
children to handle and make patterns
with. You can get sets of plastic or
wooden shapes from Galt or The Early
Learning Centre or you can make them as
a resource from coloured card.

When the children have experienced
the shapes, ask them to close their eyes,
pick one up, guess what it is and then
open their eyes to check if they were
right, and let this lead on to what it is
about a circle or square which makes
them easy to tell apart. Can a circle ever
be a square? Can a triangle ever be
round? No. It's their nature to be the kind
of shape they are.

What's God's nature? Jot up their
ideas on a chart and keep asking 'How do
you know?' Have some bibles and
illustrated bible stories at hand to show
God's nature being shown in action.

Now help the children to make this
moving model (opposite). The qualities
which come round into the mind bubble
could be taken from what the children
have just been talking about, or they can
be these, which are like Jesus expressing
his thoughts:

- we all need to love one another.
- don't be afraid - I am with you.
- trust me - I will never let you down.
- I will be with you always.
- I forgive you - go in peace.

## Young people

*Aim:* For them to discover more about the mind of Christ.

Start with this sketch about finding out how someone thinks.

**Max**   Look, the cat's climbed on top of the wardrobe. I wonder why.

**Cathy**   He doesn't look too happy. I expect he's wondering how on earth to get down.

**Max**   He's licking his lips. Perhaps he found something to eat up there that we don't know about.

**Cathy**   No, I reckon he's nervous.

**Max**   Cats don't lick their lips when they're nervous. I reckon he's eaten a spider and isn't sure he likes spiders.

**Cat**   Miaow!

**Cathy**   There you are – he's asking for us to rescue him.

**Max**   How do you know? He might be asking if we like spiders.

**Cat**   For heaven sake! I merely came up here to look down on things for a while. Sweet things, humans – so eager to please, but a little slow of brain.

Now read the Old Testament passage and look out for clues as to how Saul's mind worked. Then look at the New Testament passages to find out a) how the disciples' minds were working, and b) how Jesus' mind was working.

# YEAR 2

*Thought for the day:*
*God's wisdom turns our priorities*
*upside down.*

## Readings
Psalm 19
2 Samuel 9
Matthew 6:19-end

## Reflection

I remember once wandering round Chichester cathedral behind the high altar. The sun was pouring in through the stained glass and patterning the whole floor with colour and rich light. It struck me that it was a bit like walking around inside the mind of God, and as I walked, that meant that the whole of my life was moving around inside his mind, as indeed is the whole of the entire created world. I suppose I was understanding very vividly the meaning of 'In him we live and move and have our being'.

That memory has stayed with me and helps me hold things in proportion when they threaten to get out of hand. God is not distant from us but enfolding our lives; within the heart and mind of God is both a beautiful and a safe place to be, however alarming immediate problems may seem.

This week's readings make us wonder why people seek treasure – whether that be in the form of money and possessions, sex and close relationships or power and recognition. The obvious answer is that we want to be happy and know contentment, and we believe that the treasure we seek will give us those things. Sometimes they do. Sometimes they cheat us, and we are coaxed into seeking another kind of treasure which will really do the trick. Sometimes, particularly as the years go by, we get cynical and disillusioned with the whole idea of treasure seeking.

But we are right to seek it; the seeking is built into our design by the designer himself. All that needs checking is that we are seeking the real treasure which will truly satisfy, and not all the low-quality substitutes which won't last and never fit comfortably anyway.

## Discussion starters

1  Why do people worry? Why does being a Christian make any difference?
2  How can we live out this gospel in (though not necessarily part of) a materialistic society?

## All stage talk

*Theme:* Treasure.

Beforehand prepare three treasure maps of the building with an X marking the spot where the treasure is to be found. All three maps have the treasure in a different place. Where the first map leads, have a locked box with a bread roll in it. Where the second leads, have a locked box with a tee-shirt in it, and where the third map leads, have a large bunch of keys, which includes the (marked) keys to the other two boxes.

Begin by talking about treasure, and the way pirates used to bury their treasure somewhere secret and hope to find it later with the aid of a map. Explain that you have found three such maps and need three intrepid explorers to find the hidden treasure. Send the first group off, and as they follow the map, talk about how we all seek treasure in our lives, and our treasure may be some smart clothes from the High Street, or a new set of golf clubs, or coming first in our exams, or getting a really dishy boy/girlfriend.

When they find the treasure, and the disappointment of not being able to unlock it, explain how the things we rush after are often not as satisfying as we thought they would be. Send the second group off, full of new hope. They will also be disappointed just as people in life sometimes get. Send the last lot off, and when they find the keys, explain that this is rather like us seeking God; it's a waste of time seeking all the other treasures, because we might as well go to the one who holds all the keys, not just to our two boxes but to a rich, fulfilling life, inner peace and everything we need.

## Intercessions

Father, we call to mind the church and its leaders, all who minister in word and sacrament; a church divided, with problems, hopes and responsibilities.

*Silence for prayer*

My God and my all:
**my God and my all**

Father, we call to mind the barren areas of our world and the areas of abundance and wealth; the crowded cities and isolated communities, the squalid, the fashionable, the oppressed and the endangered.

*Silence for prayer*

My God and my all:
**my God and my all**

Father, we call to mind our parents and all whom we love and care for; all who cause us concern, all who make us laugh and all whose lives touch our own.

*Silence for prayer*

My God and my all:
**my God and my all**

Father, we call to mind the malnourished and the starving; those living in inadequate housing and those with nowhere to live.

*Silence for prayer*

My God and my all:
**my God and my all**

Father, we call to mind the dying, and those who have finished their earthly life; those who die alone and those who grieve alone.

*Silence for prayer*

My God and my all:
**my God and my all**

Father, we call to mind all that is good and lovely in our lives; all that builds us up, eases our loads and strengthens our faith.

*Silence for prayer*

My God and my all:
**my God and my all**

## Other ideas

Have the New Testament passage read chorally by a mixed group of voices, including men, women, girls and boys. Or have this passage read while two or three people interpret it in mime. The actions need to be simple and stylised, with the actors freezing in position until they go on to the next 'move'.

## In the crèche

*Aim:* For the children to experience the fun of seeking and finding treasure, and discover that it's easier if you have someone to help you.

Beforehand, hide various treasures around the room and let the children hunt for them and find them. Now show them something that isn't treasure at all – such as a rotten apple – and something everyone would love to find, such as a lovely, sweet, crunchy apple. Which would they like to seek most? Everyone hides their eyes while you hide this, and then you help them by saying when they're getting warmer or colder. Jesus tells us to seek what is good every day, and he will help us.

## Children

*Aim:* For the children to understand the way seeking God and his righteousness can free their lives from worry and strain.

Have one child walking around the circle looking more and more worried as the other children call out things to make him worried. (i.e. 'You're all on your own in the dark'; 'you've forgotten your swimming kit'; 'you're out shopping and suddenly realise everyone's gone home without you'.) Talk with the children about the things that worry them. This may lead into a time of prayer, and may also provide leaders with insights which will help them to pray more specifically for the children during the week.

Now look at what Jesus has to say about worrying. Either read the passage from Matthew, or tell it in your own words with the children acting out dressing and eating and so on, so that you can then go through the reading again in actions, which will help them remember it.

Now split the children into small groups to go on a treasure hunt. Each team is given a coded clue to start them off, and when they have solved it they go to the leader, who gives them the next clue to find from somewhere else. Eventually the clue words should make up the message:

STORE UP RICHES FOR YOURSELF
IN HEAVEN.

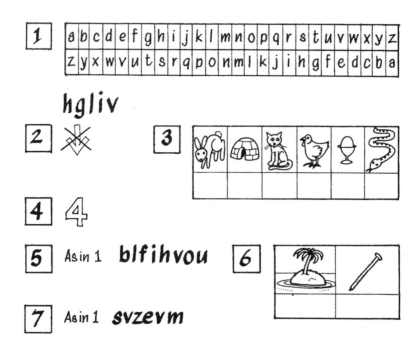

## Young people

*Aim:* For them to look at the practicalities of what Jesus' teaching implies.

First split into small groups of two or three and make a list of the things people their age worry about, and what they think the very old and the very young worry about. Share these ideas in the full group. Talk about the value of a certain amount of anxiety, but the imprisoning effect on our lives that constant worrying has.

Now read the passage from Matthew, looking at Jesus' teaching about this. Some of it they may immediately respond to; other parts of it may seem foolhardy or difficult to practise. Follow the progress of the discussion on a flip chart. Lead the discussion into the area of our responsibility for providing for those who lack food and clothing , and work on planning an event to help in this.

# 11th Sunday after Pentecost

## YEAR 1

*Thought for the day:*
*It's not God's will that we burn ourselves out, but that we support and encourage one another as we serve those in need.*

### Readings
Psalms 123,124,125
Exodus 18:13-26
Acts 6

### Reflection

The three psalms set the scene for today's theme, with their affirmation of our dependence on God, and his faithfulness so that we can always trust him to care for us. God regards us all as special and precious, and that shows in the way he founded the church – a whole mixture of people with different strengths and weaknesses. The 'famous superstar' model doesn't sit comfortably with the vision of the church as the body of Christ; the whole point of a body is that every single organ and cell is important, and needs to be in working order for the body to be running with full vitality. The head is not some other organ grown grotesquely out of proportion, but Christ himself, governing the working of the whole body. From time to time the news erupts with terrible, tragic stories of Christians turned superstars who have been tempted to pretend they are the head, rather than a little finger or an armpit.

Moses is becoming overburdened with the work of sorting out everyone's problems and disputes, and the good sense of Jethro, his father-in-law, prevents him from suffering burnout in the service of God. Moses, being the godly person he is, takes Jethro's good advice happily on board; clear proof that his heart is in the right place. However good and conscientious we are, we still need to let others help us out from time to time, and learning to delegate is not only wise but vital for our health. If you haven't been doing this, then start!

The early church soon found the need to delegate and spread the load, so that God's work was strengthened as the church grew; if this hadn't happened, the churches couldn't have grown much larger. Similarly in parishes without full lay ministry the number of committed members never grows larger than clergy can cope with.

Within our communities we need to check that we are constantly training up future leaders and that every part of ministry has prayerful and practical support, so that we don't get burnt out cases, or dreadful gaps when one person or one family moves away. We need to check, too, that those of us who are leaders are not hogging the leadership or seeking personal glory; any sense of being threatened by spreading the workload is a danger and can help us put things right.

## Discussion starters

1  What can we learn about Jethro and about Moses from the first reading? Is there a situation you know of where similar advice is needed?

2  Notice how the seven assistants in the early church were chosen from the group of those complaining. Why was this a) a sensible, and b) a courageous move?

## All stage talk

*Theme:* Burn out.
Beforehand, arrange for two piles of extremely bulky, cumbersome items to be put at the front of the church.

Explain that you would like these two sets of equipment/junk moved down to the back of the church, out of the way.

Invite three or four people to work on one lot, and one person on the other. Invite everyone else to watch what happens. It should become apparent that the group of four found it both easier and quicker than the person on his/her own, who is probably left struggling and tired at the end of the operation. Suggest that many of us have felt like that struggling, weary person, when everything feels too much to cope with, and yet we know the job has to be done.

That's how Moses felt, sorting out everybody's problems, and teaching them God's ways. The job had just become too big for one person to cope with, and that's why Jethro sensibly suggested the load sharing by other wise, trustworthy people.

We need to look out for anyone struggling on their own in ministries within our church, and offer to help. (If there are any particular needs, why not mention them here.) It doesn't make God happy to see a few of his children burning themselves out unnecessarily when there are others to share the load. Load sharing doesn't just get things done quicker; it builds up the love and fellowship of the church as people work together, encourages a deepening of faith and joy in believing, and guards against the onset of resentment and bitterness which are so often born of overwork.

## Intercessions

For all church leaders, bishops, priests and deacons; for all who are overworked and stressed; for all who feel they are doing an impossible job; let us pray.

*Silence for prayer*

Our help is in the name of the Lord:
**who has made heaven and earth**

For all world leaders and their advisers; for judges, and all who work to uphold law and order; for leaders of oppressive and corrupt regimes; let us pray.

*Silence for prayer*

Our help is in the name of the Lord:
**who has made heaven and earth**

For families coping with difficulties; for children suffering abuse or neglect; for those we love, and those we dislike; let us pray.

*Silence for prayer*

Our help is in the name of the Lord:
**who has made heaven and earth**

For all who are dependent on others for everyday care; for the crippled in body and the confused of mind; for the victims of violence, carelessness and hatred; let us pray.

*Silence for prayer*

Our help is in the name of the Lord:
**who has made heaven and earth**

For those who are dying, even as we pray; for those facing death with terror; for all who have recently gone through the journey of death; let us pray.

*Silence for prayer*

Our help is in the name of the Lord:
**who has made heaven and earth**

For all that lightens our lives with laughter, for all that blesses our lives with peace, let us give God thanks and praise.

*Silence for prayer*

Our help is in the name of the Lord:
**who has made heaven and earth**

## Other ideas

Have a time of praying in groups for people in particular ministries in the parish, and for particular parish needs.

## In the crèche

*Aim:* To help the children know that Jesus likes to see us helping one another. Prepare some light refreshments for everyone to enjoy after the service, making pretty paper table cloths, icing biscuits or decorating cakes, folding napkins and so on. As everything is being prepared, explain how we can all work together to do something nice for everyone and that means that no one has to work too hard. Have a Christian song tape of music on while you all work together.

## Children

*Aim:* To think about how we can be a serving community.

Begin with an activity which can only work when everyone pulls together, such as parachute games, or creating a structure out of bodies (as in the Halifax building society advertisements). Then read or tell the events of Exodus 18, with the children acting it out. They can all do the queuing up for Moses and then make several queues once the other leaders have been chosen.

Talk together about how we can help people with their difficulties of housing, or not having fresh water, using atlases and aid organisation materials to anchor the discussion in reality.

Work together on creating posters for the event you plan to help.

## Young people

*Aim:* To help them understand how important it is for Christians to be helped and supported by each other in their work for Christ.

Start by giving them out a really hard maths sheet to do entirely on their own, and wait for the outcry. Let this lead on to talking about how it feels to be up to your eyes in work which you know is too hard, and yet you feel you've got to do it. Now that they know how Moses felt, read the passage from Exodus together, noticing how tactfully Jethro advises his son-in-law.

Talk about how easy/difficult you all find it to accept advice, even if you know it is good advice.

Now read about what was happening in the early church, and how the complaints were sorted out. They may have examples of situations which they feel have been well sorted out, and others which have not been dealt with sensibly.

Make a radio news report such as might have been on the day after the seven assistants were appointed. Interviews may be with some of the widows, the complaining Greek Jews, an apostle or two, and with one of the newly appointed assistants, such as Stephen. If you have time, record the radio news item on tape as a parish resource.

# YEAR 2

*Thought for the day:*
*It's not God's will that we burden one another, but that we give one another encouragement and support.*

## Readings
Psalms 123,124,125
1 Kings 12:1-20
2 Corinthians 9

## Reflection
Sometimes we are well aware that the course of action we choose will have far-reaching consequences. We would give very careful thought, for instance, before deciding to marry someone, or kill someone. Yet often our apparently trivial, everyday decisions can cumulatively have consequences far greater than we imagine, and in areas we might not even have considered.

It was largely due to Rehoboam's decision to follow rash advice that the kingdom of Israel was drastically split into the northern and southern kingdoms, his insensitive treatment of a restive, burdened people proving to be the last straw. Perhaps Rehoboam had become used to ignoring advice from the elders and had got into the habit of behaving in a callow, tough-guy manner. What is certain is that he was way out of touch with the feelings and needs of the ordinary people.

Paul, who has been leaping around the Mediterranean on his missionary journey, has a remarkably global view of the church, and well understands the importance of each pocket of Christians helping one another out in time of need. In his letter to the Corinthian Christians it is apparent that Paul sees giving as much more than fishing in your pocket for some loose change. He sees that there are far-reaching consequences from living in a giving manner. Firstly, giving not only blesses the receiver, but also gives glory to God, so it is a very sacramental thing – a form of worship. Secondly, since it is pleasing to God, he always provides us enough to be generous with. That smashes on the head the idea of spending what you have to first and giving out of the dregs that are left. Paul suggests that if we get our giving priorities right first, the rest will follow without leaving us destitute. Thirdly, our generosity will be a witness to the richness of our faith, and through that others will be drawn to seek God and worship him.

## Discussion starters
1 What do you think lay behind the advice given by the elders and the young men? Is all advice 'loaded'?

2 It is often said that the last part of people to be converted is their wallet. How far do you think this is true? What help does Paul's letter give us in working out how we should give?

## All stage talk

*Theme:* Lightening one another's burdens
Beforehand, ask someone to walk up the centre of the building when the talk begins, carrying a fully packed backpack, as if they are going camping.

Begin by saying we are going to be thinking about heavy loads, and when the camper arrives, interview them about the best way to pack things so that you don't put your back out before you start. Unpack some of the items so that everyone can see the weight-saving that goes on and the care that is taken in making the load as easy as possible. But it's still pretty heavy!

In our lives we are probably all carrying a load of some kind. A load is something which makes you weighed down, and we may feel weighed down from our concern about a close friend or relative who is suffering or is in with the wrong crowd. Or the pressure of work demands may weigh us down, or the strain of living in an unhappy environment, or the fear of a bully at school. All these things can feel like heavy burdens. For many in the world the burden is not having enough to eat, not being able to feed your children, not having your home any more, or not being able to get treatment for a loved one who is very ill. Some of these weights can be made a little easier by ourselves, but for most of them we need to share the weight with others, who can help take the strain. To do that, two things are needed:

1 For us to be willing to share another person's load. (Let a volunteer come and pick up an empty backpack.)

2 For us to be willing to let others help us. (The camper agrees to be helped, and together they share the load.)

## Intercessions

Father, we bring to you the disunity in the church which so many are dedicated to heal; we bring the efforts for reconciliation, and our longing to live out your will in our lives.

*Silence for prayer*

With our God:
**nothing is impossible**

Father, we bring to you the fragile nature of our humanity, our efforts and mistakes in caring for this world; our leaders, our talks and conferences, our decisions.

*Silence for prayer*

With our God:
**nothing is impossible**

Father, we bring to you the homes and families we represent; the homes in our neighbourhood; the children attending our local schools.

*Silence for prayer*

With our God:
**nothing is impossible**

Father, we bring to you all who carry burdens and have no one to share the weight; we bring the ill, the weary, the frightened and the homeless.

*Silence for prayer*

With our God:
**nothing is impossible**

Father, we bring to you those who have died and those who grieve at their going. We bring those who die unnoticed and in despair.

*Silence for prayer*

With our God:
**nothing is impossible**

*Continued overleaf*

Father, we bring to you our thanks for your unchanging love and your affection for us; we bring our desire to love you more and more.

*Silence for prayer*

With our God:
**nothing is impossible**

## Other ideas

In view of the reading from Corinthians about giving to support one another, make the time of gift offerings special today. Most of the aid agencies are happy to supply posters and other materials for display, and a time of prayer before the giving is valuable, so as to provide everyone with a real focus. Instead of having people walking round the congregation to collect the money, try having a time of music and worship during which everyone who wants to give walks up to put their offerings in a receptacle placed near a cross.

## In the crèche

*Aim:* To help the children see that some things we do make life easier/harder for others.

Have a skipping rope and lay it across the floor and let everyone walk over it. Then lift it a little off the ground and everyone tries again. Or have two ropes to represent a river which everyone tries to cross, and gradually you make it wider and wider. Gradually the task gets harder until no one can do it at all. Have an assistant offer to help the children over, and see how the help makes all the difference. God wants us to make life easier for one another. Talk about ways they can do this.

## Children

*Aim:* To help the children see that some things we do make life easier/harder for others.

Begin with a similar game to the crèche activity, or have a beanbag thrown round the group. If you don't catch it, you have to catch it next time with one hand, then on one leg, then kneeling on one knee, then kneeling on both knees. Each time you catch the ball you can work your way up to catching it standing up with both hands again.

Talk about how difficult it is when the game gets harder and harder, just when you need a bit of help. Life sometimes feels like that. Talk together about some of the things that weigh them down and make life difficult, and then think of things that weigh other people down. Pray for these people. Now read the passage from 2 Corinthians 9 and think of ways they could help some of the people they have been praying for. Plan what to do and start working towards it.

## Young people

*Aim:* For them to look at the value of taking good advice and being sensitive to complaints.

Begin by sharing in small groups any times they have had to make a complaint about something they have bought, or the way they have been treated, and explain to one another how they dealt with the problem, and how they would like to have coped with it. (It's always afterwards that we think of the choicest things to say!) Have a role play of a customer complaining to his friends that his elderly mother has been unfairly treated, with them advising him about what to do.

Now read the events of Rehoboam asking different people for advice, and stop when he has received both pieces of advice. Decision time! What do they think Rehoboam should do? Then carry on to see what actually happens, and what the outcome is. Talk about how we can learn from this when we have a problem. It's always a good idea to ask God to put you in touch with people who will be able to give good, sensitive advice. By all means ask two or three different people, but weigh up their advice in prayer before you take action you might later regret. Don't ask advice only of someone you know will suggest what you *want* to do, rather than what you *need* to do.

# 12th Sunday after Pentecost

## YEAR 1

*Thought for the day:*
*It is both our privilege and our responsibility to spread the good news wherever we are put.*

## Readings
Psalms 145,150
Ezekiel 33:1-9,30-end
Acts 16:1-15

## Reflection

All the prophets feel the burning necessity of speaking out God's word whether they want to or not, and whether they think it will be well received or not. If they don't do this (as Jonah chose not to, for instance) nothing in their life is right or settled until they pass on the work God has given them. The sad thing is that they know they are speaking words which can bring people life, but they are often heard without understanding, so that the chance of full life is rejected along with the prophets themselves.

Ezekiel does not shrink from speaking out the unwelcome words God gives him; he can do no more, and after this it is up to his hearers as to whether they change their lives or not. We cannot do that part for anyone apart from ourselves. Nor need we take a long guilt trip if someone we have done our best with decides to turn away from following Christ. There are some occasions when it is important to be able to wipe the dust from our feet and go forward to the next situation in peace.

What about when people do listen? This week's reading from Acts lets us in on the very inauspicious beginning of a new church at Philippi, which eventually grew to be strong and full of blessing. It could well be that the little party of missionaries are not particularly thrilled to be in this dead end kind of place with only a tiny group of women to talk to. But God makes great things happen, beginning with Lydia, who listens to the word attentively and immediately becomes a follower of this surprising, fulfilling God.

## Discussion starters

1 Why do you think people don't listen properly to Ezekiel – or to most of the prophets?

2 Work through Acts 16:1-15 as it might be told by a grumpy pessimist. (It might help to know that there was an excellent Roman road going directly

into Asia from where they were.) Use this exercise to talk about our habits of cynicism, and highlight the missionaries' positive attitudes and prayerful expectancy. Any challenges here?

## All stage talk

*Theme:* Witnessing.

With a couple of people warned beforehand, stage a crime, such as a handbag snatch, in front of everyone's eyes. Then accuse an innocent person of committing the crime. S/he appeals for witnesses. Interview a couple of witnesses and let everyone vote on the strength of their eye witness accounts as to the person's innocence. (Hopefully the person should be proved innocent – if s/he isn't, I suggest you go on quickly to the next hymn, or trade your congregation in for a different model!)

Point out how important witnesses are; if they have seen something and don't speak out about it, they are partly to blame for a miscarriage of justice. If we have seen what a difference Jesus makes in our lives and know that he really is alive, then we are called to be witnesses to that, so that all those in our lost and weary world may find the joy of his love for themselves. If we don't, how are they to know?

So, how do we witness? a) By our lives, b) by our words.

Going back to the crime that was committed here this morning, could those a long way off be effective witnesses? No. In this case that was out of their control, but being Christ's witnesses, the closer we get to Jesus, and the more time we spend with him, the more effective witnesses we shall be.

## Intercessions

We pray for all missionaries and evangelists, particularly those who are ridiculed or persecuted for their faith; we pray for all who hear your word, that they may receive it with joy.

*Silence for prayer*

In your strength, Lord:
**make us strong**

We pray for those in local, national and international government; for integrity and sensitivity in all debates; for right judgements, good counsel and fair laws.

*Silence for prayer*

In your strength, Lord:
**make us strong**

We pray for our homes and all who live or visit there; that each room may be blessed with your love to nurture forgiveness, mutual respect and compassion.

*Silence for prayer*

In your strength, Lord:
**make us strong**

We pray for those whose bodies are weak, whose minds are blurred, whose spirits are listless; we pray for comfort, healing, refreshment and peace.

*Silence for prayer*

In your strength, Lord:
**make us strong**

We pray for those whose life on earth has ended, that you will welcome them with mercy into your kingdom; we pray for those who have died violently and for those who struggle to forgive.

*Silence for prayer*

In your strength, Lord:
**make us strong**

We pray for the truth of your astounding love to reach deeper into our understanding as we praise and bless your name in our lives.

*Silence for prayer*

In your strength, Lord:
**make us strong**

## Other ideas

• Have the psalm accompanied by music as it is said by two halves of the congregation, but in these chunks, rather than in alternate verses:
v1-3 . . . v.4-6 . . . v.7-9 . . . v.10-13
v.14 . . . v.15-16 . . . v.17-20 . . . v.21, all.
• Think of one person whom you want to know Jesus. Write their Christian name on the palm of your hand with your finger, then cup this hand with the other as you pray for them, and offer yourself to be available for God to use in the process. Commit yourself to doing this every day until that person comes to know for him/herself new life in Christ.

## In the crèche

*Aim:* For the children to know the urgency of spreading the good news of God's love.
Bring with you a number of postcards you have received from your friends on holiday, and show them around, talking together about how nice it is when you hear good news from people who love you enough to let you know about it.

The best news of all is that Jesus is alive and loves us. Give the children labels to draw on and decorate which have a Christian message on. Tie the messages to helium balloons and send them off.

## Children

*Aim:* For them to know the urgency of spreading the good news of God's love.
Beforehand prepare some letters, cards and bills in envelopes, some of which bring bad, unwelcome news, and some which bring good, encouraging news. Put them in a bag, and have one of the children as postman, delivering the post. As each item is delivered, it is opened up and read out. Everyone can make a suitable groan or thumbs up sign according to the news it brings.

Explain how some bad news is necessary, even if we don't like it, because it can help us put things right. Read or tell the events from Acts 16, where Paul, Timothy and Luke travel around wherever they feel God wants them to go, in order to bring people the good news of God's love which they know can fill their lives with colour and joy.

What kind of message would we like people to know about Jesus? Work on writing (or scribing) the messages, and illustrating them, before putting them in envelopes and sending them off to someone they know.

## Young people

*Aim:* For them to realise the urgency of spreading the good news of God's love.
First read the passage from Ezekiel, drawing attention to the way the prophet feels the necessity of speaking out, even if the people are not likely to receive the message. Ask someone to stand up on their own in the group and say that they believe in Jesus, so that they can feel how uncomfortable it is to stand up and be counted even in a group of sympathetic Christians. It isn't worth pretending that witnessing is easy – it is often embarrassing and very scary. Spend time looking at these misgivings, and at the importance of not doing anything in our own strength, but in God's strength, God's way and God's timing.

Split into groups of three, where one pretends to be someone who is not a believer, and the other two work together to evangelise him/her. This exercise can be quite light-hearted, but will be very valuable in highlighting areas of difficulty. Come together as one group and gather some points which have come to light, noting them so as to provide further input in those areas.

# YEAR 2

*Thought for the day:*
*It is both our privilege and our*
*responsibility to spread the good news*
*wherever we are put.*

## Readings
Psalms 145,150
Amos 5:14-24 (or 6-24)
Romans 15:14-29

## Reflection

Not all news is what we want to hear, and it is usually a lengthy job to learn to accept criticism gracefully. Our usual reaction begins as a survival instinct mechanism. Criticisms pick holes in our personality and so are considered as threats. We either put up our defences of righteous indignation, digs at the critic, or distraction, or we collapse in a spate of self flagellation as we join forces over-enthusiastically with the critic. Neither response is very healthy, though both are very human.

We all react out of our past experiences, and deep healing may be necessary before we can hope for a changed behaviour pattern. Still, I have seen too many people healed in this area to be pessimistic. What a close relationship with Jesus gives us is the assurance that we are completely loved and valued. It is this knowledge that enables us to see genuine criticism as an exciting opportunity for growth, rather

than as a destructive threat. We can talk it over with the God we love, while he holds us secure, and think of it much as we might embark on a physical fitness session – possibly painful, but positive and very useful.

The prophets speak out words for our good, and we dare not close our defences against what we hear. The church is a witnessing community; we may as a body need to speak out against the evils in our society and many people will prefer not to hear, so they will respond with ridicule or hostility. To speak out may cause us embarrassment or even danger, but we are privileged to be given the task.

## Discussion starters

1  Time and again it is hypocrisy which galls the heart of God. Why do you think this is so? Is there anything that smacks of hypocrisy or double standards which needs addressing among Christians today?

2  It almost makes us tired just reading about Paul's enthusiastic travel plans in order to win Gentiles for God. Are we as passionate for the spread of the gospel? Why/why not?

## All stage talk

*Theme:* If nobody tells them, how will they know?

Arrange beforehand for someone to be wearing their coat or sweater inside out, and for someone's bag to be mislaid.

Start by saying you need a volunteer, and choose the person with their clothing on inside out. Pretend you are rather embarrassed at having to tell them something, and then tell them about their clothing and help them put things right. Ask everyone if they think you should have mentioned it, or whether you should have kept quiet. If your sound system makes it possible, allow a few people to put their points of view.

Explain that if we can see something that is really wrong, and don't tell the person lovingly about it, they won't be able to put things right. And if we're on the receiving end, we might wish we did know where we are going wrong, or hurting someone, because then we are in a position to do something about it.

The prophets were shown what God wanted them to say to the people, and the ones who listened were the ones who saw God's word as an opportunity for growth, rather than as a destructive threat.

Now ask if anyone has mislaid their bag this morning. Ask if anyone knows anything about this. No one does. Point out that if we are in possession of good news and don't let on, then this person will stay worried and upset. Now the person who knows where the bag is stands up and tells the good news, and the bag is found. (A round of applause if you're that kind of congregation; polite smiles if you're not.)

There are lots of people in our world who are lost, and confused and scared inside or lonely because they haven't yet met anyone who introduced them to the living Jesus. And if you meet them, and don't share your good news with them, they will have to go on being miserable. Ask people to turn to the person next to them, and in twos and threes tell one another why they love God already, or why they are interested in finding out more about him. After a minute or two, ask if any four people would be brave enough to stand up on their own and say why they love God. Point out how difficult this is to do in the middle of sympathetic listeners, let along with a hostile audience. We need to remember that being a witnessing community is not easy, and we need to keep close to God the whole time, supporting one another with prayer.

## Intercessions

Whenever we face obstacles in living God's way; whenever the church is called to stand for what is right; whenever we find God using us for his glory,
Father, we need your help.

*Silence for prayer*

At all times and in all places:
**we praise the God of love**

When past wounds keep nations from working together; wherever power threatens to corrupt; when injustices need righting, Father, we need your help.

*Silence for prayer*

At all times and in all places:
**we praise the God of love**

When the children squabble and the grown-ups nag;
when anyone feels left out or unacceptable,
Father, we need your help.

*Silence for prayer*

At all times and in all places:
**we praise the God of love**

When pain takes over, and normality is only a dream; when carers grow weary and tempers fray; when sleep won't come and waking is unwelcome,
Father, we need your help.

*Silence for prayer*

At all times and in all places:
**we praise the God of love**

When the stars or sunlight touch our hearts with wonder;
when we catch a glimpse of your tenderness or power,
Father, we give you our thanks.

*Silence for prayer*

At all times and in all places:
**we praise the God of love**

## Other ideas

• For a different statement of faith, use the baptismal questions, ending altogether with: 'This is our faith. We believe and trust in one God, Father, Son and Holy Spirit.'

• Or use this question and answer form:

Who was there before anything else?
GOD WAS!

Who decided to make our universe?
GOD DID!

Who is in charge of our universe today?
GOD IS!

Who was walking on earth as Jesus?
GOD WAS!

Who loved us so much that he died
for us all?
GOD DID!

Who is alive in us now through his Spirit?
GOD IS!

Who do we believe in?
WE BELIEVE IN GOD!

• At the time of penitence, focus on the opportunities we waste for bringing others to know Jesus for themselves. If there are empty seats around, have everyone praying for the people God longs to be there. Or have groups of people praying for different streets in the parish. During the coming weeks people could undertake to walk these streets, praying for the homes as they pass them.

## In the crèche

*Aim:* For the children to understand that as Christians we have very good news to spread around.

Play a 'passing on' game such as 'Pass the parcel' or 'Pass the hat'. Make sure that everyone has a chance to open up a layer. Inside the parcel is some very good news – popcorn or raisins that everyone can share. Teach the children this clapping game which they can use to spread the good news.

4 claps: Jesus loves me
clap both hands to a partner x 3:
He loves you too!

Once you have been chosen as a partner you can go off and find someone else to share the good news with, until everyone is involved.

## Children

*Aim:* For the children to understand the importance and fun of spreading the word.

Prepare a paddling pool of water if you have outside space, or a baking tray of water if you are inside. Watch how the ripples spread right out to the edge when we drop something into the centre. Let plenty of people have a go at this. Then look at how ink, dropped onto wet blotting paper spreads and makes lovely patterns as it does so. Everyone can try this.

Now tell the children about Paul, in a 'cricket highlights' rundown of his travels and adventures. If you draw a rough approximation of the Mediterranean with chalk on the floor, and have card labels of the main place names, two or three children can move around it as the adventures are told. Put a card down wherever Paul got a new group of Christians going, so everyone can see the way the gospel was spreading.

Now give each child a small jar and a label on which they write 'DON'T KEEP THE FAITH – SPREAD IT!' When they have stuck their label on their jar, let them fill the jar with an individually chosen spread from an assortment of ingredients, such as raisins, honey, jam and chocolate chips. They can take these home and follow the instructions on their jar in the coming weeks.

## Young people

*Aim:* To explore the practicalities of spreading the faith.

Begin by looking at a selection of estate agency brochures for houses in the area. In groups of two or three, choose a favourite for a family/a bachelor/an elderly couple. Share the results of the discussions.

Point out that unless the news of those properties had been made available, the potential buyers would never have known about them; very few would go to the trouble of driving round every street and knocking on doors, asking if the house was for sale. Yet sometimes, we keep the good news of our faith shut tight in our churches, where no one hears of it. How can we make sure that people know about Jesus in a way which they understand, and which doesn't frighten them off?

Have a brainstorming session for plans of how the church can witness to different groups of people, and have the resulting list of ideas presented to the next PCC. Finish with Paul's letter to the Romans, hearing his plans for the spread of the early church, and pray together for the people in the area who have yet to be introduced to Jesus.

# 13th Sunday after Pentecost

## YEAR 1

*Thought for the day:*
*Being a Christian doesn't take all the suffering away, but transforms our way of dealing with it.*

## Readings
Psalms 130,137:1-6
2 Kings 19:8-19
Acts 16:16-end

## Reflection

All through history we have seen how martyrs, dying noble deaths, have inspired surges of deeper faith and growth among those who have been impressed and probably shocked by the extraordinary way such people have faced suffering. Most of us are cowards at heart and shrink from getting involved with anything which might cause us pain, and I suspect most martyrs have felt the same. Yet when suffering is inevitable and their deep conviction of faith is on the line, God provides ordinary people with remarkable staying power and even cheerfulness.

In our own lives we may not have touched the martyrdom zone, but there may well have been times when we know we could never have coped with a situation in our own strength, and are well aware of God's quiet, reassuring presence in the most unlikely circumstances.

I love the way Hezekiah reacts to Sennacherib's letter by taking it to the temple and laying it out physically before God as he prays. I have followed this example on several occasions with distressing letters, or bills that seem impossible to pay. It helps, and I can recommend it.

Paul and Silas don't have a great deal to sing about after their severe flogging and public hostility, with their legs clamped in iron in the squalor of a Roman prison. Yet sing they did, and this peculiar acceptance of suffering and lack of the expected bitter indignation at their treatment impressed the guard so much that he and his household became Christians that very night.

## Discussion starters

1   Do we still behave as if this life isn't the end, or have we lost that abandoned, reckless joy of these early Christians?

2   Can we just decide to care less about the things that go wrong, or does there have to be a deeper change of priorities in our whole personality before our behaviour can change?

## All stage talk

*Theme:* Coping with the outrageously awful.

Beforehand collect together several scummy-looking cartons, and label them with such things as 'Bitter disappointment', 'Unfair criticism', 'Severe irritation', and 'Personal failure'. Also provide lots of dried flowers, stickers, coloured paper, scissors and glue.

Begin by talking through the Paul and Silas story, pointing out their unexpected reaction to a very nasty state of affairs. Then show everyone the boxes which represent those awful times we sometimes get when the very last thing we'd think of doing would be praising God or singing. We feel perhaps that it wouldn't be honest if we did.

Ask some people to use the materials you have provided to make the boxes beautiful – without actually mending the boxes at all. While they work talk about how some terrible circumstances are beyond our control, and we can't change them; like when the train we need to catch is cancelled, when we have to live with a relative who drives us crazy, or when we don't get the grades we have worked so hard for. They are like Paul and Silas' prison, or like these boxes. If we can fill those times with praise, those awful situations will become beautiful. It's not a question of pretending that we're happy and that everything's wonderful – that would be ridiculous. It's a question of getting in touch with God, feeling, with him, the horror or ugliness of the situation and then deciding to praise him exactly where you are, which may well be through your tears. That is honest praise, praise that recognises God's beauty and his presence in the dreadful as well as the easy, the painful and well as the uplifting.

Try it next time you miss the bus, get let down by a friend or the washing machine pours filthy water all over the floor, and make those desolate places beautiful.

Have the finished boxes placed around the church to remind people.

## Intercessions

We call to mind our brothers and sisters in Christ who are imprisoned or suffering persecution simply for believing what we believe.

*Silence for prayer*

Trust in the Lord:
**for with the Lord there is mercy**

We call to mind those whose lives are caught up in war, political unrest, family feuds or nationalistic grievances.

*Silence for prayer*

Trust in the Lord:
**for with the Lord there is mercy**

We call to mind refugees and all who do not know whether their loved ones are safe or not; all whose homes are places of violence and all whose homes are havens of love.

*Silence for prayer*

Trust in the Lord:
**for with the Lord there is mercy**

We call to mind those imprisoned by guilt, addiction or bitterness; and all those who undergo suffering bravely and bring joy to those who care for them.

*Silence for prayer*

Trust in the Lord:
**for with the Lord there is mercy**

We call to mind those who have recently died and those who miss them; those who are nearing death, and those who support them.

*Silence for prayer*

Trust in the Lord:
**for with the Lord there is mercy**

We call to mind the times when God has carried us through difficult times, and thank him for his faithful love.

*Silence for prayer*

Trust in the Lord:
**for with the Lord there is mercy**

## Other ideas

• The reading from Acts can be acted out effectively, or dramatised using different voices.
• Incorporate a letter and open envelope into the flower arrangements today, so that the arrangement expresses Hezekiah's trust in a God who listens and gets involved.

## In the crèche

*Aim:* To help them understand that God loves us all the time, not just when we're happy.
Use puppets – two children, and a parent who is working in the garden while the children play. First they play very nicely, and the parent says how nice that is, and how happy s/he is that they are happy. Then the children quarrel and start being nasty to one another until something gets broken. One of the children cries. The parent comes and comforts the child, asking what the matter is. The child is afraid the parent won't love them any more as they've messed things up. The parent reassures both children that s/he may not always like what they do, but the love is always there. Explain that God is like that – he loves us all the time, however we feel, and whatever we do.

## Children

*Aim:* To introduce the children to the story of Paul and Silas in prison.

Have a few ball and chains made from card circles and paper chains made with black or shiny paper. Prison bars can be oven shelves, held up in front of the prisoners.

Begin by sharing memories of some of the worst times in their lives, and how they felt during those times. Then tell or read the story of Paul and Silas, with the children making the appropriate sounds for the whipping, and the doors clanging shut. Have some of the children fastened up with the ball and chains, and then think how Paul and Silas must have felt. Yet they sang! (They can sing their favourite songs at this point.) Have some children using instruments such as shakers, drums and cymbals to create the earthquake, and call out above the noise, as Paul did, so that the children can sense the panic and confusion with Paul in control.

After the story (which the children may well want to do twice, to get it really lifelike) talk about how we can sing our praises in those worst times, knowing that God is good, even if we are in a sticky patch, and giving God praise in those times is one of the best presents we can give him.

Have a time of prayer for all those who are in prison for believing in God at the moment, and help the children make these balls and chains to take home.

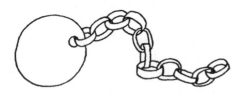

## Young people

*Aim:* To explore the way Christians react to suffering.

First read the Old Testament passage, and share times when they have had very frightening or disappointing letters. Suggest they try Hezekiah's idea. Look at the stages of Hezekiah's prayer, too, so that it can become a model or pattern for them. Then look at the Paul and Silas story, having different people to read

different characters in it. Pause at the point they are thrown into prison and talk about how they might have felt at this point, and then go on to read about the way they dealt with the situation. We can do the same, odd though it may feel at first. To get the sense of praying in various situations, make a praise trail round the premises, where labels are put up on places such as the rubbish dump, a dark, crowded cupboard, the loo, a bramble patch and so on. The labels suggest situations which are very unpleasant or worse, such as those suggested in the All stage talk, but it's best if you make your own up so that they are particularly relevant to your group. Then people can walk round and praise God in each setting, in practice for the real thing.

# YEAR 2

*Thought for the day:*
*Being a Christian doesn't take all the suffering away, but transforms our way of dealing with it.*

## Readings
Psalms 130,137:1-6
Isaiah 49:13-23
Matthew 11:20-end

## Reflection

I have a disastrous memory and have tried all kinds of ways to remember things. What works better than anything is to write 'paint stripper' or 'bank' on my hand; it's surprising how often you catch sight of the memory jogger, and it is conveniently joined on to you 24 hours a day.

What a reassuring picture it is that God gives to the exiled people of Israel, of their names being written on the palm of his hand. It suggests that he wants to remember them and will never forget them; they are constantly brought to his mind and he has their lives and their futures safe for ever. The people needed such reassurance in the misery of exile. They were beginning to feel that God had forgotten about them. Through Isaiah God tells them of his continuing love for them and gives them hope again.

Matthew quotes Jesus' open invitation to anyone at all who feels weighed down by problems, work responsibilities or difficult circumstances. They do not have to be Jewish – the whole world is included in the invitation now, and all we need to do is to take him up on his offer and let him into our lives.

Yet, simple as it may sound, there are many, many people who groan at their burdens but choose not to let Jesus in to relieve them. Matthew is anxious to make the point that if we will only come to Jesus in our suffering he will lovingly refresh, comfort and restore us, and we need not fear God as a fanatical slave driver; his yoke is easy, and his burden light. But if we insist on turning our backs on him, even in the face of obvious spiritual hints, then Jesus will not be able to help us, and we will be fully in charge of our own continuing misery and potential downfall.

## Discussion starters

1  Why do you think that people in the area where Jesus lived and worked didn't believe, in spite of all those miracles? What makes us sceptical and prejudiced?

2  In what ways have you found Jesus' burden to be light?

## All stage talk

*Theme:* Burden sharing.

First ask for two volunteers to take part in a memory game. Explain that you will reel off a list of numbers and then see how many people in church can remember the list. The two volunteers are given biro pens and told to write the numbers down on the palm of their hands as you say them. When you ask if anyone can tell you the numbers, probably the only ones able to will be those who had written the numbers on their hand to remind them.

The Old Testament reading is explaining that God never forgets us – it is as if he has our name written on the palm of his hand, so that he is always lovingly calling us to mind. What God offers us is the chance to be yoked up with him as we stumble and plod our way through life. Show everyone a cut out yoke, and explain how it worked, with the stronger, more experienced animal helping to guide the younger one in right way so that the load is less painful to carry.

## Intercessions

Father, we remember those whose faith is fresh and fragile, those who labour faithfully in your service through difficult times; all who minister by word and sacrament throughout the church.

*Silence for prayer*

Come, Lord:
**comfort your people**

Father, we remember the needs of the world and the unbalanced spread of wealth; we remember the leaders and advisers, the peace makers and the law makers.

*Silence for prayer*

Come, Lord:
**comfort your people**

*Continued overleaf*

Father, we remember our own relatives and friends, our neighbours and those we meet week by week; we remember the laughter and tears we have shared, the hopes, dreams and fears.

*Silence for prayer*

Come, Lord:
**comfort your people**

Father, we remember the weary and heavily burdened, the anxious, and those who have lost their way; all whose lives are filled with suffering; all who do not yet know Jesus.

*Silence for prayer*

Come, Lord:
**comfort your people**

Father, we remember those who have come to the end of their earthly life and those who have nursed and cared for them and will miss their physical presence.

*Silence for prayer*

Come, Lord:
**comfort your people**

Father, we remember your kindness and mercy to us at every stage of our journey, and offer you our thanks and praise.

*Silence for prayer*

Come, Lord:
**comfort your people**

## Other ideas

The Isaiah reading works well with a group of voices. Go through the group listening out for the particular 'shade' of voice each has, and split into 'dark', 'medium' and 'light'. Now work through the passage, breaking it into sections which can be read by the different sub-groups, soloists, or by everyone. If you want a passage to build up, for instance, have the first phrase read by 'light', the next by 'light' and 'medium' and the last phrase by everyone. You will find that working through the passage like this turns into an accidental bible study, because you are forced to look at the meaning so carefully. Begin the planning time with prayer, and be attentive to God's ideas about things, rather than pushing your own!

## In the crèche

*Aim:* For the children to know that God never, ever forgets them.

Play a simple version of Kim's game, with two or three objects on a tray. After you have seen the objects, cover them over, and guess what is on the tray. Talk about some people and animals with good memories and some who are always forgetting everything. If we have good memories, we can help those who haven't. One person who never forgets us is God, who thinks of us all day long and all night long as well, so whenever we need him we can always talk to him straight away and know that he knows who we are by name.

## Children

*Aim:* For the children to know that Jesus knows us by name and can really help us if we let him.

Start by providing strips of material or scarves for the children to try walking about three-legged with a partner. This doesn't have to be a competitive race – it's really the experience of learning to walk 'yoked up' to someone else that is important.

Now show the children some pictures from the library history books of oxen yoked up together, and explain how the farmers would put a young, inexperienced animal yoked to a strong, experienced ox, so that the young one would learn how to work and the load wouldn't be so hard to pull. Talk together about their three-legged walks. They will probably have noticed how difficult it was at first with both pulling different ways, and how much easier it was once they had learnt to walk exactly in step with each other.

Now read the part from Matthew about Jesus' invitation to all the weary and heavily burdened. Why will it help to be yoked up with Jesus? Pray together for those who don't yet know they can let Jesus take the strain in their lives, and for all who carry burdens of some kind.

Then help the children to make this model of oxen yoked together.

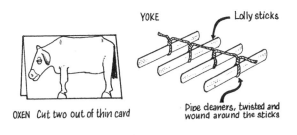

YOKE     Lolly sticks

OXEN Cut two out of thin card

Pipe cleaners, twisted and wound around the sticks

## Young people

*Aim:* For them to look at what Jesus offers, and why his offer is often refused. First read the passage from Matthew straight through, but then concentrate on the end part first. It is important that everyone knows how a yoke worked, and understands that it eased the burden to be yoked up with a strong, experienced ox. Talk together about how Jesus'

invitation works. How do we know God makes our loads easier to carry? Does the yoke image suggest that he takes the load away from us or shares it with us? How much of our load is the load itself, and how much our feelings of grumpiness about having to carry it, and what does Jesus do about this if we let him? It is important that doubts and questions are aired and that the conversation is open and honest; there may well be times when we wish Jesus would do things differently! If our young people are going to deepen their faith they need to know the implications of choosing to accept Jesus' invitation for themselves, and not do so just because we have told them to. Now go back to the earlier part of the reading. If Jesus did all those amazing things, why wasn't he believed? Why don't people today take up his offer of an easier life when it sounds like an obvious good bargain? Keep track of ideas raised, and include the point that we keep wanting to go our own way, and we can't do that and stay yoked with Jesus at the same time. Yokes are not that elastic. Have a time of prayer for desperate situations and people who are heavily burdened in various different ways. Choose one to pray for each day during the week. If there is time, finish with a go at three-legged walking to experience the need to choose to walk in step with the one you are yoked to.

# 14th Sunday after Pentecost

## YEAR 1

*Thought for the day:*
*Whatever our age or marital status,*
*we are all children in God's family,*
*brothers and sisters bound together*
*by love.*

### Readings
Psalm 103
Genesis 29:1-20
2 Timothy 1:1-14

### Reflection

This week's readings focus our attention on some tender, affectionate moments of family life. For those who live in a family, much of the time we are so involved with the jobs and chauffeuring, the normal in-house bickering and general survival, and then there are those delicious times of a quiet snuggle, an unexpected home-coming, helpless laughter, or faithful support through a time of tragedy, which remind us of the value of family life. Others have loathed family life so much that they avoid it at all costs, and the damage inflicted from early bad family experiences can miserably affect us far into adult life. Others, living singly, find themselves left out whenever the word 'family' is mentioned. So it is a sensitive area.

Nevertheless, it is a beautiful thing to live in harmony with others, and whatever our household it is a good idea to ensure that we regularly associate with others from different age groups, since we all have so much to offer one another. We are all members of God's family – all sons and daughters of God, our loving parent - and that means that everyone we meet at church is a brother or sister. Quite a prospect! 'Family worship' does not mean 'worship for families' at which many feel outsiders, but God's family of all Christian people coming to meet their parent and worshipping together.

Timothy has received so much from his mother and his grandmother. It is intriguing to wonder how Lois herself came to know about Jesus. What we can be certain of, is that the growing Timothy must have picked up the truth of the good news through living with such people. The people who live with us will also be picking up hints as to what rules our life and is of most importance to us. It might be worth taking a candid look at our lives to check what we are inadvertently passing on to those who spend time with us.

## Discussion starters

1   Notice how Jacob chose his wife. How do we go about choosing our partners? How far do we involve God in the process?

2   What do you think makes for good family life? Do we give enough support to parents who want to bring their children up as Christians?

## All stage talk

*Theme:* Family matters.
Begin by asking various groups of people to stand in quick succession: brothers, sisters, mothers, fathers, grandparents, grandchildren, aunts and uncles, nephews and nieces, cousins, sons and daughters. Some people will have stood up several times – that's fine. Everyone should have stood up at least once. (If the congregation is wary of standing up like this, I find it is less embarrassing for

everyone to stand, and then the different categories sit.) So in our human families we may be several things at once – a dad may also be a cousin, a brother and a son, for instance.

We are also members of God's family. God is our father – our parent – and, whatever our age, we are all his children. That means that everyone around us is a brother or sister. If you thought you didn't have any brothers and sisters, take a look around at some of your family!

What we need to do is to invite God into our homes – not as an occasional guest, but as a resident. We need to ask him to live with us. That way, our household will be filled with love, and we will find that we are able to treat one another with more love and care, and less irritability.

## Intercessions

Father, we bring to you our longing for unity, our desire for a closer walk with you and our concern for all our Christian brothers and sisters.

*Silence for prayer*

God is full of compassion:
**full of compassion and love**

Father, we bring to you our longing for a world of peace and integrity; a world of mutual respect and international understanding.

*Silence for prayer*

God is full of compassion:
**full of compassion and love**

Father, we bring to you our love and concern for our families, friends and neighbours; particularly those facing change or feeling isolated.

*Silence for prayer*

God is full of compassion:
**full of compassion and love**

Father, we bring to you our desire for healing and wholeness in those who are distressed, uncomfortable or in great pain; we bring our willingness to help wherever you want to use us.

*Silence for prayer*

God is full of compassion:
**full of compassion and love**

Father, we bring you our loved ones who have died, and those who are dying with no one near them.

*Silence for prayer*

God is full of compassion:
**full of compassion and love**

Father, we bring to you our thanks for life and all its blessings; for the experiences we learn from and grow through.

*Silence for prayer*

God is full of compassion:
**full of compassion and love**

## Other ideas

• Have a parent and child, a brother and sister (of any age), a grandparent and grandchild, or two close friends doing various jobs today. These might be leading the intercessions, or collecting the offering, reading one of the bible passages or leading part of the worship.

• Have friendship cake mixture ready to dish out to a number of people, and suggest that in two weeks the resulting cakes are brought to share over coffee after church.

## In the crèche

*Aim:* To think about being part of a family, and being a member of God's family.

Use an animal families set of cards and jumble them up, so that the children can sort them out into family groups. Talk about their own family groups – those who they live with and those who look after them. Don't push the 'Mum, Dad, children' set up, as this may not be the situation they recognise. The 'household' idea is very Hebrew anyway, and all the children will have someone who looks after them. Tell them that we are all children in God's family, and go round the group by name with the children joining in. 'Thomas is one of God's children . . . Naomi is one of God's children . . . Jessica is one of God's children . . . and God is our Father in heaven.'

## Children

*Aim:* For the children to feel part of God's family.

Begin by the animal family game. Everyone is told in a whisper what type of animal they are, and whether they are the Mum, Dad or Baby of that animal. Then everyone makes their animal noise, trying to meet up with the rest of the family. When they are ready, Dad stands behind a chair, Mum sits on the chair, and Baby sits on Mum's lap.

Now talk together about the things they like doing at home with their family – the people they live with. Write these up on a sheet of paper. Then talk about the things they don't enjoy and write these up on another sheet. It is important that the children accept that no home life is perfect; sometimes children think theirs is the only home where people shout at each other, and are quite relieved to find it's quite a normal part of family life for people to get cross with one another sometimes. In the discussion, talk about ways of making up and putting things right, and if children don't want to contribute, don't draw attention to this. Let the children pick something from each list to draw, and stick the pictures on to the inside and outside of a paper plate.

Round the rim write GOD'S LOVE . . . GOD'S LOVE . . . GOD'S LOVE . . . on both sides, so that they know that their own human family is held in the love of God, both at the good and the difficult times.

Paper plate

## Young people

*Aim:* For them to look at the way people choose partners.

Start with a role play version of Blind Date, with three boys being given a few minutes to work out answers to three questions. Then rig up a partition and have a girl sitting on one side, asking the three questions and choosing a boy. The 'holiday prize' is to do the washing up together after church, or something similar. The questions might be:

1  If we went out for a meal, what would you choose to eat?

2  If you had 50 pounds, what would you spend it on?

3  If you were going to take a year out after school, what kind of thing would you choose to do?

Now read the story of Jacob meeting Rachel, picking out the things that Jacob went for when choosing a wife, and making a note of them. How do people choose life partners in our society – are any of the factors still the same?

Finally, think about Christian marriage and the importance of letting God in on the choice, so that we end up with the partner God knows is right for us. Bear in mind, too, that some people are called to marriage and others to living as singles; there is often great social pressure to get married, but if we stay close to God, he will guide our lives in the way which is most fulfilling for us.

# YEAR 2

*Thought for the day:*
*Whatever our age or marital status,*
*we are all children in God's family,*
*brothers and sisters bound together*
*by love.*

## Readings
Psalm 103
Genesis 47:1-12
Colossians 3:12-21

## Reflection
This week we are standing at an important stage in the great plan of God's salvation – the point where Jacob's family is poised to become a nation. God spoke his promise and called one person originally – Abraham. Now his great-grandson Joseph gets the family settled in the land of Goshen, well catered for but separate from the Egyptians. God has been able to redeem all the family feuds, jealousies and misunderstandings so that good comes from them in the end, and the family bonds are still holding.

All families get the same treatment; all those jealousies, feuds and misunderstandings that have been woven into the fabric of our own families can be redeemed so that good comes from them. All the wounds can be healed and the damage put right and used for good. It may not happen overnight, (we would probably be unable to cope if it did!) but as we begin to pray seriously for change, things will start to happen, often in ways we would not have thought of. And how can we make our family life work? Paul has some very practical advice, based on Jesus' teaching about love. So many arguments are caused by someone's selfish behaviour, or someone's refusal to forgive. If we were to remember to treat one another as special, then peace would rule instead of the loudest voice or the worst temper.

True as this is we need to remember that we all act and react out of our own woundings. Love, practised in prayer, helps us respond to the need and the wound, rather than the bristles and prickles which show.

## Discussion starters
1 Notice how the very elderly Jacob takes it upon himself to bless the mighty king of Egypt, even though his own status is only that of nomadic shepherd. What is our society's attitude to the elderly? What about our church community? Any changes needed?

2 If Paul were writing today, what do you think he might say to us about family life?

## All stage talk
*Theme:* Family life for Christians.
On a large sheet of paper or on an OHP have two columns, headed like this:

**FAMILY LIFE**

| The nice things | The nasty things |
| --- | --- |
| | |

Give people a minute to talk in pairs about the nice things before collecting ideas on the chart, then do the same with the nasty things. Reassure people that all families have both, and that helps us learn to forgive, because we get lots of practice.

Point out that God had used the jealousy and double dealing in Jacob's family to bring good in the end. Joseph is now able to help the family in a crisis and the stage is set for the nation of Israel to form in Goshen. Even the things which threaten to split a family apart can be used for good if we let God in to work. Family life is to do with helping one another. Do we make life easier for others in our home, or harder? Do we pull our weight as part of the team, or expect someone else to do everything for us? Talk it over with God and listen to what he puts into your mind over the next few days.

Today could be the first day of you changing things and helping to make your home a happier place.

## Intercessions

Father, we thank you for welcoming us into your family; for treating us as special and forgiving us. We pray for all our Christian brothers and sisters worshipping today all over the world.

*Silence for prayer*

Thank you, Father:
**for loving us so much**

Father, we think of our parents and all who have helped and looked after us through our life; we pray that you will make your home in our homes.

*Silence for prayer*

Thank you, Father:
**for loving us so much**

Father, we pray for those damaged through bad relationships; those who are lonely, rejected or broken-hearted; we pray for the newly born and their parents.

*Silence for prayer*

Thank you, Father:
**for loving us so much**

Father, we remember those who have reached death and ask that you will welcome them into your kingdom.

*Silence for prayer*

Thank you, Father:
**for loving us so much**

Father, we thank you for the opportunities to practise forgiveness; for the different times that have enabled us to grow; for the light-hearted times that have made us happy.

*Silence for prayer*

Thank you, Father:
**for loving us so much**

## Other ideas

• Have the first reading acted out, with voice parts and simple costumes.
• In the passage from Colossians have a cluster of wives, husbands and children to read the appropriate parts.

## In the crèche

*Aim:* To think about family life, and our part in it.

Have some toys to help the children play 'families'. Play out a family being nice, and then a family being nasty. Sprinkle some loving powder over everyone so they play as a nice family again. Help them to notice how everyone helped and looked after one another, and that's how God loves us to live, so that everyone gets cared for and no one is left out.

| God calls Abraham | Isaac born | Jacob and Esau born | Esau sells his birthright | Jacob marries Leah and Rachel | Joseph born | Joseph sold to Egypt |
| --- | --- | --- | --- | --- | --- | --- |

## Children

*Aim:* To see the settling of Jacob's family in Egypt as part of the whole bible story.

Have a timeline drawn on a long strip of paper and fill in the main characters and events on it as you go on a whistle stop tour through to Joseph and his brothers. The children may be able to help you, filling in details of individual stories as you go. When you get to Joseph, slow the pace and increase the detail, getting the children to join in the acting out of the story, or using the 'carpet tiles' method of story telling. Make sure the children are aware of the change of place, and the geography of it.

Then make a communal model of the whole family plus animals in Goshen, using upturned bowls and plates under a large cloth to make hills and valleys, pipe cleaners and cloth for people and paper cut-out sheep.

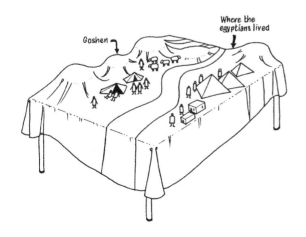

Goshen

Where the egyptians lived

## Young people

*Aim:* To see how one man was becoming a nation, as God had promised, and to look at family life.

Use a family tree chart to trace the way God was making a family grow into a nation. Then read the Genesis passage together, with different voices for the speaking parts. Notice how Joseph, Jacob and the brothers act towards one another and towards the king of Egypt. What has the family learnt through their experiences?

Now get into small groups and make a list of the plus and the minus side of family life. After a few minutes, gather their thoughts onto a chart.

Read the passage from Colossians to see what advice Paul gives about living in harmony with others, and see how this could apply to the list of good and bad aspects and of family life. Have a time of prayer for those finding home life particularly difficult at the moment, and those who have been separated from their families through war or famine.

# 15th Sunday after Pentecost

## YEAR 1

*Thought for the day:*
*God is the One who has power over*
*our lives and everything we do.*

### Readings

Psalm 50
Daniel 5
Acts 25:1-12

### Reflection

When Belshazzar ordered the sacred cups from the temple to be used at his pagan feast, he was making a clear statement. He trusted so confidently in his own power that he was deliberately and arrogantly dismissing God's power altogether. Just as Nebuchadnezzar, his ancestor, had done, Belshazzar laughs in the face of God and finds out too late that God is not to be mocked. The elderly Daniel can interpret the writing on the wall because he understands God's language, through living daily in his presence. And that very night, as the king feasts, Belshazzar is overcome and killed by the attacking Persians. God is in charge, whether people recognise this or not.

Before this week's passage from Acts, Paul had been hounded and nearly killed by the Jews in Jerusalem, and held in prison for two years. During this time the governor, Felix, had talked with Paul often, but never got as far as allowing religion to interfere with his life-style. He could not cope with the consequences of God taking charge of his life.

Now there is a new governor, and Paul's case is aired again. After two year's imprisonment, Paul sounds weary with the false charges, but his faith shines clear as he trusts in the only one who has real authority.

Life is not a question of fighting in our own strength. When we trust in God, and get caught up in terrible situations, our reaction as Christians is to honour God by staying obedient to him, and watching with interest and excitement as God turns each situation to his glory. In Paul's case, through the imprisonment he is taken safely to Rome, spreading the good news there and at every opportunity on the way.

### Discussion starters

1  It is helpful to read over the preceding chapters of Daniel so as to see things more in context. Notice throughout these chapters how God is able to use Daniel because Daniel honours God, makes himself available and in humility is happy for God's will to be done in any way God pleased. How can we learn from all this?

2  Are there any areas in the world and in our lives where we could witness more faithfully? What holds us back?

### All stage talk

*Theme:* Who's in charge here?
Beforehand, collect together one of those cocktail stick umbrellas for decorating drinks, a small/child's umbrella and a huge golfing umbrella.

You will also need to make a crossing patrol lollipop, out of card fixed to a broom handle or bamboo cane.

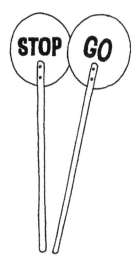

Begin by setting up the centre aisle as a road with a crossing patrol at it. A group of children show how it works, while the rest of the congregation watch or make traffic noises.

Ask who was in charge in that situation. How do we know? What might happen if the lollipop man/lady wasn't in charge?

Explain that lots of people are in charge. Perhaps some of the people here are in charge of people at their work, in charge of certain jobs at home, or in charge of looking after a person or a pet. When we're in charge we can sometimes get bossy, and think we have lots of power. Sometimes we use our power of being in charge to do what is wrong – as when people are put in charge of money and fiddle the books to steal the money, or when powerful leaders of a country use their power to make themselves very rich while the poor in their country starve. And that is wrong.

The one who is in charge over everything is God. Even when we are put in charge, God is in charge over us. Some people think God's power is no bigger over them than this. (Put the cocktail umbrella up over someone's head.) So they get bossy and greedy, and don't bother about what is a right, caring way to be in charge. Some people think God is in charge, but only about this much. (Put the small umbrella up over someone's head.) So they act responsibly some of the time, but if they feel like using their power badly, and don't think they'll be found out, they go ahead. But other people know that however important they get in life, it's God who is really in charge totally and completely. (Put up the golfing umbrella over someone small.) So when they are put in charge of anyone or anything they do it God's way – in a caring, honest and humble way.

## Intercessions

We pray for the churches which are thriving and those which have lost a sense of your direction; we pray for a reckless giving of ourselves to God.

*Silence for prayer*

Lord, our God:
**let your will be done in us**

We pray for those in positions of power and authority; we pray against all corruption and personal ego-trips; we pray for justice, mutual respect, peace and humility.

*Silence for prayer*

Lord, our God:
**let your will be done in us**

We pray for those who make us feel happy and comfortable, and for those we find it hard to get on with; we pray for all who take care of children.

*Silence for prayer*

Lord, our God:
**let your will be done in us**

*Continued overleaf*

We pray for those whose minds or bodies are trapped in illness, those who lack freedom of movement; we pray for all involved in medical research.

*Silence for prayer*

Lord, our God:
**let your will be done in us**

We pray for the dead and the dying, for those dying without care or comfort; for all victims of violence.

*Silence for prayer*

Lord, our God:
**let your will be done in us**

We pray for a deeper understanding of God as we remember with thankfulness the constant faithfulness and love which surround us.

*Silence for prayer*

Lord, our God:
**let your will be done in us**

## Other ideas

• Have the words 'Mene, Mene, Tekel, Parsin' written up in large letters on the wall for the service. They can be cut out of black paper and fixed to the wall with sticky putty.

• Have a small flower arrangement which incorporates metal chains and a simple crown, and spreading over this arrangement have another which suggests God's authority over all earthly power.

## In the crèche

*Aim:* For the children to learn that God is in charge.

Play the game of 'Follow my leader', where one person moves in a certain way and all the others follow, doing the same. Let everyone who wants to have a go at being the leader. Talk about who's in charge in different places, such as at home, at play group, on a bus, at the hospital or when Mum/Dad goes out for the evening. Who's in charge of everything in the whole wide world? God is. Go through some of the things he's in charge of. Paint, draw or model them and display them on a board labelled 'God's in charge!'

## Children

*Aim:* For them to see how Paul's reaction to his hardships showed that Jesus was Lord of his life.

First play the 'Simon says' game, in which they have to listen out for the authority of 'Simon' before carrying out the orders.

If possible have a man to tell Paul's story from Paul's point of view, putting on the appropriate headgear to do so. If you have no men on the team, try to borrow someone for the morning. Whoever does the telling will need to prepare the story from Acts 20, when Paul goes to Jerusalem and the Jews attack him. The children can be brought into the story as the Pharisees and the Sadducees. Have a question time afterwards, with the children questioning Paul (still in character) about his adventures.

Point out that what made the Jews so angry was that Paul was saying Jesus was Lord - that a human was God. It is an amazing thing to claim, but it's true. Go over the things Jesus did which make it clear that Jesus really is the Christ everyone had been waiting for, and try this simple creed. The responses need to be really loud.

Who was there before anything else?
GOD WAS!

Who created the entire universe?
GOD DID!

Who is in charge of our universe today?
GOD IS!

Who was walking this earth as Jesus?
GOD WAS!

Who loves us so much that he died
   for us all?
GOD DOES!

Who is alive for ever and living in
   his people?
GOD IS!

Who do we believe in?
WE BELIEVE IN GOD!

Help the children to make some bracelets, anklets and neck bands to wear. (See bottom of page.)

## Young people

*Aim:* For them to explore the nature of God's Lordship in our lives.

First have people in pairs, and tell one of each pair a destination within the teaching area. They are to give directions to their partners so that the partner manages to reach the right place. Then they swap over so that everyone has a go at being in charge.

In their pairs, ask everyone to make a list of what they feel makes a good leader, and then share these qualities in the whole group. You will probably find that the qualities you are looking at have a lot in common with the qualities of God, who is ultimately in charge, and from whom all authority comes. The trouble in earthly leadership happens when we start putting ourselves in God's place.

Read together Daniel 5, listening out for what was wrong in Belshazzar's leadership, and have a time of prayer for all world leaders, and any areas of the world where corrupt leadership is causing terrible suffering.

Finally look at Paul, living with Jesus as his Lord. What effect has this had on his life?

# YEAR 2

*Thought for the day:*
*God is the One who has power over*
*our lives and everything we do.*

## Readings
Psalm 50
1 Samuel 8:4-22a
1 Peter 2:11-end

## Reflection

Obedience and submission to authority are alien concepts in our culture. We even have to teach our children that it's OK to say 'no', because there are too many adults who might abuse them if they think obedience is essential. What a

terrible reflection on our society that is. We have brought two generations of children up to question authority all the way along the line because we still recoil from the horrors of atrocities committed in the second world war through people obediently following corrupt orders.

And yet we all know that a society without obedience runs wild and is no longer a safe place to live in. Many children with severe behavioural problems respond positively to a highly structured system where obedience to the rules is central. Gradually we are learning to trust obedience again, providing it is rules we obey, and not people, whom we have learnt to distrust.

The people of Israel wanted a monarch, and Samuel could see the dangers of power in the hands of a human turning to greed and corruption. A national leader would be alright so long as the people never forgot who their real leader was – God himself. As the American people say, it needs to be 'one nation under God'. And so often through history this truth, rejected, causes destruction and decay.

Peter, probably writing from Nero's Rome, still emphasises the calling of Christians to honour their leaders and obey the rules. Obviously there will be times when the rules are opposed to God's law, and ultimately it is God's law that we follow. But often, our honour and respect for those in authority – including those we disagree with – can be a way of witnessing to our belief that all people are worthy of respect, since in God's sight they are special. And in our lives we need to work to change what is unjust, cruel or corrupt.

## Discussion starters

1  Why did the people want a king? What were Samuel's objections?

2  Why does Peter insist on us putting up with authority, even if it treats us badly? At what point do we fight against evil, and what form should such a battle take?

## All stage talk

*Theme:* What it means for Jesus to be Lord. Beforehand prepare some sheets of paper in large zigzags – computer print out paper is perfect. On the sets of sheets, write the words LEADING, ORGAN-ISING, RULING and DIRECTING, so that when the sheets are folded up you only see the initial letters of the word, and when they are let down you see the whole word. Fasten the top edges with paper clips.

Begin by reminding everyone of how the people wanted to have a king, like all the other nations did. They wanted someone important, who would tell them what to do, and ride into battle with them and so on. Samuel wasn't so keen. A king might give them a hard life, and anyway, if they have a king they might forget who is really in charge. Who is that? God himself is really in charge.

Ask four people to come out and arrange the letters you give them into a word. When it says LORD, explain that we are always talking of Jesus as Lord, and today we are going to explore what that means.

Unfasten the letter L so that the word LEADING can be seen. That's one thing about Jesus; when we let him be Lord of our life he will be leading us through all our difficult decisions and hairy, scary moments. Unfasten the O. When we ask Jesus to be our Lord he will be organising our priorities and the things we feel are important, so that our lives fit in with God's plans. Unfasten the R. When Jesus is Lord of our life he will be ruling over us; all the different parts of our territory will be in his kingdom and subject to his law of love. Even those rebellious outlying districts of bad temper, greed or critical gossip can be brought under his rule. Unfasten the D. When Jesus is Lord in our lives he will be directing us, at those tricky decisions, those awkward dilemmas and those nagging temptations.

So when we say 'Jesus is Lord', we mean that Jesus is Leading us, Organising us, Ruling us and Directing us every moment of our lives.

## Intercessions

We call to mind all church leaders and the problems they face; all ministers, evangelists, teachers and healers; all who come thirsting and searching for God.

*Silence for prayer*

We are your people, O Lord:
**and you are our God**

We call to mind the nations and their leaders; the temptations that accompany power and the people's needs and hardships.

*Silence for prayer*

We are your people, O Lord:
**and you are our God**

We call to mind each home in this area; the squabbles and tears, the laughter and affection.

*Silence for prayer*

We are your people, O Lord:
**and you are our God**

We call to mind those in hospital and at home who are in pain; those who are frightened by their illness; and all who care for them.

*Silence for prayer*

We are your people, O Lord:
**and you are our God**

We call to mind those who have recently died and can meet you face to face; those for whom death is terrifying and all who are unprepared.

*Silence for prayer*

We are your people, O Lord:
**and you are our God**

We call to mind the glimpses of glory you show us; the times when we have known your presence close to us; the times of unexpected joy.

*Silence for prayer*

We are your people, O Lord:
**and you are our God**

## Other ideas

The first reading can incorporate different voices, with all the congregation joining in the words of the people.

## In the crèche

*Aim:* For the children to learn that obedience is God's way.

Make two circles of card, one red and one green, and label them STOP and GO. Fix them on to a stick so that you can turn either one side or the other to the children. Get everyone moving in a certain way while the green side is showing, and tell everyone to stop when they see the red sign.

Talk together about doing what we're told so that we make life happier for everyone. That is a loving way of living, and God wants us to be loving to one another because he loves us.

## Children

*Aim:* For the children to learn about obedience to God, and to those who look after us.

Have everyone moving round the room in the ways you direct – forwards, backwards, sideways, slowly, quickly etc. From time to time tell them to stop and then go again. Talk about obeying orders and making an effort to do this without arguing! Talk about how difficult it is to obey when you really want to do something else instead, and suggest ways to improve this for everyone. (Asking for it to be made known before the final deadline for finishing a game and going to bed; having a family rota for house jobs, so that everyone agrees what is fair; deciding in advance on bedtimes, getting up times and hair wash days.)

Listen to what Peter has to say, and pray together for our own world leaders. Then everyone can help make a large painting of all kinds of different places we come across in our lives. Over each is stamped or stuck a JESUS IS LORD.

## Young people

*Aim:* To explore our attitude to authority as Christians.

Begin by reading the Old Testament passage from 1 Samuel. Talk together about why the people wanted a king, and why Samuel wasn't so keen. Remember that they were surrounded by pagan societies. Now read the passage from 1 Peter, so that they can see Peter's advice as to the way we should behave. At that time the Christians were living in a strongly pagan society, and facing increasing persecution for their faith.

What about in our own time, when it is supposedly accepted that people shouldn't put up with bad treatment, but protest loudly until things are changed. Do they think this is actually true? Are there some categories of people in our society who do not, or cannot complain? (Such as the mentally vulnerable, the homeless or, in some countries, women and children or those of a low caste.) Keep a track of the discussion by jotting down main points, and suggest that they finish the session by expressing some of their feelings in paint or creative writing. Let the sharing lead on to a time of prayer, proclaiming the Lordship of Jesus in all the sadness, neglect and corruption of the world.

# 16th Sunday after Pentecost

## YEAR 1

*Thought for the day:*
*Treat others as you want them to*
*treat you.*

### Readings

Psalm 107:1-32
1 Kings 21 (or 1-23)
Matthew 7:1-12

### Reflection

We don't usually choose our neighbours, and they can make all the difference to our quality of living in a particular home, or working at a particular place. Acceptable noise levels, junk levels and space invasion levels are all very important, both to us and to the neighbours who have the pleasure of living or working next door to us.

Ahab and Jezebel do not rank highly in the register of good neighbours. Since Naboth refused to sell his vineyard Ahab sulked, until his wife sorted things out for him by having Naboth viciously murdered. What shines out is their total disregard for the value of human life, which can be brushed aside whenever it is inconvenient.

Such action never happens out of the blue, but is the accumulated evil from years of habitual selfishness. I sometimes wonder if some families are helped or hindered by being able to afford several televisions; the daily practice of sharing, negotiating and compromising our own wants is no longer there. Selfishness needs no practice at all, but reaching outwards to consider the needs of others around us takes a good deal of practice before it becomes a habit.

We know that it is often hard to get along well with certain people, but whenever we are put out we should be thankful, because whoever has irritated or upset us has given us another chance to practise our forgiving. Or they might have revealed to us a patch of self we are still jealously guarding and have not surrendered to God – concern to be thought intelligent, perhaps; the assumption that our methods are the only right ones; or the concern to keep our good image unchallenged.

Yet if anyone had cause to be affronted, Jesus did, and he chose the path of the servant, giving up all rights to search out the needs, rolling up his sleeves and setting to work to put things right, whether he was thanked for it or not. That's what he calls us to do - look out for the needs and get in there, keeping ourselves available so that God can use us in emergency encounters, daily conversations, and persevering loving behaviour with all those we live and work with.

### Discussion starters

1 Have a go at tracing the possible steps and behaviour patterns which eventually led to this act by Ahab and Jezebel.

2 Work through the advice Jesus gives about the way we treat one another, trying to keep open minded and attentive to what God may be saying to you, the parish, or the community in which you live. Each section seems obvious at first sight through familiarity, but be ready to be challenged.

## All stage talk

*Theme:* Good neighbours.

Begin by playing the theme tune of *Neighbours*, if you can stand it! Point out how the words are all about good neighbours becoming good friends – all very noble stuff – and yet most episodes are largely taken up with the feuds and grumps of those living around the Ramsay Street area. Quarrels, we suppose, are far more lifelike, and make better viewing.

Talk everyone through the Ahab and Jezebel 'bad neighbours' plot, where Naboth gets a very raw deal through the king's sulks and the queen's efficient cruelty. How do we react when people won't give us what we want? Learning to accept that we can't have things we want is often a hard, though very valuable lesson to learn. The more we work at accepting other people – whatever they look, sound or smell like – the less we shall find ourselves being driven crazy by them. We may not agree with what they do, but we won't be holding grudges, nurturing resentment or waging guerrilla warfare.

## Intercessions

Where the church is weakened by doubt or apathy, by confused priorities, or lack of self discipline, we commend it to the Father's love.

*Silence for prayer*

Father, we ask not for what we want:
**but for what you know we need**

Where the world is morally off course, bogged down in ancient feuds, and overwhelmed with disaster, we commend it to the Father's love.

*Silence for prayer*

Father, we ask not for what we want:
**but for what you know we need**

Where homes are harassed and over-busy, where children are frightened or adults are coping in difficult circumstances, we commend them to the Father's love.

*Silence for prayer*

Father, we ask not for what we want:
**but for what you know we need**

Where patients wait for and recover from operations, where the helpless are learning dependence and today's new babies are struggling into the world, we commend them to the Father's love.

*Silence for prayer*

Father, we ask not for what we want:
**but for what you know we need**

Where the dying are entering eternity, and the suffering bodies are at last relieved of pain, we commend them to the Father's love.

*Silence for prayer*

Father, we ask not for what we want:
**but for what you know we need**

Where experience has taught us more of God's love; where friends and neighbours have enriched our lives, ·
we offer, Father, our thanks and praise.

*Silence for prayer*

Father, we ask not for what we want:
**but for what you know we need**

## Other ideas

For the passage from 1 Kings 21, have the story acted out in a series of 'stills'. Work out the 'pictures', such as when Ahab is sulking, or when Naboth is accused at the special feast, and act your way into them, freezing when you get to that spot. Then act into the next 'still'. Keep it simple, and make sure that the congregation can see what you are doing – don't act to one another, but out to the front.

## In the crèche

*Aim:* For the children to learn that we are to treat others as we would like to be treated ourselves.

Use puppets to act out someone being nasty to someone else, but getting upset when they get treated the same way. (Being pushed away from their game, for instance, because someone else feels like playing with it.) Then have the puppets meeting up with a similar situation, where they remember to treat others the way they would like to be treated.

## Children

*Aim:* To hear the 'bad neighbour' story and look at Jesus' teaching on how to live peaceably with others.

Begin by playing games of 'piggy in the middle', using beanbags. This is actually an excellent example of how the problem of being left out and then spoiling a game has been solved by it being made into a game.

Now tell the story of Naboth's vineyard. You could do this effectively by having it told three times from different viewpoints – first the king's, then the queen's, then Naboth's. Or you could have pictures of the main characters and display them on the floor, or on an OHP whenever they come into the story. Or you could have the children acting it out as you do the narrative, with everyone joining in the crowd scenes. Whichever way you do it, bring out the underhand and cruel way Naboth was dealt with, and after the story talk with the children about what a bad and unjust thing it was to do. What do they think Ahab should have done? And suppose he had still gone all sulky, what do they think Jezebel should have done?

Now look at what Jesus said we should do - treat others as you would want them to treat you. See if they can learn this off by heart by singing it over and over again to the tune of 'Twinkle, twinkle little star'. It fits in squashily, so long as you make 'treat others' fit with 'twinkle' like this:

| Twin-kle, | twin-kle, |
| Treat oth-ers as | you would-want |

| lit-tle | star |
| them to-treat | you |

It makes a tongue twister!

## Young people

*Aim:* To explore the Naboth story and how Jesus taught us to treat one another. First read the Naboth story in small groups with different people taking the different parts, and then in the full group have a role play, with Ahab, Jezebel, Naboth and the hired men giving their accounts of the events.

On a large sheet draw some steps going down, and try to work out together what stages Ahab and Jezebel might have gone through to reach this point of total selfishness without concern for others. It may alert us to the dangers of the early steps in our own lives.

Now look at the passage from Matthew 7. Do our laws reflect these teachings? Does our behaviour as a country, a church and as individuals? If you find any glaring inconsistencies draft letters, or plan other action which seems appropriate to bring about a change for the better.

# YEAR 2

*Thought for the day:*
*Treat others as you want them to treat you.*

## Readings

Psalm 107:1-32
Proverbs 25:6-22
James 2:1-13

## Reflection

The nomadic Hebrews are so practical! These wise sayings from the book of Proverbs don't assume that people are perfect, but help us muddle along together with those we have to live and work with, respecting one another's space, but at the same time available for reliable help when needed. The sayings have obviously been born of generations of experience, and have a wonderful freshness about them, so that we can almost see the characters.

One of my elderly teachers at school always seemed very fond of us all and really enjoyed our company. If one of us was ever upset after getting into trouble she used to say, 'Ah, never mind, love; write it on the wall with a big E for experience!' And she was very wise – we do learn so much by getting things wrong. If we make mistakes in our dealings with one another it isn't the end of the world, though it may seem so at the time. Next time we will hopefully remember what we've learnt, and understand a little more, and act a little more wisely. The important thing is to be humble enough to recognise our need to learn.

Humility in our dealings with one another is a kind of earthiness – the word has the same root as 'humus' – so that we are like the earth, open to the rain, frost and sun; open to seeds which can then grow in us. This is what will keep us free of prejudice and narrow mindedness, bigotry and hypocrisy. If we are open always to God's way of looking at things, our churches will be places where strangers of any kind feel welcomed with natural warmth. There will be no rigid seating arrangement, no jobs held on to on lifetime leases, and no complex book shuffling where you need 'A' levels in filing skills to keep up. What there will be in plenty is a vibrant love for God and all his children which is infectious and speaks through every tradition of worship.

## Discussions starters

1  In what way do Jesus' stories and actions reinforce and fulfil the teaching in the Proverbs? Pick out specific examples as you talk about this.

2   It is so easy to fall into the way of only associating with 'neighbours' who are like ourselves. How can we ensure that we stay open to all?

## All stage talk

*Theme:* How open is open?

Beforehand arrange with two people from another church to come to your church as strangers today, asking one to dress in a way which fits in well with the people in your congregation, and the other in a way which might be difficult for the congregation to accept. This needs some careful thought! Ask them to come into church separately, and make it clear to the sidespeople that they aren't used to coming here.

At the beginning of the talk have a box with a closed lid. Is it open or closed? Now open it a little. Is it open or closed now? Then open it up fully. Is it open or closed? We are like this with other people and with God. With some people we are very open, with others we are a little open, and with others, we shut up tight. God's teaching today advises us to be wide open to God, so that we are able to be open and welcoming to others.

Now invite the two 'strangers' to the front, and explain the awful truth that you invited them specially to help us look at our own hospitality. Ask them how it felt to be coming in as strangers, and what would need to happen (or happened) to put them at their ease. This needs to be done with sensitivity, humour, and without any sense of accusation, of course. Point out how it is natural for us to find some people easier to get on with than others, and that as we realise God's love for us more and more, we shall be more and more able to reach out to others, even those who would not naturally be our friends.

## Intercessions

Father, we remember our brothers and sisters in Christ as they worship in large and small groups all over the world.

*Silence for prayer*

O give thanks to the Lord:
**for he is good**

Father, we think of the world's peace makers and all who spend their lives working constructively for good; all who uphold Christian values and stand firm for what is right.

*Silence for prayer*

O give thanks to the Lord:
**for he is good**

Father, we remember all who are bringing their children up carefully and lovingly; all who care for elderly neighbours and relatives; all who work to build community where they live.

*Silence for prayer*

O give thanks to the Lord:
**for he is good**

Father, we think of the sick and those caring for them; we think of those who rarely get a break, but need one; those who are offering their suffering for you to use.

*Silence for prayer*

O give thanks to the Lord:
**for he is good**

Father, we remember those who are dying and those who have crossed from time into eternity; we think of the example of their lives and we remember those who love them.

*Silence for prayer*

O give thanks to the Lord:
**for he is good**

*Continued overleaf*

Father, we think of the beauty of all you have made and the daily miracles of life and love.

*Silence for prayer*

O give thanks to the Lord:
**for he is good**

## Other ideas

Have the passage from James acted out by people in appropriate dress, with the sidespeople doing the obsequious and disparaging bits, while a Highway code 'Not allowed' sign is displayed. Then have a 'Take 2' sign displayed as the actors retrace their steps backwards to where they started, and then do it properly, welcoming both people equally.

## In the crèche

*Aim:* For the children to learn to treat others as they would like to be treated. Use teddies and soft toys, some grand and some moth-eaten and scruffy, to act out being unkind to each other and not enjoying receiving the same treatment back. Then go through the same situation doing it properly, after one of the characters has pointed out how much happier they will be if they treat others as they like being treated themselves.

## Children

*Aim:* For the children to understand the teaching of James and to look at our own behaviour in the light of it.

First have a game where one end of the room is 'Being a good neighbour', the other end is 'Being a bad neighbour' and the middle is 'Names of people who are our neighbours'. As you call out

something from the categories, everyone runs to the appropriate position. Good neighbour qualities may include such things as taking turns in a game, sometimes playing the game their friends want to play, helping at home without arguing, and making a get well card for someone in hospital. Bad neighbour qualities may include sulking if you don't get your own way, moaning about having to tidy your room, cheating at a game, and getting someone else into trouble when it's really your fault.

Names of neighbours may include the names of people in the parish (including some of the children's names), those they live with, share a table with at school, teachers they like and dislike, and friends and relations.

Then read the passage from Proverbs, using different voices for the various sayings, and act out together the teaching in James, so that they can see what ought to be done as well.

Finally help the children to make this circle of people joined in God's love, which could be taken home to use as a table centrepiece, putting a candle in the middle.

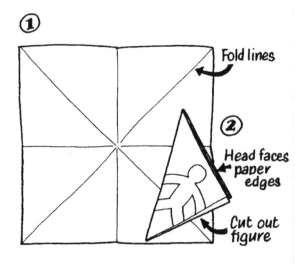

① Fold lines

② Head faces paper edges

Cut out figure

# *17th Sunday after Pentecost*

## YEAR 1

*Thought for the day:*
*Work for God's glory, not your own.*

## Readings

Psalms 91, 93
Judges 7:1-8,19-23
John 7:1-24

## Reflection

There are some good things to be learnt from this story of Gideon. It's quite likely that the original sized army would have been able to defeat the enemy, though this would have involved many casualties and the price of victory would have been high. But in any case, this wasn't the way God wanted it to be. He wanted to show Gideon and all the people his lordship, and that wouldn't happen unless Gideon was prepared to trust him. Gideon did put his complete trust in God's way, listening out for his instructions bit by bit as they went on. And although the instructions must have seemed strange – even foolish – Gideon's soldiers won the day, without even having to fight.

In the New Testament reading we find Jesus hanging on to every word his Father tells him to say, utterly obedient, no matter how much of a dangerous rebel that made him appear. Jesus' values, words and behaviour were proof that he was not out for self glory.

We need to be aware of wanting recognition and praise more than following God's will, however odd or

## Young people

*Aim:* To explore the bible's teaching about real neighbourliness and relate it to their own experiences.
Begin by making a communal list of what they consider makes a good neighbour. Take neighbour to include those we share desks or lockers with, rather than just those we live next door to. Then read what the wise sayings from Proverbs have to add – they may well overlap. Notice how all the qualities bring out the importance of respecting one another's space, but at the same time being a reliable help when needed. Talk about any examples they may have experienced of helpful and/or unhelpful neighbourliness.

Now broaden the idea of neighbour to include those we find it hard to accept, and read the example from James' letter about some being better welcomed than others. Talk about the kind of partiality they have noticed in our society, and what could be done to change and improve matters. Keep the discussion positive as far as possible, and don't let it develop into a 'them and us' moan. On the other hand, take note of genuine grievances, either for themselves or on behalf of others, so that something positive can be done to put things right. Pray together for each different cluster of people who have been mentioned.

uncomfortable that may be. There is a story of Bernard, one of St. Francis' earliest companions, who went regularly to a town telling people of God's love. He was regularly insulted and despised, but he went on going out of love for the people and obedience to God's will. Gradually the people started to listen and then to honour him, and this was what frightened Bernard, so that he begged Francis to send someone else instead!

Obedience to God grows from our trust in him; in our conviction that his ways may be unusual, but there's always a good reason behind them which we may or may not eventually be aware of. And equally, our trust in God grows as we set ourselves to be obedient to him. It is worth remembering that the word 'obedience' actually means instant and alert listening.

## Discussion starters

1  What hints do we have of Gideon's faith in this story? What about us – do we prefer to see the end before we start to follow? Why does God show us only a bit at a time?

2  What was it in Jesus that made the people love him and their teachers find him so threatening? Are we, as a church and as individuals, ever threatening to others through our obedience to God's will?

## All stage talk

*Theme:* Faith shows in our actions.
Beforehand get a box or case with a lock, and put a bible in it. Lock it up and give the key to someone sitting on the end of a row, asking them to hold it out discreetly on the palm of their hand during the talk.

Begin by asking everyone to stand up, and then sit down again with their eyes fixed on you. They will just have demonstrated their faith in the chair still being there, because they were prepared to sit down without checking that the chair hadn't disappear-ed. Gideon trusted God and so obeyed his instructions.

Give someone an instruction to go to the back of the church. When they get there they find a box which they can't open. Ask them to come back to the front, explaining as they do so how this is how we often act; we hear God's first calling, or instruction and then stop listening or looking. Explain the root meaning of obedience (instant and alert listening) and send them off again, reminding them to be alert, listening and looking, as they go. This time they will probably notice the key (reminding them to look, if they seem to be ignoring it) and can open the box. Explain how God keeps in touch all the way, if only we will be alert to what he is saying through events around us. When the box is opened the bible is found. That's another way God speaks to us and helps us, but it only works if we read it!

We need to keep in constant touch with God; if we aren't, it probably means we don't reckon much to God's power, and don't think he's worth taking seriously.

## Intercessions

Father, we entrust to you the small and the complex problems facing your church throughout the world; we think of all those in lay and ordained ministry and of each person worshipping somewhere today.

*Silence for prayer*

You are my refuge:
**God in whom I trust**

Father, we entrust to you the local issues
where feelings run high; the national and
international matters of concern
and our longing for your kingdom to
come on earth.
*Silence for prayer*
You are my refuge:
**God in whom I trust**

Father, we entrust to you our loved ones;
those who are constantly on our minds;
those who frighten us;
and all who need us to listen to them better.
*Silence for prayer*
You are my refuge:
**God in whom I trust**

Father, we entrust to you all who feel lost
or disillusioned; those whose lives are
plagued by resentment or guilt;
all who suffer and need comforting.
*Silence for prayer*
You are my refuge:
**God in whom I trust**

Father, we entrust to you those who have
died and those who will die today;
all who mourn and all who minister to
their needs.
*Silence for prayer*
You are my refuge:
**God in whom I trust**

Father, we entrust to you ourselves
and the rest of our lives; all our decisions,
hopes, sorrows and joys.
*Silence for prayer*
You are my refuge:
**God in whom I trust**

## Other ideas

In order to express the idea of us being
moved along by God's Spirit from one
stage of our journey to the next, and from
one instruction to the next, have someone
being directed along a route marked out
by other people. One person, expressing
God's Spirit, arrives to direct and point
the way when it isn't clear. This
mime/dance could take place all round
the church so that everyone can see part
of it close up. Another way of expressing
this theme is to have one person walking
around and being led on different stages
of the journey by different people who
just get up out of their seats to direct that
part and then sit down again. Have some
music playing which your congregation
will relate to. It may be an Indian raga,
Pachalbel's Canon, or some Celtic music,
for instance, but should have a sense of
steady progression.

## In the crèche

*Aim:* For the children to understand that
God is someone who won't let them down.
Have a time of free play with building
towers out of bricks or an assortment of
junk, seeing how high the towers can get
before they crash.

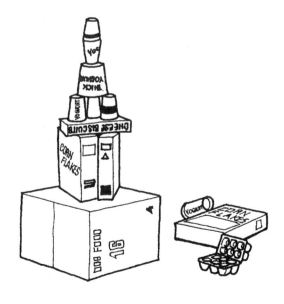

Then talk to the children about the way we get let down sometimes by toys that don't work properly, or friends who say they'll help and then don't, and sometimes we let other people down by not keeping our promises. While you are talking, play the fool – leaning against things that let you down and give way. As you find something strong at last that doesn't let you down, tell them how God never ever lets us down.

## Children

*Aim:* For them to understand the truth behind the Gideon story – faith shows in action; God knows what he's doing.

Begin with a sorting out game, such as all those wearing yellow run to the back wall; all those who ate cornflakes for breakfast hop to the centre; all who watch Superman leap across to the front wall etc.

Now tell the story of how God sorted out the soldiers and by following God closely, Gideon led his army to a rather clever victory. During the telling, hold a large version of the card the children will be making later, and break open the seal at the appropriate moment to reveal the light inside. We have a nativity play 'shepherds' fire' which also comes in handy at different times of the year; if you have one hidden away, bring it out and use it for when Gideon creeps down to hear what the enemy are saying. These few props really focus attention, making the story telling very realistic.

Then help the children to make this card model of the hidden lights. As you all work on the models, talk informally about how we need to keep looking and listening to God, so that we notice what he is trying to tell us. You may be able to share a personal example of this so that the children understand that it really happens now.

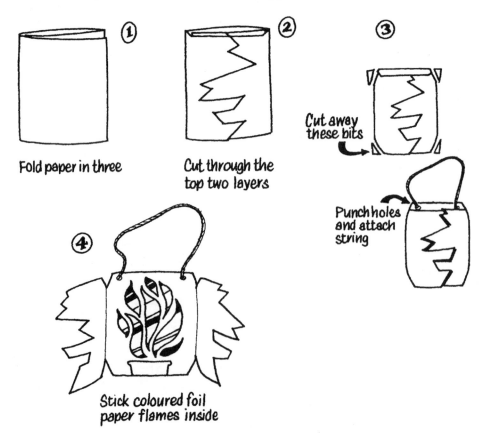

① Fold paper in three

② Cut through the top two layers

③ Cut away these bits

Punch holes and attach string

④ Stick coloured foil paper flames inside

## *Young people*

*Aim:* To explore the way God leads us 'mysteriously' but we can trust him to know what's best.

Beforehand prepare a trail of clues which make a message. Use this one (NIV), or one of your own.

Find the missing words.

- Psalm 20:7 Some _ _ _ _ _

- Genesis 1:1 In the beginning _ _ _

- Exodus 2:3 coated it with tar _ _ _

- John 2:5 His mother said to the servants _ _ _ _ _ _ _ _ _ _ _ _ _ _ _ _ _ _ _ .

(Solution: Trust God and do whatever he tells you.)

Point out that if they had stopped half way they wouldn't have found the answer to the puzzle. If we stop listening out for God in our lives he won't be able to complete the excellent plan he has for us and all those he was planning to bless along the way by our action.

Read the Gideon story together, checking each instruction to see how Gideon's faith kept him listening, even when God wasn't suggesting the accepted way of going on.

Then read the passage from John and notice Jesus' obedience which kept him alertly listening, so that he spoke and behaved in harmony with his Father, and not as the teachers and experts expected him to behave. Make a space for a discussion/question time of areas they may be exploring in their own lives - such as how we are to be sure what is God's voice and what is just ourselves; how God actually communicates with us; a natural wariness of it all being a con and so on. Finish with a time of quiet prayer and music.

# *YEAR 2*

*Thought for the day:*
*Work for God's glory, not your own.*

## *Readings*
Psalms 91, 93
Joshua 5:13-6:20
John 6:51-69

## *Reflection*

The soldier/angel was a sign to Joshua that whatever happened, God would be leading, and Joshua was happy to follow God's instructions, however weird and wonderful they were. Often in the closed capsule of the present moment God's instructions sound divergent, if not downright foolish according to normal expectations. But of course God is not closed in by time or space, and that is why his routes can be so perfectly devised. The part of the route you are on at the moment may seem to have no meaning and good purpose. It might even be making you angry with God. But it may be that God needs you to go via this section so as to help others or forge friendships which will later in time bring blessing.

Sometimes this inner conflict in us is caused by God having a different agenda from ours. For instance, I always pray my way round the supermarket and when I am nearing the checkout allow God to lead me to the queue he would like me to join. Now *my* criteria might be that the best queue will be the one that gets me out quickest. God often has other ideas; *his* choice of queue may well be one with problems, and someone in it needs some help that I can give – even if it's only God's love ministered in ordinary friendliness. But many 'deep and meaningfuls' (as my daughters call such surprising spiritual conversations) have taken place in the carpark or by the empty trolleys! God will use anyone who admits they're available. Sometimes he says what we would prefer not to hear, and sometimes what he wants us to do is painful. But he never discards what we offer, and never leads us up the garden path. We can be assured that where he leads us is the right place to be.

## Discussion starters

1   What factors in the Jericho story enable the city to be taken so thoroughly and so easily? How could you use these lessons in tackling strong, walled problems in your own life?

2   When Jesus spoke directly of himself as the living bread, many couldn't take it. They voted with their feet and walked no more with him. Why do you think they found his words hard to accept, and yet the disciples were able to acknowledge Jesus as God's Holy One?

## All stage talk

*Theme:* What's on God's agenda?
Begin by asking people to forget they know the end of the Jericho story, and imagine what an unusual set of instructions they must have seemed for taking the city. A bit like being told to walk round your car shouting loudly if you've forgotten your car keys. Perhaps the soldiers thought Joshua was going mad. And yet God knew what he was doing; he knew that the walls weren't as secure as they might have been, and through prayer he allowed Joshua to use this hidden information.

We are used to interpreting things. Show some travel brochures and ask two people to come to the front. One reads an expression you might find inside, and the other reads out what we know it really means:

cosy = cramped

quaint and traditional =
the plumbing doesn't work

very new hotel =
building loudly in progress

sea view from some rooms =
sea view from the bathroom

Sometimes we think we have the same agenda as others, but in fact we haven't. Ask two adults and two children to read this out.

**Adults**      We go for the children's sake.

**Children**   We go because we're told to.

**Adults**      It's a nice rest for us all.

**Children**   They sleep on the beach all day.

**Adults**      They loved all the animals at the farm.

**Children**   We loved the slot machine – if you wiggle it you get an extra chocolate bar.

The more we spend time with one another and listen to one another, the less misunderstanding there will be. And it's the same with God. Our ideas are often different from his.

Our idea might be: If I catch this bus I'll be home extra early. But God's idea might be: If she misses this bus she'll meet Mrs. Merry and be able to help her with her shopping bags.

Our idea might be: If I don't pass this time I can always try again – I'm not going to kill myself over it. But God's idea might be: If he does pass this time he'll drive Terry and Pete to Scotland and meet his future wife.

Our idea might be: If I commit myself to a bible study I'll miss my programme, and anyway, I'm too shy. But God's idea might be: If she goes to a bible study I'll be able to help her sort out her shyness, and give her a lifelong friend who will look after her when her mother dies.

Our idea might be: If I make that phone call and he doesn't even remember me I shall look a complete idiot. But God's idea might be: He needs re-assurance and encouragement, and she is the most appropriate person to give it – this phone call will stop him falling apart. So if as you pray, God's ideas come to you, be prepared to act on them.

## Intercessions

Father, we ask you to strengthen and purify your people; teach us to be better listeners to each other and to you.
Speak to our inmost being and show us your will.
*Silence for prayer*
When we call:
**we know you answer us**

Father, we ask you to unravel the tangled problems of our world; help us to follow you, step by step, towards harmony and peace.
*Silence for prayer*
When we call:
**we know you answer us**

Father, we ask you to live in our homes and in all hostels and orphanages.
Remind us to value the time we spend with our friends and listen to one another with full attention.
*Silence for prayer*
When we call:
**we know you answer us**

Father, we ask that the sick and injured will be aware of your comforting presence; that the very old and the very young may know they are safe and loved.
*Silence for prayer*
When we call:
**we know you answer us**

Father, we ask you to welcome into your kingdom those who have recently travelled through death
from lifetimes all over the world.
*Silence for prayer*
When we call:
**we know you answer us**

Father, we ask you to sharpen our awareness of all that is beautiful, hopeful, precious and eternal.
*Silence for prayer*
When we call:
**we know you answer us**

## Other ideas

So as to practise listening out for instructions, teach a dance to groups of people who gather in the aisle. Choose simple steps – perhaps barn dance ideas – which can then be danced while everyone sings a song or hymn. Suitable hymns include 'O O O How good is the Lord', 'Jubilate', 'All things bright and beautiful' and 'Freely, freely', but there are plenty of others, and the quiet, worshipful ones are particularly helpful to express in movement.

• Practise listening to each other in pairs. One speaks for a minute while the other listens. Then the other person tells back what they have heard. Then you swap over roles.

Make the subject matter something that everyone finds easy to talk about – how they spend each day of the week, for instance, and which days they like best and why.

## In the crèche

*Aim:* To help the children learn to listen.
Gather an assortment of things which make different noises, and make the noises in turn hidden from view by an

upturned table. Talk together about what the sounds might be before showing the answers. Also, try having some music of different moods played, and let the children either sit and listen or move around. With older children in this group you could try a time of silence, asking the children to listen to the silence and then talk about the sounds they have heard. Have a prayer time in the quietness.

## Children

*Aim:* To help the children listen to God.
Begin by playing the 'keys' game, where everyone sits in a circle and one person sits blindfolded in the middle. Someone creeps round the outside of the circle, holding the keys, and the person in the middle has to listen for where they are. If they point directly to them, someone else can go in the middle.

Then have a time of quietness, listening to the sounds, and praying through them. Explain that Joshua, in today's story, listened to God and carried out his instructions, even though they were very strange instructions indeed.

Tell the story from a soldier's point of view, and have children standing up as the walls of Jericho, so that when the army give their huge shout the walls can fall down.

Afterwards, help the children make these trumpets.

## Young people

*Aim:* For them to understand the need for constant, expectant listening.
Start with a game where one person in each team is blindfolded, given a task and the equipment needed, and the rest of the team can give instructions as they try to beat the clock. A possible task might be to fill a box with scattered objects and take it to someone, but you may well have better ideas for your particular group.

Now read the Jericho story, noticing the way Joshua followed God's instructions carefully and made sure the soldiers did as well. They will have seen how the person in the game had to listen intently all the time to complete the task, and we have to do this too. Prayer is just as much an attitude of listening and watching as it is saying things to God. If we don't expect to hear him we probably won't; if we do listen expectantly, we'll find he starts using us.

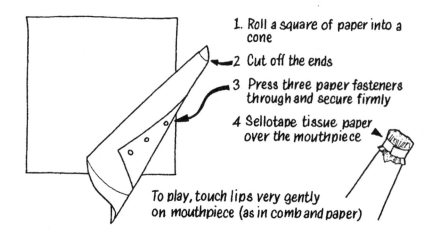

1. Roll a square of paper into a cone
2 Cut off the ends
3 Press three paper fasteners through and secure firmly
4 Sellotape tissue paper over the mouthpiece

To play, touch lips very gently on mouthpiece (as in comb and paper)

# 18th Sunday after Pentecost

## YEAR 1

*Thought for the day:*
*Live every day of your life to the full.*

### Readings
Psalm 118
Ecclesiastes 11 and 12
Luke 12:1-21

### Reflection

Whatever else we may think of Ecclesiastes, he was certainly frank. 'Make the most of your life', he advises, 'because it's the only one you get, however awful it is.' Not exactly uplifting stuff. On the other hand, there are those miserable, depressing times in our lives when we can see his point. Perhaps we also see what is wrong in our society but feel too weary to work at changing it any more. Perhaps there are times when we get exhausted from caring for others, and feel in need of a bit of cosseting ourselves for a while. At such times we may shrug our shoulders at grand hopes and dreams, recognise that we might as well accept things as they are, and then get on with making the most of it.

Jesus picks up on the theme of futility – the futility of amassing material wealth or prestige because we never know when we are going to die and lose it all, or when some catastrophe might wrench our plans from us.

But in contrast to Ecclesiastes, Jesus doesn't leave us in this gloomy thistle patch. He suggests that, rather than being let down and depressed by all this, we change our way of building; instead of fixing our hopes and dreams on things which are bound to let us down sooner or later, we set our hearts on the things which last right through death, and which keep dishing out regular bonuses of joy, even while we are saving.

### Discussion starters

1 If you come across someone feeling as disillusioned as Ecclesiastes, how would you cheer them up? (Or perhaps you wouldn't treat them in a 'cheering up' way at all?)

2 Is it really possible to live simply in a materialistic society? And how can Jesus suggest we live joyfully when there are so many people suffering in the world?

### All stage talk

*Theme:* Making the best of things.

Ask everyone to turn to someone close to them and try counting the hairs on their head. (This will be easier for some than for others!) Ask if anyone can give a definite answer. Most probably no one will be able to. Pretend to be surprised, and disappointed that they aren't very clever this morning, then give them another chance with another question – really easy, this time. How many sparrows died in (your town) yesterday? Be amazed that they don't know the answer to that easy question either. Try them once more with a really easy question – who can add one day (not a week or a year, or anything difficult; just a day) to their lifetime? Show your disappointment and then explain how Jesus asked these questions, and none of his listeners could answer them either, so they are in very good company with the Galileans of 2000 years ago.

Draw attention to Jesus' teaching, that if we can't even do simple things like this, there's really not much point in worrying about everything.

Pick up a glass of water and ask if anyone feels thirsty. (If no one does, ask them to imagine they've just spent the last two days in a desert with the sun beating down – that should do the trick!) Give the person the water to drink and then ask them what their favourite drink is. Point out that water isn't their favourite, but when you're thirsty you enjoy any drink, without wasting time grumbling about what you can't have.

Worrying and grumbling are habits that we can get into and they spoil our enjoyment of this life which God has given us. Thankfully they are also habits we can get out of – listen to yourself during the day and find out if you're addicted to either of them. If you are, recognise it and allow Jesus to help you break the habit.

## Intercessions

Father, we give you thanks for your constant care of the church in all its strengths and weaknesses; for your sensitive guiding, pruning, anointing and enabling.

*Silence for prayer*

The Lord is my strength:
**the Lord is my strength and my song**

Father, we give you thanks for your love which binds up the world's woundings, protects and defends us against evil, and works unceasingly for what is right and just.

*Silence for prayer*

The Lord is my strength:
**the Lord is my strength and my song**

Father, we give you thanks for your presence in our homes through the nights and mornings, afternoons and evenings, each day, each week, each year.

*Silence for prayer*

The Lord is my strength:
**the Lord is my strength and my song**

Father, we give you thanks for your comfort which refreshes and soothes, supports and sustains all who are sick in body, mind or spirit.

*Silence for prayer*

The Lord is my strength:
**the Lord is my strength and my song**

Father, we give you thanks for life which is not taken away at death but brought into fullness and everlasting peace.

*Silence for prayer*

The Lord is my strength:
**the Lord is my strength and my song**

## Other ideas

When people come in, give them each a piece of wheat, or a flower and while some quiet music plays, ask people to hold this symbol and think of one particular thing they want to give thanks to God for. Then have everyone coming up to present their offering of thanks-giving, either into a basket, or (if flowers) into a vase at the front of the church.

## In the crèche

*Aim:* For the children to know that God loves to see them enjoying themselves and living life to the full.

It is so important that children never get the idea of God being a crusty old person who frowns on ordinary, natural enjoyment, since this couldn't be further from the truth. I suspect that most children don't need to be told to live life to the full – they do it naturally anyway! So today can be a time to celebrate being alive as God's children in a lovely world. If you have access to an outside area, wander round with small groups of children for them to find a 'favourite', special place, and decorate it with leaves and stones, and pictures made with outdoor materials. Then each group can invite the others to see their special place and enjoy it with them. Sing a favourite praise song in each place.

## Children

*Aim:* For them to appreciate the lasting things and see the way other things don't last.

Start with blowing bubbles and enjoying them, noticing how we don't get terribly upset when they burst because we know that bubbles aren't built to last, and we don't expect anything more from them. If we did, we'd get very disappointed every time one popped.

Explain how sometimes people set their hearts on things they think will last - like money and power. How long do these things last? Only to death, at the very most.

Now tell the story from Luke, introducing it as it is in the bible – coming straight after two brothers wanting Jesus to sort out their squabble. (You may well have a couple of real squabbling brothers who would be happy to explain this part.)

During the telling of the story introduce some sound effects of the old barns being pulled down and the new ones built. Either have these previously taped, or have them being made by the children.

Then help them to make the three dimensional picture (shown overleaf), which you can either look at or through, just as we can either fix our attention on this world and get disappointed, or we can look deeper into it and find real, lasting meaning.

## Young people

*Aim:* For them to explore things which are lasting and worth building on and working for.

Begin by reading Ecclesiastes. Is this how they feel sometimes, or their friends? Talk together about the things which do make us depressed and hopeless. Now read the passage from Luke and notice the similarities and contrasts when compared with Ecclesiastes. Once again, relate Jesus' teaching to their own way of thinking and that of their friends.

Using various cardboard boxes, tape, lining paper and pens, work in groups of twos and threes to create a three dimensional model to express the futility of setting our hopes on such things as fame, money and possessions, and the good sense of setting our hopes on God, the maker, judge and rescuer.

Have the finished models displayed in church.

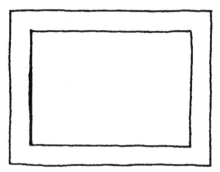

**1** Make a card frame

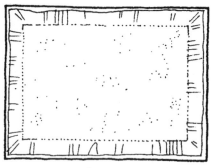

**2** Stick coloured tissue paper on to the frame

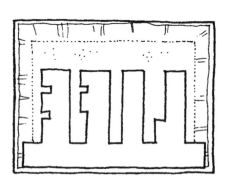

**3** Cut out card shapes and stick on the back of frame

**4** Look down at the picture and it is just a nice colour. Look up to the light and see LIFE

# YEAR 2

*Thought for the day:*
*Live every day of your life to the full.*

## Readings
Psalm 118
Jeremiah 26:1-16
Philippians 1:12-26

## Reflection

Not surprisingly Jeremiah's prophecy that the city and the temple will be destroyed does not go down too well. We can easily imagine everyone's indignation as they busily collect together all kinds of reasons why Jeremiah must be wicked, rather than searching in his message for the unpalatable truth. And don't we do this all the time – this bridling of righteous indignation which rapidly turns into attack? Yet Jeremiah is actually giving a very positive warning, allowing the inhabitants of the city to take a sober look at their behaviour and change it so as to avoid the devastation.

What is interesting is the way that Jeremiah is quite casual about his own life, knowing that he has to do what God has called him to, whatever the response. It may well be partly this lack of personal fear which helps sway the officials in his favour.

Paul shows the same casual attitude to his own life in this letter to the Christians at Philippi. He isn't terribly bothered by being in chains in prison with no immediate prospect of release. What's really important to him is the task of telling people the good news that will set them free, and in a way, the chains seem actually to be helping that. So, odd though it may seem, Paul is quite happy to be living his life chained up, and doesn't see the infringement of liberty in a vengeful or resentful way at all.

Then Paul has this little conversation with himself about which is better – to live or die – and he can't easily make up his mind because both have such excellent advantages! It certainly makes us shamefully aware of how much most of us still cling to the importance of staying alive in this world, rather than thinking of ourselves as people who have already passed from death to life, and therefore whether we spend the next week or year on earth or in heaven is of little consequence.

But when we do grasp this, what a difference it makes to our attitudes, our need to prove things; our willingness to speak out or face danger. All the usual fears and restrictions disappear and we are truly free to live.

## Discussion starters

1  Think of the people you would usually avoid mentioning your Christian activities to and try to discover what honestly puts you off. If it is anything at all to do with fear of rejection, for instance, pray for courage to speak out God's words, and the opportunity for it to happen.

2  Do we live too much in the 'if only' zone, instead of offering every situation for God to use, and then living through it fully and thankfully? Or does such talk make you want to run and hide somewhere where no demands will be made?

## All stage talk

*Theme:* The good life – even in chains.
Beforehand prepare four official-looking files, labelled on the front in large letters, A,B,C and D. The information in the files reads something like this:

File A: A is very bitter at being taken prisoner, and vows that he will get revenge as soon as possible. A spends his time cursing the waste of his life, and makes life as difficult as possible for everyone else in the prison.

File B: B was very bitter at being taken prisoner, but then decided that he was only making his life worse, so asked God to use his imprisonment in some way for good. Over the year two other prisoners have met Jesus through talking to B, and their lives have been transformed. Many prisoners come to B when they feel down, because he makes them feel better.

File C: C is a gifted runner with an excellent physique. He lets nothing at all interfere with his running. Through this his marriage is breaking up and he never keeps friends because he is always letting them down. His parents are frail, but he never has time to visit them.

File D: D is a gifted runner with an excellent physique. He has offered his running gift to God to use. Now that D is famous, he often gets asked about his life, and uses these opportunities to talk about how important Jesus is to him and what a difference being a Christian makes in his life. As a result, many of his followers have been introduced to the God of love.

First have two people running up and down the aisle, labelled C and D, and two people sitting chained up, labelled A and B. Ask everyone which two people are in chains and which two are free.

Now explain that while that certainly looks obvious, we'll just check a few details out from their official files. Read out each in turn, asking/pointing out which ones are actually chained up, spiritually, and which are actually free. So our job is to live life to the full – however trapped or free we may physically feel.

## Intercessions

Father, in all our preparation for worship, in our committees and various groups and meetings, be among us to work in us, with us and through us.

*Silence for prayer*

Holy God:
**take charge**

Father, in all our political debates and congresses, in the hidden agendas and the gaps between words, work your will and prepare our hearts to work with you.

*Silence for prayer*

Holy God:
**take charge**

Father, in all our times of shared laughter and shared tears, in our efforts to reconcile, and our failures to please, · touch our lives with your compassion and affection.

*Silence for prayer*

Holy God:
**take charge**

Father, in all the pain and suffering of our brothers and sisters, in the times which come close to despair, lift us on your shoulders and carry us to safety.

*Silence for prayer*

Holy God:
**take charge**

Father, as we release into your everlasting protection those who have recently died, renew and deepen our understanding of what it means to have the gift of eternal life.

*Silence for prayer*

Holy God:
**take charge**

Father, in all that we say and do during this week may we know the freshness of your love and the security of your hold on us.

*Silence for prayer*

Holy God:
**take charge**

## Other ideas

• Give out percussion instruments for the children to play during one of the hymns and have some music which really allows everyone to sing their hearts out as they celebrate our Christian calling to live life to the very brim.

• As a way of focusing on the offering of our whole selves, ask people to write their name on a piece of paper and around it write or draw the different areas of their lives. These are folded up and brought out to offer at the same time as the money collection, so that all of it is blessed to God's service.

## In the crèche

*Aim:* For the children to enjoy living to the full in Christ.

Young children know this week's teaching instinctively; one of the marks of a young child is that they only have two speeds – fast forward and stop. It's only as they get older that they learn to pace themselves, not only physically, but emotionally and spiritually as well.

Today they can simply enjoy themselves in their Father's company. Use a children's praise tape or have a time of singing and dancing to your own music. Decorate the room a bit, too, so that there is quite a festival atmosphere. The occasion? Just because God is so wonderful and loves us so much!

## Children

*Aim:* To help the children understand about living to the full in Christ.

Begin, as with In the crèche, in a lively praise and worship time, with a real sense of celebration. Explain that although we could all think of lots of reasons for not celebrating, we're going to celebrate the sheer perfection of God loving us, and the fact that he can bring good out of every situation, however bad or terrible.

Tell the story of Jeremiah, and get them all to close round you, in a hostile, threatening way, before the officials give their verdict. Show the children how Jeremiah wasn't too bothered about their threats – he was far more bothered that they took some notice of his warnings, and got themselves right with God again. Have a bowl of water labelled LIFE, and using a Sindy and an Action man, dressed suitably, show how lots of people only dip their toes in life, never letting themselves go or getting deeply involved. As Christians, we are called to live life fully, getting ourselves totally immersed in it, and enjoying all the good things God gives us. That means an exciting life is in store for all who decide to follow Jesus – you just never know where or how you will be used next! Help the children make these sliders which transform a very dull life into a very colourful one.

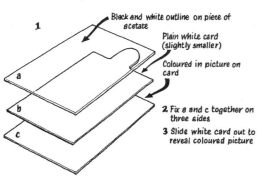

1

Black and white outline on piece of acetate

Plain white card (slightly smaller)

Coloured in picture on card

2 Fix a and c together on three sides

3 Slide white card out to reveal coloured picture

## Young people

*Aim:* To help them understand the implications of living in Christ.

Start by having some bowls of melted chocolate over hot water, some marsh mallows and cocktail sticks. Dip the marsh mallows in the chocolate and make sure they are well and truly coated, before cooling them off. They should be ready for eating in a few minutes.

Read the passage from Jeremiah, and then the passage from Philippians, noticing how both people are unperturbed by their dangerous situations, so long as God's work is being done, and the message getting through. (Or a passage from Brother Andrew, Corrie Ten Boom or Jacquie Pullinger could be read instead.)

Talk about how Jesus calls us to get totally involved, not just one tiny corner of us. We need to do the job properly, as we did with the chocolate marsh mallows. These should now be ready to enjoy to the full!

# 19th Sunday after Pentecost

## YEAR 1

*Thought for the day:*
*Commit your ways to God; he*
*promises to look after your needs and*
*he will not let you down.*

### Readings
Psalm 37:1-22
Job 23:1-12
2 Corinthians 1:1-22

### Reflection

Ours is a very pragmatic culture. We like and expect everything to be proved. Hours and hours are now spent writing up assessments and keeping highly detailed records to prove what professional people probably knew anyway. Everything everywhere has to be proved and backed up with conclusive evidence. Much of this is probably very valuable, but it does highlight an aspect of our society which is, I suspect, based on a breakdown of trust and mutual respect. And a people increasingly cynical about trust will be finding it increasingly difficult to come to faith. Interest in religion, or knowledge of Jesus is all very well, but there is no definitive proof (of the ordinary sort) which we can give people so they can avoid the step into space which involves faith. Real faith only starts when we can't see proof – it is a leap in the dark. And we are not faced with such a leap only once, at the beginning of our faith journey. It may happen at other times along the route, and shock us with its insistence and terrify our assumptions.

Sometimes it seems to lead us, via an agonising route, more deeply into God; he has been giving us an experience of his presence by the ache of his absence.

Sometimes what looks like a lapse of faith into strong, muscular doubt, is in fact the confrontation of our unGodlike behaviour with the nature of God. We are faced with either surrendering this part of our life, or withdrawing ourselves from God's presence, and explaining it to ourselves as doubt.

Yet when we live within faith, the yoke is so much lighter, and the peace so much less ruffled. If only we remember to keep our eyes fastened on Jesus, rather than letting our glance shift to the deep and threatening water below us!

### Discussion starters

1  How would you describe faith? How does it link with such things as trust, wishes, optimism or brainwashing?

2  What do you think Paul means when he talks about God giving us both suffering and consolation? Have you ever found that times of great distress have actually been learning times when you have understood more of God's love and increased your faith?

### All stage talk

*Theme:* Is 'faith' living in cloud cuckoo land?
Explain that we are going to find out what faith is by discovering what it isn't. To make a point, have the word 'FAITH' drawn really faintly on a large sheet of paper.

As each thing that isn't faith is talked about, some of the outside is coloured in, until the whole word appears in white, through the background being filled in.

Suppose you jumped out of an aeroplane, feeling sure that God would stop you getting killed; or you were sure that when you got up in the morning, God would have arranged for all the washing up to be done; is that real faith? No – it's certainly odd, though. Faith in God isn't magic.

What about having faith that God will give us everything we ask, so we ask him for a bike or a new car. When we don't get it we can safely say that God doesn't exist. Is that real faith? No, all that proves is that God isn't a slot machine, which we knew already.

Or what about faith being a kind of wishful thinking. God doesn't really exist, but if we want to pretend he does and that makes us feel better, then we can, so long as we don't take it too seriously. Lots of people think like this. They think of us with a sort of pity, and wonder when we'll grow up. So is faith in God wishful thinking? No, faith would only be a 'let's pretend' game if God didn't exist.

Faith in God means recognising the truth that God is real, alive and active. When we have faith in him we are prepared to trust him to lead us, advise us, heal us and even use us so as to let more people have the fulfilment they long for.

Ask everyone to shut their eyes. Now they can't see the church around them. But it doesn't mean it isn't there. (Open eyes to check!) Sometimes we can feel God's presence very strongly, and that's exciting. Sometimes we can't feel anything but that doesn't mean God has disappeared – it just means we aren't aware of him at the moment. The more we listen and watch for signs of his presence, the more we will notice them. And the tragedy is that those signs are staring people in the face sometimes, and because they are so sure God doesn't really exist, they do not see him reaching longingly out to their misery, in love.

## Intercessions

Father, increase our faith;
help us to grow closer and closer to you
as we live and pray and worship.

*Silence for prayer*

Lord, we believe:
**help our unbelief**

Father, open the hearts and minds of all leaders so that your will is done
and your kingdom spreads throughout the whole world.

*Silence for prayer*

Lord, we believe:
**help our unbelief**

Father, speak your love through our voices and our actions, in our homes, our places of work, and wherever we go.

*Silence for prayer*

Lord, we believe:
**help our unbelief**

Father, let your comforting and healing presence touch those who suffer and those who are frightened,
to fill them with peace.

*Silence for prayer*

Lord, we believe:
**help our unbelief**

*Continued overleaf*

Father, gather to yourself the souls of
those who have finished their earthly life,
and comfort those who mourn their going.

*Silence for prayer*

Lord, we believe:
**help our unbelief**

Father, we offer you our thanks and
praise for all the signs of your glory we
experience and cherish.

*Silence for prayer*

Lord, we believe:
**help our unbelief**

## Other ideas

Use an alternative creed today, or
introduce each section of the creed with a
question, rather like the baptismal
promises.

## In the crèche

*Aim:* For the children to experience
trusting others.

Have an activity such as making sweets
(the no cooking sort). Beforehand explain
the rules of washing hands and not
licking fingers and then set to work. The
children will have to work along with
others, trusting them to put in the right
ingredients and so on. Arrange the sweets
on small paper plates, then hand them
round, trusting everyone to take only
one, so there are enough to go round. Talk
about the way we can trust God, and the
way he is always happy for us to work
with him in loving people better.

## Children

*Aim:* For the children to deepen their
understanding of what faith means.
Beforehand set up a length of wool
around the room, or outside on a trail.
First of all send people off in pairs to
walk the trail. One of the pair is blindfold
and holds on to the wool for guidance;

the other person is there to encourage
and direct, but not touch, unless really
necessary. They then swap round. This is
an excellent exercise for noticing how
vulnerable we feel when we can't see and
don't know where we are going.

When everyone has had a go, talk
together about how they felt and what
scared them. In our faith we can't always
see very clearly, and have to feel our way
through life bit by bit. But God has
promised that those who seek will find,
and he will always be there helping and
guiding us and encouraging us as we go.
Then help the children to make a sign
which says JESUS IS LORD, which they
can even read with their eyes shut,
because the letters are cut out of different
materials.

## Young people

*Aim:* To help them understand what faith
is.

Begin by reading the passage from Job,
and Corinthians. In small groups find
two different definitions of faith from

these passages, and then discuss the findings in the full group.

Look at these images and see in what ways they are right, and in what ways they don't give the true picture.

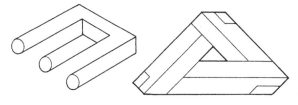

Then go back into small groups to write a few words to explain what faith really is, and share these definitions in the full group again.

# YEAR 2

*Thought for the day:
Commit your ways to God; he promises to look after your needs and he will not let you down.*

## Readings
Psalm 37:1-22
Joshua 23
2 Corinthians 11:16-31

## Reflection

Joshua is old, and the land is for a while at peace. One thing that stands out for Joshua, as he thinks over all the past battles of life, is that God keeps his promises and has never ever let them down. It is this that Joshua wants to leave with the people as he approaches death – that God's love goes on and on, and they can look back over the past and see the truth of this. The other side of the same coin is that if the people separate themselves from God, God will be faithful in this promise, too, and allow them to experience the painful and destructive consequences of going their own way. Perhaps Joshua could see ahead the human tendency to stick close to God while the battle is raging, and drift off once there is peace.

Although Joshua is speaking for the good of those who follow him, his words still give a clear, reflected image of Joshua's own life and values, full of ready obedience and Godly wisdom, gained through the years.

Then we have Paul, quite agitated and passionate as he tries to sort out problems and false accusations to clear the air before his visit to Corinth. Happily for us, this means that we are given a glimpse of what the life of faith has been like for Paul. Otherwise we may never have known of this hair raising catalogue of disasters and dangers. For Paul they were just an accepted part of the cost he was happy to pay for the sake of introducing Jesus to the world.

## Discussion starters

1 Much of what Joshua says is to do with being in the world but not of it. How does this apply to us today?

2 Paul's life was exceptionally danger-ous, but even so, does it challenge our expectations of living quietly and comfortably as Christians?

## All stage talk

*Theme:* The Christian adventure.

Begin by asking about some of the adventures people have had, so that they share them around. (Just one-liners, like 'I was trapped in a lift once'; 'I got dragged along by a runaway horse' etc.) Have a collection of adventure stories, including books that every age group will recognise, and have amongst the collection the Bible, and *Pilgrim's Progress*. Read snippets of exciting bits from the books, including a short passage from today's reading in Paul's letter to the Corinthians. Point out how Paul wasn't really the James Bond type, but as he went around telling people about Jesus' love for them, the adventures seemed to come and meet him!

That may already have happened to some people in this congregation. They may have mentioned Jesus and been teased at school, or insulted at work or at home because of it. When that happens, don't let it put us off – it's actually an exciting sign that we're on the right track, and are involved in an adventure story. Try writing it down, praying lots for people involved, and wait and see how God works in them. The Christian adventure is exciting, can be dangerous and should probably carry a government health warning! Try it.

## Intercessions

Through the adventures of Christian witness and the dangers, insults, mocking and anger we may meet, keep us, and all your church, loyal and strong.
*Silence for prayer*
Come with us, Lord:
**and we will go with you**

Through the local, national and international tensions, through rows in the community and distortions of the truth, keep us and all people honest, just and compassionate.
*Silence for prayer*
Come with us, Lord:
**and we will go with you**

Through the interrupted nights, the quarrels and celebrations, the unspoken needs and wounds, keep us and our children safe and loving.
*Silence for prayer*
Come with us, Lord:
**and we will go with you**

Through the dark hours of pain, the struggle with guilt and the damage of hatred, keep us trustful and open.
*Silence for prayer*
Come with us, Lord:
**and we will go with you**

Through the last journey of death and the ache of separation, keep us both in and out of time, held firmly by your love.
*Silence for prayer*
Come with us, Lord:
**and we will go with you**

Through the sunlight and shadows of each day, through storms and stillness, keep us thankful and rejoicing.
*Silence for prayer*
Come with us, Lord:
**and we will go with you**

## Other ideas

• As a central flower display of rich red and orange flowers, incorporate a selection of adventure books which include the Bible and *Pilgrim's Progress*. (See All stage talk.)
• From a wide selection of Christian adventures, such as lives of the saints, both past and present, write up small sections and display around the walls so that people can walk round the church while music is played, or sung, and be inspired.

## In the crèche

*Aim:* For the children to know that following Jesus is an adventure.
Have a time of sharing one another's news – which will lead on to adventures. Then play this adventure game, based on the idea of *Pilgrim's Progress*. Set up different places in the room such as blue

paper lake that they 'swim' through, a small step ladder or a couple of chairs to climb over, a blanket to wriggle under, and so on. Call the obstacles such things as 'feeling jealous of your brother/sister', 'trying not to show off', 'other people tease you' and so on. Let the children take it in turns to go through the course.

## Children

*Aim:* For the children to see that life as a Christian is an adventure.

Begin by playing a game like 'block', where everyone has to try and get back to a prearranged place without being caught by the keeper of this place.

Look at some of the adventures Paul had, just because he set out to tell people about Jesus. Have them written on different sheets of paper, and spread the children around them so that all the pictures are drawn and painted, or expressed in modelling clay or collage. The whole lot becomes an exhibition which can be spread around the room, so that everyone can walk through it, finishing with prayer.

You will need one or more pictures of Paul being beaten and left for dead, being beaten with rods, and being whipped. One of him being stoned, several of him being shipwrecked and one of drifting out to sea. You will need pictures of swollen rivers, Paul being attacked by bandits, sleeping rough and looking hungry. And, though Paul doesn't mention it here, you could include a picture of him in prison.

Eventually the pictures and models might become part of an exhibition in church, or a book, or part of a flower festival.

## Young people

*Aim:* For them to see how dangerous/exciting the Christian life is when we live it fully.

Start by reading the passage from Corinthians and then showing a section from *The Cross and the Switchblade*, so that they can see that the dangers were not just there during Paul's life. It still gets dangerous today when people speak out for what is right, and experience hostility.

If you have never experienced one of the young people's Christian adventure holidays, this might be a good time to introduce the idea. Such experiences are especially valuable if you are small in numbers. Or suggest the possibility of planning a hike with other churches in the area, praying your way through the town or getting involved with a local evangelism project.

Pray together about where God is leading you as a group, and be prepared for ideas which may surprise, or even disappoint you.

---

# 20th Sunday after Pentecost

## YEAR 1

*Thought for the day:*
*If we endure, we shall reign with him.*

### Readings
Psalm 51
Job 1
2 Timothy 2:1-19

### Reflection
Now these weeks of teaching on how to live the life of faith darken in mood and explore the shadowed area of perseverance.

While the adrenalin of fear and excitement may flood during specific acts of noble bravery, perseverance can be gruelling and tedious, sapping our energy and wearing us down. Those who persevere are not usually those who hit the headlines, and perseverance has about it a quality of humility which many possess as they keep going in a difficult situation week after week and year after year. It is not a grim determination they have, but a quiet acceptance that they are in the right place and have a job to do there. That job may be that they are among those who 'stand and wait'. Certainly there are many frail or house bound perseverers who are a tonic to visit, and give so much.

The story of Job locks into this quality of perseverance. God and Job have been building a deep relationship for years, so that Job knows his comfort and health are not the basis of hope. God is, and remains so, through all these sufferings which pile up like Satan's frozen laughter. Paul knows it too, as he writes to advise the young Timothy, and many of us know it as we live one day at a time, unable to face the long-term bleakness, perhaps, but finding resources provided miraculously from the reserves of God's love.

Perseverance is beautiful because it is a reflection of God's enduring faithfulness, and whenever we are entrusted with it, we can be assured that through the experience God is sharing with us the hidden qualities of his loving nature.

## Discussion starters

1  How can we train ourselves for the lean, dark times, so that they won't throw us off course?

2  What is it about Jesus that makes people willing to endure and persevere in such suffering? Is it really worth it?

## All stage talk

*Theme:* Grace to persevere.

If possible, beg or borrow a cycling or rowing machine, but don't worry if this is impractical.

Start by showing someone having a workout on the machine, gradually increasing the resistance to make it harder work. If you aren't using a machine, have people skipping without stopping, or doing sit ups. As they work, point out how in order to get fit we put in a lot of effort, and when the going gets difficult, we struggle on, and put up with it, because we consider the effort worthwhile.

Let the volunteers have a rest, and explain how we are also called to endure things in our Christian life. This may mean the daily effort to get on with someone in our family whom we find difficult; the constant battle against temptation of some sort; the regular, tiring care of someone who depends on us. Often the nasty part is not having any idea when this difficult part of our life will end, and if that gets us down, we are better off thinking just of today, or even just for this moment. God loves us, and will not let us suffer on and on in our own strength. He will be right there, providing exactly what we need to cope with the situation. And one last thing: God has promised us that we will never be tempted beyond our endurance, and there will always be an escape route if necessary.

## Intercessions

God of holiness, cleanse the church
from all that is selfish, complacent and
worldly.

*Silence for prayer*

His love goes on:
**his love goes on and on**

God of wisdom and honour, give our
leaders integrity, and our world the
openness to listen, and the courage
to forgive.

*Silence for prayer*

His love goes on:
**his love goes on and on**

God of tenderness and understanding,
may our children be brought up in the
knowledge of your love and every
member of every family be valued.

*Silence for prayer*

His love goes on:
**his love goes on and on**

God of healing and wholeness,
give to those who are in any pain or
suffering all that they need, both
physically and spiritually.

*Silence for prayer*

His love goes on:
**his love goes on and on**

God of eternity, as you welcome into your
kingdom those who have endured to the
end, we thank you for the example of
their lives.

*Silence for prayer*

His love goes on:
**his love goes on and on**

God of joy and serenity, we thank you for
your constant help and loving presence,
and offer you our lives, however things
turn out.

*Silence for prayer*

His love goes on:
**his love goes on and on**

## Other ideas

• Use 2 Timothy 2:11-13 as a responsorial
section, perhaps after the sermon or talk.
Set it out like this:

| | |
|---|---|
| **Leader:** | Here is a saying you may trust: <br> If we died with him, |
| **All:** | we shall live with him; |
| **Leader** | if we endure, |
| **All:** | we shall reign with him; |
| **Leader** | if we disown him, |
| **All** | he will disown us; |
| **Leader** | if we are faithless, |
| **All** | he remains faithful, <br> for he cannot disown himself. |

• Have one arrangement of different
kinds of evergreens, which are a beautiful
symbol of faithful endurance. The
thought for the day could be written as a
sign to go with it.

## In the crèche

*Aim:* For the children to experience
persevering to the end of a task without
giving up.

First play a game like 'Peep behind the
curtain', where the children keep having
another go, even if they have to go back
to the beginning. Then have a salad
making session, where there are lots of
different stages to go through, but if you
keep going, you end up with a reward.

## Children

*Aim:* For the children to learn abut the
value of enduring and persevering.

Start with a guessing game, such
as 'I spy', where we sometimes admit
defeat, and give up. As you are playing,
notice whether people give up easily, or
keep pressing on, and mention this
afterwards.

Tell the story of the first chapter of Job,
using the carpet tiles method, and cut
outs of Job, his family and all his herds of
animals. As each disaster strikes, the
appropriate cut out is taken away, until
Job is left all on his own.

Talk together about how hard it is to
stay cheerful when things keep going

wrong, and how Job refused to let his sufferings turn him away from God. Then help the children to make this model to help them remember.

2.

Job went JOB on trusting

cut

3.

Join the two at the edges

## Young people

*Aim:* For them to understand the value of endurance and perseverance.

Start with a fitness session, so that they feel in their bodies the sensation of persevering when the muscles are beginning to ache. Then read the first chapter of Job and talk together about how difficult it is to keep going when everything goes wrong. Yet many Christians do this long-term perseverance and God helps them by providing times of refreshment, and strength and courage for the really gruelling parts.

We can train ourselves for such hard times by disciplining ourselves, much as we train ourselves for a rugby match by doing all those press ups and squat jumps. Think of ways we could do this spiritually, and write out a daily schedule.

# YEAR 2

*Thought for the day:*
*If we endure, we shall reign with him.*

## Readings
Psalm 51
Jeremiah 38:1-13
James 1:1-15

## Reflection

Being a prophet is a lonely business. Jeremiah burns inside if he doesn't speak out God's word, and yet when he does, it gets him into all kinds of trouble, because God's work is not always what people want to hear. Putting a prophet down a well is rather like reaching for the off switch when you can't stand what someone's saying on the telly.

Whatever must have been going through Jeremiah's mind as he slithered down into the stinking mud? People who endure suffering for their faith do not bypass the ghastliness of their situation, and they never stop being human. But there is something that keeps them going through everything. They are convinced, overall, (allowing for times of personal doubt and misgiving) that what they are doing is right and necessary.

James actually tells us to be happy when everything goes badly and we are mistreated, because all this is a training ground for patience. During the times of training we may well wish ruefully for an easier way to acquire this virtue! James' teaching follows Jesus' words in the beatitudes, where we are called blessed when we are persecuted for his sake.

The other thing which is good to notice is the loving way Jeremiah's friends lift him out of the well, stuffing rags and clothes under his armpits to protect him from the soreness of the ropes. In any prolonged suffering for Jesus' sake there is always loving assistance given, or encouragement, or a short time of respite, just as the angels ministered to Jesus after his time of temptation in the wilderness and at the agony in the garden.

There may be times when we are on the receiving end of all this, and survive because of it; there may be times when God needs us to be the encouragers or practical helpers. Praying constantly means that God can call on us whenever and wherever he needs us. If we are not available, someone who badly needs our help may not get it.

## Discussion starters

1 Could you share with one another the times when God has ministered to you in the middle of a difficult time, to enable you to carry on?

2 Have you noticed any difference in the way you cope with things going wrong if they happen because of your belief in Jesus, rather than through your own sin or foolishness?

## All stage talk

*Theme:* All the way through.
Beforehand get two sticks of rock which have a name going all through them. If you find these impossible to get hold of, use two Swiss rolls instead.

Begin by showing everyone a rock and get someone to read what it says at the top. Break a piece off and give it to them. Surprise, surprise, it still says the same thing! Break this piece off and so on, until all the rock is given away, and we have found that the writing is there all the time, through every part of the rock.

Now remind everyone of Jeremiah, being thrown down the well and left for dead. Before he went down he was telling

the people God's message. Even when they pull him up, he's still telling the people God's message. (Doesn't give up easily, does he?) He's like the piece of rock (show the unbroken one), keeping to God's message all the way through, during the good times, the dangerous times and the painful times.

What about us? Are we God's friends just at the beginning, when we're all excited by the faith, or have just got baptised or confirmed? Or are we still God's friends when we get into trouble? (Snap off a piece of rock.) When everything is going really well for us? (Snap.) When life is full of pressures? (Snap.) When our friends aren't interested? (Snap.) If we are real friends of Jesus, we will stay his friends all the way through.

## Intercessions

Father, let your church be freshly inspired to spread the gospel and serve the world without thought of personal safety or comfort.

*Silence for prayer*

At all times and in all places:
**you are our God**

Father, raise up leaders in each community who are honest and trustworthy, and rekindle our enthusiasm for honour and mutual respect.

*Silence for prayer*

At all times and in all places:
**you are our God**

Father, breathe into all our relationships patience, understanding and affection, keep marriages strong and friendships open-hearted.

*Silence for prayer*

At all times and in all places:
**you are our God**

*Continued overleaf*

Father, ease into wholeness the sick and the confused, calm the fearful, soothe the sobbing, unfasten the chained and let your love pour in.

*Silence for prayer*

At all times and in all places:
**you are our God**

Father, receive into your presence the travellers who have come home to you, and out of all evil and suffering bring good.

*Silence for prayer*

At all times and in all places:
**you are our God**

Father, may our praises and joyful thanks be a sweet, fragrant offering at every part of our lives.

*Silence for prayer*

At all times and in all places:
**you are our God**

## Other ideas

• In a flower arrangement have a clear line of one colour winding through a split level arrangement, so as to highlight the quiet perseverance through good and bad times.

• During a time of penitence and reconciliation, explore the areas where we reach the limits of our patience, and fly off the handle or give up. Pray God's presence into these situations, so that next time you are supported and protected.

## In the crèche

*Aim:* For the children to learn about helping their friends, and not giving up. Use puppets to act out the story of someone trying to make something and getting very cross because it is all going wrong. They are just about to give up, all angry, when a couple of friends come to cheer them up and help them. Talk together about how we sometimes feel like giving up, but our friends help us, and sometimes we can be the ones to help. Play a clapping game, which you can only play with a friend. Clap to the chant:

You are my friend, I am your friend.
Good friends always help each other.

## Children

*Aim:* For the children to hear the story of Jeremiah, and understand about not giving up.

Start with a fitness session of running on the spot, jumping, skipping and sit ups. While everyone relaxes, have some quiet music, and talk about how hard it is sometimes to keep going on something we find difficult, but God will help us, often through our friends.

Tell the story of Jeremiah, using a large scale version of the model the children will be making. Then help the children to make a model of Jeremiah being pulled out of the muddy well. You will need a large plastic pot (yoghurt type), some plastic from other bottles and pots to cut Jeremiah out of, some bits of material, string and scissors. Either make the sloshy mud yourselves by adding water to some earth from outside, or have this already made.

Paint outside stone colour

YOGHURT

Mud inside

Thick cotton thread

Paper clips to weight

## Young people

*Aim:* For them to look at ways of enduring and persevering when it is difficult.

Start by reading the story of Jeremiah in the well and his rescue. Talk about times when their friends have managed to get them out of a tight spot, or times when they have felt abandoned, as Jeremiah must have felt in the mud at the bottom of the muddy well. (They may remember that Joseph was also dumped in a well.)

Now read the passage from James, picking out his words which link up with Matthew 5:11-12. Talk about our different strategies for keeping going when things are difficult and list the ideas so everyone can learn from one another. Look, too, at the way Peter managed to walk on the water – and what made him start sinking. (Matthew 14:29) Have a time of prayer for those who are enduring persecution and hardship for Jesus at the moment; Amnesty International has special details of specific people to whom you can send encouragement, and letters asking for their release.

# 21st Sunday after Pentecost

## YEAR 1

*Thought for the day:
In his own good time, God is drawing all things to perfect completion.*

### Readings
Psalms 23,24 or 78:1-24
Ezekiel 34:11-24
2 Peter 3

## Reflection

This week our attention turns from the present to the future. Where is it all leading? What is God's plan for us?

Every morning our cat conducts me on a special journey from my bedroom to a particular cupboard in the kitchen. She gets more and more excited, the closer we get, and when I open the cupboard, can contain herself no longer. It always takes far longer to get her food out because she keeps getting in the way! Cats aren't the only creatures with a built in impatience syndrome. I sometimes wonder if our constant, impatient hassling of God slows the kingdom from advancing.

Ezekiel's prophecy uses the hopeful and comforting image of the sheep and their shepherd, with God himself taking over care of the flock, and sorting out from the sheep those who have been making themselves rich and strong through corrupt dealings and cruelty. At last, says Ezekiel, God will take charge, bring justice and lead his own flock to safety. A prince of the line of David will put this into effect on earth.

And that is exactly what Jesus did,

calling himself the good shepherd and leading his followers to good pastures. Any who strayed were not abandoned but searched for until they were found and then carried home on his shoulders. That was not only true while Jesus walked the roads of Galilee, as we know from our own experience. His shepherding continues through the generations and in every part of the world.

It was widely expected that the end of the world would come shortly after Pentecost, and those in the early church, lived ready and waiting for the great day. But when time went on and nothing seemed to be happening, the scoffing began, and followers themselves were confused. Peter's letter to explain things, shows how much God's Spirit had changed him from the early days.

Here is the impatient, impetuous Peter, who has grasped the long-suffering nature of God; he understands God's view of time compared with ours and sees that all things will happen in God's good time. Our job, in the meantime, is to keep close to his thinking in prayer, and live out our lives moment by moment in his presence, so that whenever the end of all things comes upon us we shall be ready.

## Discussion starters

1 Go through the Ezekiel passage, linking up each section with its remarkable fulfilment in the life and teaching of Jesus.

2 We are now about 2000 years on from the time of Jesus, and the church has had a stormy and sometimes shameful journey through time to the present. What do you think we have learnt through all this, and what should we be concentrating on in the next few years, do you think?

## All stage talk

*Theme:* Waiting in hope.

Beforehand get a kitchen timer, and one of those automatic timers which you fix on a lamp.

Begin by explaining how you are going to set the timer for X minutes, at which time the talk should be finishing. You are also setting the light to come on half way through the talk. (Do this.)

Talk about the way things seem to take ages coming, because we want them so much – like birthdays, Christmas, holidays, pension day or tea time. Other things seem to come too fast – like telephone bills, exams or dentist appointments – because we aren't looking forward to them at all.

The early Christians were really looking forward to Jesus coming back in glory, and it seemed to be taking for ever. People who expected it to happen before they were sixteen, grew to seventy-five and died, and still Jesus hadn't come. It has been about 2000 years now, and he still hasn't come.

Now as soon as we start measuring the time for something, it seems to make us impatient. 'A watched pot never boils', they say. Because you know this talk will end when the ringer goes, you are probably all waiting for it to ring at any moment, especially as the light will remind you that it's all being timed. Peter told the people not to think God was slow in coming; he was just patiently waiting for the right time, and that might be any time. That's still true – Jesus could come again at any moment, on any day. All we know for certain is that he is definitely going to return in glory, and we can't give an exact time and date to it. Meanwhile, we can live our lives to the full, living the life of love that God shows us, and keeping in close contact with him through prayer and worship, so that we are ready when he does appear.

## Intercessions

Father, deepen our awareness of your presence in the moments and days, sorrows and joys, and keep us ready and attentive.

*Silence for prayer*

Through time and eternity:
**God is**

Father, open the eyes of all leaders and their advisers to seek wisdom, hold to what is right, discern needs and care for the weak.

*Silence for prayer*

Through time and eternity:
**God is**

Father, be in our childhoods and our parenting, be in our friendships, and those we shop and work with.

*Silence for prayer*

Through time and eternity:
**God is**

Father, feed our needs, give us hope, heal our sickness and bring us to lasting wholeness.

*Silence for prayer*

Through time and eternity:
**God is**

Father, walk with us through the journey of death, welcome home those who have recently died to this earthly life, and cradle those who mourn in the comfort of your arms.

*Silence for prayer*

Through time and eternity:
**God is**

Father, accept our thanks and praise for your unchanging love pulsing always under the activity of our lives.

*Silence for prayer*

Through time and eternity:
**God is**

## Other ideas

• The first reading is very effective if done chorally, with light, medium and dark voice tones. Work through the passage together after prayer, and let the voice tones bring out the meaning by building and emphasising the phrases.
• After the talk, have the acclamation: Christ has died, Christ is risen, Christ will come again!

## In the crèche

*Aim:* For the children to learn that Jesus looks after us as a shepherd looks after his sheep.

Play at being sheep and lambs, following the shepherd, going to drink at the stream, being taken to a new pasture etc. Then tell them how the shepherd looks for the sheep if they get lost, and looks after them very carefully. That's how Jesus looks after us.

## Children

*Aim:* For the children to see how Ezekiel's prophecy came true in Jesus, and look forward to the second coming of Christ.

Begin with setting out a whole lot of things that measure time, and work out together their order, starting with the smallest time measurement. So your assortment might include a stopwatch, egg timer, watch or clock, and calendar or diary. Use a simple time line (showing us, Jesus, Ezekiel, Moses and Abraham) to make it clear what time Ezekiel was writing and who he was. Then have the passage read out by two good readers.

Ask the children if it reminds them of anything Jesus said or did. No matter if they don't make the connection on their own. Look at a picture of Jesus, the good shepherd, and read or tell the children about how in Jesus, Ezekiel's prophecy came true, some time after it was written.

Now remind the children that Jesus is

going to return to us in glory some time – we don't know when, but we know it will happen because he said this would happen and he speaks the truth and always keeps to what he says. If they want to talk and ask questions about this, answer simply and honestly – including 'I don't know' if you don't.

Help them to make this stand up model of looking into the distance at the same time as seeing the immediate present.

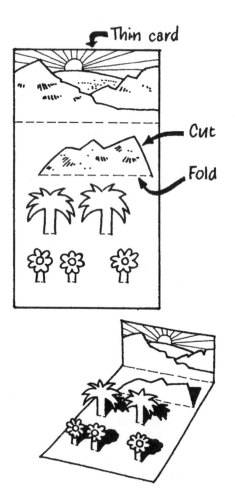

Thin card

Cut

Fold

## Young people

*Aim:* For them to explore the nature of the hope to which we are called.

First read the passage from Ezekiel, picking up any ideas here that they recognise from the New Testament. Join these together, so that they can see how Jesus' ministry brought to fulfilment the hopes and longings of the people of Israel.

Now read the letter from Peter and explain the climate of feeling at the time he was writing. Talk together about how they feel, knowing that Jesus could return at any time. Are there any areas in our lives which we need to sort out with God before we can look forward to it? We need to clear up anything outstanding every day, as we never know when it might happen. Have a time of quietness and worship, perhaps jotting down anything they want to put right with God on a piece of paper which is then put in a sealed envelope and only thrown away when completed.

# YEAR 2

*Thought for the day:*
*In his own good time, God is drawing all things to perfect completion.*

## Readings

Psalms 23,24 or 78:1-24
Job 4:1 and 5:1-16
Hebrews 10:19-end

## Reflection

Job was a good and upright person, and the terrible onslaught of troubles was, in his case, nothing to do with resentment or sin. Eliphaz knows nothing of the conversation between God and Satan, of course, so he counsels Job as if he were indeed steeped in sin. So even though his advice must have gone down like a lead balloon with Job, it does give us some very useful and sound teaching on how our sin can separate us from God, and how we can put our trust in God, who is able to do wonders and will surely save us.

The writer of the Hebrews gives some excellent sermon material as he tried to explain the sacrifice of Jesus in language and imagery which his readers would easily relate to. Through his teaching shines excitement and enthusiasm; he is not theorising, but speaking out of the exuberance of personal experience. His message is full of urgency, because he cannot bear to think of those who have travelled so far in Jesus' company turning aside from him and throwing their heritage away.

If either of these readings rings a bell with your own life, then God may well be quietly suggesting that now is the time to sort it out. Nothing else can compete with the joyful peace that comes only from knowing that we are doing God's will. It is a peace which not only surrounds us as we walk in the present, but also stretches out in front of us, full of hope for the future, so that all fear is blotted out by its light.

## Discussion starters

1  So many people are paralysed or distorted through fear of one sort or another. So many aggressive, violent people have fear in their eyes. Is there any way that we can speak to this fear the word of God's peace so that they understand?

2  We often find a drop out in church membership a year to two after confirmation. Why do you think this is, and what do you think we could do as a church to prevent the 'soul drain'?

## All stage talk

*Theme:* Turning to trust.
Beforehand collect four shoe boxes, and in one of them place a pair of binoculars.

Ask a volunteer who wears glasses to help you with the talk this morning. Ask her to stand where most people can see her, and put a chair at four points round her, not near enough for her to touch. Blindfold the volunteer, or ask her to close her eyes. On each of the chairs place a box, and in the box containing binoculars place her glasses. Turn her to face another chair. Point out that Helen needs her glasses, and life is very difficult without them. She can't see much (even when she's not wearing a blindfold!) and she feels very vulnerable. We may feel like this if we suddenly lose something important to us. Perhaps our best friend moves, or we lose our job, or we have a row at home, and suddenly we don't know exactly who we are or which way to turn.

The secret is to turn in the right direction, because God is the one who has both power and inclination to help. His motive is ardent love for his precious child. If we turn any other way and walk in that direction, we will face emptiness and disappointment. (Help Helen to turn in each wrong direction, open the shoe box and find nothing.) But if we turn in the right direction – turn towards God and walk his ways, (turn Helen the right way) then we will find fulfilment, often far more than we dared hope for. (Helen opens the box and finds in it not only her glasses but a pair of binoculars as well.)

## Intercessions

Father, in all the decisions and activities of the church, make us slow to rush ahead of you, yet quick to follow where you lead.

*Silence for prayer*

We will not forget what you have done:
**in you we put our trust**

*Continued overleaf*

Father, in all areas of conflict and injustice, keep us clear sighted, and attentive to your will.

*Silence for prayer*

We will not forget what you have done:
**in you we put our trust**

Father, with our friends, neighbours and loved ones, with those we are tempted to despise, give us opportunity to serve.

*Silence for prayer*

We will not forget what you have done:
**in you we put our trust**

Father, on those who are ill and frail, place healing hands; in those who live fearfully breathe peace.

*Silence for prayer*

We will not forget what you have done:
**in you we put our trust**

Father, to the dead and dying bring rest; to those who die unwanted and alone give knowledge of their brothers' and sisters' concern.

*Silence for prayer*

We will not forget what you have done:
**in you we put our trust**

Father, with joy we call to mind your love, and marvel at your affection for us.

*Silence for prayer*

We will not forget what you have done:
**in you we put our trust**

## Other ideas

The passage from Job works well read chorally with a group of voices including men, women, girls and boys.

## In the crèche

*Aim:* For the children to know that God can do all things and does not let us down. Sticking time! Have a large sheet of paper prepared with the words 'SEE WHAT GOD HAS DONE' on it. Have a supply of pictures, roughly cut out, of all kinds of things that remind the children of what a wonderful, generous and powerful person God is. The pictures might include calendar scenes, greeting cards, seed catalogues, and parenting magazines, so as to include people behaving lovingly as well as nature.

Have a good time cutting the pictures out and sticking them on the paper.

## Children

*Aim:* For the children to know that with God nothing is impossible, and we can put our hope in him.

Bring a vacuum cleaner in with you today.

Begin with that excellent eating game, where you throw a dice in turn and when you get six you run up to the front, put on thick gloves and a scarf, and start to eat a chocolate bar with a knife and fork. As soon as someone else throws a six they take over.

After the game, talk about how we were all living hopefully as the dice came round, hoping that we would get a six. We are going to look at a hope which won't make any of us disappointed, because we can all win.

Now ask someone to do a spot of vacuuming, but before they start, ask the children how they know the vacuum will clear up the mess. Their trust in it will be based on past experience. (Try the cleaner to check that it really does work.) It is our past experience of God that makes us know he is worth trusting, and can do the impossible in deadlock situations.

Take the children on a whistle stop tour of the wonders God performed (as in today's psalm) in Egypt, and share any more recent wonders that have happened in your own experience.

## Young people

*Aim:* For them to know that with God nothing is impossible, and our hope in him is never disappointed.

Bring along a photo album of pictures which include parish events through the years, or family events of some of those in the group. When you have all had a good laugh, talk about the way a community builds up its love and commitment by all the things it has laughed and struggled through together. In God's family it is just the same. At every anniversary of the great events of their history the people of Israel would relive the way God had lifted them out of trouble.

As Christians we remember the main events of Jesus' life, death and resurrection each year, because they have changed our outlook and given us hope.

Read Psalm 78:1-24 together, and then the passage from Hebrews. Finish with a prayer and worship time, reaffirming their trust in God, and welcoming his power into their lives.

# 22nd Sunday after Pentecost

## YEARS 1 AND 2

*Thought for the day:*
*You cannot live with self and God both at the centre of your life; you will have to choose between them.*

## Readings
Psalms 42,43
Proverbs 14:31-15:17
James 4:13-5:11

## Reflection

Most of us live with forward planning and a crowded diary, our eye on the clock and a systematic controlling of how each day will be spent. Without all this, how would we be able to survive in today's world? Yet James brings us up sharply, pointing out that such a way of living can kid us that we are the ones in control of our lives, rather than God. Such an attitude, if it gets deeply rooted in us, will block our ears from hearing God's advice, and anchor us so that we can no longer be blown by the Spirit wherever it moves.

The vehemence in today's reading against self indulgent oppressors all stems from the battle in us of who has control in our lives; so often we try to enthrone self and God, side by side, and it simply doesn't work. Why do we do this, when we know with our heads that God is the better option to go for?

The story of disobedience in the garden explains it in the universal language of pictures. The fruit from the tree of knowledge looks particularly attractive to us; we are jealous of God's power and want it for ourselves. We like the idea of being like gods – in control of our lives, and able to control other people's lives. So we eat, but the fruit does not set us free. God is about love, and love is not about control. We can become like God, but only through the lengthy, paradoxical route of obedience – there is no short cut.

We are so often terrified of losing our identity if we allow Jesus to reign over the territory of our being. But God does not work like that. God has this uncanny knack of rolling things inside out and turning things on their head. Instead of crushing our personality and abusing our submission, he starts to work on us and make us more ourselves than ever. That's why it feels so natural and comfortable to be in harmony with him – he isn't squashing us into a character that barely fits, but clothing us with robes which settle comfortably all round the proportions of our own character.

## Discussion starters

1   When does it seem like a straight choice between God and self, and when is the distinction blurred?

2   Should Christians get involved with social and political issues? To what extent should they work for Christian morality in a largely non-Christian society?

## All stage talk

*Theme:* The big choice.
You need to get hold of someone who can juggle (however badly) with two balls today. If the juggler is really bad, rolled up socks will be better than balls as there is less retrieval time!

Explain that the readings have been all about choices, and the way we choose to live our life. We can choose to live life exactly as we want, buying loads of unnecessary clothes, sweets and luxury goods, yet unable to find more than small change for the Christian Aid collection. Or we can choose to live life exactly as God wants, sharing what we have with other people, being happy to help at home, whether we get paid for it or not, and putting all our time and money at God's disposal.

Perhaps we have already definitely chosen one or other of those ways; for many of us, we try to do it this way. (The juggler does his stuff. It's actually better if he keeps dropping the socks.) We try to juggle our choices, so that sometimes we are holding God at the centre of our lives, and sometimes self. As you can see, it doesn't really work. Sometimes we get into a muddle, all tangled up as we try to serve both God and self at the same time. And we never get to hold on to God long enough to get to know him and understand his will for us in our lives. Having self at the centre of your life will make you possessive and bitter, discontented and miserable. Having God at the centre will make you fulfilled, light-hearted and at peace with yourself. Juggling will make you confused. It's time to make the choice.

## Intercessions

Father, take our faith and deepen it,
take our church and renew it,
take our need and supply it.
*Silence for prayer*
My God and my All:
**let your kingdom come**

Father, take our community and revitalise it, take our government and guide it,
take our world and protect it.
*Silence for prayer*
My God and my All:
**let your kingdom come**

Father, take the young and empower
them, take the old and refresh them,
take the damaged and restore them.

*Silence for prayer*

My God and my All:
**let your kingdom come**

Father, take the suffering and comfort
them, take the frightened and reassure
them, take the lonely and befriend them.

*Silence for prayer*

My God and my All:
**let your kingdom come**

Take the dying and whisper peace to
them, take the dead and welcome them,
take the mourners and grieve with them.

*Silence for prayer*

My God and my All:
**let your kingdom come**

Take our minds and think through them,
take our mouths and speak through them,
take our lives and live through them.

*Silence for prayer*

My God and my All:
**let your kingdom come**

## Other ideas

Have one flower arrangement incorporating a signpost to other arrangements,
one expressing full and exuberant life,
and the other a burst of colour which
turns into deadness.

## In the crèche

*Aim:* To explore the idea of choosing
between good and evil; between what I
want and what God wants.

In the play time, emphasise choosing -
which toys to play with, where to sit,
which book to read etc. Then have each
caller choosing another child to be the
next caller when they are playing a game
like 'Traffic lights'.

Now call out some situations. If the
children decide it is doing things God's
way they run to one wall, and if it's
selfish they run to the other. Situations
might include going to bed when you're
told to, taking sweets from the shop
without paying for them, giving Nana a
hug when she looks tired, enjoying a
swim or helping someone.

## Children

*Aim:* For the children to understand the
choice we have to make in the way we
live.

In pairs play the 'Stone, paper, scissors'
game, where each child makes a choice at
the same time, and shows the appropriate
hand sign. Stone wins over scissors
(because it can break them), scissors wins
over paper (because they can cut it), and
paper wins over stone (because it can
wrap around it).

Now have the James passage written
as if it is a real letter, in a stamped
addressed envelope, and explain how

James was writing to all the scattered Jewish Christians, and was very bothered about some unchristian behaviour. See if they can spot what this is. Use a translation such as the *International Children's Bible* where the shorter sentence structure makes it much easier to understand.

List all the things the children can remember, and then work out together how James is really wanting them to live. List these things next to the bad things in a different colour.

Talk together about how hard it is to choose to live God's way. For instance, we may know we should be honest, but when we want to stay out of trouble and get frightened of what will happen if someone finds out what we've done, we really want to tell lies. Explain how we can ask Jesus to give us the courage to choose the right way, and he will help us.

Now help the children to make this model to remind them each day. They can choose which centre to put into their life – God or self.

## Young people

*Aim:* For them to recognise the choice they can make, and the consequences of that choice.

Begin with a game involving choice, such as the 'Stone, paper, scissors' game, or 'Forfeits' based on spinning a coin. Some choices we make in life are quite arbitrary, and we have no idea whether we will be choosing profitably or not. Many people love the excitement they get from this kind of choice, and gambling is addictive.

Other choices are based on assessing the situation and reasoning your next move – like choosing your secondary school, deciding how to play the next shot, or deciding which socks to buy.

Some choices are really important, because they affect a large part of your life – choosing who to marry, or whether to go for promotion. The most important decision of all is the one that affects us not only in this life, but after death as well. Are we going to choose God or self to reign in our lives?

Now read the passage from James' letter, looking at the kind of differences this choice makes in our behaviour. If we want the world to be a better, happier place because we have lived we will have to make a conscious decision not to have self at the centre of our lives.

1. Roll out self-hardening clay.

2. With a pastry cutter, cut out two 'plugs'.

3. Make and decorate a shape with a hole in the middle.

4. Write on one plug 'GOD' and on the other 'SELF'.

5. Keep the plugs next to the model. Each morning choose which plug to put in.

# Last Sunday after Pentecost

## YEAR 1

*Thought for the day:*
*Heaven is our home.*

### Readings

Psalm 89:1-18
Daniel 10:2-19
Revelation 1:1-18

### Reflection

When salmon sense that it is time to mate and have young, they somehow taste, in all the water around them, the scent of home; and they manage to find their way back to one particular mountain stream which they originally came from. This strikes me as being a very powerful picture of our own spiritual journey. Heaven is our home – we came from it and are, as I write, all struggling our way back to the place we belong. All of the 'homes' in this life, precious as they may be, are only resting places on the journey.

The passages chosen for this week are, in a way, uncomfortable to read, because they force us to open our spiritual eyes and see sights which are not of this ordinary, familiar world. We are not the only ones to feel out of our depth; both Daniel and John the Divine went weak at the knees and felt all strength ebb out of them as they were confronted with their visions of heaven, in the presence of God.

The temptation for us is to snap our visors down as fast as possible, and perhaps dismiss what we don't understand. Both writers are trying to describe in word pictures the indescribably mystical and awesome experience of heavenly things. It is not the details of the imagery we need to study, any more than we might spend hours peering at Pisarro's brush strokes. Rather, we need to stand back and sense the wonder and majesty of these encounters; the weakness and fear which is so lovingly ministered to. And in both visions appears this Son of Man, bright beyond human brightness, and with great authority and tenderness. We are often blinkered, seeing only what we think it is possible to see. Yet this narrows our vision to the meagre limits of the human brain, and our God is far greater than this. Heaven is as real as your finger nails; it is simply beyond our imagining, much of the time.

### Discussion starters

1 Why do you think the vision makes Daniel so weak? Notice how the vision comes after Daniel's prayer, which God has been answering over a number of years. How can this help us to understand our own seeming lack of answer from time to time?

2 What difference does it make to the way we act during life, to know that we are making our way home to heaven?

### All stage talk

*Theme:* No place like home.
First show some colourful travel brochures, reading out snippets from them, and then talk about how nice it is to go home after a holiday, because home, for most people, is very special.

Ask everyone to think of the first home they remember. Imagine walking up to the front door, and looking in the rooms that they may not have visited in their imagination for a long time, or they may have left that same home this morning. Take them through various rooms, drawing their attention to things like the furniture, the kitchen window and so on, which will help bring their memories flooding back. That was the home they started out from on a journey which has brought them to Sunday morning, and the particular pew they are sitting in. Heaven is our spiritual home, and although we don't know any details, like the furniture and the windows of our earthly homes, we do know that it is a place of deep happiness and fulfilment, free from all tears and anxieties, lit with love and contentment. (Sounds good, doesn't it?)

If this was on the holiday programme, they may well be waiting now to hear the bad news of how expensive it is to go there, and how little chance ordinary people have of getting in. The wonderful news is that Jesus has already paid for us to go, and the fare was death by crucifixion, with the sins of the world heavy on his shoulders. What is more, we are not counted as tourists, but citizens of heaven. If we choose to walk with Jesus, he will bring us safely through our own death journeys to live in heaven. If we want, heaven can be our home for the whole of eternity.

## Intercessions

Father, let us notice not what we want to see so much as what you want to show us, for you are our God and we are content to be led by you.

*Silence for prayer*

Father, you hold us safe:
**safe in the palm of your hand**

Father, let us value not just those who agree with us, but all whom you died to save.

*Silence for prayer*

Father, you hold us safe:
**safe in the palm of your hand**

Father, let us care not just for those we get on with, but also those we find difficult and those who have hurt us through the years.

*Silence for prayer*

Father, you hold us safe:
**safe in the palm of your hand**

Father, let us look for the signs of your kingdom not just in the beautiful but also in what is ugly. Let us intercede for both victim and attacker, both the tortured and the torturers.

*Silence for prayer*

Father, you hold us safe:
**safe in the palm of your hand**

Father, may the dead waken to the glory of heaven and may we one day join them there to live in your company for ever.

*Silence for prayer*

Father, you hold us safe:
**safe in the palm of your hand**

## Other ideas

• Have quiet music playing as a background to the passage from Daniel. Music has the great gift of being able to lift our spiritual eyes so that we are better able to understand the vision Daniel describes.

• Have one radiant arrangement of flowers set on a mirror, with 'precious stones' around it, so as to express something of the serenity and glory of heaven.

## In the crèche

*Aim:* For the children to know that they are citizens of heaven – princes and princesses of the kingdom.

Tell the children simply and straight-forwardly that Jesus has made it possible for us to live for ever in heaven when our bodies die and won't work any more. Tell them what a lovely place heaven is, where you don't feel sad, no one is nasty, you feel warm and well loved by all your family and friends and are never lonely or frightened. In the kingdom of heaven we are all princes and princesses. Help the children make and/or decorate crowns to wear.

## Children

*Aim:* For the children to learn about heaven.

Strangely enough, one of the only parts of the Christian faith nominal Christians tell their children is that people (and often animals) who have died are in heaven, living with Jesus. It is, after all, a comforting story. Yet in church this is the area least covered, I find. If we don't talk much of this area of faith, children will sooner or later think of heaven as a baby story which they have to grow out of. So let's go for it, and bring all those secret questions into the open.

Start by asking the children what they think happens when a person's body wears out and dies. Listen carefully to their answers, so as to address any worries or misunderstandings you hear hinted at. Talk to them about what heaven is like, homing in on the qualities, rather than on what it may or may not look like. What is important is that they begin to get a sense of a place which is happy, welcoming, loving and suitable for all ages! Make it clear that people do not turn into angels when they die, they won't have to hang around on clouds getting bored all day, and it isn't somewhere you could reach by spaceship. The only way in is by dying, after choosing good, rather than evil, through your life. Read to them Daniel's vision of heaven, and point out how lovingly Daniel is treated.

Then let them express their own ideas of heaven in painting, drawing, creative writing or clay.

## Young people

*Aim:* For them to think about the implications of being citizens of heaven.

Start by reading the two visions, noticing how they affect Daniel and John as they are taken over by the Spirit of God. Talk about this - some of the group may have seen the Spirit acting so powerfully in people that they have shaken, or their knees have given way. Notice, too, how this vision didn't come out of the blue, when Daniel was on an emotional high, but as a direct result of faithful, earnest prayer, as a result of which God was able to use him.

Talk together about the clues we have in the bible of what heaven is like (and what it isn't like) and ask them what difference it makes to think of going on to heaven after death, rather than death being the end of everything.

Work together to create a collage to express their ideas of heaven. This can include blocks of colour, words, pictures and textures.

# YEAR 2

*Thought for the day:*
*Heaven is our home.*

## Readings
Psalm 89:1-18
Ezekiel 11:14-21
Hebrews 13:1-21

## Reflection

God's promise to lead us home to heaven applies to everyone. Whether you're dazzling or frumpy, witty or serious, left or right handed, thin or on the round side, God's promise is for you. It is for all those who feel they have been wandering in exile for years; and for those who are stuck in ravines and are suddenly crying out to be rescued. God's promise echoes in the shape of the cross, back through the generations of prophets and forward through the generations of Christian history, bringing hope, drying tears and drawing many to know the extraordinary joy of God's companionship.

The whole of our living here is like a great journey towards that kingdom of heaven, and yet we travel as citizens of the kingdom already, sometimes sensing its closeness and sometimes painfully aware of the distance between God's humility and love and our own brash self-centredness.

We need to behave like citizens of the kingdom as we travel, and that means self disciplined behaviour out of which the spontaneous love and joy can grow. They do not grow well in shallow soil, and the discipline side of things is not to be lightly dismissed. That is particularly difficult to keep to in a permissive, flabby society, just as it was hard for the people of Israel to behave in accordance with God's will when all the surrounding nations were full of exciting wrong behaviour. Now as then, things can seem okay to indulge in because everyone else does it.

But for God's people that isn't the right standard to go by. We are to behave according to the maker's instructions – according to the way we were designed to function best in all ways - physically, mentally, emotionally and spiritually. God doesn't point accusing fingers at us, though. He opens his arms wide to welcome us home.

## Discussion starters

1  Through the generations the church wobbles its way, trying to keep its balance between condemnation and forgiveness. Where do you think we are at the moment and what attitudes need changing?

2  Although the kingdom is other worldly, and to do with what happens spiritually, it is also a social gospel. Why are both important?

## All stage talk

*Theme:* Living as citizens of heaven.
If you have anyone in uniform present, ask a few to come to the front, one each of various sorts of uniform, including a choir member and server as well as the cubs and brownies. They can sit down, and when you mention an activity they might expect to do, they stand up. Sometimes several people will be standing up and at other times only one person.

Explain how we do expect to behave in particular ways - even if we're not wearing uniform. A car driver needs to behave as a responsible person, for instance, or he might be a danger to himself and others.

Every citizen is expected to act reasonably, and keep to the country's laws, so that life is safer for everybody. We are citizens twice over (twinned citizens, rather than twinned cities) because we are citizens of our earthly city of Bromsgrove or Plymouth, and also citizens of heaven. So we have to make sure we behave like citizens of the kingdom of heaven, and be quite strict with ourselves about this, working at the parts we find hard and exercising the parts we manage more easily.

## Intercessions

Father, look on your church and bless its work in your name and power; prune it and discipline it where necessary and keep it safe from all evil.

*Silence for prayer*

Only in you, O Lord:
**can we find rest**

Father, look with mercy on this damaged, ravaged world and bless the work to conserve resources and repair forests.

*Silence for prayer*

Only in you, O Lord:
**can we find rest**

Father, teach us to be good partners, friends, parents, sons and daughters so that our behaviour reveals only your love.

*Silence for prayer*

Only in you, O Lord:
**can we find rest**

Father, we stand alongside the outcasts and the mentally frail; the disheartened, the angry and the vulnerable.

*Silence for prayer*

Only in you, O Lord:
**can we find rest**

Father, we stand alongside those who mourn and those who die alone and unwanted.

*Silence for prayer*

Only in you, O Lord:
**can we find rest**

Father, we have known your peace and tranquillity and want nothing more than to worship you for ever.

*Silence for prayer*

Only in you, O Lord:
**can we find rest**

## Other ideas

As the Ezekiel passage is read, have a few people starting to move slowly from different parts of the church to the front. They start to move at verse 17 and gather at the foot of the cross or round the altar, with one arm raised in worship and the other round the shoulders of another person in the group.

## In the crèche

*Aim:* For the children to enjoy acting as children of the kingdom.

Have different kinds of dressing up clothes, and dress different children up in them. Talk about the jobs this person might do, and everyone joins in with some of the suggestions. Then give the children citizen of heaven badges to decorate, and act out some of the behaviour we expect from people who are citizens of the kingdom of heaven.

## Children

*Aim:* For the children to enjoy behaving as citizens of the kingdom of heaven. First try guessing what job people have from the mime they perform. Then explain that we are citizens - both of our own city, and of heaven. Jesus has opened the way for us. How should we not behave, as children? How should grown ups not behave?

Have a large sheet of paper with a journey drawn on it (as shown below), and some separate cards. Write the children's suggestions for both kinds of behaviour on the cards, in different coloured pens, and then play the game, taking turns to throw the dice. They will no doubt notice that we have only one counter, so although it's a journey we're on it isn't a race. Every time you throw the dice you pick a card. If it is right behaviour the counter is moved forward; if not it's moved backwards.

Then the children can make their own pocket version to take home.

## Young people

*Aim:* For them to look at the implications of being citizens of heaven.
First look at some local road maps, and ask them to work in twos or threes, finding the way to various places, and jotting down the route. Then the instructions are swapped, so that they have to find their way from each other's directions.

Now read the passage from Ezekiel, and talk about the way God calls his people back home from far away. It isn't just a physical distance, but a spiritual one as well. Explain how Jesus is the way for us to travel home to God, and because he paid the price of death, he has opened up the possibility of heaven to us. We are citizens of heaven, and need to behave like that on our journey home.

Now read the passage from Hebrews and look at the kind of behaviour which does and doesn't seem appropriate for sons and daughters of the living God. Talk over any they want to look at more carefully, and end with a time of prayer.

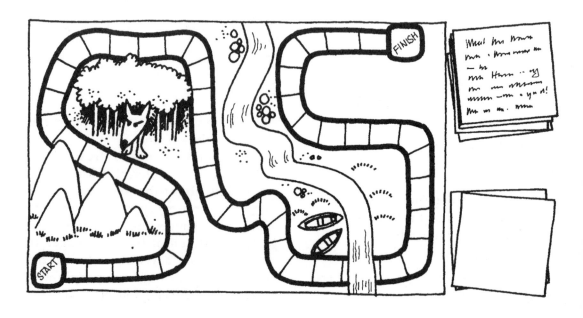

# Thematic Index

# Thematic Index